As Through a Veil

MYSTICAL POETRY IN ISLAM

LECTURES ON THE HISTORY OF RELIGIONS
sponsored by the
American Council of Learned Societies
New Series, Number Twelve

As Through a Veil

MYSTICAL POETRY IN ISLAM

ANNEMARIE SCHIMMEL

Columbia University Press
NEW YORK
1982

Library of Congress Cataloging in Publication Data

Schimmel, Annemarie.
As through a veil.

(Lectures on the history of religions;
new series, no. 12)
Bibliography: p.
Includes index.
1. Islamic poetry—History and criticism.
I. Title. II. Series.
PJ827.S3 892'.71'009 81-12302
ISBN 0-231-05246-4 AACR2

Columbia University Press
New York Guildford, Surrey

Printed in the United States of America

Clothbound editions of Columbia University Press books are Smyth-sewn and printed on permanent and durable acid-free paper.

Sometimes I call you Cypress, sometimes Moon,
And sometimes Muskdeer, fallen in the snare . . .
Now tell me, friend, which one do you prefer?
For out of jealousy, I'll hide your name!

—ʿAinulqudat Hamadhani

THIS VOLUME is the twelfth to be published in the series of Lectures on the History of Religions for which the American Council of Learned Societies, through its Committee on the History of Religions, assumed responsibility in 1936.

Under the program the Committee from time to time enlists the services of scholars to lecture in colleges, universities, and seminaries on topics in need of expert elucidation. Subsequently, when possible and appropriate, the Committee arranges for the publication of the lectures. Other volumes in the series are Martin P. Nilsson, *Greek Popular Religion* (1940), Henri Frankfort, *Ancient Egyptian Religion* (1948), Wing-tsit Chan, *Religious Trends in Modern China* (1953), Joachim Wach, *The Comparative Study of Religions,* edited by Joseph M. Kitagawa (1958), R. M. Grant, *Gnosticism and Early Christianity* (1959), Robert Lawson Slater, *World Religions and World Community* (1963), Joseph M. Kitagawa, *Religion in Japanese History* (1966), Joseph L. Blau, *Modern Varieties of Judaism* (1966), Morton Smith, *Palestinian Parties and Politics That Shaped the Old Testament* (1971), Philip H. Ashby, *Modern Trends in Hinduism* (1974), and Victor Turner and Edith Turner, *Image and Pilgrimage in Christian Culture* (1978).

Contents

Acknowledgments

The five lectures published in this volume were delivered under the auspices of the American Council of Learned Societies during the Spring Term of 1980. They were—in full or in part—given in the following institutions: Rice University (Houston); Trinity College (San Antonio); University of Tennessee at Knoxville; Duke University (Durham, N.C.); University of North Carolina at Chapel Hill; MacMaster University (Hamilton, Ont.); University of Toronto; Princeton University; McGill University (Montreal); Columbia University and Union Theological Seminary (New York); University of Colorado (Boulder and Denver); University of Chicago; Northwestern University (Evanston, Ill.); and University of Alberta, Edmonton. I would like to thank the American Council of Learned Societies as well as the American Association for the Study of Religion for arranging an excellently planned program. Dr. James N. Settle and Dean Joseph M. Kitagawa were the masterminds in the layout of my journeys, which had to be fitted into a tight teaching schedule at Harvard. My gratitude is due to all my colleagues in the various institutions, who did everything possible to make my stay in their respective places most enjoyable.

During the semester at Harvard, I was conducting a seminar about Indian popular mystical poetry together with Professor Charlotte Vaudeville (Sorbonne), the results of which were very useful for the contents of the fourth lecture; the same is true for our seminar on the Sindhi poetry of Qadi Qadan, in which Dr. Motilal Jotwani from Delhi University actively participated. My thanks are also due to the students, at Harvard and at the various campuses where I lectured. Their stimulating questions at times opened up new vistas.

During the preparation of the lectures for publication, Carl W. Ernst of Harvard University helped in retrieving some of the bibliographical material. Dr. Peter J. Awn of Columbia University kindly volunteered to assist me in preparing the manuscript for publication.

I thought it useful to leave the text of the lectures largely as they were delivered, adding only a few more examples, mainly poetry; as a consequence, the notes have grown to "cumbersome unwieldiness," and it would have been easy to extend both them and the bibliography even more. They are meant as mere guidelines for further research because the topics touch so many different aspects of poetry (bordering at times on philosophy, folklore, or literary criticism) that none of them could be dealt with in full. I hope that the reader will be able to pursue his own interests in one aspect or the other of the incredibly rich world of mystical poetry in the Islamic lands.

Introduction

THE MYSTICAL POETRY of the Islamic countries, particularly Iran, has attracted European scholars for some 200 years; it was, in fact, the first source for their acquaintance with the spiritual aspects of Islam. To be sure, some of the earliest students of Islamics were extremely critical of the poetical utterings of the Sufis (as they were critical of anything Islamic): we may think of Friedrich A. D. Tholuck's verdict in his thesis of 1821, *Ssufismus sive theosophia persarum pantheistica*, which paved the way for the constantly repeated misunderstanding that Sufism was nothing but pantheism. And some forty years later (1867) Ernest Trumpp made some poisonous remarks about one of the masterpieces of classical Sindhi poetry, Shah ᶜAbdul Latif's *Risālō,* which he edited with great pains although he thoroughly disliked anything that smacked of mysticism. Yet even he could not help admitting that some of Shah ᶜAbdul Latif's verses were worth reading. Another thirty years later, René Basset spoke in the introduction to his very useful translation of Busiri's *Burda* of "Soufisme qui commençait dès lors à exercer son influence si néfaste sur la poésie orientale" (p. x).

Despite such deprecatory remarks, mystical poetry continued to fascinate some orientalists and certainly many non-orientalists who were lucky enough to have some superb German translations at their disposal,[1] and who in the course of the late nineteenth century became acquainted with a number of studies which are still useful, and some of which have long since become classics. The mystical aspects of Islam understandably appealed more to non-Muslim readers than did the legal and dogmatic aspects of Islam, and it was particularly the poetry of Maulana Jalaluddin Rumi which attracted German and British orientalist poets and was regarded, by the Scottish clergyman William Hastie, as an antidote to Omar Khayyam's frivolous verses, which were so amazingly successful in their very free renderings by FitzGerald. The work of Reynold Alleyne Nicholson, to whom we owe excellent editions of classical Sufi works in both Arabic and Persian and who was at the same time a sensitive translator and historian of literature, facilitated the work of those who were interested in the development of classical mystical literature from Sarraj to Ibn al-Farid and Maulana Rumi, and the numerous works of Louis Massignon, though often difficult to read, opened the way for a new understanding of the martyr mystic al-Hallaj, and even ushered in a renaissance of Hallaj in Arabic literature. Among the German-speaking pioneers in the field of Islamic mystical poetry the name of Hellmut Ritter outshines all others, and his studies in Persian poetical language as well as his monumental work on Fariduddin ᶜAttar (which constitute only a fragment of his vast scholarly achievements) will be models for all later generations.

Soon the history of religion turned to translations of Islamic mystical poetry; no less a scholar than Nathan Söderblom discovered the depth of Rumi's description of the *oratio infusa,* and Rumi's verse in general served those who discussed the phenomenon of mystical poetry, and is found in practically every anthology of mystical texts—generally in Rückert's free but congenial translations.

At the same time, the problem of mystical experience and its expression was being discussed by those scholars working in the fields of the phenomenology of religion and the philosophy of religion. Evelyn Underhill's *Mysticism* is still outstanding because of her clear and sympathetic understanding and classification of the mystical experience. For her, mysticism is a practical life process, in which the One is the object of love, and a living union with this One is the goal of the mystical path—the theories of "pantheistic" mysticism, or the theosophic approach to religion, are only briefly touched in her work. The various definitions of the concept of "mysticism" have been dealt with elsewhere, and need not be repeated here. For the interpreter of Sufi poetry Underhill's scheme certainly offers a fitting framework, and poetical metaphors as used by the Sufi writers can well be explained in the light of her descriptions. The study of the mystical language, and the relation between mysticism and expression, has been studied by many scholars, but generally for the Christian world; only recently has the problem of the metaphor been discussed afresh. When Karsten Harries states that "all metaphor that is more than an abbreviation for more proper speech gestures toward what transcends languages; thus metaphor implies lack,"[2] he says in scientific terms what Rumi meant when he compared his poem to the scent which makes the absent Friend present, and gives information about him (as the scent of Yusuf's shirt gave good tidings to his blind father). Harries also stresses the importance of the sound pattern for metaphysical success and touches here a problem which is particularly important in the mystical poetry of folk poets, which certainly implies a much stronger use of sound patterns than is usually found in "high" mystical poetry; again, Rumi's way of using vowels and consonants comes immediately to mind. In this connection, it seems important to note, as Hermann Pongs has done, that the term metaphor "has hitherto not been so alive in German idiom as the related words symbol on the one hand and *Bild* on the other."[3] *Bild* still implies the act of *bilden*, of "forming" something, and the mystical poet, translating purely spiritual matters into the sphere of sensuality, certainly tries to form out of the formless ocean of the Godhead something which may represent at least a small "image" of the Reality, for "good metaphors . . . are active, lending the energy of animated things to whatever is less energetic or more abstract."[4] Typically, the word *Einbildung* was coined by the medieval German mystics to point to the act of forming images of (imagining) the Divine in the mystic's mind. The medieval Christian mystical poet found his images, *Bilder,* in "God's two books, in Nature and Scripture," and Alan de Lille's verse,

> Omnis mundi creatura
> quasi liber et pictura
> nobis est et speculum,
> nostrae vitae, nostrae mortis,
> nostri status, nostrae sortis
> fidele signaculum,[5]

can be applied to a large part of medieval Islamic mystical poetry as well. Hans Heinrich Schaeder has given the best description of this lyrical poetry, "incredibly full of tension and yet—at least in its best representatives—presents a relation between the spiritual and the mental sphere, between the sensual and the suprasensual, which has attained to the highest possible harmony";[6] for one finds that certain religious ideas which are predominant in Islamic thought can grow into symbols of truly esthetic character, can become changed and variegated, and yet are not cut off from their religious roots. Every image in this poetry opens a new vista, and the rose, so often praised for its loveliness, yet allows a look into the fire of the living God that is hidden behind her smiling.

Islamic mystical poetry is, at least during the first seven centuries, many-faceted. It begins with the simple ascetic songs of the early mystics and soon develops into chaste and lucid verses which speak of the eternal love between man and God, finally reaching full bloom in the grand odes of Ibn al-Farid, which unquestionably form the climax of classical Arabic mystical verse.

In Iran, both the lyrical forms and, additionally, the religio-didactic epic grew first in the eastern fringe of the country, present-day Afghanistan, and later in the central south, in Shiraz, with its influence soon extending to India and later to Turkey, both of which elaborated the intricate network of allusions and verbal play by adding words and forms taken from their respective linguistic backgrounds. Besides the genre to which we have devoted our main interest in these lectures, i.e., lyrics and mystical epics, Iran and the countries under her influence can boast of a variety of literary genres which we mention only in passing—the philosophical poetry of writers like the great Ismaᶜili thinker and missionary Nasir-i Khusrau has been left out, as has the whole complex of the *marthiya,* the poems and dramas connected with the death of the Prophet's grandson Husain in the battle of Kerbela in 680. Both of the above have been discussed lately in books and articles by specialists. The poetry of the Hurufis, which was particularly prominent in medieval Turkey, has also not been dealt with in detail because most of its features resemble the traditional Persian models.

When we singled out Maulana Rumi from the Persian and Persianate tradition, it is because of his tremendous influence on most writers in subsequent centuries. Rumi is one of the very few poets about the background of whose mystical poetry we are fairly well informed, even though—as in most religious biography—history, legend, and myth are almost indistinguishably interwoven. Although nobody has ever attempted to establish a chronology of his more than 40,000 lyrical verses, one can perhaps draw a few guidelines which, I hope, will prove useful for further research.

Rumi's work is inexhaustible, and though I have just published two books, one in English and one in German, about this favorite mystical poet, I confess that at every reading of the *Dīwān* new insights flash up so that I am constantly faced with the problem of how to organize this seemingly endless amount of material. In reading Rumi's verse, which reveals so much of his personal problems and yet transports them to a higher, spiritual, and hence immortal level, one sometimes thinks of Dr. Samuel Johnson's statement comparing Shakespeare to other, truly "classical" poets:

> The work of a correct and regular writer is a garden accurately formed and diligently planted, varied with shades and scented with flowers; the composition of Shakespeare is a forest, in which oaks extend their branches, and pines tower in the air, interspersed sometimes with weeds and brambles, and sometimes giving shelter to myrtles and to roses; filling the eye with awful pomp, and gratifying the mind with endless diversity.[7]

A German writer might see in Rumi's high-soaring, strongly rhythmical verse similarities with Beethoven's music (I think here especially of the Seventh Symphony, called by Nietzsche the "apotheosis of dance"): the very personal way of transforming suffering and love into something tangible that enraptures the listener and opens new worlds to him seems, at least to me, very similar in both artists.

Johnson's remark about Shakespeare points to one more peculiarity of Rumi: although he has been acknowledged as the undisputed master of all later mystical writers, I feel that he does not belong completely to the "classical" Persian tradition. To be sure, his knowledge of the traditional forms, of classical works, of the most refined rhetorical devices is as great as that of any other Persian or Turkish writer, but his lyrical poetry differs from the ideal *ghazal,* which consists of verses which follow each other like pearls on a string without needing a "logical" sequence (the inner logic, however, is always discernible). Rumi's *ghazals* usually constitute a unity, even though his thoughts may wander to the most diverse topics during the whirling dance out of which most of them emerged. One can often follow the process of inspiration in a poem quite clearly, and even feel when the true inspiration stopped and the poet was carried on by the momentum of the rhyme and the rhythm. The use of pronounced rhythmical forms, although following the Arabo-Persian metrical rules, almost invites the reader to scan them according to stress, or at least accompany them by hand-clapping. They are thus much closer to popular poetry as it was used in the dervish *tekkes* during the *samā*ᶜ than to the ideals of classical, courtly poetry. Besides, Rumi's vocabulary is taken from all walks of life and he does not shun crude or obscene words. He also introduced Turkish and Greek expressions, as they were close at hand in the Anatolian city of Konya, where he spent most of his life.

Rumi's poetry is full of paradoxes which again would merit a special study—his visions, which are sometimes alluded to, or his paradoxical tales are a far cry from the complicated but always perfectly measured ideals of poets like Saᶜdi or Hafiz. Thus, Rumi, whose poetry corresponds in the realm of the visual arts to the grand miniatures of the Tabriz style (very fittingly, since Tabriz was his spiritual home!) belongs, in a certain way, more to the popular than to the "high" tradition. The noted Turkish scholar Abdulbaki Gölpĭnarlĭ, who is certainly one of the greatest experts in the Mevlevi tradition, has pointed out some of the peculiarities which place Maulana Rumi in a category different from other mystical writers. (It would be possible to track down his influence on the poetry written in Persian or Turkish among the members of his order, the Whirling Dervishes, and trace a history of his influence on urban and popular literature in Turkey, Iran, and Muslim India east to Bengal, but this again would be a different task which could easily fill a whole volume.)

While Western scholars devoted much time to the study of mystical poetry written in Arabic and even more to that in Persian, and to a lesser extent that in Turkish, the mystical poetry in the regional languages has largely been neglected. I avoid here the term "folk poetry" because as much as this literature is meant for the masses, many of its authors were literate people, who were proud of their acquaintance with Islamic learning and sometimes liked to show off. Of course, illiterate bards are also found, who took up the popular tradition founded by the masters, and helped the ideas of mystical poetry reach into popular literature, to lullabies and wedding songs, riddles and even jokes. But the songs of illiterate dervishes and their styles of recitation have only rarely been studied in detail. Each mystic who turned to the native tongue of his area—from Mulla Da'ud in India, Yunus Emre in Anatolia, Pir-i Roshan in the Afghan-Indian border zone to the Bauls of Bengal—knew that the nonurban Muslims needed religious instruction in an idiom which they could easily understand, and in images with which they could identify. It is largely thanks to them that languages like Panjabi, Sindhi, Pashto, etc. grew into vehicles for poetry and literature. The rhythmical power, the freshness and simplicity of many of these poems often appeals to the Western reader more than the all too perfect later Persian verse. It should always be kept in mind that this poetry is mostly sung by members of Sufi orders and fraternities, and therefore shares certain features with post-thirteenth-century Arabic poetry—features which arose only after Ibn ᶜArabi had developed the very handy system of a mystical "Unity of Being," whose vocabulary was taken over even by those mystics who theoretically disagreed with Ibn ᶜArabi's thoughts. Hence, popular poetry all over Islamdom is very similar in its character, but it still preserves the local peculiarities which reflect the landscape out of which it grew.

In most poetry of the three traditions—the Arabic, the Persian, and the "popular"—the feeling of all-embracing love is predominant, as is characteristic of mystical poetry all over the world. It is the feeling that "the goal of love is loss of awareness of all but God," and many of the later Sufis would at least claim, if not practice, that "the distinction between good and evil is an illusion and does not exist for the mystic who sees the world from God's perspective."[8] This attitude is, as Joseph N. Bell has recently shown very lucidly, typical of the *eros*-oriented type of religion, which basically contrasts with the *nomos*-oriented core of Islam. Muslim mystics and orthodox theologians always knew that it is the second half of the profession of faith, i.e., "Muhammad is the messenger of God," which makes Islam a distinct religion and draws the borderline between Islam and other religions, members of which could certainly agree with the first clause of the profession of faith, "There is no deity save God."

Logically, the *nomos*-oriented attitude becomes most conspicuous in poetry addressed to the Prophet. Not that the Prophet is not loved—in later poems he, or rather the *ḥaqīqa muḥammadiyya,* the "archetypal Muhammad," appears sometimes as the beloved of the bridal soul; but on the whole the relation of the poets to the Prophet is more sober, as the "prophetic" approach to religion is the "way of sobriety," not that of "intoxication," as in the case of the mystics. When in *nomos*-oriented religion "the goal of love is obedience to God with awareness of the world,"[9] this is exactly the attitude of the poet who sings about Muhammad and addresses him full of trust and hope, notwithstanding the endless descriptions of his miraculous birth, or his ascension into the presence of God. In fact, the experience of the *miʿrāj,* the heavenly journey, serves to prove the uniqueness of Muhammad's experience: he *returned* from the Divine Presence, which he endured without fainting, while Moses swooned at the vision of only so much as the Burning Bush, and while the true mystic, as ᶜAbdul Quddus Gangohi put it, "would never like to return" from this highest bliss. In this remark about Muhammad's ascension and his return in order to work in the world, a modernist thinker like Muhammad Iqbal found the difference between "mystical" and "prophetical" religion expressed in a nutshell: the Muslim mystics have been long aware of this dichotomy which was defined, in Western scholarship, by Nathan Söderblom and Friedrich Heiler.

In the poetry composed by the mystics, even the "mythical" Muhammad still maintains his personal characteristics; he is God's beloved as he is the intercessor of those who trust in him and are fortunate enough to belong to his community. One could easily compose a parallel to *The Poets' Life of Christ* by collecting poems about Muhammad's birth, marriage, family life, miracles, victories, his ascension, and his family: sophisticated Arabic writers and simple villagers have expressed their loving trust in him, and others have woven veils of colorful descriptions around him, the meaning and end of creation. To understand Muslim piety in full, one has to take into account the poetry written in honor of the Prophet, for much of the "mystical" poetry composed in all Islamic languages bears strong similarities to mystical poetry in other religious traditions; but in the trusting and dedicated songs and hymns written in honor of the final Prophet—the model of the faithful—Islamic literature has gained a very distinctive flavor.

One / Flowers of the Desert:

THE DEVELOPMENT OF ARABIC MYSTICAL POETRY

THE LAST VERSES of Sura 26 (v. 224 ff.) in the Koran contain a sharp criticism of the poets "who wander distracted in every valley and say what they do not do." To be sure, this criticism was directed against the pagan poet-soothsayers with whom the Prophet Muhammad was sometimes compared by his adversaries (an allegation rejected in another place in the Koran); yet, the Koranic verdict has inspired much criticism of poetry among orthodox Muslims. It was greatly supported by a number of alleged traditions in which the Prophet condemned poetry as *nafth ash-shaiṭān,* "what Satan has spit out," or told his followers: "Verily it would be better for a man to have his belly filled with pus until it destroys him than to fill himself with poetry."[1] Such remarks were interpreted as pertaining to poetry in praise of sensual love, of the charms of women (and later, youthful boys), or of verses singing of the enticing beauty of the "daughter of the grape," i.e., wine—things strictly prohibited by Islamic law. The utterances of Indo-Muslim reformers of the late nineteenth century against flirtatious or dreamy Urdu poetry echo the Koranic and Prophetic aversion to "worldly" poetry and translate it into modern literary criticism.[2]

Yet, in spite of all the hostile remarks about poetry, the world of Islam is extremely rich in poetical expression. When we speak of Sufism, we think of the enormous poetical output of the Sufis in Arabic and even more in Persian and Turkish verse, as well as in the various languages of the Indo-Pakistan Subcontinent, a literature which has supplied the West with most of its ideas about the characteristics of Islamic mysticism. To be sure, even the greatest of all Muslim mystical poets, Jalaluddin Rumi, deemed it necessary, toward the end of his life, to devaluate his poetical activity in an unusual statement:

> By God, I care nothing for poetry, and there is nothing worse in my eyes than that. It has become incumbent upon me, as when a man plunges his hands into tripe and washes it out for the sake of a guest's appetite, because the guest's appetite is for tripe.[3]

However, at the beginning of this very passage he had noted the fact that he sang poetry when inspired by his mystical friend. This remained a common excuse for many religious poets who claimed that their verse was not comparable with profane poetry, which often contained praise of ritually prohibited things or eulogies for rulers who would pay for them. Regarding themselves as inspired by some higher power, they gave lively descriptions of the "birth" of poetry which poured out spontaneously. Again, the Koranic statement that the poets "say what they do not do" led some poets to declare their "immoral" songs as sheer play, or to explain their use of grand hyperboles by quoting the maxim that "the best poetry is that which is most untrue." Other poets would cite the *ḥadīth* ascribed to the Prophet, *inna min ash-shiʿr ḥikma* ("There is wisdom in poetry"), in order to defend their verse, or claimed that "God has hidden treasures under the tongues of the poets," and as even the worldly poets usually headed their collections of verse with the epigraph "In the name of God," thus later writers, especially in the Persianate tradition, began every work with hymns to praise the Creator and the beloved Prophet.[4] Thus, many ways were found to circumvent the Koranic disparagement of poetry, although a slight feeling of guilt lingered on in orthodox minds, so that biographers of pious theologians who, like most educated Muslims, indulged in poetry, made remarks like "the learned scholar condescended to committing to paper some verse, which is beneath his dignity."[5]

Despite the attempts by later poets to rehabilitate poetry and despite the fact that "no people in the world . . . are so moved by the word . . . as the Arabs,"[6] it cannot be denied that the words of Sura 26 point to an important truth, namely, the strong tension between the words of revelation and the words of poetry. This difference has been stated in a beautiful image by Goethe in the *Noten und Abhandlungen zum West-Östlichen Divan,* where he says that poet and prophet are both obsessed by the same spirit, but while the poet squanders his talents in multifaceted, colorful verse, the prophet concentrates on the one truth and repeats the same message ever so often that people may gather around it "as though it were a flag."[7] Indeed, the straight, linear monotony of the prophetic message is necessary to preserve the inspired contents without any change, and when in later times Muslim poets wrote verse in the "prophetic" tradition they would use remarkably simple forms to hammer their message into the minds of their audience.[8]

It must be further admitted that in the Arabic tradition proper religious prose literature is on the whole more expressive than most religious poetry, and the masterpieces of rhymed prose such as Hallaj's *Kitāb aṭ-ṭawāsīn,* the *Nahj al-balāgha,* and Ibn ᶜAta'ullah's *Ḥikam* display the peculiar genius of the Arabic language much better than most mystical poetry.[9] Louis Massignon has correctly underlined the central place of the *iᶜjāz qur'ānique:* the most essential feature of Islam is, in his view, the Arabic language of the Koran. Probably it was just the feeling of being confronted with an overwhelming miracle, i.e., the linguistic unsurpassability of the Koran as well as its verdict against poets, together with the Arabs' pride in the great heritage of pre-Islamic poetry which slowed down the development of Islamic Arabic poetry in the full sense of the word. Was not poetry lastly *siḥr ḥalāl,* "lawful magic"?

To be sure, the Prophet himself had to admire Kaᶜb ibn Zuhair's poem *Bānat Suᶜād,* which in later centuries became the model for those who hoped for the Prophet's forgiveness, and he was extolled by Hassan ibn Thabit. Hassan was primarily a descriptive poet who defended Islam; however, his poems are formally so much in tune with the pre-Islamic tradition, that they do not even avoid allusions to wine and love. It has even been claimed by the grammatician Asmaᶜi that Hassan's verse deteriorated after he embraced Islam, because his poetry entered the gate of virtue, *bāb al-khair,* but, as Meir J. Kister rightly states, his eulogies on the Prophet breathe a true Islamic spirit (see chapter 5).[10] Hassan's verses are important in connection with early Islamic history, however, for they were used in the biographies of the Prophet and thus served as important source material.[11]

The poetical activities of some members of early Islamic sects such as the Kharijites and the Kaisaniyya, who extolled ᶜAli,[12] are worth mentioning in passing. The verses by the Kharijite Qatari ibn al-Fujaᶜa (d. 697) belong to the category of heroic songs rather than of "pious" poetry, in as much as his strong personal involvement in the defense of his religious ideas is evident in his powerful lines.[13] One may also think of the *Hāshimiyyāt* of al-Kumait ibn Zaid (d. 743) in the time of the Omayyads, which however should be regarded as political rather than religious statements.[14]

Around the year 800, a trend toward ascetic verse emerged among some Arab writers,[15] and the poet Abu'l-ᶜAtahiya turned from frivolous love songs to *zuhdiyyāt,* in which he recalls the glory of old days and remembers those who have passed away—ancient kings and castles in ruins. From that time on, poems with the anaphora *aina aina,* "Where . . . where . . . ?" (or in Persian *kujā . . . kujā,* the classical topos of *Ubi sunt qui ante nos in mundo fuere*), became a distinctive feature of the ascetic tradition.[16] Abu'l-ᶜAtahiya advises his readers to retire from this passing world, to be content with a loaf of bread and a sip of cold water instead of dwelling in luxurious mansions and enjoying things prohibited, for this brief pleasure will certainly end in Hell.[17] His contemporary, the great jurist ash-Shafiᶜi, wrote also some poems of this sort in which he, understandably, used religious and legal terminology.[18] But his and similar scholars' well-meaning rhymed admonitions are a far cry from the truly religious literature which began to appear at approximately the same time, around the year 800. This was the period when early Islamic asceticism, with its austere and world-detesting outlook, began to turn into love mysticism, a development in which Jaᶜfar as-Sadiq, the sixth imam of the Shia, and his younger contemporary, the Iraqi woman Rabiᶜa al-ᶜAdawiyya, seem to have taken the lead.

Sufism was in its early stages what Nathan Söderblom calls *Persönlichkeitsmystik,* a personal relation between God and man, Creator and creature, Lord and slave, as grounded in the Koranic teachings. It was voluntaristic mysticism, aiming at the complete unification of man's will with the Divine will, not yet a gnostic approach as it became later, partially under the influence of Neoplatonic-gnostic ideas. Père Nwyia has highlighted the immense importance of the mystics' constant preoccupation with the Koran, the uncreated word of God, so that a complete *qoranisation de la memoire*[19] was achieved by which the mystic finally saw everything in the light of the Koranic revelation, took his inspiration in every moment from the Koran, and applied its images to his own experience. The constant recurrence of Koranic images and figures such as Abraham, Moses, or Jesus in the work of later Persian and Persianate Sufi poets can be explained by this central position of the Koran in the life of the Sufis; simple lines in any Islamic language, even in folk poetry, can contain allusions to a Koranic verse which the Western reader may detect only much later.[20]

This life in and through the Koran helped the mystics shape both their experiences and their languages. The experience of the love that exists between God and man was found expressed in Sura 5/59: "He loves them and they love Him"; and slowly, "the language of experience became," as Nwyia says, "the language of love."[21] And the Koranic story of God's speaking with Moses in an ineffable speech in which the person of the prophet disappeared from in between, formed the first step to the Sufi theory of the *shaṭḥiyāt,* the theopathic locutions, which were to become an important and much-discussed feature of classical Sufism, containing the most daring expressions of loving union or *Vergottung.*[22]

At the beginning of mystical poetry another problem posed itself. The mystic is basically a solitary wayfarer; his goal is to be in the company of God, and in the loving intimacy with the Divine Beloved during nightly vigils he would call Him no longer: "O my Lord!" as he did in the community, but rather, "O my Beloved!"[23] Who could and who would tell what was going on in the blissful solitude of love, in prayer and ecstasy, when the lover does not want anything *from* God but only God Himself? Was not poetry therefore a treason to mystical experience, and complete silence the only legitimate way a Sufi could choose?[24] Sumnun, a Baghdadi Sufi around 900, gave the problem its classical form: "A thing can be explained only by what is more subtle than itself: there is nothing subtler than love—by what, then, shall love be explained?"[25]

The poet, however, is a sociable person, "wandering in every valley"; he is the mouthpiece of the society whose dreams, hopes, aversions, and ideals he reflects and expresses, praising or blaming the rulers and always being in contact with people, even if only in court circles. How then could a Sufi be a poet?

Yet the Sufis also wanted to attract people, wanted to tell them of the marvellous experiences on the way to God, and were often compelled by an inner urge to do so. The contradictory sayings, "Who knows God, his tongue becomes dumb" and "Who knows God, his tongue becomes long," were well known among the Sufis, and although they often professed to abhor books and bookishness, the amount of literature produced by them is certainly as great as and not always more enjoyable than that written by those theologians and jurisconsults whom they liked to attack for their lack of spiritual insight. Furthermore, Sufism soon developed into a social movement. Even during its formative period, during the ninth and early tenth centuries, when only a small number of worthy disciples gathered at the masters' houses and regular fraternities had not yet developed, it was common to discuss mystical problems among initiated friends, and already in those days novices would be warned not to care too much for the *turuhāt aṣ-ṣūfīya,* the half-technical, verbose talk of the Sufis.[26] Even more importantly, as early as in the mid-ninth century, the institution of *samāᶜ*, mystical concert, was known at least in Baghdad, and verses were recited or sung in connection with music and often whirling dance. This was a starting point for one kind of Sufi poetry.

The earliest mystical verses are ascribed to Rabiᶜa (d. 801), who sings of her love of God, a love which is absolute and does not grow or diminish by the thought of Paradise or Hell. The absoluteness of devotion which she introduced in her poetry and which reminds the Western reader of sayings of medieval Christian women mystics is echoed later in innumerable Arabic and Persian songs. Her little artless poem on the two loves has often been quoted:

> Two ways I love Thee: selfishly,
> And next, as worthy is of Thee.
> 'Tis selfish love that I do naught
> Save think on Thee with every thought.
> 'Tis purest love when Thou dost raise
> The veil to my adoring gaze.
> Not mine the praise in that or this,
> Thine is the praise in both, I wis.[27]

And even more typically, she takes refuge with God, the only goal of her life, whom she loves to the exclusion of everything else, even to the exclusion of the Prophet:

> O Beloved of hearts, I have none like unto Thee,
> Therefore have pity this day on the sinner who comes to Thee.
> O my Hope and my Rest and my Delight—
> The heart can love none other but Thee.[28]

Such lines cannot be called great poetry—the author's feeling is stronger than her art. Rabiᶜa's contemporary, Rabiᶜa ash-Shamiyya, is also noted as a poetess who expressed her changing mystical states in little verses,[29] and in the course of the ninth century various forms of mystical verse developed which remained popular in the Arabic-speaking world through the centuries. We may discern here descriptive poems, in which the Sufis tried to tell of their experiences and their mystical "states" (*aḥwāl*); technical poems with often complicated word plays, puns, and allusions; and popular poems which, as will become clear, often prefigure the mystical poetry in the non-Arabic areas.

Classical Arabic poetry had taken a new course in the Abbasid period, and instead of—or besides—high-sounding Bedouin poetry, which culminates in the long, sonorous *qaṣīda* with its descriptions of the poet's journey towards the person whom he wants to praise or to satirize, shorter love poems and wine poems and especially the art of descriptive poetry (*waṣf*) became fashionable in the cities of Iraq, Syria, and Egypt. It was this kind of poetry which the early Sufis adapted to their own purposes; as far as we can see the classical form of the *qaṣīda* with its traditional framework was used by them only much later. In their descriptions the mystics used a rather simple, memorable style to describe not flowers, animals, and wine, as worldly poets did, but rather the state of the lovers who are distinct from everyone else:

> The bodies of those who are sincere in love and contentment—
> The sincerity of their love (*wadād*) becomes evident through their leanness.[30]

Or, as the same Egyptian mystic, Dhu'n-Nun (to whom ᶜAli Safi Husain ascribes the first truly Sufic love poems in a light, clear style)[31] says in another poem:

> The domain of the gnostics' hearts is in a garden,
> Heavenly, beneath which are the veils of the Lord.
> In their camping place: a crop of their fruits,
> Gently blows from proximity the breeze of intimacy with God . . .[32]

Thus he continues singing of the spiritual happiness of those who are close to their Lord and feel already here on earth the bliss of more than Paradise, for

> As was said, the Law of Islam has in view the posthumous salvation of the individual, with all that this implies in the way of the beatific vision of the Divinity in Paradise; while Sufism has in view the love and knowledge of the Divinity here and now, implying a liberation or salvation that is effective immediately, in this very life . . .[33]

Long poems are devoted to the *dalā'il,* the signs by which the true mystical lover can be recognized:

To these signs, it belongs that you see him turning up
In two cloaks on the banks of the river;
And to these signs belong his sadness and thinness
In the center of darkness, and there is no one to reproach him.
And to those signs, it belongs that you see him traveling
Towards the Holy War and toward every virtuous action . . .
And to these signs belongs that you see him giving in
All his affairs to the Just King . . .[34]

These poems take up a prose form which was sometimes regarded as a *ḥadīth* or even a *ḥadīth qudsī,* such as, "Verily God has servants who . . ." or, "Verily I have servants who . . . ," in which the lofty qualities of the lovers are described—to be honest, in much more poetical words than in most of these rhyming exercises. Moral advices were also sometimes expressed in verse, as it remained common in later Sufi poetry all over Islamdom.[35]

Sometimes, these early little poems assume the quality of real love verse, and some of them, as they were used for instance by some Sufis in their correspondence, have a touching sweetness—like those that describe the constant weeping of the lover "out of fear of separation or out of longing." They might complain, as did Junaid (d. 910):

My affair has become strange near every stranger,
And I have become an odd thing with everything odd.[36]

He ascribes this strangeness to the fact that the gnostics are of various ranks and nobody can plumb the depth of his (Junaid's) experience—a statement which foreshadows similar claims by later mystics, who were anything but modest when it came to point to their high spiritual rank.

More poetical are descriptions by Junaid's uncle, Sari as-Saqati (d. c. 867), to whom we owe lines the imagery of which, again, was taken up by later poets everywhere:

> When I claimed love she said to me: "You tell a lie,
> For I do not see any of its apparel in your limbs!
> There is no love until the skin sticks to the intestines,
> And you become so thin that you do no more answer a caller,
> And dwindle so that passion does not leave for you anything
> Except the pupil of the eye by which you weep or confide."[37]

The poor lover, in Sari's poetical description, is in a sad state:

> His heart burnt and tears constantly flowing,
> Pains assembled and patience inundated . . .[38]

For, as another Sufi sings:

> When people's eyes are altogether asleep,
> I knock the door with my distressed heart![39]

Besides these rather unassuming descriptive poems and sighing poetical prayers another genre became common in which the Sufis skillfully used their recently developed technical vocabulary and played on all the possible derivations of Arabic words, with their three radical consonants, to attain a highly complicated web of words which could be disentangled only by the initiated. They spoke of the different stages on the mystical path, of intoxication and sobriety, of gnosis and love, of finding and being found in ecstasy; and the experience of the central concept of Islam, that of *tauḥīd,* was hidden under verbal play.[40] For *tauḥīd* has both a declarative and a factitive meaning: it means in the first instance "to declare God as one," i.e., to profess that He is the sole Agent, Creator, Sustainer, and Judge who works without secondary causes, and that He is the sole and only goal of man's life. Islamic predestination is thus the complete trust in the wisdom of this sole agent rather than a purely dogmatic concept.[41] But among the mystics the feeling soon grew stronger that man had "to render God One," i.e., to annihilate himself before the only real Being who alone has the right to say "I."[42] Finally the formula of the creed "There is no deity save God" could be converted by radical mystics into the phrase *la maujūda illā Allāh*, "There is nothing existent save God." The existential experience of this Unity and Oneness—in which the created human being seemed to be annihilated at least for a moment in the everlasting God, becoming "as he was before he was"—could not possibly be told in plain words to the normal believer.

Junaid, the leader of the Baghdadian school around 900, was a master of cryptic verses and sayings, for he, following his teacher Kharraz, was well aware of the necessity of hiding one's mystical thoughts and experiences in a time when the government became increasingly suspicious of the activities of the Sufis.[43] However, in this kind of poetry, which sometimes seems so elusive, we cannot always be certain of the writers' true intentions, and we may well agree with Temple Gairdner, who once asked: "Do we not take their language too seriously? It parades as scientific; it is really poeto-rhetorical"; and the "wilful paradox" plays an important role in this type of Arabic mystical poetry as it does in later Sufi writing.[44] The Lebanese poet Adonis therefore calls early Arabic mystical poetry "surrealism before surrealism,"[45] while Massignon speaks of the *sapientèle plus que philosophique* quality of the Arabic language, which permits an understanding on various levels. *Taḍmīn*, "inclusion," which he describes as the "germination of the spiritual roots of a word into different branches" is certainly a very important aspect of Arabic Sufi poetry,[46] and Paul Nwyia has shown how Massignon himself translated Hallaj's line *yā sirra sirrī* in the three editions of Hallaj's *Dīwān* in three different ways, each of which can be defended and makes perfect sense.[47] Massignon's musings about the consonants being the body of the word and the vowels, which change according to the meaning, being the spirit, lead further into this area of enigmatic Arabic sayings, and when he states that every word has a *ẓāhir* and a *bāṭin*, an external and an interior sense, this holds true for mystical poetry in the whole Islamic world. For every Arabic root evokes of necessity many reminiscences in the listener's or reader's mind and may lead him back to the words of the Koran and the tradition; it is, as Arnold Steiger says so aptly, like a lyre in which the movement of one string makes all the others vibrate and thus evokes the secret harmonies of related concepts.[48] Thus, the vocabulary of even the simplest verse is highly charged with meaning and can therefore barely be adequately translated into any other language. The metallic hardness and crystalline luminosity of Arabic words is able to catch, in two simple-looking lines, a whole system of thought.

A third genre of early Sufi poetry is more easily accessible; that is what I would call the popular style. These are verses which immediately sound singable and must have been used in *samāᶜ* meetings; they usually consist of rather short lines in light meter.[49] A typical example is the Cameldriver's Song, which Sari quoted in a letter to Junaid:

> *abkī wa hal tadrīna mā yubkīnī*
> I cry, and do you know what makes me cry?
> I cry out of fear that you may go away from me
> And cut off our relation and leave me alone . . .[50]

This verse is certainly not great poetry, but its two long *ī*'s in the rhyme, which can be prolonged *ad libitum* by the singer, express well the longing of the lover: it is a song that fills the vast desert with melancholy during a lonely journey.

Poets might also learn songs from the mouths of strangers whom they allegedly met by chance on the seashore or in the desert (a favorite topos with Dhu'n-Nun and others),[51] or quote a singer reciting a verse of love and separation which deeply moved them and evoked religious feelings:

> The day of separation is longer than the day of Resurrection,
> And death is more beautiful than the pain of being separated.[52]

Love poems, interpreted in a mystical sense, inspired them to ecstasy and more than once caused the death of a lover, be he Sufi or layman.[53] Muslim orthodoxy instinctively recognized the danger inherent in the

Doppelglück der Töne und der Liebe—

i.e., the danger of breaking out of the well-ordered world of the *nomos,* the Divinely inspired law, into the vast fields of *eros* in all its shades;[54] hence the Muslim orthodoxy's fierce reactions to the introduction of music in Sufi circles.

Some mystics during the mid-ninth century, such as Yahya ibn Muᶜadh, began to write little dancing verses themselves:

> The truth we have not found,
> So dancing, we beat the ground.
> Is dancing reproved in me
> Who roves in love with Thee?
> In Thy valley we go around,
> And therefore we beat the ground![55]

Some of the short, concise poems by Dhu'n-Nun, who otherwise was more expressive in enthusiastic prose than in poetry, sound very singable:

> *man lādha billāhi najā billāh*
> He who seeks shelter with God is saved by God,
> And the bitterness of God's decrees makes him happy.

If my soul were not in God's hand
How would I follow God's decree?[56]

One of his short poems has a form which is still used today by the *qawwāli*. This form includes a first line which can be repeated by the chorus and different second hemistichs:

Who tastes the nourishment of love (*wadād*)
    denies all human beings.
Who tastes the nourishment of love,
    hates all human beings.
Who tastes the nourishment of love,
    forgets all human beings.
Who tastes the nourishment of love,
    becomes familiar with the Lord of human beings.[57]

This poetry rarely uses complicated images; its central theme is love in its various shades. Dhu'n-Nun's line:

amūtu wa mā mātat ilaika ṣabābatī
I may die, but my passion for you does not die[58]

forms the keynote for innumerable poems in the various Islamic languages, as does his complaint to the beloved God, with its unusually long rhyme, a poem which he allegedly heard from some hermit in Lebanon:

I had tears, and You have annihilated them,
And I had eyelashes, and You have made them bleed,
And I had a body, and You have afflicted it,
And I had a heart, and You have consumed it,
And I had, O my Lord, an eye
With which I saw the Divine Truth, and You have blinded it.
Your servant is seriously ailing, O Lord:
If You want You could cure him before today![59]

This last line presents a frequent image, the beloved as the physician who alone can heal the wound which he has inflicted. How then could the lover complain of his ailment since the physician himself is the cause for his pain?[60]

The early Sufi poets sing of a suffering in love which would make the hard rock melt if the mountains had to bear it,[61] and in later Sufi poetry there is no end of hyperboles of this kind because "there is no one more complaining than the lover" who weeps constantly and is burnt by the fire of love, dissolved in tears so that even if he wanted to write to his beloved about his pain, the heart's fire would burn the pen, and the eyes' water would wash off the ink.[62]

> Fear made me ill, and longing burnt me,
> And love fettered me, and God revived me.[63]

Thus says Dhu'n-Nun in a form which was taken up by later poets who loved to juxtapose pairs of concepts in order to point to the Divine kindness and beauty, *jamāl*, and the Divine wrath and majesty, *jalāl*, which work together in the world and act upon the lover to make him die to himself and gain a new life in God. And the feeling that the true lover sees only the Divine Beloved was poetically symbolized in images taken from traditional love stories:

> I pass by the region, the dwelling place of Laila,
> And kiss this wall and that wall.
> Yet it's not love for the houses which enraptures my heart,
> But love of her who dwells in the houses.[64]

During those years of the late ninth and early tenth centuries some mystics composed tender love poems without using images from worldly love. Such verses speak of the feeling of being completely safe and secure in God's hands, or they speak of the trust in Him who is closer to man than his jugular vein and who is, at the same time, praised by everything created.

The way toward You has now become clear,
And no one who intends You needs ask for a guide;
For when winter arrives, there is summer in You,
And when the summer comes, You are the shade.[65]

"Let moons rise or set"[66]—the mystic has a moon which does not change with the change of times, for:

Your beauty is in my eye and Your remembrance in my mouth,
And Your love in my heart—how could You be absent?[67]

Or, as Sumnun the Lover from Baghdad says somewhat earlier in an unforgettable image:

I have diverted my heart from the world and its pleasures,
You and my heart are nothing separate,
And never are my eyelids pressed together by slumber
But I find You between the eye and the lid.[68]

The Sufi poets knew that they had to hide their feelings, but that is impossible: even though they may keep their tongues, their tearful eyes reveal their state,[69] for the tears

. . . write on the cheek lines
Which someone can read who does not know well how to read,[70]

as Shibli, a master of short songs, says in a poem about patience. Still, even though the tears may divulge the lover's secret, he keeps silent:

People know for certain that I am in love,
But they do not know whom I love—[71]

a line which has become the model for later love lyrics in which the name of the beloved is never revealed, so that only allusions can help to decipher it. How often mystical (and profane) poets speak simply of *fulān,* "a certain person," or use the traditional names of Salma or Laila to hide the identity of the beloved if they do not, as do many Turkish poets, exclaim over and over again: *adīn demem,* "I don't tell his/her name!" For to know the name of something means to be able to control it: how then could anyone be allowed to use the sacred name without proper initiation?[72] The truth that God Himself is surrounded by the 99 Most Beautiful Names while His essential name—the Greatest Name—is hidden, points to this secret of the name. In the same way the Sufis assume unusual or "heavenly" names known only to the innermost circles of the initiated.[73]

The lover himself is so dissolved in love that:

> Nothing has remained of him but his name:
> One calls him Lover, that's all![74]

Mystical poets know that this Divine love is not connected with time and space:

> My heart loves You as long as I am alive, and when I die,
> Then my bones, decayed, love you in the dust.[75]

But even to claim that the heart loves God, as Shibli does in this verse, is not enough; he says in another line:

> There is no special heart from me that points at You:
> Every limb of mine is a heart directed at You.[76]

One may think here of the experience of *dhikr,* the recollection of God, during which not only the tongue and then the heart are filled with the name of God, but the whole body of the meditating Sufi is permeated so that his blood and each of his limbs is replete with the name of God and practices, as it were, its own *dhikr.*[77] Shibli has pointed to this secret of constant recollection in another simple verse, which takes up an idea by which Hallaj shocked his contemporaries and whose beginning, again, foreshadows one of Rumi's most ecstatic prayer poems:

> Today I forgot my ritual prayer due to my excessive love,
> And I do not know whether it's morning or evening;
> For Your recollection, O Lord, is my food and my drink,
> And Your face, if I see it, is the cure of my ailment.[78]

The early Sufis had claimed, as had all legalistic Muslims of the ninth and tenth centuries, that love between man and God should be understood exclusively as obedience. As Ibn Mubarak says:

> You are disobedient to God and pretend to love Him—
> That is, by my life! a very novel action:
> If your love were sincere, you would obey Him,
> For the lover is obedient to him whom he loves.[79]

This obedience is indeed the central quality of the lover, and Ghazzali quotes an earlier verse which prefigures thousands of later Sufi poems in which the ideal lover is described:

> I want union with him, and he wants separation from me:
> Therefore I give up what I want for that which he wants.[80]

The lover has no right to have his own will, not even an existence of his own, as a much-quoted verse says, a verse which Junaid considered to represent almost the quintessence of Sufism:

> When I said: "What have I sinned?" she said in reply:
> "Your existence is a sin with which no other sin can be compared."[81]

And at the same time that Junaid quoted this verse from an unknown source, his compatriot Ruwaim (d. 915) defined the lover's state:

If you would say, "Die!" I would die in perfect obedience,
And would say to the one who calls me to death: "Welcome, welcome!"[82]

This longing for death—death being the bridge which finally unites the lover with the Beloved—was to be the central topic of all later Sufi poetry, particularly in the Iranian world,[83] and has engendered the innumerable cruel descriptions of the lovers dying on the path towards the beloved, because the Sufis would have subscribed to Suso's remark that: "To love belongs according to the old custom, suffering."[84] Even more, they too claimed to die *fī sabīl Allāh,* on the path of God, as martyrs; but that meant not, as in orthodox Islam, during the Holy War against the infidels, but rather in the "major holy war," the struggle against their lower selves, in mortifications and by willingly taking upon themselves all afflictions in the hope of being sacrificed by a glance of the Beloved, to become true martyrs of love.[85]

The mystic who became the primary model of this martyrdom in love is Hallaj. Louis Massignon has devoted his whole life to the study of this mystic, Husain ibn Mansur al-Hallaj,[86] a disciple of Sahl at-Tustari and a contemporary of Junaid, who was cruelly executed in Baghdad in 922 for religious and political reasons. Massignon has proved that it was not so much his famous sentence *anā'l-ḥaqq,* "I am the Absolute Truth," which brought about his execution, but rather some of his religious theories. Yet, in later Sufi literature Hallaj is celebrated as the great lover, as the one who "without fear divulged the secret of the unity of man and God,"[87] and who had to pay with his life for his excessive love. Indeed, Hallaj was the first to discover that the mystery of creation lies in the dynamic love which is the very essence of God.[88] He was by no means a pantheist, as his teaching was interpreted later; rather, he

"l'essentiel désir"
Massignon.

F. Tholuck.

maintained the Divine transcendence, although he experienced that God might, in rare moments, lift the barrier between Him and man so that the uncreated Divine spirit could descend into the created spirit of the lover. Hallaj's poetical works are, therefore, as Massignon says,

> conversations of his spirit with the Divine spirit about their common love. . . . No other mystic of his time has shown himself more familiar with God than he, using constantly the pronouns I, Thou, and We, and yet, he did not apply, as did later poets, any symbols from profane love. . . . There is no mystical poetry which is at the same time more ardent and more radically dematerialized than that of Hallaj.[89]

At times, he reverts to the letter symbolism which had been developed by earlier Sufis,[90] and his verse in general takes up trends developed in the Sufi poetry of the ninth century. He likes short, four-line poems which sometimes suggest the later genre of *rubāʿī*, the quatrain that became so popular among Persian-writing Sufis.

Hallaj saw God everywhere:

> O Sun, Full Moon, and Day—
> You are for us Paradise and Hellfire![91]

Can any place be empty of God? And yet people do not see Him due to their blindness, although God sees them gaze openly at Him.[92] Once the mystic has given up human concerns and is exclusively devoted to recollecting God, the Beloved will fill his heart completely, uniting all his various hopes and thoughts into one single thought, that of love and devotion.[93]

> Verily the sun of the day sets at night,
> But the sun of the hearts never disappears.[94]

The lover feels the extreme nearness of God, whom he addresses:

You run between the heart and its sheath
As tears run from the eyelids. . .[95]

and in loving confusion he asks over and over again:

Ah, is it me and you? That would make two deities![96]

and therefore beseeches God to take away by his "I," the human "I" which is so painful. Out of this feeling grew Hallaj's famous poem *uqtulūnī yā thiqātī* in which he calls people to kill him—for him, as for many others, death seemed to be the only way to achieve lasting union with the Divine Beloved. That is why this *qaṣīda,* with its amazing paradoxes in its second half, was often quoted by later mystics. The words

Kill me, O my trustworthy friends,
For in my being killed is my life![97]

formed the basis for their meditations about the secret of *Stirb und werde,* about spiritual death and resurrection, and Maulana Rumi uses them in both his lyrics and his *Mathnawī* to point to metamorphosis through the repeated act of sacrificing oneself.

In dark, heavy verses Hallaj sings a threnody for all those who are deprived of the experience of God because the true witness has gone away,[98] and again, he expresses the union of the Divine and the human spirit which he experienced in rare moments of bliss:

I saw my Lord with the eye of the heart
And said: "Who are you?" He answered: "You!"[99]

or:

Anā man ahwā wa man ahwā anā
I am He whom I love, and He whom I love is I[100]

so that he and the Divine Beloved have become inseparable like amber and musk,[101] like water and wine—verses which have been imitated by numberless later mystics.

> Your spirit is mingled with my spirit as though
> Wine were mixed with limpid water,
> And when something touches You it touches me,
> For I am You in every state.[102]

Hallaj was daring enough to speak out that in the highest ecstasy of love "the ritual prayer of the lovers is infidelity."[103] Hallaj's poems have been repeatedly quoted by later authorities, often without mentioning the author, for he was disliked among the orthodox and suspect even in some Sufi circles. His attempt to rehabilitate Satan certainly shocked the legalists as it estranged also many of the mystics. In a famous poem, he made Satan declare that his refusal to fall down before Adam (see Sura 2/31) means in reality his acknowledgment of God's holiness and unicity, for did not God will that one should not worship anything but Him?[104] How, then, could an obedient lover follow God's order to prostrate himself before the newly created Adam? To be cursed by God on account of this seeming disobedience is, according to Hallaj, more agreeable to Iblis than to enjoy God's grace, for, as he sings in another poem:

> *urīduka, lā urīduka li'th-thawābi*
> I want You, but I do not want You for recompense,
> Rather, I want You for punishment.[105]

For: "Suffering is He, and Grace comes from Him."[106]

Hallaj's rehabilitation of Satan, which was taken up in later centuries by some Persian and Indian Sufis (Ahmad Ghazzali, ᶜAinulqudat Hamadhani, Sarmad in Delhi, Shah ᶜAbdul Latif in Sind)[107] is found in his *Kitāb aṭ-ṭawāsīn,* a small work in superb rhyming prose with interspersed verses. It contains also a glowing hymn in honor of the Prophet as well as the allegory of moth and candle which inspired ever so many Persian and Turkish poets. This allegory reached Europe around 1800 to find there its most famous expression in Goethe's poem *Selige Sehnsucht,* which translates into German verse the secret of being transformed into Divine light and fire by lovingly sacrificing one's transient, external existence.[108]

Hallaj's poetry, although not acceptable to more moderate mystics, became perhaps the most important ferment for later, particularly Persianate, poetry. Many of his metaphors as well as his statement, *anā'l-ḥaqq,* "I am the Absolute Truth," or "I am God," were taken over by numerous later writers,[109] and he became the model for all those who were in conflict with the authorities and suffered or died for their convictions, be they religious or political.

In Hallaj's verse, we also find allusions to the secret of the *oratio infusa:* God's address to man precedes man's calling to God (as God's every activity precedes human activity):

> I call You, nay, rather You call me to You. . .[110]

A few decades later Hallaj's Iraqi compatriot Niffari expressed the secret of God's preceding love and grace in his *Mawāqif,*[111] and in the thirteenth century it was Jalaluddin Rumi who most eloquently sang of the prayer of grace.[112]

Again, Hallaj speaks of the importance of *dhikr,* but he knows that it is God as remembered in the *dhikr* who throws him into utter confusion, and not the act of recollection:

> *Dhikr* is a means [or "a central pearl"] which hides You from my view.[113]

Niffari too discusses this very problem, because this is the question with which every serious mystic is confronted: to what extent can words, prayers, and recitations serve at all to unveil the Divine? Niffari, more than any other mystic of his time, has "unmasked the idolatry of the letters," as his modern interpreter, Père Nwyia, states.[114] And Hallaj's friend Shibli, who threw a rose at him when he went, dancing, to the gallows,[115] expressed the same central problem of the relation between silence and words in a more popular style. His verse often takes up Hallaj's ideas and couches them in light, singable words:

> Praise be to God that I am
> Like a frog that dwells in the sea:
> When he utters something his mouth is filled with water,
> But when he is silent he dies from grief.[116]

With Hallaj, Sufi history and, in a certain way, Sufi poetry reached its first climax. Shortly after his death, a mystic complained:

> The people of Sufism have passed, and Sufism has become only a patched frock,
> The sciences have passed; there are no sciences left and no illuminated hearts.[117]

Indeed, in the following centuries we rarely find any great Sufi poetry in Arabic; rather, handbooks of Sufism were composed which constitute our main sources for early poetry and for the apophthegmata of the fathers. Poetry on a higher level appears again in the thirteenth century, a time when the Muslim world once more saw an unrivalled spiritual activity which seems to have outweighed the political and social destructions caused by Genghis Khan and his successors from 1220 onward. This is the century during which the greatest master of theosophical Sufism, Ibn ᶜArabi, appeared on the scene; also, mystical poetry in Persian reached its apex in Rumi's work, and the Sufi orders, which were just beginning to crystallize, carried the message of Divine love into the various lands of Islam so that from Morocco to Transoxania, from Central Anatolia to Bengal an almost uninterrupted chain of mystical centers was established, on the framework of which all later mystical movements as well as literary activities developed. Since profane Arabic poetry had also had its last important masters with Mutanabbi in the tenth and, on a different level, Maᶜarri in the eleventh centuries, a literary critic like Gustave E. von Grunebaum sees in the mystical poetry which grew in the thirteenth century "a growing form of self-expression when the creative impulse in the other branches of Arabic literature had long been fading."[118]

An Egyptian scholar, ᶜAli Safi Husain, has devoted a book to Sufi poetry in Egypt during the seventh century hijri (thirteenth century), Egypt being the only major country that was spared a Mongol invasion and remained therefore the leading cultural center of the Arab world. The author distinguishes in this period "practical Sufis," who wrote *shiᶜr aḍ-ḍamīr wa'l-wijdān,* poetry born out of religious sentiments, and "theoretical Sufis," who composed *shiᶜr al-kashf wa'l-ilhām,* poems relying upon inspiration and mystical revelation.[119] Using further classifications he speaks of those Sufis who wrote in *ghazal* style, in which the subject was Divine love; those whose verse was inspired by the theories of the *ḥaqīqa muḥammadiyya* and the Muhammadan Light (*nūr Muḥammad*); and finally the sober, unsophisticated poetry of those who were strict Sunnites before entering the mystical path.[120] The latter are, in his opinion, the poets of the Shadhiliyya order which, as is known, represents the sober trend grounded in the teachings of the school of Baghdad, particularly those of Junaid. However, the only major writing for which the Shadhiliyya is remembered is not poetry but prose; it is Ibn ᶜAta'Allah's *Ḥikam,* "the last miracle of Sufism on the shores of the Nile,"[121] as Nwyia calls this small but weighty book of meditations and prayers. The poetical tradition of the order is most conspicuous in Muhammad Abu'l-Wafa ash-Shadhili and his sons, who belonged to the leading Egyptian poets of the fourteenth century.[122] Busiri, the author of the most famous encomium for the Prophet, the *Burda,* was an early member of the Shadhiliyya in Egypt (see chapter 5).

What Dr. A. S. Husain calls "poetry inspired by the *ḥaqīqa muḥammadiyya*" is, in fact, typical not only of Egyptian or Arabic poetry but of virtually all poetry composed in the Sufi orders.[123] In these verses the founder of a fraternity—such as Ahmad al-Badawi and Ibrahim ad-Dasuqi in Egypt—claims to be the *quṭb* or *ghauth,* the highest member of the mystical hierarchy. United with the Light of Muhammad, he claims to have existed well before Adam, to have known Idris on his way to heaven and Noah during the flood. This model was taken over into most post-thirteenth-century popular poetry. It is remarkable that the language of these medieval Arabic poems is generally no longer classical but uses popular phrases and forms without following strictly the rules of inflection or metrical exigencies; however, it always maintains the rhyme, a feature typical of popular Sufi poetry. Thus not only the contents but even formal characteristics of mystical folk poetry outside the Arabic world are preformed in thirteenth-century Arabic verse.

This type of poetry would probably not have developed without the overwhelming influence of Ibn ᶜArabi (d. 1240), whose numerous works in prose as well as his Diwan *Tarjumān al-ashwāq* became the spiritual staple of the Sufis because they offered a very logical world view which was condensed by most poets to the simple phrase "Everything is He." Of course, Ibn ᶜArabi's system—generally called *waḥdat al-wujūd*, "Unity of Being"—is much more complicated and should not be interpreted as pure pantheism, as much as verses such as

> When my Beloved appears,
> With what eye do I see Him?
> With His eye, not with mine,
> For none sees Him except Himself,

suggest this interpretation.[124] But according to Ibn ᶜArabi, the creatures in their actual existence are not identical with God but are solely the reflection of His attributes.[125] Lately, scholars like Henry Corbin and Seyyed Hosseyn Nasr have interpreted Ibn ᶜArabi's theories of "the Pathetic God Who yearned to be known" and have dwelt upon the mystery of the *unio sympathetica* between the Divine Names and the named things, and have reached novel conclusions.[126] But whatever the Spanish-born mystic who soon became known as *ash-shaikh al-akbar* (Magister Magnus) might have intended, there is a world of difference between his approach to religion and the dynamic, personal religion of Hallaj. With Ibn ᶜArabi, Islamic mysticism comes close to the mysticism of infinity, and his approach is theosophical or gnostic rather than voluntaristic, for his goal is to lift the veils of ignorance which hide the basic identity of man and the Divine, while in early Sufism the element of personal love between man and God was predominant.[127]

There is, however, one poem by Ibn ᶜArabi which has influenced not only millions of Muslims but also European students of religion because it seems to express the "tolerance" of the mystic in the most poetical words:

> My heart is capable of every form,
> A cloister for the monk, a fane for idols,
> A pasture for gazelles, the pilgrim's Kaᶜba,

The Tables of the Torah, the Koran.
Love is the faith I hold: wherever turn
His camels, still the one true faith is mine.[128]

The poem is, however, a glowing tribute to Islam, for, as Ibn ᶜArabi himself explains:

I accept willingly and gladly whatever burden He lays upon me. No religion is more sublime than a religion based on love and longing for Him whom I worship and in whom I have faith.

This is, as Ibn ᶜArabi's learned interpreter, Reynold A. Nicholson, says, "a peculiar prerogative of Moslems, for the station of perfect love is appropriated to Muhammad beyond any other prophet, since God took him as His beloved, *ḥabīb*." Besides, the verse shows that Ibn ᶜArabi boasts of having reached the highest possible station on the mystical path, a station which is beyond the limited forms of peculiar religions, and has realized in himself the pleroma of Divine Names.

Ibn ᶜArabi's prose writings, particularly the comprehensive *Futūḥāt al-makkiyya* and the small, very dense *Fuṣūṣ al-ḥikam*, were commented upon and translated until our day (the *Fuṣūṣ* even into Urdu verse during the eighteenth century!).[129] On the other hand, orthodox theologians often regarded his work as dangerous, if not outright heretic, and its perusal was prohibited once more in February 1979 in Egypt by the authorities of al-Azhar.

Ibn ᶜArabi's poetry, inspired by his meeting with a learned young Persian lady in Mecca, has some charming sides to it although R. A. Nicholson feels that "the book is too abstract and remote from common experience to give pleasure to others who do not share his visionary temper or have not themselves drawn inspiration from the same order of ideas."[130] This remark is gently but firmly contradicted by Martin Lings in his brief introduction to the new edition of the translation of the

Tarjumān al-ashwāq. To be sure, the introductory poem, *kullamā adhkuruhu*, where the poet remembers the beloved in ever-changing new words and forms, is quite charming despite its somewhat technical language, but one has only to compare it with a related poem in Rumi's *Mathnawī* (the great monologue of Zulaikha who sees her beloved Joseph in everything) to feel the difference in poetical depth and warmth.[131] Ibn ᶜArabi indeed found it necessary to comment upon his own love poems, which use for the first time in Arabic Sufi poetry the imagery of the classical Arabic tradition although popular preachers had employed already before him the names of Salma or Lubna, the traditional heroines of Arabic poetry, to allude to the Divine beauty. One could innocently enjoy Ibn ᶜArabi's descriptions of travel in the desert, of charming women in camel litters and of animals and natural phenomena as profane love poetry, but the commentary makes this interpretation impossible.

The poet himself admits "that in some passages of his poems the mystical import was not clear to himself, and that various explanations were suggested to him in moments of ecstasy."[132] And thus, the feminine name Salma is explained as an allusion to a Solomonian ecstasy (*ḥāla sulaimāniyya*) which descended upon the author by virtue of a prophetic heritage from the station of Solomon,[133] and the simple phrase "They journeyed continuously" means: "Since the object sought is infinite, the return from it is also a journey toward it. There is no migration except from one Divine Name to another."[134] A "tender playful girl" is a form of Divine wisdom, essential and holy, which fills the heart with joy,[135] while a "slender girl" in another verse is explained as the single, subtle, and essential knowledge of God,[136] and a "maid of fourteen" is the perfect soul, since 4 is the most perfect number, and 10 is the sum of 4 numbers, 1,2,3, and 4, while 14 is 10 plus 4.[137] The "married women" are the forms of Divine wisdom already realized by gnostics who preceded the poet,[138] and the "fair women" of another poem are the Divine names.[139] Natural phenomena like dew, rain, and flowers are similarly explained, and one wonders whether the constant interpretation of *barq*,[140] "lightning," as a center of manifestation for the Divine essence has not caused the extremely frequent use of the motif of lightning in Indo-Persian poetry.

Ibn ᶜArabi's style of interpretation deeply impressed later mystics, and many of them tended to put a heavy philosophical and theological coat of mail over their (often charming) verses, thus canceling their beauty. However, this method of interpretation, perfected in the Arab world by ᶜAbdul Ghani an-Nabulusi (d. 1731) and used in the Persian-speaking areas by authors like Muhsin Faid Kashani, became a vehicle that carried the teachings of the Ibn ᶜArabi-school into every corner of the Muslim world, because it enabled poets to give even the most worldly poem a "spiritual" interpretation, and thus avoid the wrath of the orthodox. The interpretation of Hafiz's poetry is the most telling example of this trend.

While Ibn ᶜArabi's influence rests mainly upon the colossal number of his prose works, his contemporary, Ibn al-Farid, left only a few exquisite Arabic odes which have been studied, recited, and enjoyed ever since the early thirteenth century.[141] Contrary to the Sufis in early times, whose language carried hardly any reminiscences of classical, "worldly" love poetry, Ibn al-Farid employed the whole heritage of traditional poetry: the address to the faraway beloved, the description of the landscape, and the complicated web of images. He mentions the *raqīb*, the watcher, and the *wāshī*, the slanderer who advises him to give up his love because he himself is "unmoved of heart", and the true Divine beloved is hidden behind the names of Salma and Hind. The historian Ibn Khallikan mentions Ibn al-Farid with the rather shallow remark:[142] "He has a collection of charming (*laṭīf*) poetry, and his style therein is lucid (*rā'iq*)" while the traditionist and mystic ᶜAbdur Ra'uf al-Munawi (d. 1621) calls him "the absolute master of the poets of his age," a judgment with which a modern reader would probably agree. Orthodox theologians, on the other hand, liked to criticize him; in the late fifteenth century a fierce fight raged in Cairo between those religious scholars who supported his views and those who regarded him as a heretic.[143]

This criticism was primarily directed toward his *Tā'iyya*, the *qaṣīda* rhyming in *t*, called also *Naẓm as-sulūk*, "The Order (or: the Poem) of the [mystical] Journey" which describes in some 750 verses in high-flown imagery the states and stages of the soul on its way to God. Louis Massignon saw in the *Tā'iyya*, which appeared to him as a *lourde tapisserie de brocade mordante*, a *kiswa* for the spiritual journey: just as the Egyptian government used to send every year the black, gold-embroidered veil for the Kaᶜba to Mecca, thus Ibn al-Farid has woven his poetical *kiswa* for the pilgrimage of the soul in a poem which, according to Massignon, reaches the heights of "transcendental esthetics."[144] While the French scholar visualizes the *Tā'iyya* as a brocaded tapestry, Ibn al-Farid's masterly English interpreter, R. A. Nicholson, states that: "His style and diction resemble the choicest and finest jewel work of a fastidious artist rather than the first fruit of divine inspiration."[145] And yet, we are told and have every reason to believe that most of his poetry was recited in a state of trance as a result of inspiration. Although the Egyptian mystic follows the tradition of classical Arabic poetry, which on the whole rarely moves a Western reader, he reaches in some passages such a perfection, such a unity of feeling and expression, that his verse can be fully enjoyed even in translation and comes closest to what we would consider to be true *Erlebnislyrik.* Here is a fragment of the poem rhyming in *j:*

> Every limb (of my body) sees him, even if he be absent from me, in every delicate, clear, joyous essence:
> In the tune of the melodious lute and flute when they blend together in trilling strains,
> And in luxurious pasturage of gazelles in the coolness of twilight and in the first rays of dawning,
> And in misty rains falling from a cloud on a carpet woven of flowers,
> And where the breeze sweeps her train, guiding to me most fragrant attar at sweet dawn,
> And when I kiss the lip of the cup, sipping the clear wine in pleasure and joy,
> I knew no estrangement from my homeland when he was with me; my mind was undisturbed where we were—
> That place was my home while my beloved was present; when the sloping dune appeared, that was my halting-place. . .[146]

Ibn al-Farid's most famous poem besides the *Tā'iyya* is the *Khamriyya,* the ode praising the primordial wine of love which inspires everything created:

> *sharibnā ᶜalā dhikrā'l-ḥabībi mudāmatan*
> We once drank wine to the memory of the Beloved
> Before the vine was created. . .[147]

This is the first full description in Arabic of the wine of love, which was offered to the souls on the day of the Covenant when God addressed the not-yet-created souls with the words *alastu bi-rabbikum,* "Am I not your Lord?" (Sura 7/171). The very scent of this wine is quickening and healing; its veiled bottle makes the blind see; the sound of its libation makes the deaf hear, and its radiant color shows the way like the polar star. Importantly, the beloved who is mentioned in the first lines of the poem has been interpreted to be the Prophet as the essence of the Creator, which leads to speculations about Muhammad's role as the Perfect Man. As for the symbolism of intoxication, it is common in the mystical traditions of both the East and West.[148] Already Shibli sang:

> Verily the love of the Merciful has intoxicated me—
> Did you ever see a lover who was not intoxicated?[149]

And the topos of the wine quaffed at the "banquet of *alast,*" as Persian poets would call the primordial covenant, became an integral part of later mystical literature, especially in the Persianate world.

But it was the great *Tā'iyya* to which commentators and translators returned time and again, beginning with Joseph von Hammer-Purgstall's first attempt at producing a German rhymed translation which, despite the beautiful print in oriental style (Vienna, 1854) gives only the faintest idea of the content of the poem.[150] R. A. Nicholson's interpretation doubtlessly does best justice to the difficult poem, and he rightly points out that the pantheistic trends which aroused the anger of the theologians are expressions of a state of feeling rather than a system of thought, as is the case in Ibn ᶜArabi's verse. One of the most famous parts of the *Tā'iyya* is the description of the shadow play, where the world is a screen on which the showman makes the puppets move, only to take them back, in the end, into the undifferentiated unity. Ibn ᶜArabi had used the same image,[151] and slightly before the two Arabic writers used it, it had formed the subject of ᶜAttar's Persian *Ushturnāma,* where the hero is a Turkish puppet player.[152] The image, so fitting to explain that "everything is the work of the One" remained a favorite symbol in later mystical writings too.[153]

Lo, from behind the veil mysterious
The forms of things are shown in every guise. . .

says Ibn al-Farid, who closes this part of the poem (vv. 680–706) with the line:

Whatever you have seen, it was the work of the One—

a slight variation of one of the favorite verses of the Sufis in early days:

wa fī kulli shay'in lahu shāhidun
yadullu ᶜalā annahu wāḥidun
And in everything there is a witness for Him
Which points to the fact that He is One.[154]

Ibn al-Farid was a lover of beauty in every form, and his love was sometimes also kindled by beautiful human beings. For instance, he wrote a verse in popular style about a handsome butcher boy, as Ibn Khallikan remarks.[155] However, his fame rests exclusively upon the highly refined odes which are, along with the poems of Hallaj, the only truly great mystical poetry in Arabic.

Ibn al-Farid was not the only major poet in the thirteenth century to sing of his love; the name of ᶜAfifuddin at-Tilimsani (d. 1289), a Sufi of pantheistic tendencies, is connected with easy-flowing poetry in which, however—as his critics claimed—"some poison was hidden."[156] Busiri composed his numerous poems in honor of the Prophet, a genre that became more and more popular (see chapter 5). Sufis in the Arabic-speaking areas took over the tradition of composing didactic verse in the simple meter *Rajaz*,[157] and popular lyrical forms came in to use: the strophic *muwashshaḥ*[158] and *zajal*, and 4- or 5-lined forms such as *billīq*,[159] *dūbait*,[160] and *mawāliyā*[161] were applied to mystical poetry in the following centuries.

A typical example of a late Sufi writer who wrote in most

of the various genres of mystical poetry is ᶜAbdul Ghani an-Nabulusi, at the turn of the eighteenth century. He excelled as a commentator of classical Sufi texts in the vein of Ibn ᶜArabi, and was regarded as the leading religious poet of his time. His voluminous *Dīwān* contains every type of mystical verse, from playful little *muwashshaḥ* to variations on earlier Sufi poems, from a censure against tobacco[162] to *qaṣīdas* studded with the terminology of Ibn ᶜArabi, whose *Futūḥāt al-makkiyya* he praised in a little poem which expresses the feelings of many mystically minded people in the Islamic world:

> The Book of God contains everything,
> And the *sunna* of Ahmad the Elected is a commentary [on it],
> And the commentary for both of them is the *Futūḥāt* through which
> A spiritual triumph [or "donation," *futūḥ*] arrived from the All-Holy.[163]

ᶜAbdul Ghani sings of drinking wine in the monasteries[164] and writes lofty panegyrics for the Prophet, but his verse does not breathe the bittersweet happiness of the immediate, loving experience as found in the simpler lines of some early Sufis, nor does it attain the superb rhetoric of Ibn al-Farid.

While true inspiration seems to be lacking in most of the post-thirteenth-century mystical poetry, the Sufis indulged in writing extensions of and variations on classical poems. A typical example is the art of *tashṭīr* and *takhmīs,* i.e., adding two verses of one's own to a hemistich of a well-known poem, or filling up each of its distichs with three new lines. The *takhmīs* remained a favorite form with the Sufis because it could serve as a kind of poetical commentary on a classical poem: even Ibn ᶜArabi composed a *takhmīs* for a didactic *qaṣīda* by Abu Madyan of Tlemcen, a poem which formed the basis for numerous elaborations by later mystical writers.[165] This kind of second-hand poetry, which required considerable technical skill, was not restricted to the Arab countries proper; Muslim India produced an enormous output of religious poetry in classical forms, faithful to the traditional poetical rules, and even in the eighteenth century Indian Muslim poets and theologians competed in complicated Arabic *qaṣīdas, takhmīs,* or other forms, whether they lived in Delhi (Shah Waliullah), in the northern Deccan (Azad Bilgrami), or in the Carnatic.[166]

This tradition continued into our century, and it was only after World War II that a new kind of mystically tinged poetry emerged in the Middle East: poets who by no means stand in the current of orthodox Islam but have tried to find a new religious base in the mystical tradition of their religion have interpreted afresh some of the figures of classical Sufi history. Salah ᶜAbdas Sabur's drama, *Murder in Baghdad* (as its translator calls it),[167] shows the martyr mystic Hallaj as a social reformer, not as a religious hero, and yet captures some of the mysterious quality of his life and death. And in the verses of Adonis and even more of ᶜAbdul Wahhab al-Bayati he appears in his seeming contradictions, in strange but genuine paradoxes.[168] The recourse of these poets, some of whom politically are leftists, to the Sufi tradition seems to me an important development even though it may not be more than a passing phase in contemporary Arabic poetry. It is all the more interesting since some poets have revived the mythical notions of the ancient Near East, and Hallaj's death and survival is seen as a parallel to that of Tammuz and other dying and resurrected deities,[169] or as allegories of dying and resurrected nations. We have here a first attempt to create a truly mythical poetry in Arabic, but also an example of sociopolitical criticism, since Hallaj stands always for those who have been persecuted by the establishment and yet is still much more alive then those who put him to death.[170]

The fact that such verse was written in our time shows that there is still a possibility of rescuing mystical poetry from the fetters in which it was kept more or less from the turn of the fourteenth century, and it also shows, as it appears to me, that the message of love and sacrifice, of metamorphosis through death, which was the central theme of the early generations of mystics in their unassuming little poems, is alive and meaningful even today.

Two / Tiny Mirrors of Divine Beauty:

CLASSICAL PERSIAN MYSTICAL POETRY

"ALL POETS CAN envy that country, that Persia, where neither forms nor thoughts nor languages change, and where nothing falls into oblivion." Thus wrote Pierre Loti a century ago, expressing the feeling of those Western readers who had become acquainted, if only very superficially, with the works of two or three great Persian poets in translation. It was particularly Hafiz's poetry which fascinated Europe from the late eighteenth century onward and was instrumental in shaping the general notion in the West of Persian poetry as something that expressed uninhibited sensual love, religious freedom if not outright heresy, and that sang mainly of wine, roses, and nightingales. Its peculiar lyrical form, the *ghazal,* was introduced to Europe in the early nineteenth century in Germany, in a masterly way by Friedrich Rückert.[1] A short time before this ingenious orientalist poet published his *ghazals,* which were inspired by Jalaluddin Rumi, Goethe, deeply impressed by Joseph von Hammer's rather shapeless translations of Hafiz's verse, had composed lines which show a deeper understanding of the character of Persian poetry than do the very free and often faulty "translations" and imitations by most other Western writers on Hafiz.[2] I refer to his poem in the *West-Östlicher Divan* (1819):

Dass du nicht enden kannst, das macht dich gross,
und dass du nie beginnst, das ist dein Los.
Dein Lied ist drehend wie das Sterngewölbe,
Anfang und Ende immerfort dasselbe,
Und was die Mitte bringt, ist offenbar
Das, was zu Ende bleibt und anfangs war.[3]

In these lines Goethe points to the character of the *ghazal* with its monorhyme which, like arabesque decorations or the pattern of a carpet, seems to be able to continue beyond the physical boundaries of the design;[4] but he knew also that in this poetry the rhyme determines, to a certain extent, the poet's choice of words and figures of speech and thus provides the poem with a basic unity around which thoughts and ideas are woven in various colors. Again, when Rainer Maria Rilke, a hundred years after Goethe, sings in his *Sonette an Orpheus* of the

Wasser und Gärten von Ispahan oder Schiras . . .
    wie in Glas
eingegossene Gärten . . .[5]

he emphasizes the somewhat static, precious character of Persian lyrical poetry, which in its best examples (like Hafiz) approaches absolute perfection—like a well-cut diamond which shows a different color every moment and yet preserves its transparency. With the image of the carpet, which occurs at the end of the same sonnet, Rilke speaks of the Great Weaver in whose design man is only a tiny thread that, however, has its specific place in the whole pattern. Rilke remains very close to Persian imagery, and seems, at the same time, to allude to the carpetlike quality of a Persian poem, with its multiple focal points and the schematization of figures and design.

Persian poetry, and particularly mystical poetry (whose wings are too heavy with beauty, as someone said) developed at a time when Arabic poetry, on the whole, was on the decline.[6] Mystical ideas and feelings had been alive in Iran from the early days of Islam; eastern Iran, Khorasan, and present-day Afghanistan were the homes of the first ascetic movements in Islam, which perhaps were influenced in some way by Buddhism, whose old center was Bactria. During the Abbasid period many Persian-born mystics came to Iraq, as did Persian courtiers and politicians; then the tradition of al-Hallaj was carried to Iran by Ibn-i Khafif of Shiraz, who was the last to visit the martyr-mystic in prison before his execution in Baghdad on March 26, 922. With the growing of Persian national feeling the Persian language too became a vehicle of poetry, and even though we can no longer accept the traditional view that the first Persian mystical quatrains were composed by Abu Saᶜid-i Abu'l-Khair, the saint of Maihana (d. 1049)[7] it is a fact that mystical literature in Persian developed first in the Eastern Lands of the Caliphate, namely in Herat and northwest India, in the second half of the eleventh century.

The *Kashf al-maḥjūb* of Hujwiri, who spent his last years in Lahore, is the first major treatise on Sufi theories in Persian,[8] and at approximately the same time another mystic, ᶜAbdullah-i Ansari, translated not only Sulami's *Ṭabaqāt aṣ-ṣūfiyya,* a collection of biographies, into his native tongue but also wrote the first devotional booklet in Persian, the *Munājāt.*[9] These short prayers and invocations in rhymed prose with interspersed verses are among the finest in the Islamic world. In these confidential addresses, which, full of love and trust in God, swing between fear and hope and always return to the threshold of the Almighty, Ansari has expressed the feelings of millions of pious souls. Therefore the *Munājāt* are used, though in different redactions, to our day, and its form became a model for many later writings, among them Saᶜdi's *Gulistān.* The change in emphasis in Sufi thought between the late eleventh and the late fifteenth centuries can be understood best by comparing Ansari's *Munājāt* with a booklet in a similar style, written in the same city of Herat and by the scholar-poet Molla Jami, who reworked Ansari's hagiographical work, retitled *Nafaḥāt al-uns*. Molla Jami's *Lawā'iḥ* are a typical expression of the theosophical mysticism formulated by Ibn ᶜArabi and his school, and the difference between the heartbeat of Ansari's warm orisons and Jami's more cerebral *Lawā'iḥ* is very telling.[10]

When Ansari died in 1089 another poet in Afghanistan was still writing rhetorically superb panegyrics for worldly rulers. That was Sana'i of Ghazna, after his conversion to Sufism the first poet to compose a *mathnawī* on mystico-didactic lines.[11] The form of *mathnawī*, rhyming couplets, was unknown in Arabic writing circles;[12] its most famous example in Iran is Firdausi's *Shāhnāma*, the heroic *mathnawī* that was composed in the same city of Ghazna one century before Sana'i. It was followed in the centuries to come by innumerable imitations out of which the genre of romantic *mathnawī* developed, perfected in the twelfth century by Nizami of Ganja, while the ethical *mathnawī* with a soft Sufi hue attained perfection in Saᶜdi's *Būstān*.[13] The form allows the poet to extend his thoughts and tales as long as he deems it necessary—from a couple of hundred verses to tens of thousands of lines. Sana'i's *mathnawī Ḥadīqat al-ḥaqīqat*, "The Garden of Truth," has been considered by orientalists and even by modern Orientals a rather boring piece of literature because its meter is somewhat halting, and its diction is quite straight in spite of the author's amazing rhetorical skill. The *Ḥadīqa* is a storehouse of Sufi lore and contains numerous anecdotes known from earlier prose sources. These are used to explain ascetic or mystical truths in a language which is not exactly "poetic," but rather earthbound and at times outright vulgar. But even Sana'i's greatest spiritual disciple, Maulana Rumi, often borrowed expressions from his works which were widely read and studied among the mystics of Iran. Sana'i's poetic skills are much more conspicuous in his lyrics and his panegyrics on the Prophet, a genre which he seems to have introduced into Persian literature (see Chapter 5).

Sana'i's example was followed by ᶜAttar of Nishapur,[14] whose mystical epics were much more appreciated by later generations, and whose prose work, the *Tadhkirat al-auliyā,* furnished innumerable poets in Iran, Turkey, and India with stories about the lives of earlier Sufis, particularly Hallaj, by whom ᶜAttar was spiritually initiated. His lyrics too contain many expressions which were to become standard topoi in later Sufi poetry, including some *ḥadīth qudsī,* which seem to appear with him for the first time. ᶜAttar's *Manṭiq uṭ-ṭair,* "The Birds' Conversation," and his *Muṣībatnāma,* "Book of Affliction," deal with the development of the human soul on its pilgrimage toward God until the seeker discovers his identity with the Divine, while the *Ilāhīnāma* expresses rather ascetic trends.[15] ᶜAttar is an excellent storyteller; his anecdotes are logically inserted into the framework of the main story, and the meter of his most famous epics is easy-flowing; it was taken over by Rumi for his great *Mathnawī* and subsequently became used in most mystical and didactic poems in the Persian and Persianate tradition. ᶜAttar's *Ushturnāma,* the story of a Turkish puppet player, shows already some disintegration of style; ecstasy, it seems, overwhelms him often in his later compositions. At every stage, his poetry contains long chains of anaphora and is, much more than that of Sana'i, the expression of endless sadness and yearning; he is indeed, as he himself says in the *Manṭiq uṭ-ṭair,* "the voice of pain."[16]

Sana'i and ᶜAttar were the masters of Jalaluddin Rumi, whose *Mathnawī* became the standard work of Persian mystics, "the Koran in the Persian tongue"; Rumi, however, is in a class by himself (see Chapter 3). The allegorical novel in verse, as it developed among later Sufis (like ᶜArifi's *Gūy u jūgān,* "Ball and Polostick," Hilali's *Shāh u gadā,* "King and beggar," etc.)[17] as well as the poetical epistles that deal with technical problems of mysticism (such as Shabistari's *Gulshan-i rāz,* "The Rosegarden of Mysteries") should be mentioned here only in passing.[18]

A contemporary of ᶜAttar, but more representative of the central Persian tradition, was Ruzbihan-i Baqli of Shiraz. Though not primarily a poet, he is extremely important as the author of mystical works like the *Sharḥ-i shaṭḥiyāt,* an interpretation of the theopathic locutions of early Sufi masters, in particular al-Hallaj. Ruzbihan, who stands in the mystical *silsila* of Ibn-i Khafif, tried to communicate the experience of pure love in his *ᶜAbhar al-ᶜāshiqīn,*[19] and here he follows love mystics like Ahmad Ghazzali (the younger brother of the more famous mystical theologian Abu Hamid al-Ghazzali) and his disciple ᶜAinulqudat Hamadhani, who was executed in 1131. In his meditations on Love in all its shades, the *Sawāniḥ,* Ahmad Ghazzali aimed at translating into melodious, undulating sentences the secret of that relation in which the lover, being the mirror of the beloved, is "more the beloved than the beloved himself,"[20] and ᶜAinulqudat's work became, from the early fourteenth century onward, one of the important stimulants of Indo-Muslim mystical literature.[21] In Ruzbihan's writings, the Persian language, refined to almost silken smoothness and transparency by Ahmad Ghazzali, reaches its most sublime form. In these rhapsodic descriptions of the various stages of chaste love, fantastic images follow each other like waves of red roses. The pure and chaste love of which Ruzbihan sings in his work aims finally at a transformation of the soul into Love, and his theories form the basis for our understanding of most Persian mystical poetry. One may think in this connection of Fakhruddin ᶜIraqi's charming lyrics of the late thirteenth century and of his interpretation in graceful poetical language of Ibn ᶜArabi's theories in the *Lamaᶜāt;* [22] these theories form the background for Hafiz's verse in the fourteenth and Jami's lyrics in the late fifteenth century, although in Jami's verse a stupendous rhetorical skill often hides the poet's real concern.

A similar style of mystically tinged love poetry, with exactly the same imagery and poetical forms, developed from the fifteenth century in the Ottoman Empire. As a result, Turkish "Divan Poetry" was often regarded as a mere imitation of Persian models, and E. H. W. Gibb's introduction to his useful *History of Ottoman Poetry* is valid for most of Persian poetry as well.[23] India too contributed to this literature—in fact, the Subcontinent produced more Persian works than Iran proper. India was the home of poets writing in Persian as early as the eleventh century, shortly after the conquest by Mahmud of Ghazna of its northwestern part (now Pakistan). In the thirteenth and fourteenth centuries mystical and mystically inclined poets like Amir Khusrau[24] and Hasan Dihlawi created a highly refined lyrical poetry, and Khusrau also wrote important epical works. The literature of the Sufi urban orders was generally composed in Persian, the standard language of literature and, from the late fifteenth century, of administration. During Moghul times numerous poets, many of whom were immigrants from Safawid Iran, developed the complicated and in the end almost incomprehensible Indian Style, *sabk-i hindī,* which, despite its intrinsic difficulties, has moments of extreme beauty.[25] Poetry in Urdu—in which only Mir Dard in eighteenth century Delhi composed truly mystical verse—is unthinkable without the Persian literary tradition.[26]

The poetical forms that developed in Iran were well suited

to the expression of religious ideas. The *mathnawī* could be extended almost infinitely, and the poet could easily introduce endless anaphora to point to the mysteries of God's creative power which is visible everywhere in the world. In the introductory praise poems of their epics the poets liked to allude elegantly to the content of their work by addressing God with relevant names or fitting descriptions: in a heroic epic He would be called predominantly by names of wrath, like *al-qahhār* (The Wrathful), or *al-jabbār* (The Overpowering), while in romantic epics He would appear as the one who kindles the flame of love, as *al-laṭīf* (The Tender), or *al-wadūd* (The Loving), or similar names of grace. In the *qaṣīda,* the long praise poem with monorhyme which was taken over without major change from the Arabs, the poet could richly orchestrate his feelings about God's wonderful actions. Since Persian poetry frequently uses the *radīf,* one word or a number of words after the actual rhyming letter, the writer could easily insert many repetitions of the same exclamation or question and thus express his love and longing, or ask the Lord's forgiveness, or praise His greatness in regularly repeated rhymes. Often closely related to litanies (as are some of the religious introductions to epics), such *qaṣīdas* circumscribe with constantly changing metaphors the Numen without ever plumbing Its abysses. The use of daring hyperboles is part of the *qaṣīda* tradition and is appropriate for the praise of God's marvelous works, in which the aspects of *jalāl* (Majesty), and *jamāl* (Beauty), work together to create the patterns of the mysterious yet meaningful carpet of life. In such *qaṣīdas* the poets exclaimed that their tongues had no other work than praising the Lord[27] whose power presses its seal on the sun,[28] and the more learned and complicated their poems were the more eloquently would they say that they were incapable of praising God with appropriate words. Sana'i has beautifully translated God's answer to such praise when he has Him say:

> Whatever comes to your mind that I am that—I am not that!
> Whatever has room in your understanding that I would be like this—I am not like this!
> Whatever has room in your understanding is all something created—
> In reality know, O servant, that I am the Creator![29]

The *ghazal,* the shorter poem with monorhyme, which probably developed out of the erotic introduction of the *qaṣīda,* uses a softer instrumentation, and *ghazal* writers concentrate on their love of God or their longing for the beloved who is as beautiful as he is cruel.

In later times poets would sometimes utilize the form of *tarjīᶜband* for religious poetry, which is a series of *ghazals* bound together by one verse repeated after each *ghazal,* like Hatif's oft-quoted poem on Divine Unity:

> He is One and there is naught but He,
> There is no God save Him alone.[30]

A late, more "scholarly" poem of this genre is the well-known *tarjīᶜband* of the Turkish poet Zia Pasha (d. 1880), who exclaims again and again in the Arabic *band:*

> *Subḥāna man taḥayyara fi ṣunᶜihi 'l-ᶜuqūl*
> *Subḥāna man bi-qudratihi yaᶜjizu'l-fuḥūl*
> Praise to Him by whose workmanship the intellects are stunned!
> Praise to Him by whose power mighty stalwarts are rendered incapable![31]

This form is also very fitting for musical performance, where the repeated verse can be taken up by the chorus to form a kind of continuo.

The *rubāʿī*, quatrain, in the form aaxa, offers the poet the opportunity to express mystical thought or feeling in a succinct, epigramatic form in which ideally the first two lines set the theme; the third, nonrhyming line contains a kind of antithesis, and the fourth line offers the summary.[32]

All these different genres are strictly determined by quantitative meters, which were inherited from Arabic but slightly changed according to the exigencies of the Persian (as well as Turkish and Urdu). The rhetorical devices which are an integral part of that poem, are very carefully observed: *murāʿāt an-naẓīr* requires that the images in a verse stand in a well-defined relation to each other. When the rose is mentioned, we can definitely expect a nightingale, and probably one or two more images from the garden. If a Koranic prophet appears, his specific qualities or those of some other prophet are likely to appear. It is the art of the great masters to maintain a perfect equilibrium of images in such a way that they seem perfectly natural, as exemplified in the work of Hafiz. This technique gives the verse a certain symmetry and, as in a perfect classical Persian miniature, everything has its place so that, as in miniature painting, one may speak of a two-dimensional system of signs that have equal, or near-equal, value.[33]

The other favorite rhetorical figure, *ḥusn-i taʿlīl*, the fantastic etiology, allows the poet to make everything alive: when the rose opens, the poet sees this natural act as an expression of the rose's tearing its fragrant shirt because the beloved, beautiful as Yusuf, has come to the garden. According to the Koranic tradition (Sura 12/26–28) Yusuf's shirt, in turn, had been torn by Zulaikha and later served to heal his blind father by its very fragrance. The combination of the rose with the shirt forms a kind of mirrored image—the rose is both as beautiful and fragrant as Yusuf and yet envies the Yusuf-like beloved. This artistic form enabled the poets to put everything into a kind of mythological setting and to express psychological moods by esthetic means; thus all nature becomes alive and active in this poetical cosmos.[34]

Persian poets also loved the art of *tażādd,* contrasting pairs of words, which is especially applicable to the description of God, who manifests Himself in the world under the dual aspects of *luṭf* and *qahr,* kindness and wrath, of *jamāl* and *jalāl,* the *fascinans* and the *tremendum.* This dual aspect of the Perfect One Divine is necessary to maintain the flow of life, as are *yang* and *yin,* the positive and negative poles, and, in the Persian poetical tradition, Beauty (as a static concept) and (dynamic) Love, which are interdependent and appear here on earth in various manifestations.

The predilection of mystical poets for contrasting pairs of concepts shows itself also in another frequently used phrase, namely the bipartite profession of faith, *lā ilāha illā Allāh.* This formula is used by many Sufi orders as *dhikr,* and has been connected by Ibn ᶜArabi with Divine breathing: *lā ilāha,* "there is no deity" is the existentialization of the world which is outside God, and *illā Allāh,* "save God," is the taking back of the Divine breath into the eternal and unchangeable Divine essence. In the poets' eyes, *lā,* which looks in its graphic form like ᶜAli's famous two-edged sword Dhu'l-fiqar, or like scissors or a broom, serves to clean the heart from everything that is not God, for the full realization of mystical *tauḥīd* was the goal of all mystical poets. Therefore the *lā* was even compared, by Jami, to a crocodile which swallows everything that is not God.

After "cleaning the house with the broom of ᶜno' " the poets recognized God everywhere,[35] as their favorite Koranic phrase states: "Whithersoever ye turn there is the Face of God" (Sura 2/109). This experience (or, in many cases, the imitation of this experience) led the poets to sing that God manifests

Himself under different guises, as the color of the bottle colors the water in it, an image Junaid had used and ᶜAttar had repeated in a fine passage in the *Ushturnāma*.[36] And when Hallaj had complained of those who look at the sky without perceiving God while the true lover finds Him in every sip of water, Amir Khusrau sings:

> It is nothing but Your goblet which the lovers drink in the taverns;
> It is nothing but Your name which the ascetics recite in the monasteries.[37]

However, in most cases this was rather the expression of an overwhelming feeling of God's omnipresence, not the kind of theoretical pantheism that became so prevalent in post-Ibn ᶜArabi poetry. And one can interpret in both ways Jami's famous lines:

> So constantly are you in my stricken soul and sleepless eyes
> That whatsoever should appear from afar, I should think that it was you,[38]

for the true lover sees everything as pertaining to his beloved.

ᶜIraqi had sung of the primordial wine of love which was borrowed from the cupbearer's intoxicated eyes. His charming Persian poem with the Arabic beginning:

> *a-ku'ūsun tala'la'at mudām*
> Cups are these a-flashing with wine,
> Or suns through the clouds a-gleaming?
> So clear is the wine and the glass so fine
> That the two are one in seeming,

describes the perplexity of the intoxicated lover who can no longer discern between vessel and content:

> The glass is all and the wine is naught,
> Or the glass is naught and the wine is all—

and finally discovers

> That all that is, is He indeed:
> Soul and loved one and heart and creed.[39]

The formula *hama ūst,* "Everything is He," was already in use before Ibn ᶜArabi laid down the foundations of the theory of *waḥdat al-wujūd;* it is found more than once in ᶜAttar's lyrics, while in later mystical poetry it was to become pivotal. Persian poets never tired of inventing new images to express this all-embracing and all-pervading unity:

> Sometimes we call You goblet and sometimes wine,
> Sometimes we call You grain and sometimes snare.
> There is no other word but Your name on the tablet of the world—
> By which name, then, should we call You?[40]

It goes without saying that, for this feeling that everything is part of the Divine life, the image of the ocean and the waves offered itself comfortably.[41] The mysterious effect of the contemplation of running water is often discussed in the history of religion (the Buddha, Ignatius of Loyola), and so is the transforming power of water when man is immersed in it for a moment.[42] Likewise, the ocean of the Godhead is an image common to most religious traditions, particularly the more impersonalistic mystical currents: are not the waves and drops identical with the sea even though they look different? River and brook, rain and ice are all part of the infinite ocean out of which foam may come up in strangely shaped figures, remaining at the surface for a moment and then responding again to the call, "Come back!" (Sura 89/27), disappearing in the eternal abyss.[43] Ibn ᶜArabi had contemplated the Godhead as a green ocean, and for him and his followers the world was like ice, crystallized out of the Divine sea.[44] Persian poets loved the symbol of the rain drop which emerges from the water, travels for some time through the clouds and then returns to be reunited with the water.[45] However, mystical poets in the more personalistic tradition saw still another possibility: the drop returns to the sea to find a home in an oyster where it will grow into a precious pearl, living in the ocean and yet distinct from it. But the general feeling was that the heart of every drop is filled with "dropsy," as ᶜAttar calls it, namely the longing to become the ocean itself.[46] Then Hallaj's sentence *anā'l-ḥaqq* "I am the Absolute Truth" could be interpreted by more critical mystics as the call of the drop that impudently voices the claim that it has already *become* the ocean.

From early days Sufi poets voiced the feeling that in true *tauḥīd, kufr* and *īmān* (infidelity and faith) are basically unimportant because both of them are created, hence transient. Sana'i sings with words that are to become mere conventions in his successors' verse,

> Rosary and religion and monastery is the order of asceticism;
> Infidels' girdle and infidelity and tavern is the order of love.[47]

But while he points, with this verse, to the eternal conflict between "love" and "law," he goes even further in the beginning of the *Ḥadīqa,* where he states:

> Infidelity and faith are both running to and fro in Your way,
> Saying: "He is alone and has no companion."[48]

He in fact adopts Hallaj's remark that "*kufr* and *īmān* differ in name, but in reality there is no difference between them," which may be interpreted as the mystics' statement that all contrasts fall together in God, the perfect *coincidentia oppositorum,* or that both guidance and error are created by God.[49]

Sana'i is, theologically speaking, closer to the second interpretation, but in Sufi poetry the mystical *tauḥīd* became gradually more prominent, and in the course of time, more and more poets would sing of the "one dream and its different interpretations" when they thought of the Divine essence and Its various manifestations in time and space. It is only natural that these trends became paramount in post-Ibn ᶜArabi poetry. Thus poets like Maghribi (d. 1406) became the spokesmen for the conviction of the overall Unity of Being, which they tried to express in thousands of lines whose imagery soon became stereotyped.[50] The possibility of interpreting practically every sensual image in a mystical way according to the method used by Ibn ᶜArabi in the *Tarjumān al-ashwāq* made this kind of poetry easy to handle, and as the conventional topoi became more shallow and outworn, only very few poets were able to fill them with new life.

In this tradition, the inherited values of Islam were considered only as a support for the poor plebeians who had not yet reached the lofty heights of all-embracing unity, as Faizi says condescendingly:

> Don't destroy the Kaᶜba, O Love, for it is there
> That those who have stayed behind alight now and then.[51]

This attitude is one reason for the aversion of Muslim modernists to this poetry, which seemed to lull their compatriots into sweet slumber instead of inciting them to new activity on the Path of God. For the dynamic love-relation between God and man had been replaced, in most cases, by a theosophic *tauḥīd* expressed in sweeping statements about the relation between unity and plurality.

Evelyn Underhill has shown that in every religious tradition mystics try to explain their experiences in three major categories of symbols.[52] Sometimes they see themselves as pilgrims to a better country or as travellers home, to the eternal Jerusalem or whatever their native land might be, living on

> The hope of the City of God at the other end of the road,

as John Masefield says. Others, those who primarily hope for sanctification of their lives, prefer the images of alchemy: Persian poets love to speak of the copper which becomes gold when it is touched by the alchemy of Love or by the hand of the beloved, and of the necessity of suffering in the crucible for the sake of purification. Then, the lover's face shines like gold, i.e., is pale and translucent, and the mystical guide acts upon him like *kibrīt aḥmar,* red sulphur, the most precious ingredient for producing gold.[53] A third category of symbols, used mostly by those who long for God as the Beloved, use the imagery of human love. But these three categories are only rarely used exclusively; Persian mystical poets use and interweave them often in a single verse even though the center of their thoughts is always Love.

Among those who have described the spiritual journey most eloquently are Sana'i, with his little philosophical *mathnawī Sair al-ᶜibād ilā'l-maᶜād,* "The Journey of the Servants to the Place of Return,"[54] and ᶜAttar, whose poetry consists entirely of the story of the soul's longing for home. Both he and Sana'i knew this journey to be extremely long: it begins with the lowest forms of life and leads finally to man, and among men, to the Prophet as the Perfect Man. Much patience is required to see created beings develop to their final stages, as Sana'i writes:

> It takes days that the wool of a sheep
> Becomes a cloak for the ascetic or the bridle for a donkey;
> It requires a lifetime, naturally, until a child
> Becomes a good scholar or a sweet-worded poet;

It requires centuries until out of the semen of Adam
A [mystic like] Abu'l-Wafa Kurd or an Uwais-i Qarani comes into being.[55]

And ᶜAttar sees how in these long periods of growing and waiting thousands and millions of creatures are destroyed until the longed-for Man of God appears:

A hundred thousand creatures were fire worshippers
Until the Friend of God (Abraham) was saved from the fire.
A hundred thousand hearts and souls were destroyed
Until Muhammad one night reached ascension to heaven.[56]

The mystical poets were well aware that the caravan of life is constantly moving, and with images taken from the Arabic tradition they taught their listeners to follow the call *ar-raḥīl*, "Let's travel!" and not to close their eyes in the sleep of heedlessness lest the caravan leave them in the desert. And the sound of the caravan bell which guides them to the sanctuary, Mecca, where the Beloved dwells, is awaited eagerly (even if this pilgrimage is understood, as it is by many, as a metaphor for the journey into one's own soul). But once the caravan has reached its goal, the bell will be silent, for in perfect union no words are possible.[57] But these poets, headed by Sana'i and ᶜAttar, knew also that

Every time this road is more endless,
Every moment people are more confused in it.[58]

For once the journey *to* God is finished the journey *in* God begins, as is stated at the end of the *Manṭiq uṭ-ṭair*—and that is a mystery never to be told. ᶜAttar is here close not only to his coreligionists but also to Meister Eckhart, who, after speaking of God as the complete, pure One, closes his discourse with the words: "And in this One we are to sink from nothing to nothing, so help us God."

This infinite way, however, can be traversed only by Love, for every stage on it requires a loving sacrifice from the wayfarer.

> Heaven has no prayer direction but Love,
> The world has no glamor without the matter of Love,[59]

says Nizami, who, in commonly used phrases, praises the power of Love, which is visible in the magnet attracting the iron, in the amber attracting the straw. Love is, as Hallaj had determined for the first time, the inner principle of Divine life, and hence without beginning and without end.

> Love is what has no end;
> It has had neither a beginning nor has it an end.[60]

The resurrection which the common believers fear so much is, according to ᶜUrfi, only the first station in Love,[61] a love which obliterates everything and is, in itself, death and resurrection. For being the innermost essence of God, Love is, like God, an endless ocean, but:

> The water of this ocean is fire;
> Waves come so that one would think they were mountains of darkness;
> In the midst of its waves it has three hundred crocodiles,
> On the shore a hundred dragons full of majesty . . .[62]

Thus Sana'i describes the ocean of Love, and the image of the sea of fire remained a favorite with all later mystical poets—how could intellect with wooden legs enter it!

The Persian poets never ceased to contrast Intellect and Love.[63] Just as in the early Arabic tradition Majnun claimed that Laila's beauty could be appreciated only by his (the demented lover's) eyes but not by those who cleverly compared her to others, thus the mystics, anti-intellectual despite their great learning, repeated time and again that reason, or intellect, leads to talk while Love silently reveals the inside of the mysteries; intellect is blind when it comes to the street of Love, and should be left to Avicenna.[64] Thus said Sana'i, who—probably following Ghazzali's attack on Avicenna in the *Tahāfut al-falāsifa*—was the first poet to condemn his compatriot Avicenna, the philosopher-physician, as the paragon of loveless intellectualism. Avicenna is regarded this way in Persian verse to our day (e.g., in Iqbal's work).[65]

What do the jurists know of Love? Neither the Kufi, Abu Hanifa, nor Shafiᶜi know its ways and traditions.[66]

> What shall I say about the one who denies Love?
> He is a cow, a jackass, and a hard stone,

sings Gesudaraz, the Chishti saint,[67] who even at the age of 90 still enjoyed singing of his love. But he has gracefully pointed to one of the problems connected with love:

> You look at the beautiful one and see the stature and the figure—
> I do not see in between anything but the beauty of the work of the Creator![68]

He alludes here to an aspect of Sufism that had become more and more popular: to see the Divine beauty reflected in or manifested through a human being, ideally a boy of fourteen. The alleged Prophetic tradition, "I saw my Lord in the most beautiful form,"[69] which was then enlarged with the qualification "with his cap awry" (*kajkulāh*) gave the mystics the pretext not only to discover God's wonderful creative work in a lovely human being but to regard him as the true witness, *shāhid*, of Divine beauty. The root of all human beauty is God's smiling (*ḍaḥk Allāh*),[70] and when later mystical poets claim that they do not care for Paradise but are happy with the smile of the beloved, they allude to the tradition that God will be smiling at them in the Otherworld. What, then, would be the need for houris and castles as promised to the faithful in the Koran?

The veneration of young boys—branded by the orthodox as a kind of manicheism—developed into a highly refined spiritual art, but could also degenerate into a more or less crude homosexuality. The sober Sufis were always aware of the danger of "looking at the unbearded,"[71] and already Sana'i accused the Sufis of his time of having no other *qibla* but *shāhid, sham*ᶜ, and *shikam* (a handsome boy, candles at parties, and their stomachs).[72] The lovers, however, maintained that such a love was licit, provided that the chastity of the glance was preserved.[73] Ahmad Ghazzali put a rose between himself and his beloved, contemplating both of them alternatingly.

> Wherever you see a *shāhid,*
> Sit before him like a mirror,

says Rumi,[74] echoing Ahmad Ghazzali's ideals. As the old proverb says, *al-majāz qanṭaratu'l-ḥaqīqa,* "The metaphor is the bridge that leads to Reality"; the Sufis knew with Ruzbihan-i Baqli that love of a human being is the ladder leading to the love of the Merciful.[75] Hence human love was called *ᶜishq-i majāzī,* metaphorical love, in contrast to the pure, true, Divine love, *ᶜishq-i ḥaqīqī.* The soul needs the wings of human love to fly toward Divine love, and thus many poets claim: "We have directed our *qibla* toward the quarter of the one who wears his cap awry."[76] This verse by Hasan Dihlawi was imitated time and again, and it is here that Persian poetry gains its specific flavor. The constant oscillation between the two levels of experience often makes it next to impossible to translate or even to understand a poem correctly. It is this ambiguity between the human and the superhuman levels which makes the Persian *ghazal* so delightful, like a two-faced brocade. Without returning to the heavy and usually quite tasteless theological interpretation of the various metaphors, one would agree with Goethe that the poetical word as used by the Persian poets is a fan that both hides and reveals the beautiful face behind it.[77]

Persian poets have sung in innumerable verses about the lover's plight. Faithful to Daqqaq's saying, "Who does not make his soul a broom at the door of the beloved is not a lover,"[78] they claimed to have honor only in so far as they had no desire for union. Sana'i rightly states:

> In the way of *tauḥīd* one cannot walk toward two *qiblas,* [namely]
> the satisfaction of the friend and one's own selfish lust.[79]

The same poet repeated Hallaj's feeling that Iblis was the true lover because he obeyed God's pre-eternal Will and prefered to be cursed by Him rather than to fall down before someone other than Him. His *Lament of Iblīs* is one of the most touching poems in Persian I know.[80] The conviction that:

> The separation which is the aim of the beloved
> Is a thousand times better than union[81]

becomes a recurring topos in Persian poetry. Hafiz perceived with deep insight that union is hidden behind separation as light is hidden in the darkness:[82] only in absolute darkness, in the dark night of the soul, can the Sun at Midnight rise or, as the poets often say, only in the Valley of Tenebrae is the Water of Life to be found. And the heart needs to be polished, the stains of worldly existence need to be removed by the constant remembrance of the Beloved, so that the heart can become a radiant mirror that reflects the beauty of the Friend without fault.

In later times, the feeling that there is no real separation possible because *everything* is the Beloved seems to prevail in many poems, and ᶜIraqi's lines:

> Lover, beloved and love—all the three are one.
> When union comes in, what has separation to do?[83]

form the model for thousands of verses, often by mediocre writers who were no longer aware of the secret of longing as the source of true poetry.

But how to reach union with the Beloved? That is possible only by death:

> It is not easy to reach the incomparable friend—
> If you hope for union, then die![84]

The dictum described to the Prophet: *mūtū qabla an tamūtū*, "Die before ye die," forms the basis on which developed a deep longing for death on the path to the beloved: the martyr of love, too, was hoping for the privileges promised to those who die *fī sabīl Allāh*, in God's way, or for His sake.

> O would that I had a thousand lives
> That I could spread out all of them before your arrows!

sings ᶜAttar's hero,[85] voicing a hope which, in different words, has been expressed by almost every poet in the Persianate world.

This longing for death is combined with longing for pain, for the pain of love is in itself the greatest happiness—an idea common to mystics in all religions. The Persian poets invented an ingenious way to prove the value of pain and affliction by pointing to the central metahistorical event, the *rūz-i alast*, when God asked the not-yet-created souls *alastu bi-rabbikum*, "Am I not your Lord?" and they answered *balā*, "Yes!" (Sura 7/171). From Sana'i onward this *balā* was interpreted to mean *balā*, "affliction." This means that the souls willingly accepted by their very *balā*, "Yes," every affliction that God would shower upon them during their lives to test their love and sincerity.[86] Affliction thus reminded them of the pre-eternal covenant in which they pledged to obey and, as the mystics soon added, love only the Eternal Lord. Pain thus becomes the most important ingredient of love.

> When you have no pain, how could the medicine come?

asks ᶜAttar,[87] for pain has been granted by the Beloved, who then will appear as the physician to heal the wound which He Himself has inflicted upon the lover. Destruction is necessary for building up: *kenōsis,* emptying oneself, complete surrender, or "being broken" is the prerequisite for a higher spiritual life. Persian poets love the image of the treasure which is found only in *kharābāt,* devastated and ruined places, and which will become evident when everything that covers it has fallen to pieces. Did not God Himself say that He was a hidden treasure that wanted to be known, and therefore created the world? And did He not say, in a later *ḥadīth qudsī,* that He would dwell with those whose hearts are broken for His sake? The allegory of moth and candle, in which Hallaj expressed the secret of *Stirb und werde,* became a standard topos in Persian poetry; the poets knew that the moth, by immolating itself in the flame, reaches union with and is thus transformed into Divine fire. Besides, the ascetic education of the *nafs,* the lower soul, could easily be expressed in images of the traveler's suffering on the Path where, in Ghalib's words, liver pieces of dying lovers turn all the thorns into rose bushes.[88] The cruelty of Persian imagery, in which every lover gladly uses his head as a polo ball for the mallet of the friend's tresses, and where roses look like fire or like wounds, and eyelashes are converted into piercing arrows, shocked Goethe when he tried to give an impartial judgment of Persian poetry.[89]

This constant emphasis on pain and suffering led the

mystics to the assertion that love is only for the strong, for the true men of God (the rhyme *mard* ["man"] with *dard* ["pain"] was helpful in this respect).

> He who is not pregnant from pain,
> He is a woman, he is not a man![90]

This true man, who seeks nothing but God alone, has to give up joyfully everything, especially his life; he has to enjoy the blame of the outsiders, and the scolding of the beloved is like music for him. His love has to be absolutely unconditional. He is constantly burning, and it is remarkable how often the rhymes *sūkhtan, sūz* ("burn") in all their variations occur in classical and postclassical Persian poetry.[91] Fire in all its aspects (flame, spark, lightning, candle, etc.) forms one of the most important ingredients of later Indo-Persian poetry (see chapter 3).

For the mystical poets knew that it is both impossible and illicit to express in plain words their experience of burning and melting, of transformation in suffering, and those who try to give a description of the Divine Reality which they tasted in a moment of ecstasy are like the blind who touched an elephant in a dark stable and could not describe anything but the part their hands had touched.[92] Maulana Rumi, who retells this Indian story, which was first used by Sana'i, expressed better than any other poet the predicament of the lover who wants and yet does not want to sing of his love. So, one of his verses in the beginning of the *Mathnawī* has become the standard motto for all later writers:

> *Khushtar ān bāshad ki sirr-i dilbarān*
> *Gufta āyad dar ḥadīth-i dīgarān*[93]
> It is better that the secret of the beloved ones
> Should be expressed in the stories of others.

For the greatest sin of the lover is *ifshā' as-sirr,* divulgence of the secret. This was at least according to the poetical tradition, the reason for Hallaj's execution. Persian poets have therefore woven a veil of symbols in order to point to and at the same time hide the secret of love, longing, and union. The world of religion offered them numerous images—the Kaᶜba and the street of the friend, the black stone and the mole on the beloved's cheek became interchangeable, and to kiss the black stone during the pilgrimage would remind the lover of kissing the mole on his beloved's cheek, or the ruby of his mouth. *ᶜId,* the great Feast, is meeting the beloved:

> We celebrate the ᶜId but once a year—
> A constant ᶜId for me: your presence dear![94]

The friend's beautiful face could be compared to the Koran, for like every copy of the Holy Book it was of perfect, flawless beauty and contained the manifestation of God's words and actions; the eyebrows, due to their shape, could then form the prayer niche for the lover. As separation is longer than the day of resurrection,

> Paradise is my beloved's face,
> Distance from him is Hell![95]

Koranic phrases were cleverly inserted or alluded to so that the whole Islamic prophetology became part and parcel of Persian poetry.

Adam, created by God's own hands and endowed with Divine breath, is the place of manifestation of that beauty which God placed in human forms, and he becomes therefore the prototype of the beloved. Abraham, who was cast into the pyre whose fire became "cool and pleasant" for him (Sura 21/69) is the lover, for whom the fire of love turns into a lovely rose-garden. And Joseph is the paragon of beauty whose appearance confused Zulaikha and the Egyptian women (they cut their hands but did not feel any pain while gazing at him). He is also a model of the soul which, after spending days in the darkness of the well, is restored to higher glory. Likewise the scent of his shirt, which cured Jacob's blindness, becomes connected with the fragrant morning breeze which the lover hopes will bring him news from his beloved and brighten his eyes, which have become blind from weeping. The waiting lover has, like Moses, to hear the Beloved's word, "You will never behold Me!" (Sura 7/139), and David's psalter is echoed in the songs of the nightingales. Jesus is endowed with life-giving breath so that he becomes the ideal beloved whose kiss quickens the near-dead lover. The idea, known from Greek and Roman antiquity, that the kiss is an exchange of souls, occurs frequently, for the poet hoped that the beloved would put his soul into his mouth, because his own soul is already on the lip, i.e., he is almost dead.[96]

Besides figures from the Koranic heritage, historical personalities too have been transformed into symbols of lovers. Mansur-i Hallaj is the ideal hero of all those who believe in the importance of daring, unrestricted love, rather than legalism, even though—or perhaps because—he had to pay with his life for his love. Thus his name is much more frequently used in Persian nonepic poetry than that of any other Muslim. More surprising is the transformation of the great warrior king of Ghazna, Sultan Mahmud, into the model of the ideal lover. This conqueror of northwest India is praised for his close relationship with his Turkish officer Ayaz, who appears as the exemplar of the "servant." But the king finally became "the slave of his slave"—a topic used still in Iqbal's poetry.[97] And in early days the heroes of the romantic epic tradition of Iran—such as Wis and Ramin, or much more frequently in post-

Nizami centuries, Majnun and Laila, or Khusrau, Farhad, and Shirin[98]—came to designate the various aspects of love. Among them, Majnun was the favorite of enthusiastic poets because he personified the loss of discerning intellect through the overwhelming power of Love.

Not only human figures served the Persian poets singing of their love and suffering; even the most insignificant parts of nature became symbols for them:

> Rose and mirror and sun and moon—what are they?
> Wherever we looked there was, indeed, Your face![99]

Since the Koran states that everything was created in order to worship God, early Sufis listened to the trees and the flowers, the birds and the fishes, each of them speaking in *lisān ul-ḥāl,* the "tongue of its whole being." Sana'i created the lovely "Litany of the Birds," in which every bird addresses God in his own language: the stork speaks with a constant *lak lak,* attesting *al-mulk lak, al- ᶜizz lak,* "Thine is the kingdom, Thine is the glory," while the dove is always asking the way towards the Friend by calling *kū kū,* "Where? Where?"[100] Such ideas were taken up by Rumi in his great spring poems. But the poet who gave classical form to the ancient idea of the "soul bird," as it is known from primitive religions onward, was ᶜAttar with his *Manṭiq uṭ-ṭair,* in which thirty birds guided by the *hudhud* (the hoopoe who once was the go-between between Solomon and the Queen of Sheba) perform the difficult journey to Mount Qaf, where the king of birds lives.[101] After passing the seven valleys they discover finally that the Divine bird, *Sīmurgh,* is nothing but themselves, being *sī murgh,* "thirty birds." With this most ingenious pun in the Persian language ᶜAttar has alluded to the final and basic union of the individual souls with the Divine, and the Simurgh, known from the *Shāhnāma* as a resourceful kind of phoenix, now becomes the symbol of the Godhead at the end of the road where every longing finds it consummation.

The soul bird assumes various forms. One is the falcon, the noble bird who is captured in the cold, dark world in the midst of ravens or crows (symbols of the lower, material world) and after much suffering is finally called back to his Lord with the Koranic word *irjiʿī*, "Come back, O soul at peace!" (Sura 89/27). For the falcon got his name, *bāz*, because he returns, *bāz āyad*, as Rumi says with another, less ingenious pun.[102] The training of the falcon at the hand of the falconer is a fine image of the education of the novice by the Pir, as is that of the "sugar chewing," sweet-worded parrot (a typically Indian bird) who learns to speak through a mirror of polished steel, i.e., the polished heart of the master who reflects the Divine light.[103] All of these birds join the poet in his question:

> When will it be that I leave this cage
> And make my nest in the Divine meadow?[104]

The ideal soul bird, however, is the nightingale, who spends his life longing for the rose. It may be that the easy rhyme *gul*, ("rose") with *bulbul* ("nightingale") has contributed to the frequent use of this image for the relation of lover and beloved.[105] But the rose was from early times connected with the Prophet or with God: created from the Prophet's perspiration during his ascension, it carries his fragrance. As the Prophet put the red rose on his eyes and recognized in it something of the divine beauty and majesty, thus Ruzbihan-i Baqli visualized divine glory as a red rose full of radiance, comparable to Dante's *Rosa mystica*.[106] To love the eternal rose, which is protected from the unworthy by innumerable thorns, makes the nightingale eloquent, for his longing can never be fulfilled in this life (as is the case with man's love of God), and only unfulfilled longing makes the soul productive, induces it to sing without end about the beloved.

Every flower in the mystical cosmos of Persian poets has a special function. The lily is silent with ten tongues, as the mystic should be. The narcissus is all eyes to look at the friend. The cypress reminds the poet of the Beloved's graceful stature, the hyacinth of his dark curls. In the spring, when all of these flowers appear again from the seemingly dead earth, prefiguring resurrection, the breeze of love brings the scent of Joseph's shirt, and in the tulip bed the burning bush appears or the bloodstained shrouds of the martyrs.[107]

Animals too figure in this cosmos: camels are human souls; lions are the saints who wander in full glory through the dark forests of this world; and musk deer leave a fragrant trace that may indicate the way to the Beloved. One of the most touching symbols for the soul's longing for home is the captured elephant who dreams of Hindustan and tears his chains to run home in a frenzy of love to be united with those whom he has loved in his native country, just as the reed flute sings of its longing for the pre-eternal reedbed.

Stones remind the poets of the activity of the Beloved. The ruby is created from coarse rock by the transforming rays of the sun, as the heart's blood, after much suffering and patience, may be transformed by love into a valuable and beautiful material. The ruby also symbolizes the lips of the Beloved. The emerald blinds dragons and serpents and is therefore connected with the charms of the Friend.

Music is seen as the resonance of eternal harmony; the flute speaks only when touched by the Friend's lips, the rebeck when caressed by his hand. Even the letters of the Arabic alphabet become ciphers for the charms of the Beloved, or point to the lover's state.[108]

In short, everything in the world is in some mysterious

way connected with Love and expresses either the longing of the lover or sings of the beauty and glory of the eternal Beloved who hides His face behind a thousand forms. He hides because the pure light is too strong to be seen; it has to be reflected in various colors—in the red of fire and blood and roses, in the green of grass which is reminiscent of Paradise, or in the gold of the lover's emaciated cheeks.[109] For the poets, the rhetorical form of *ḥusn-i taᶜlīl* was an ideal vehicle to make this poetical cosmos come alive.

In such a cosmos, discursive intellect has no place; rational thought is not allowed in the sanctuary of Love, even though the rhetoric of Persian poetry has been filtered through the intellect. But the highly developed technique of Persian poetry could still serve to describe mystical intoxication, an intoxication which is not from the wine of the grape but rather from the pre-eternal wine of love, which Ibn al-Farid had praised in his *Khamriyya.* This poetry is like Persian miniature painting, which combines an inspirational quality with the minutest detail work so as to lead us into an enchanted garden in which we finally discover deeper and deeper mysteries that go far beyond the "real" figures and extend into the spirits of leaves, flowers, and even rocks.

Intoxication is an integral part of many mystical currents, for "sobriety diminishes, discriminates, and says No, while drunkenness expands, unites, and says Yes" (William James).[110] Gesudaraz sings:

> Those who are intoxicated by the goblet of Love
> Are unconscious from the wine of *alast.*[111]

The wine-house, the old magian who operates the winehouse, and the young Christian boy of fourteen who offers the lover the cup with fiery wine are all part of this picture that signifies the preeminence of love over external rites and outward forms.[112]

The majority of the mystics would have sided with Bayezid Bistami, who once exclaimed: "Someone has drunk the oceans of the seven heavens and earths and he still calls: Is there more?"[113] That is why in later centuries the poets of the Indian style would speak of *khamyāza* ("yawning") to express this infinite thirst and longing, which resembles the longing of the shore to embrace the ocean and can never be satisfied.

It is this thirst that made the poets create. Words die when union has finally been achieved, but the never-ending yearning for the beloved made talkative those who were well aware that mystical experience cannot properly be communicated through words. They knew that they undertook an impossible task, and that all their poems were but weak attempts to circumscribe the essence of the mystical Beloved by applying to Him symbols from the word of the senses. A study of their imagery proves that the vocabulary of both personal and impersonal mysticism is used almost indiscriminately by them, and images from the three major spheres outlined by Evelyn Underhill can occur even in the same verse. A poet might sing of the journey of the soul, which might take him, in imitation of the Prophet's *miᶜrāj,* to the heights of the transcendent God, or lead him finally into the depths of the ocean of his own soul to find the beloved there, not in the market place. He could enumerate in line after line the beautiful qualities and actions of the superlucent, supersublime Beloved, using the *via eminentiae* to call out, a few lines later, that He is beyond description, that His depths are unfathomable, that He is *ᶜadam,* "positive not-being." Or else he could repeat over and over again *namīdānam namīdānam,* "I do not know, I do not know," thus applying the *via negationis* to God, who is beyond How and Why and all categories of thinking and can only be approached by ever new oxymora and paradoxes.[114] Metaphors of light, fire, and radiance, or of music and sound would perhaps be preferred by those who speak of their personal beloved God. A few lines later they might use metaphors from the silent nightly world of the Absolute Unseen and call themselves to silence, only to begin after a few breaths another glorious song in honor of the Divine Beloved. Time and again they return to the image of the mirror, which reflects the beauty of the Beloved and, having lost its own identity, has become more He than He Himself, and thus constitutes the only gift which the lover can offer to the Beloved.[115] The whole world is, for the discerning eye of the true lover, nothing but the mirror of God's eternal beauty, as Jami sings in immortal verse:

> Each speck of matter did He constitute
> A mirror, causing each one to reflect
> The beauty of His visage. From the rose
> Flashed forth His beauty and the nightingale
> Beholding it, loved madly. From that fire
> The candle draws the lustre which beguiles
> The moth to immolation. On the sun
> His beauty shone, and straightway from the wave
> The lotus reared its head. Each shining lock
> Of Laila's hair attracted Majnun's heart
> Because some ray Divine reflected shone
> In her fair face. It was He to Shirin's lips
> Who lent that sweetness, which had power to steal
> The heart from Parviz and from Farhad life.
> His Beauty everywhere doth show itself
> And through the forms of earthly beauties shine
> Obscured as through a veil. . . . Where'er thou seest a veil,
> Beneath that veil He hides.[116]

The poets often returned to the language of profane love. They spoke of tresses and rosy cheeks, of kisses and union, but every word in the colorful cosmos of Persian poetry is filled with connotations which can be understood properly only by those who carefully unravel the significance of each, even the smallest, motif in a verse. The poets might twist the meaning either of a profane word or of a Koranic saying, and it is therefore easy to interpret their verse as worldly poetry in praise of wine or love instead of mystical prayers, or vice versa. But, as I mentioned earlier, this double entendre is intended, and in the case of Hafiz one may even find a third level, that of panegyrics in the guise of love poetry. In other cases a poem that enthusiastically sings of the beauty and kindness of the beloved may be meant to be a eulogy on the Prophet. Unless one disentangles the interwoven designs in each and every verse and places the images into the context of the whole history of Persian poetical language, one neither really understands nor enjoys verses which look, to the outsider or to those who know them only in translation, often quite repetitious. But when one studies Persian mystical poetry, with a close examination of its numerous possible connotations, one may slowly come to feel the artists' genuine longing, for which they used the choicest words and images.

Perhaps one may then understand why they used the image of scent. Words are the scent of the muskdeer, which leads finally to the source of the fragrance; or they are like the scent of Yusuf's shirt, which brought his father glad tidings from his faraway son and cured his eyes, which were blind from weeping. Through the image of fragrance mystical poetry gives some news of the everlasting Beloved even to those who have never seen him, and who never realized that His beauty is hidden behind cypress and rose, behind the dark cloud and the jasmine bush. As Rumi says:

> The pre-eternal moon is his face, verse and poems are his fragrance—
> Fragrance is the part of those who are not admitted to the view.[117]

Chapter Three / Sun Triumphal—Love Triumphant:

MAULANA RUMI AND THE METAPHORS OF LOVE

Everyone who says: "Rescue him from Love!"
This prayer of his may be rejected by Heaven![1]

"WHO HAS NOT heard the name of Jalaluddin Rumi?[2] And who is not familiar with the *Mathnawī*?"[3] Thus begins the introduction of a Panjabi translation-cum-commentary of Maulana Jalaluddin Rumi's mystico-didactic poem, called by Jami in the fifteenth century "the Koran in the Persian tongue." Translations of and commentaries on this work exist in almost every Islamic language and are available, at least in part, in Western languages as well. Its author has been praised as the foremost poetical interpreter of the all-embracing Unity of Being and as a poet whose mystical flights have carried him almost invariably and without interruption to the highest level of spiritual experience.[4]

But Rumi has also been misunderstood by his most ardent admirers, for nothing could be more alien to him than a systematization of his thought, particularly when this systematization is undertaken, as in hundreds of commentaries up to our day, in the light of Ibn ᶜArabi's theosophy, which was being taught in Konya by Rumi's colleague, Sadruddin Qonawi. To understand properly Rumi's poetry, and particularly his lyrics, one has to know the major events of his life out of which his verse grew.

Muhammad Jalaluddin was born in Balkh, now Afghanistan, in 1207. His father, Baha'uddin Walad, was a noted mystical theologian whose *Maᶜārif* contain unusual, often bizarre visions and statements which seem to have influenced his son at a later stage of his life.[5] The family left Balkh before the Mongols began their attacks on the Eastern part of the Muslim world. They finally settled in Anatolia, *Rūm*—hence the poet's surname, *Rūmī.* It was the era of Sultan ᶜAla'uddin Kaikobad, under whom the Rum Seljukid capital, Konya, reached its greatest splendor; the mosque which he erected in 1220 close to the fortress is still in use. In 1228 the aged Baha'uddin Walad was called to teach in one of the numerous *madrasas* of Konya; he passed away in early 1231, and his son succeeded him in the chair. During the following decade he was introduced into mystical theories and practice by a disciple of his father, Burhanuddin Muhaqqiq, who had fled from Tirmidh to seek shelter in Anatolia, as had many other mystics and scholars. We do not know whether Jalaluddin stayed all those years in Konya or traveled for some time in Syria where a number of Sufi masters were active. Burhanuddin later settled in Kaiseri where his modest tomb beneath the majestic Mt. Erjiyas is still visited by the pious.

Rumi's life as a professor and father of two teenage sons was suddenly changed in October 1244 when he met the wandering dervish Shamsuddin, "Sun of Religion," of Tabriz, a man of at least his age, endowed with an overpowering mystical presence. The two mystics spent days and nights, weeks and months together, deeply immersed in discussing mystical love, and forgetting the world, family, and disciples. None of the masters in Syria had appealed to the passionate, demanding Shams, but in Rumi he found the friend who understood him and was ready to be consumed by his spiritual fire. For Shams claimed to have reached the station of the Beloved, *ma^c^shūq*, a claim never made, as far as we can see, by any mystic before him. The intimate relation of the two mystics aroused the wrath and jealousy of Rumi's students and his family, and after some eighteen months Shams left Konya secretly. Maulana was heartbroken, and it is at this point that he began to sing poetry. In whirling dance he poured out his longing and love, even though he had never previously shown any major interest in Persian poetry. He had of course read the classical works of Anwari, Khaqani, and others, as can be understood from allusions to and quotations from their verse in his own poetry. But now he exclaimed more than once:

> Love for you seized my rosary and gave me verses and song—
> I very often said *lā ḥaula* and *tauba!* but the heart did not listen.
> Through Love's hand I became a *ghazal*—singer, hand-clapping:
> Your love burnt honor and shame and whatever was there.
> Chaste and ascetic and firmfooted was I, like a mountain—
> Where is the mountain which your love does not carry away like straw?
> If I am a mountain, then I carry the echo of your voice,
> If I am straw, then I become smoke in your fire. . . .[6]

Love's bewitching eye turned him into a poet[7] so that:

> Every hair of mine has become through your love verse and *ghazal;*
> Every limb of mine has become from your taste a vat full of honey.[8]

After another eighteen or twenty months Shams was seen in Syria, and Maulana's elder son, Sultan Walad, was sent to bring him back; he later poetically described his father's meeting with Shams: they fell at each other's feet, "and nobody knew who was the lover and who was the beloved." Shams stayed in Konya, now even in Maulana's own house, and was married to a girl from the household, but again tension built up between him and Rumi's younger son ᶜAla'uddin. Finally Shams was called out one night in early December 1248, stabbed to death, and hastily buried close to the house—not without the connivance of ᶜAla'uddin. Rumi was told that he had disappeared once more, and after a few sighs of resignation he burst out in a long threnody with the *radīf begrīstī*—the whole world "would have wept,"[9] and yet he did not want to believe that "the sun has died." After some time he set out to search for Shams in Syria, but finally he discovered that the friend was living in him—Shams was he himself, and what he sang was in reality Shams' words.[10] By thus adopting the friend's name and using it as a pen name in his verse he assumed a new identity, entering, as it were, a new life.[11] His younger son ᶜAla'uddin, however, was no longer considered a member of the family.

At present it seems impossible to attempt an exact dating of Rumi's early verse. However, one can observe a certain change of emphasis in his lyrics, and a careful metrical analysis of the *Dīwān-i Shams* is also helpful in placing at least some poems in their proper sequence. During the earliest period, overwhelmed by the separation from Shams, Maulana sings of love, longing, and sometimes of dance. Grotesque images also appear, but the identity of the friend is not mentioned. It is an old Sufi rule not to reveal the name of the Beloved. In the beginning Rumi would therefore say:

> I gave him so many surnames, perfect and imperfect ones,
> But since he is absolutely peerless, he has a hundred times more.[12]

However, many of the poems that give no proper nom de plume speak at some point of the sun, *āftāb* or *khūrshīd,* thus pointing to the name of *Shamsuddīn,* "the Sun of Religion"; it seems that poems with astronomical imagery, in which not only the sun (preferably in Aries) but also Mars and other stars are mentioned, belong to the period in which the identity of the "Sun of Tabriz" was still hidden under subtle allusions. Certain key words appear only in early poems. The *lūlīs,* the charming, playful, and dangerous Gypsies, appear to me as part of the early vocabulary as do Rumi's ecstatic words about *ṣaḥrā,* the wide desert. Poems in which the beloved is addressed as *khidīw,* "sovereign," or with the Greek terms *efendī* or *aghapōs* (which may even constitute the *radīf*) are certainly early. Quite a few of Rumi's short, unassuming Arabic poems can probably be ascribed to that period as well. After all, he had been an admirer of the "last classical poet," al-Mutanabbi, to whose verses he alludes now and then.[13]

> Speak Persian, even though Arabic is nicer,
> But Love has still a hundred other tongues,

he says as late as in the third book of the *Mathnawī.*[14] Verses that sing of the poet's longing to die in love, to become annihilated before the overwhelming spiritual presence of the Beloved, also sound like products of the early, highly agitated period.

Then, the shift from secrecy toward open declaration is made in a delightful poem,[15] a description of the poet's destitute and miserable heart which sits at night in a lonely corner, crying and shivering. But asked who is his *makhdūm,* his master, and asked to describe him, the heart refuses to answer, until finally, after a lively dialogue with the poet, a voice from the Unseen exclaims at *sun*rise, "Tabriz!"; the heart falls down in a swoon, overwhelmed by the appearance of the Sun, and the poem ends with the jubilant lines:

> When I became unconscious, on [the heart's] face became engraved
> The name of that *makhdūm,* Shamsuddin, in that ocean of generosity!

But even then Shamsuddin's name was not yet used exclusively as a *takhalluṣ* (pen name); rather it appears in the middle of a poem[16] or in the second-to-last line. The simple name of Tabriz, without mentioning Shams, occurs also, for Tabriz is the place "where the water of life flows. . . ."[17] There is even one poem in which Rumi inserts his own name, Jalaluddin, although Shams is mentioned twice in the middle.[18] We may assume that some of the most rhapsodic poems, in which Rumi repeats the name of the beloved through a whole *ghazal,* belong to this second stage when he finally not only dared mention the blessed name but indulged in repeating it in rhythmical verse,[19] echoing the praise bestowed upon him by all creatures:

> Not alone I keep on singing
>   Shamsuddin and Shamsuddin,
> But the nightingale in gardens
>   sings, the partridge in the hills.
> Day of splendor: Shamsuddin, and
>   turning heaven: Shamsuddin!
> Mine of jewels: Shamsuddin, and
>   Shamsuddin is day and night . . .[20]

Or he admonishes himself:

> Say the name of my *makhdūm* Shamsuddin every moment
> So that your poem and verse may get luster and charm.
> See the blood in my poetry—don't look at the poem because
> In love for him eye and heart are blood-filtering.[21]

And finally, after experiencing complete union with Shams, Maulana used the friend's name as his nom de plume, so that the collection of his verse became known as *Dīwān-i Shams-i Tabriz.* Maulana praised his beloved in terms which understandably horrified the inhabitants of Konya. He not only called him *ᶜaql-i kull,* "The First Intellect,"[22] but went even further:

> I am ashamed of Love if I call him a human being,
> And I fear God when I say that he is God [*khudā*].[23]

This dilemma is also expressed in another poem which belongs to the same period before the nom de plume *Shams* was used:

> If I call you human being [*banda,* lit. "servant"], it is not permissible,
> But I fear to call you God.
> You do not allow me to be silent,
> But you do not open the way of speaking.[24]

But Shams does not only "bear the fragrance of the Overpowering Creator (*khāliq jabbār*),"[25] he is closely related to Muhammad the Prophet. The powerful, almost eschatological hymn with the beginning

> *Nūr-i Muḥammad rasīd* [The Light of Muhammad has arrived],

can probably be dated after Shams' return from Syria in January 1248.[26] For, as Maulana says in a later poem:

> Tell me, who is the intimate of Ahmad the Messenger in this world?
> Shams-i Tabriz, the king of kings, who is "one of the greatest." (Sura 74/38)[27]

Thus praise of the Prophet and praise of Shams are almost inextricably interwoven in Rumi's *ghazals.* Shams is "the radiance, *farr,* of Mustafa's light,"[28] and "the pride of the Tabrizians" is the intimate companion of Mustafa in the secrets of love.[29]

> Shams-i Tabriz, you are acquainted with the secrets of the Prophet:
> Be your sweet name the remedy for every erring person![30]

Cross relations between the name of Shams, "Sun," and Sura 93, "By the morning light" (which was generally interpreted by the Sufis as pointing to Muhammad, see chapter 5) could easily be established, and a line like

> The Sun came, and the moon was split,

is a typical pun pointing to Shams' connection with the Prophet.[31] The numerous poetical allusions to the *yār-i ghār*, "the friend in the cave," referring to the extremely close relationship between Muhammad and Abu Bakr during the night in the cave on their way to Medina, may also refer to Rumi's relation with Shams.

The radiant, fiery poetry in honor of Shamsuddin "from whose Sun the sun is just a tiny mote of dust"[32] continued for a long time, for he felt "like an egg under his wings,"[33] waiting for the time of resurrection. Yet, in the meantime Maulana found a calm, serene companion to soothe his heart's burns. It was the goldsmith Salahuddin Zarkub, who had been a friend of Rumi for some time because he was the spiritual successor of Rumi's master, Burhanuddin Muhaqqiq, and Rumi's meetings with Shams had sometimes taken place in his cell. One day, the rhythmical, melodious sound of the goldsmiths' hammers in the bazaar of Konya so enraptured Maulana that he took Salahuddin with him to whirl through the streets.[34] In him he found someone whom he could trust completely, and a number of poems are dedicated to him, but they are, understandably, less ecstatic than those written in connection with Shams. It is possible to find the moment when this new friendship manifested itself:

> When the sun has gone down to set it is not annihilated:
> From another sign of the zodiac this radiant moon has risen.
> Don't say, "Shams ul-Haqq of Tabriz has arrived!"
> From the sky of purity the moon of mysteries has risen.

The beginning of this *ghazal* describes the change which the inhabitants of Konya observed with ever greater displeasure: how could the learned professor be interested in the simple, illiterate goldsmith? But he saw it differently:

> He who came in a red frock in years past,
> He came this year in a brown garb.
> The Turk about whom you had heard that time
> Appeared as an Arab this year . . .
> The wine is one, only the bottles are different—
> How beautifully does this wine intoxicate us![35]

As Maulana introduced the name of Shams first in the middle of his poems he does the same with Salahuddin's name, the last line still referring to Shams:

> O you Weal of Heart and Religion [*Ṣalāḥ-i dil ū dīn*], you are from outside the directions . . .[36]
> Shams-i Tabrizi, you are the king of all the beautiful ones!

Maulana saw Salahuddin either as a moon, reflecting the sunlight, or as *żīā*, a ray of light from the sun;[37] this latter surname was, however, officially given to Husamuddin Chelebi a few years later.[38] Predominantly, Salahuddin was for him a faithful, unquestioning mirror:

> When you see his face, don't speak,
> For breath injures the mirror.[39]

To cement the relationship with the friend, he married his eldest son Sultan Walad to Salahuddin's daughter, and his letters to his beloved daughter-in-law are touching proofs of his humanity.

But before long Rumi's interest turned to his disciple Husamuddin Chelebi, who had been praised by Shams for his exemplary behavior. Typically, the few poems in the *Dīwān* which contain the name of Husamuddin, either in the middle or as *takhalluṣ,* are glowing praise in honor of Shams:

> Everyone who heard the name of Shams-i Tabrizi and prostrated himself,
> His soul is acceptable in the Presence, and he calls out *anā'l-ḥaqq,* ["I am the Divine Truth"],[40]

and he invites young Husamuddin to join those who do so. The most important poem of those that mention Husamuddin's name is the account of a vision of a mysterious ocean. It was written at the time that the Mongols intended a new attack on Konya; it even bears the date of this event, 5 Dhu'l-qa^cda 654 (25 November 1256).[41] During those critical days, when Salahuddin's terminal illness had probably already set in (he died after prolonged suffering in 1258 and Rumi wrote a beautiful dirge on him),[42] Husamuddin drew closer to his master. He asked him one day to compose a didactic poem that his disciples could study instead of the epics of Sana'i and ᶜAttar. We can safely place the beginning of the *Mathnawī* in this period (late 1256), for the dialogue between Maulana and the still somewhat immature Husamuddin in the beginning of the *Mathnawī*[43] shows the disciple eager to know more about Shams, whose praise Maulana had been singing time and again.[44] After the completion of the first book of the *Mathnawī* there was a break of some four years; it was the time during which Salahuddin died and Husamuddin lost his wife. Some poems of a more didactic or narrative character can probably be ascribed to this period. When the dictation was taken up again in 1262, Husamuddin had fully matured and was now officially installed as Rumi's *khalīfa.* A rather subdued poem without any nom de plume, which seems to be late, mentions him in the middle:

> Don't do it—if you have become like a grain in the earth in autumn,
> Remember Husamuddin's spring and the rosegarden.[45]

The *Mathnawī,* with its nearly 26,000 verses, which grew out of Maulana's loving relationship with his disciple, is a veritable encyclopedia of mystical lore. But it lacks a systematic structure, and some of Maulana's more philosophically minded compatriots blamed him because he did not enter into any theoretical discussions or use the technical vocabulary of the Sufis. He rather followed his own inspiration and was often carried away by verbal associations which then unfold into mystical insights. Some of the topics of his poetry are taken up in prose in his "table talks," *Fīhi mā fīhi.*[46] He not only cared for his numerous disciples from all strata of society but also wrote a great number of letters which show him as a man deeply concerned with the welfare of those who were close to him.[47] His good relations with the ministers, who for all practical purposes ruled the remains of the Seljuk empire after several Mongol attacks on Anatolia, enabled him to extend help to many poor and needy. His relations with Ibn ᶜArabi's foremost interpreter, Sadruddin Qonawi, were friendly though probably not very close, since he was not interested in the theosophical aspect of mysticism which developed under Ibn ᶜArabi's influence. And it is remarkable that practically nothing is known about his relations with Sadruddin's friend, the gifted Persian poet Fakhruddin ᶜIraqi, who lived for some years in Konya after his master, Baha'uddin Zakariya of Multan, had died in 1267.

Maulana Rumi could not finish the sixth book of the *Mathnawī;* its last story is open-ended. In the autumn of 1273 he fell ill and consoled his friends with verses that speak of the soul bird's flight from the cage of the body, and of union behind the curtain; he told them about the grain that dies and gives a hundredfold fruit, the transformation of the grain being a perfect symbol of death and resurrection[48] (as St. Paul worded it powerfully in I Corinthians 15:42). Even more, Maulana greeted death with jubilant anticipation:

> If death is a man, he may come before me
> So that I may take him very very closely to my breast!
> I'll take from him a soul, without scent and color—
> He'll take from me [only] a multicolored frock![49]

He asked his friends not to visit his tomb without drums and instruments, for his intoxication would last beyond the grave.[50] Maulana Rumi died the evening of December 17, 1273, and all inhabitants of Konya participated in his funeral, which ended in an ecstatic dance. Husamuddin succeeded him as the leader of his disciples, and after his death in 1284 Sultan Walad took over to organize his disciples into a proper order, known in the West as the Whirling Dervishes. With this organization and with his poetry about his father's life, Sultan Walad secured immortality for himself. He was the model of an obedient son, who brought home from Syria his father's first friend, was married to the daughter of his father's second friend, and entrusted the leadership of the disciples to his father's third friend.

Maulana Rumi's life is a paradigm of the ideal mystical biography as drawn up by later Sufis, i.e., the semicircle. It began with the rising flame of his love for Shams, in whom he reached complete annihilation;[51] then came the time of *baqā*, of stabilization in and through Salahuddin; and finally the *sair ilā', l-ashyā'*, the return to the created things as manifested in his friendship with his disciple Husamuddin, for whose benefit he told of the experiences of the mystical path in abundant allegories, folk tales, and metaphors.

Rumi is one of the few poets in the Islamic world who have spoken often and openly about the secret of poetical inspiration. His remark in *Fīhi mā fīhī,* that he was basically not at all interested in poetry, rather that in accordance with the tradition of orthodox Islam he considered poetry to be something despicable, shows also that he was well aware that it was "that one, that Turk" who breathed into him, addressing him (in Turkish!) *Sen kimsin,* "Who are you?," and forced him to answer in poetry.[52] Sometimes Maulana felt that he was almost talking in a dream:

> Do they not say in their sleep words without tongue?
> That is how I am speaking in my waking state![53]

His heart appears as a mirror which is silent and yet can translate the beauty of the wondrous mirror-holder to others,[54] or like a mountain which reverberates from the echo of the friend's voice.[55] This experience of inspiration continues into the *Mathnawī:*

> I think of rhymes, but my beloved says:
> "Don't think of anything but of my face!"[56]

Remarks pointing to this process of inspiration are repeated throughout the *Dīwān*. Rumi even turns to the rebeck player who accompanied his song, admonishing him not to be so sleepy but rather to listen to his words,[57] for he knew that from his mouth the song of the immortal flute is heard "even though I am bent like the back of a harp."[58]

Rumi was well aware that his lyrics were born spontaneously out of the agitation of his heart and that they should therefore be taken as sudden outcries, not as theological statements which could be ruminated upon by generations of readers or commentators:

> My poetry resembles Egyptian bread:
> When a night passes over it you cannot eat it anymore.
> Eat it at this point when it is fresh
> Before dust settles upon it![59]

But with the same food imagery (which he used most frequently in his poetry) he admits that his verse is more than ordinary bread:

> My word is the food of angels—when I don't say words
> The hungry angel says: "Speak! Why are you silent?"[60]

And although we can follow the flow of inspiration or the outburst of longing in quite a few *ghazals*, Rumi also admits that he is often fed up with the traditional metrical schemes or that he is not in good shape:

> Don't blame [me] that the *ghazal* remained incomplete,
> For the fluttering thought is faithless![61]

Or he apologizes for an overlong *ghazal* by reminding the listeners that he started out by mentioning a camel—and after all, a camel *is* long![62] But usually, especially in what I take to be poems from the earliest period, he reminds himself:

> Don't say the rest of the *ghazal*, for it is a pity
> [That] we are talking and the Friend is silent.[63]

Or after asking the friend in a longish poem to do this or that he comes again to his senses and blames himself for his audacity:

> Now it's enough, my impudence has transgressed all limits!
> Who am I to tell you: "Do this!"?[64]

Sometimes—and such poems may belong to the period after Shams' return to Konya—Rumi sings out his love and would like to say more and more:

> If I were not afraid of boring you I would sing a hundred verses![65]

But he closes his mouth so that the friend may open his; or he asks the beloved to close his ever-singing mouth, for:

> It is necessary to bind an intoxicated camel's mouth![66]

Becoming silent because the secret of Love cannot be conveyed, or in order to give room to the true king who "comes after the *ghazal* is finished,"[67] is a motif which occurs often in his early poems. The word *khāmūsh,* "silent," "quiet," is used so frequently that some scholars have been inclined to regard it as Rumi's original nom de plume. However, although many of the poems in which he calls himself to silence seem to belong to the earliest period, the combination of *khāmūsh* in the second-to-last line with the name of Shams in the last line is quite common, and a number of poems ending in *khāmūsh* can be dated to a later time, such as the wedding song for Salahuddin's second daughter and other not purely "mystical" poems.[68] A typical poem in which Rumi admonishes himself to be silent is from the early period where he says in the middle:

> Outwardly I am silent, but you know that inwardly
> I have blood-stained talk in my blood-drinking heart.
> Look, I nicely walk in my state of silence
> So that you see on my cheeks a hundred thousand traces of yours.

I have shortened this *ghazal,* its remnants are in my heart:
I will say it when you intoxicate me with your drunken narcissus eyes . . . ,

and he continues in five more verses to explain that he is silent.[69] Rumi knows that in silence he carries the fragrance of the friend's rosegarden, but when he opens his mouth to complain the whole world is perfumed, thanks to his odoriferous herbs (= words).[70] Or, in a slightly different form: by praising the beloved he transforms his soul into a rosegarden, thanks to the friend's fragrance.[71] It is important to note that Rumi often compares words to carriers of scent. Scent is the medium of reminiscence, and the remarkably frequent use of the word *bū,* "fragrance," "odor," is typical of Rumi's way of interpreting the world.

The reader of Rumi's poetry, and particularly of his *Dīwān,* is always amazed at the ease with which he uses images and metaphors from every walk of life and how, with his astounding command over the language and over all the traditional rhetorical devices, he is able to convert everything into a symbol. Seemingly banal sensual affects trigger off the highest inspiration, and out of elemental realism grows the most sublime symbolism. He uses the kitchen, the market place, hunting, medicine, children, the greengrocer with his sourmilk who toils for his daily bread,[72] as well as obscene anecdotes and the stories of the Prophets, family quarrels and a vast range of allusions to classical Sufism, to form a fabric of incredibly rich texture.

The protean character of his images poses an additional difficulty to the interpreter. Rumi's verses are often surprising in their frankness and sometimes coarseness. He does not mind telling the friend:

> When blood reaches me from your earthen vessel as though I were a dog,
> I would be a plebeian if I would not consider this to be the goblet of the elite.[73]

Or he describes his meeting with the friend in a humorous way:

> I approached him in prostration, my back curved like that of a camel;
> He opened his lips, laughing, and said: "O my long-necked one!"[74]

Dialogues and little discourses are Maulana's forte, whether he speaks to his heart,[75] to sleep, or the dream image of his friend:

> Yesterday your intoxicated dream image came with a cup in his hand.
> I said: "I don't drink wine!" He said: "Don't do it then [but] it is a pity!"
> I said: "I am afraid that if I drink, shame will fly out of my head,
> And I may put my hand on your curls, and then you'll again recede from me!"[76]

But once in a while the heady wine of love gets the upper hand, and Rumi laughs and sighs at once:

> I without myself, you without yourself—who will bring me home?
> How often have I told you: "Drink two or three cups less!"[77]

He describes his insatiable thirst for more and more love in odd images:

> I am ruined by separation from you; your dream-image is my fodder,

For my heart's stomach is suffering due to you from *jū*ᶜ *al-baqar*
["cow's appetite," i.e., voracity].[78]

But he can also be very practical when it comes to telling the uninitiated how to behave when blessed by Divine grace:

When the table arrives from heaven, wash your hand and mouth
Lest the scent of garlic and onion come from your hand![79]

Rumi constantly waits for the beloved:

Even though I am dwelling at your door like a ring [knocker]—
What is the use when you are on the high roof?[80]

And, following his father's example, he likes concrete images for the uninhibited union of the soul with the beloved:

With you I am better naked; I put away the garment Body
So that the bosom of your grace becomes a cloak for my soul.[81]

When hopelessness overwhelms him, he may complain in the traditional imagery of Persian poetry:

I am afraid that due to the long separation from you, O stone-hearted friend,
The pitcher of my patience may get broken by accident.[82]

And then again he addresses the beloved in strange but tender words by applying various rhetorical devices to the seemingly simple lines:

Sometimes you are the support of the nose like the scent of the rose,
Sometimes you become the companion of the eye and are a rosegarden.[83]

Or, more beautiful because no strange-sounding comparisons are involved:

You are not in the sky, O Moon, however
Wherever you appear, there is a heaven.[84]

In this colorful imagery Rumi sings of his love, of his absolute trust in God, and at a later stage also of man's duties in this world, where he should work so that he will be able to see the fruits of his actions on the spring day of eternity.[85] He reverts again and again to Koranic allusions and to quotations from the Prophetic traditions, and at times, mainly in the mid-sixties, he tries to discuss philosophical topics which soon dissolve again into poetical musings.

Maulana Rumi's topics cover almost every aspect of life, but the center of his thoughts is Love, which is sometimes interchangeable with the Beloved, and one often wonders whether it is Love or the Beloved that is intended by his words.[86] There is such variety in his poetical descriptions that they seem to include all the symbols ever used by mystics in East and West.

> I read the story of the lovers day and night—
> Now I have become a story in my love for you![87]

That is the quintessence of the more than 35,000 verses of Rumi's *Dīwān.* He was also well aware that people might misunderstand his praise of Love and interpret his spiritual relations with his friends in a crude manner:

> A mighty primordial light is Love before the elect
> Although it be like external form and sensuality before the ordinary people.[88]

Colorful as his imagery is in general, he becomes even more eloquent when it comes to Love. But he claims more often than not:

> When it comes to Love, I have to be silent . . .
> To describe Love, intellect is like an ass in the morass,
> The pen breaks when it is to describe Love.[89]

For he knows that Love is free from all directions and yet causes agitation in every direction,[90] and that it has therefore to be circumscribed in ever-changing images, expressed in paradox, visionary accounts, and dialogues full of oxymora—dialogues that reflect the tension between his heart and this Love which is as beautiful as it is cruel. There are jubilant poems with the words *ᶜishq* or *iqbāl-i ᶜishq* ("happiness of love") as their refrain;[91] others deal exclusively with Love's manifestations and tell the onlooker:

> If you do not know Love, ask the nights,
> Ask the yellow cheeks and the parched lips![92]

Images follow each other in breathtaking speed without apparent logical order: Love is pre-eternal—it is a magnet—it annihilates the soul for a moment, then again becomes a trap for the soul to whom it offers a sip from the wine of Reality, and all this

> Is only the beginning of Love—
> Nobody reaches its end![93]

Rumi likes to converse with Love to find out what it looks like:

> One night I asked Love: "Tell me honestly, who are you?"
> It said: "I am life eternal, I repeat the lovely life."
> I said to it: "O you who are outside every place, where is your house?" It said:
> "I am together with the heart's fire and beside the wet eye;
> I am a dyer: due to me every cheek becomes saffron-colored;
> I am a swift-footed messenger, and the lover is my lean horse;
> I am the crimson of the tulips, the value of the merchandise,
> I am the sweetness of complaints, I am the unveiler of everything veiled . . ."[94]

One of the great odes in which Maulana tries to solve the mystery of this Love begins with the question:

> O Love, are *you* more harmoniously shaped, or your garden and apple-orchard?

It continues in dancing rhythms, to tell of the miraculous actions of this Love which makes bitterness sweet, inspires every atom, and teaches the trees to dance, and without which there is no joy in life:

> I tried it for some time—but without you there was no pleasure:
> How could life be tasty without your limitless salt?
> I went on traveling, I went from the end to the beginning:
> This elephant saw in his dream the vast desert of your Hindustan!

Hindustan, as often in medieval Persian literature, here stands for the eternal home which the soul suddenly remembers in a happy dream and where it wants to return immediately; tearing its material chains, it runs toward the primordial forest like a homesick elephant. And Maulana closes this long, ecstatic poem, which seems to be one of his earlier verses, by admitting once more the incapability of his describing the mysterious power of Love, which is the perfect *coincidentia oppositorum:*

> As many doors as you may have opened in iron, mountain, and stone:
> Yet, the heart is like an ant that looks for a breach in your vessel and bowl [i.e., it cannot find a way out].
> If I should tell of your face until the day of resurrection, I would be amiss—
> How could your ocean be measured with a saucer?[95]

Love appears in some verses as the mirror for both worlds, and one would not dare to breathe on it,[96] i.e., to speak about it. It may also manifest itself as the power that polishes the steel, (the dense, opaque objects of creation), so that the whole world finally becomes its mirror.[97]

Rumi at another time sees Love as a *muṣḥaf,* a copy of the Holy Book which the lover reads in his dreams.[98] Love is also the tablet from which he copies his poetry,[99] or else, he is simply like a pen between Love's fingers, writing down what he does not know.[100] Was not Shamsuddin's name written from pre-eternity in the notebooks of Love?[101] And the bent stature of the lover resembles the twisted *tughrā* (the royal handsign) on the *manshūr* (diploma) of Love.[102]

Although Rumi has written numerous Arabic or mixed verses in praise of Love, he knows and admits more than once:

> If I should praise Love in a hundred thousand tongues,
> Its beauty is greater than all vessels.[103]

Other mystics and poets, like Rumi, have described Love as being both manifest and hidden,[104] without beginning or end; for since it is coeternal with God or, to use Hallaj's expression, is the innermost dynamic essence of God, it has, like God, no limits.[105] Maulana's love for Shams also has no limits; rather, there are thousands and thousands of porticos behind it[106] so that the lover can "travel in Love"[107] and find more happiness the farther he progresses. And when Love itself begins to run about, hundreds of thousands of heavens and earths are too narrow for its roaming.[108]

Love, as mystics and philosophers know, is the reason for every motion:

> If the earth and the mountains were not lovers,
> Grass would not grow out of their breasts . . . .[109]

This idea is repeated in the *Dīwān* and in the *Mathnawī.* Rumi also shared with other poets the frequent comparison of Love with amber,[110] which attracts the tiny straw (it is so powerful that the mighty mountain, *kūh,* is transformed into straw, *kāh,* before it)[111]—a comparison which at the same time alludes to the yellowish, "strawlike" cheeks of the emaciated lovers. The magnet, which attracts hearts like pieces of iron, is a common image for Love even in philosophical writings such as Avicenna's. It is common also among nonmystical poets, particularly Nizami.[112]

Rumi's predilection for images from daily life is well known. For instance, he saw Love as a school.[113] Here he is not unprecedented, for the Sufis (and particularly Ruzbihan-i Baqli) had spoken of the educational value of human love, which prepares man for Divine Love: the hero gives his little boy a wooden sword so that he may learn to wield it until he becomes old enough to use the real weapon.[114] Love's school, in which the spirit matures, where the teacher is God Most Majestic (*dhū'l-jalāl*) Himself,[115] and where worldly scholarship is ignorance,[116] is made of fire.[117] Love seizes man's ear to drag him every morning to this school, which is called, with an allusion to Sura 13/20: "They are faithful in their promises."[118] In this school even the villagers—in Rumi's poetry usually representing man's base instincts—are taught to read from the Tablet of the Invisible World.[119] Is it not through Love that the skies are joined together and the stars eclipsed, and that the crooked letter *dāl* is transformed into a straight *alif,* while without Love an *alif* turns into a bent, miserable looking *dāl?*[120] And Love writes a thousand fine points on the poet's face, which other lovers can read.[121]

Rumi at one time hears Love tell him that he is fire, kindled by Love's wind;[122] but his favorite imagery, though taken from the fiery sphere, depicts the situation in reverse:

> Love is a fire which would turn me into water if I were a hard stone![123]

and in the beginning of the *Mathnawī* he exclaims:

Fire is that voice of the reed, it is not wind,
Those who have not got this fire may be noughted![124]

It is indeed, as with Juan de la Cruz, the *Llama de amor viva,* which inspires Rumi. Here the imagery is, as it so often is with him, ambivalent. He sighs,

It's a thousand fires and smoke and grief,
And its name is Love.[125]

Or he claims that the sun and thousands like him have their wings burned by the friend's (Shamsuddin's) love,[126] but he always realizes that this fire turns into a rosegarden for the true lover, as for Abraham the pyre became "cool and pleasant" (Sura 21/69).[127] He rather enjoys this fire, for his "soul is a salamander," meaning it cannot survive outside fire.[128] And yet the soul may sometimes want to flee when it finds itself surrounded by a threefold fire, i.e., that of the friend's rosy face, that of red wine, and that of Love.[129] The lover can appear as sulphur or dry kindling,[130] ready to catch fire, and more frequently as a reedbed which has been burned up. This idea was most prominently expressed in the lines about the fiery reed in the beginning of the *Mathnawī,* an image that was taken over by numerous later Persian poets, particularly in the Indo-Persian tradition.[131] As the fire of Love burns every picture and form[132] it thus annihilates all man's faults and defects,[133] so that all the thorns of the friend's (here Salahuddin's) rosegarden disappear and the lover can strew roses before the beloved.[134] Such images go back to ancient rites of purification through fire, and lead, in turn to the vocabulary of alchemy.

Is not Love a lightning that burns the cloud which hides the moon?[135] For it destroys everything that stands between man and the eternal beauty of the beloved and is thus "a ladder to heaven."[136] Hearts and livers roasting in the fire of Love[137] are common with Persian poets, as is the scent of their burning livers (comparable to burnt offerings), rising to the beloved's house. The lovers enjoy burning in the flames of Love, like aloes-wood exuding sweet fragrance in the friend's sanctuary, or like wild rue placed in the flames to avert the evil eye from his beauty.[138] "Is not the cotton set aflame by Love?" asks Rumi with an elegant allusion to the fate of the martyr-mystic al-Hallaj, whose name means "cotton carder."[139] The oven, *tannūr,* of Love warms those frozen in the hibernal world of matter,[140] which will melt one day like ice,[141] and it serves to purify man as ore is refined in the crucible to become gold.[142]

Maulana does not frequently use the favorite image of most Persian poets, that of "moth and candle," but when it occurs is has a special depth:

> The moth casts itself into the kindled fire
> Because the fire appears to him as a window![143]

On the other hand he speaks of the "lamp of Love" or of Love as the candle of the heart,[144] and in an ecstatic dancing poem he invites the lovers to have their bodies and brains thrashed so that they may become oil in the lamp of Love.[145] Even more grotesque is his recurring comparison of the lovers with the ostrich, a bird which, according to Oriental belief, swallows live coals. Thus in an enrapturing *ghazal* with the beginning:

> When Love comes: "Do you hand over your soul to me?"
> Why don't you immediately say: "Yes, yes"?

he has the vision of:

> Love like a tower of light—
> Inside the tower of light—what a fire!

> Like ostrichs, the souls around that tower;
> Their food: a very tasty fire. . . .[146]

In this fiery sphere, the sun most adequately represents both Love and the Beloved (Shamsuddin). It is both beautiful and dangerous and thus a perfect manifestation of God's *jamāl* and *jalāl,* the *mysterium fascinans* and the *mysterium tremendum,* as Rumi explains to young Husamuddin in the initiatory scene of the *Mathnawī.*[147] The sun, always connected with Shams, the Sun of Tabriz, thus becomes the most comprehensive symbol of Love's twofold nature: it is the true morning before which thought and anxiety disappear like the "false morning,"[148] or it suddenly shines up like the Sun at Midnight.[149] It transforms stones into rubies[150] and makes grapes ripe and sweet[151] and yet it would burn everything if it were to draw closer to our planet. Often, the lovers are seen dancing around this sun like dust particles, held together by its magnetic field,[152] for it was the Sun of Love that made them appear from not-being.[153] At times, Rumi's poems sound almost like the powerful odes which were sung in ancient Egypt and Assur to praise this central light of life, and they are reminiscent of medieval hymns to Christ, the *sol verus et dies verus.*

But as Love is fire, it is also water:

> Every inhabitant of Hell who was burnt and fell into this Love,
> Fell in the *kauthar,* for your love is a *kauthar,*[154]

a paradisiacal pond. It is indeed "a fire of which the Water of Life is ashamed."[155] Love, being God's essence, is symbolized as an ocean without end,[156] an ocean whose water may be blood or fire,[157] and whose waves are pearls.[158] Therein the lover is either drowned or swims around like a fish without ever getting tired,[159] and no matter how much the fish may drink, the ocean never diminishes.[160] Sometimes Rumi sees strange visions of a fish which itself is the ocean, a model of the lover who lives only in and because of Love.[161] In this ocean is the beginning and the end of everything—out of love, the rivers flow to the sea,[162] and human words are nothing but water from this ocean.[163] Then again, Love appears (like Mme. Guyon's *Torrents spirituels*) as a powerful torrent which washes away everything and destroys man's external being completely.[164] Love as fire burns away man's every fault while Love as water purifies everything; it even longs for the dirty to wash away their sins.[165] Rumi once more becomes rather concrete:

> Since there is no veil for the souls in the hot bath of his love—
> I am not a picture in the bath house—why should I not rend my clothes?[166]

Love, or the Beloved, can also be rain, for "the clouds are pregnant from the ocean of Love," as is the lover.[167] This metaphor, often used in connection with the Prophet, is particularly appropriate, for when the clouds of Love come the dead earth will be fertilized:

> How happy is the meadow where roses and eglantines are grown
> From the water of Love, and where yonder gazelles are grazing![168]

Therefore grass and leaves, symbols of man, should happily endure the rain although it may thrash them heavily for a while.[169]

Understandably, the positive, wholesome aspects of Love are more prominent in the watery than in the fiery sphere. Comparisons offer themselves easily: Love is the veritable Water of Life which is hidden in the darkness.[170] Eternal Love can also be an ark for Noah to carry him safely through the floods of this world.[171] Does not the lover sleep peacefully in the boat of Love, moving along while unconscious?[172] Water brings life:

> In the middle of the burning sand in the desert road
> You see the water-carrier Love shouting with a voice of thunder,[173]

and soon, the dead desert will be filled with green and flowers. And, closely connected with water imagery is that of gardens:

> The spring of Love came to the garden of the soul![174]

Here, Rumi's descriptions become even more lively, especially when he sings of the spring breeze of Love which makes the trees dance. He sees that

> The wind of Love makes us [like trees] yellow or green.[175]

Love itself is a garden, and an immortal garden indeed:

> Whatever is born in spring will die in fall—
> The rose parterre of Love needs no support from spring![176]

This marvelous garden is "watered by the sea of the eyes,"[177] i.e., it blossoms when the lover sheds tears of longing, and its every thorn is more wonderful than all the roses.[178] Rather, one thorn from this garden which pierces the lover's liver is worth a hundred other gardens. That is why Rumi, prefiguring scores of later Persian and Urdu poets, can claim that "Love has rosegardens in the midst of veils of blood,"[179] and those who are gardeners there "pluck fruits from their hearts."[180]

Rumi's numerous spring poems combine various aspects of this imagery. At times Love itself appears as the garden,[181] or it creates flowerbeds and meadows out of dust;[182] then it appears as the spring breeze,[183] or the beloved comes in paradisiacal robes. Whenever gardens are mentioned they are connected in one way or other with Love, for

> In the garden of Love, longing for the mystical dance
> Those with cypress-statures come hand-clapping like plane-trees,

as Rumi sings in an early, playful *ghazal.* [184]

Love can be seen as a tree while the lovers are its shade, moving with the branches as they swing.[185] The tree of Love, which cannot be described in words, is higher than anything created and can be explained only in paradoxes:

> The branches of Love are in pre-eternity, its roots in eternity:
> This tree does not lean upon the Divine Throne nor on the earth
> nor on a leg![186]

And again, Rumi invents comparisons which, though seemingly absurd, make perfect sense in his cosmos of Love: Love acts as a creeping plant which completely surrounds the dry tree, i.e., natural man, covering him to the last twig.[187]

The garden imagery includes almost every aspect of life. But Maulana sees Love also as a kingdom,[188] a town,[189] or a beautiful city[190] which is wider than both worlds.[191] In rare cases he specifies this town—it may be Damascus, the place where he discovered the lost Shamsuddin and which therefore is praised as *dimashq-i ᶜishq,* [192] or Egypt, the place where Yusuf, the paragon of beauty, dwells and whence caravans with loads of sugar arrive to make the lovers happy.[193] It is a secret Baghdad where the residence of Love is situated[194]—during those days, Baghdad was still the capital of the Abbasid Empire. But whether Love be a strong castle[195] or a vast steppe that stretches along the ocean of the eye,[196] it is always full of wonders: in its streets[197] one sees, on long iron rods, cut-off heads which will be miraculously revived.[198] The house of Love[199]—once called the House of God[200]—has roofs and doors made of *ghazals* and songs,[201] and one may find the moonlike beloved on its roof.[202] In rare cases, Maulana sees Love as a monastery, *ṣauma*ᶜ*a-i kirām*, as a cave for monks,[203] but also as the cave in which the Prophet and his friend Abu Bakr spent the night of their emigration to Medina as "two names and one soul."[204]

In many of Rumi's verses the powerful, often cruel aspect of Love prevails—the pangs of separation, the subconscious memory of Shamsuddin's blood near his door are often palpably present in his images. He knows from experience that there is no way out once Love has taken over the human heart:[205]

> For Love has grasped my hem and drags it
> As a hungry man clutches to the edge of the tablecloth.
> Who could spring out of Love's hand that my heart could spring?
> The handle of the shimmering sword was in Love's fist![206]

Love appears often as a trap or a net for the soul bird. What bird could or would flee from the grains, sugar, and almonds which are its bait?[207] Indeed:

> He who is far away from the net of love
> Is a bird that does not have a wing![208]

For only the lovely birds fall in Love's trap—not the owl,[209] which belongs to the ruined places and refuses to look at the sun. The paradox of Love is that man becomes the freer the more he is captured by it, for only thanks to Love will he be able to fly heavenward. Therefore, even the Simurgh, that divine bird, does not fly any more toward his residence, Mount Qaf at the end of the world, once he has fallen in Love's snare.[210] Love's strong hand seems to spare no one; even lions tremble and are captured by it,[211] and elephants become like helpless cats in Love's bag.[212]

Only by experiencing this cruelty of Love can man become happy: he eagerly awaits the moment when the beloved will sacrifice him, for love of Shams is the great Feast of Offerings, *ᶜīd al-aḍḥā*.[213] Rumi's central idea, repeated in hundreds of verses, that growth is possible only through constant self-sacrifice, is conveniently expressed in such comparisons to Islamic ritual.

But Love not only slaughters the lover at *ᶜId* day; it is in general a man-eating monster.[214] That is why the lover is urged repeatedly to become a "man" so he will constitute a good morsel for Love,[215] and the combination of Love with heroism occurs as often in Rumi as in other Persian poets from Sana'i onward. The whole road toward Love is full of blood shed by those who have felt its sword:[216] after dragging the poor intoxicated lover with a hook,[217] Love eats his liver,[218] and although it is the host of men[219] it finally devours them.

> The whole world would become a morsel
> If Love had got a mouth![220]

Love is bloodthirsty; it becomes fat[221] from drinking the blood of the lover or of Muslims in general,[222] and it also makes the lover drink his own blood, so that his task is

> To become blood, to drink one's own blood,
> To sit with the dogs at the door of faithfulness.[223]

The lover becomes like a flask filled with blood[224] and is finally transformed into "blood in the veins of Love, tears in the lovers' eyes"[225] and thus reaches the highest station on the path, that of complete transformation into Love.

Similarly, Love also appears as a cupper to bleed man,[226] or it uses needles, like the physician,[227] since bleeding implies purification. By means of this rather painful operation man becomes spiritually healthier. But sometimes Love is just nasty: it may come, intoxicated, and scratch the face of the one whom it has selected.[228]

Maulana loves images from the animal kingdom, and here the lion[229] is a perfect symbol of the triumphant love that roars in the forest of the soul[230] and scares away the flock of grief.[231] Love may be a black lion,[232] a panther,[233] or, in an inverted image, a meadow where lions dwell.[234] It certainly is not the cunning, cowardly fox![235]

Unusual in the context of Persian poetry is the image of Love as a unicorn which impales the elephant (i.e., man) on his horn. Still, the legend of the unicorn killing the mighty elephant was common in the Middle East, and is represented in a stone carving on the walls of the palace in Konya, where Rumi must have passed frequently. It may even have inspired his verse.[236] Love also appears as a dragon,[237] but likewise as the emerald that blinds and scares away all dragons on the road.[238] More often it is a crocodile,[239] a dangerous beast from whose very sight sleep flees as a fish flees from an alligator. This crocodile can swallow the whole world[240] or at least shatter the fragile boat Intellect in the ocean of Love.[241] It is natural that Maulana also sees Love as a falcon that carries away the heart which, foolishly enough, had laid a trap for the royal bird, not anticipating how much stronger it was than expected![242] More outré is his idea that Love is a worm which lives inside the tree Man and destroys him from inside to grow out of him[243] (as the creeper covers him from outside). But if Love, radiant as a peacock, should fly away, then the heart becomes a house full of serpents "as you have seen."[244]

Love is also depicted in various human forms. Love is the Sultan,[245] the Shah through whom one becomes checkmated, the proudly riding prince, *shāhsuwār,*[246] or the *ghāzī,* the fighter for the true faith through whom those slain in battle are quickened again.[247] In a more concrete image it appears as the emperor of Byzans, *Rūm,* who defeats laziness as though it were the army of the Ethiopians[248] (*rūmī,* Byzantine, and *zanjī,* Ethiopian, form a traditional contrasting pair as do *turk* and *hindū*).

Following behind such a king, tears arrive like little coins strewn at festive occasions or in parades.[249] This king or Khusrau is sometimes qualified as *ᶜayyār* ("wild," "roguish"), a term which suggests the vocabulary of the *futuwwa* circles with whom Rumi may have had some contact; the term also assumes an almost cosmic dimension, as do the related terms *rind* and *qalandar*.[250]

The emperor Love often appears with a huge army[251] after he has sent out his spy to ask for man's submission;[252] sometimes only its dust is visible.[253] In front of this army the souls are arrayed, numerous as grains of sand, the props of the soul-tents being of pure light.[254] The warrior king and his army besiege the human heart[255] and destroy the city of intellect,[256] offering something better as a substitute;[257] the king also takes prisoners in the country of the infidels.[258] In a different approach, but again using the martial tone, Rumi describes Love blowing the clarion, playing the triumphal tune *innā fataḥnā* (Sura 48/1): "Verily We have given victory."[259]

The hero Love carries with him his sword,[260] an Indian sword of good quality,[261] and orders it to cut off the head of everything that exists beside him:[262] this is the traditional image of the negation, *lā,* with which the profession of faith begins and which in its graphic form is interpreted as a double-edged sword. It is comparable to ᶜAli's famous Dhu'l-fiqar. Rumi knows, however, that not everyone is worthy of being slain by the sword of Love, for "would the blood-thirsty lion drink the blood of dogs?"[263]

Sometimes Love is a shield-maker to protect man;[264] at other times a Sultan with strong bows[265] and arrows[266] (a favorite symbol of mystical love poetry all over the world) to pierce man's heart and liver:

> This liver has become from arrows like the back of a porcupine—
> If Love had a liver, it would have pity![267]

Love carries with him his flag to protect the lovers,[268] or has a hundred drums and flags[269]—how could a skinny mule carry the burden of Love's mysteries?[270] And with all this martial glory Love can easily plunder the country of the heart, for as a true Turkish hero Love is used to *yaghmā,* plundering.[271] *Turk* is here, as elsewhere, the designation of the powerful, radiant, and cruel beloved, the princely rider who can even tame the restive mustang Heaven![272] And when Love rules supreme like Nushirwan, the city's inhabitants will gladly spend their lives like Hatim, the Arabic paragon of largesse and unquestioning generosity.[273]

> How happy is the town whose king Love is!
> There, every street is feasting, every house a festivity![274]

It is therefore not surprising that man, or his soul, is Love's servant[275] or slave-girl,[276] or becomes its disciple.[277]

But while the personification of Love as a king ruling supreme or even as a cruel Sultan is not unheard of in poetical language, other images in Rumi's work are uncommon and verge on the grotesque. Who else would see Love as the police chief, *shiḥna,* who goes to the town to exact confiscation from everything living?[278] And confiscation in the Middle Ages, as is well known, was connected with all kinds of humiliation if not torture. In another, vigorous poem the police chief Love cuts the throat of both repentance and the repentant[279]—for what has repentance to do when Love appears on the scene? As a police chief, Love is also able to open the door of the prison,[280] i.e., of this world, to free the soul. But it also can brand man like an animal is branded by its owner; those who have received such a brand of Love will be exempt of all taxes.[281]

In a similar image, Love appears as the judge who extorts taxes[282]—but since the village of the heart is completely in ruins, how could the poor lover pay taxes? From here it is not difficult to see Love as a highwayman before whom everyone becomes naked.[283] Or Love breaks down the doors and steals everything from the house,[284] or is just a cutpurse:

> Love cut off my purse. I said: "What do you do?"
> It said: "Is not my boundless grace enough for you?"[285]

For mystical love means leaving the colorful but shallow mundane life to enter into the abyss of "positive nothingness" in God. In another image, after Love has come and taken everything away to the ocean "He," the ragman calls in vain (and Maulana has him speak Turkish): "Who has got old shoes?" for nothing that reminds man of this outworn, transient world is left to him.[286]

Rumi dramatically describes how the personified love for Shamsuddin runs about everywhere, its eyes filled with blood and a sword in its hand, searching for the lover's soul while people are fast asleep:

> Sometimes it shone up on the roofs like a moon,
> It went from lane to lane like the breeze,

and finally "the lover's vessel fell from the roof," i.e., his secret was revealed, and everyone became alerted and understood that a burglar must have intruded.[287]

Now and then, Love is a bleacher who breaks the fragile bottle of repentance by his cruel treatment[288] (the washerman-bleacher hits the laundry repeatedly on stones). Love is also a bottle-maker of mysterious qualities,[289] or the carpenter who builds the ladder that leads to Heaven,[290] or the ladder itself.[291]

Rumi's favorite imagery is that of the kitchen and cooking. Love invites man to a table where dry and wet food is procured by the lover's dry lips and wet eyes,[292] or Love simply places a flaming table before its guest.[293] The heart becomes an iron pot on the fire of Love.[294] And Love is the great Baker,[295] for it is thanks to Love (which appears also as a kitchen)[296] that the raw becomes cooked, as Maulana repeats over and over again. Images connected with the kitchen, the pan of the liver or the kettle "heart" and all kinds of edibles, occur frequently.[297] The Sufis' use of the term *dhauq*, "tasting," for the immediate mystical experience has possibly contributed to this imagery. Love is even seen as the nourishment of the lovers, who "eat Love."[298]

> If sugar would know how sweet Love is,
> It would become water from shame and not show its sugary
> nature![299]

And whosoever has eaten salt from Love's table will "swallow himself," i.e., be completely annihilated.[300]

One such "kitchen poem" is one of Rumi's most paradoxical *ghazals* and like many of his paradoxes it tells of a vision or a dream. It translates into verse some of the strange events the great cook Love brought about:

> One night, seducing Love came beside me:
> "[Eat!] In the name of God! I have cooked a *tutmāj* for you!"
> It brough a *tutmāj* so that I lost the thread's end,
> Immediately broke the needle and tore my shirt.
> When I drank from its *tutmāj* it stamped me like garlic;
> I became bitter-faced like pickles due to the separation from
> that sweet one.
> In my hand there came nothing from this *tutmāj* but a spit—
> But I am sharp like a spit in what I have gained.
> On every leaf there opened another kind of rose from this *tutmāj*,
> Every garden opened its blossoms when I began to blossom . . .

1. *The execution of al-Ḥallāj. From a* Dīwān *of Ḥāfiz, Iran, probably Shiraz, second half of the sixteenth century. Courtesy Staatsbibliothek Preussischer Kulturbesitz, Berlin (Ms. or. fol. 108).*

2. *The* hudhud *(hoopoe) and the birds. From a manuscript of* ᶜ*Aṭṭār's* Manṭiq uṭ-ṭa
Courtesy Metropolitan Museum of Art, New York. Folio 11 recto, detail, painting by Ḥa
Allāh. The Ms. was copied in Herat by the calligrapher Sultān ᶜ*Alī of Mashhad and dated 8*
A.H./A.D. 1483. This painting was added c. 1600, at the order of Shāh ᶜ*Abbās, in Isfahan*

3. *Worldly and otherworldly drunkenness. From a* Dīwān *of Hāfiz, by Sulṭān Muḥammad, Iran, sixteenth century. Private collection. Courtesy Fogg Art Museum, Harvard University, Cambridge, Mass.*

4. *Poet and angel. India, late sixteenth century. Courtesy Fogg Art Museum, Harvard University, Cambridge, Mass.*

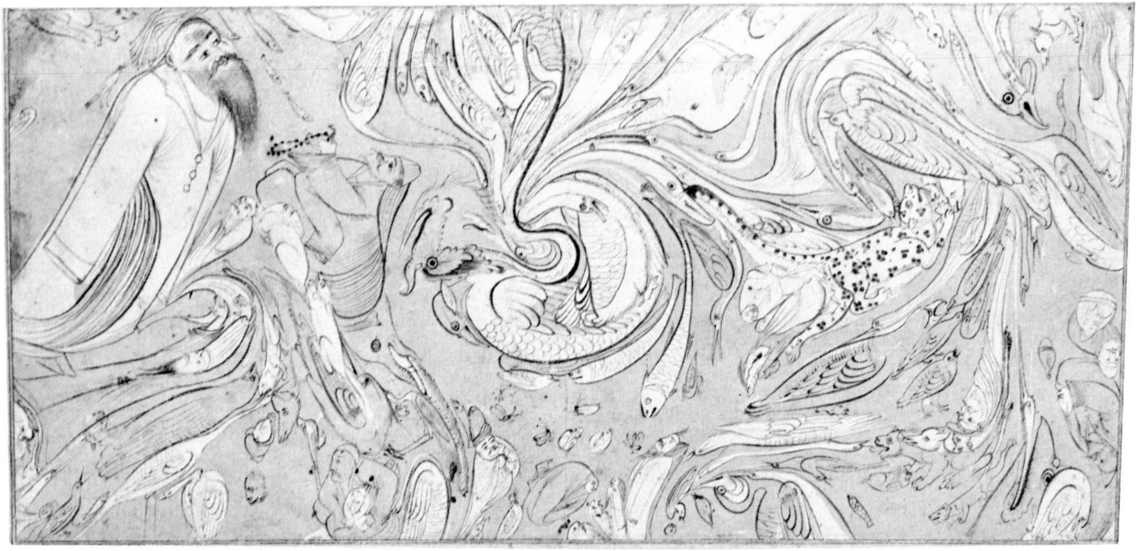

5. *Mystical journey. Isfahan, c. 1650. Courtesy Fogg Art Museum, Harvard University, Cambridge, Mass.*

6. The Prophet enthroned. From a Marzubānnāma, *Iran, fourteenth century. Istanbul, Archeological Museum, Ms. 216.*

فان نفسي قد خافت معرتها
وقد رجت منك منجاها ونصرتها
فاشفع لها وازل عنها مضرتها
إن من جودك الدنيا وضرتها ومن
علومك علم اللوح والقلم
من عفو مولاي آمالي قد انصرمت
وانما النفس مما قدمت المت
يا نفس لا تقنطي من زلة عظمت إن
الكبائر في الغفران كاللمم
فانت نفس عصت من كان يكرمها
وزاد عصيانها عدوا وما ثمها
وليس شي سوى الغفران يعصمها
لعل رحمة ربي حين يقسمها تأتي على حسب
العصيان في القسم

7. *Page from a* takhmis (*quintuplet*) *of al-Būṣīrī's* Burda, *written for the Mamluk Sultan Qaitbai (d. 1496). Egypt, late fifteenth century. Courtesy Staatsbibliothek Preussischer Kulturbesitz, Berlin (Ms. or. fol. 1623).*

8. Sindhi folk musicians, playing mystical songs. Photo Gräfin zu Dohna, Bonn.

and he goes on to tell in strange combinations of images that only by losing oneself one can attain eternal life.[301]

As Love is a cook it can also be a weaver or a tailor: its thread goes through a needle's eye[302] and it can also stitch things together without thread and needle.[303] Maulana has invented a delightful description of the "tailor of the lovers" who cuts pieces from black material, i.e., melancholia.[304]

Rumi is not clear as to whether the one whom Love has denuded will or will not be given a garment;[305] but he clearly states that Love is the robe of honor for the soul and the necklace of *karramnā* (Sura 17/70): "We have honored the children of Adam."[306] And he knows:

> Whatever is woven without you in the factory of Love—
> By God! neither warp is left; by God! nor woof is left![307]

Only the beloved weaves the carpet of true life.

Love can also appear as the great sorcerer who seizes the lover's ear like the handle of a pitcher and drags him into a corner to cast a spell over him—and who could tell how his soul was transformed then![308]

Love has more respectable professions as well. It very often acts as a physician and is then interchangeable with the beloved.[309] It is the Galen of the heart,[310] although the poet soon discovers that Galen and Plato cannot compare with this eternal, wise physician who both gives and takes away the heart's ailment and is able to give man a tranquilizer, *mufarriḥ*.[311] In a little dialogue the lovesick poet's soul asks forgiveness from Love for some fault he has committed:

> [Love] said laughingly: "I have taken your hand
> So that I know you completely without hand and feet.
> I have ordered for you a diet—I am the physician,
> For you are sick of this hope and fear.

Keep the diet so that I may prepare a drink
That you do not come to yourself till eternity![312]

This means that fear and hope are stages of the beginners; when they are overcome man will reach annihilation in love-intoxication. Love is also the Imam, and when this Imam appears, a thousand mosques are filled.[313]

After so many different general personifications it is natural that Love is also represented more specifically as the Koranic prophets. Most frequently Love appears as Moses and his miracles. His wand, which brought forth water from the rock[314] or, more importantly, turned into a powerful serpent,[315] offers the poet fine analogies, for Love can change things into their contraries—the body, dry as a wooden stick, becomes like a miraculous serpent once Moses, i.e., Love, takes it in his hand,[316] and Love's serpentlike rod is certainly able to swallow the whole world. The Koranic tales of Pharaoh, the embodiment of false pride and selfishness, are well suited to show that Moses "Love," *kalīm-i ᶜishq,* can do away with the conceit of the worldly.[317] And the immensely rich but unspirited Korah (Qārūn) becomes bankrupt in Love.[318]

Love can also appear as Abraham,[319] before whom the lover is like Isaac,[320] ready to be sacrificed. And the identification of Love with Yusuf, due to whose beauty the Egyptian women cut their hands (Sura 12/31), was common to all Persian poets.[321] For Rumi, Love is also manifested in Jesus, the prophet with the life-bestowing breath, "who gives happiness to the dead and medicine to the sick,"[322] and the poet invites his listeners to:

Die before his beauty![323]

a sentence which leads back to his favorite theme, that of death and resurrection through Love.

Love is Solomon,[324] whose seal subdues djinns and fairies,[325] and in an unexpected turn the *samāᶜ* is once called his army.[326] Love is David,[327] for in his hand human hearts become soft and pliable as did the iron;[328] "Love is to give up free choice."

For the Muslim mystic the absolute source of Love, and the perfect manifestation of Divine Love, is the Prophet Muhammad, for whose sake heaven and earth were created:[329] Love comes "like Mustafa in the midst of infidels."[330] A full study of this aspect of Rumi's prophetology, which again leads back to Shamsuddin's connection with the Prophet, is yet to be done (see alst chapter 5).

Love, cruel and overpowering as it generally is, can at times be a feminine concept, for it is the mother who gives birth to man[331] and to the four elements.[332] Maulana sometimes ponders the mysterious relation between Love-as-mother and man:

> First I was born from his Love; in the end I gave my heart to him,
> As the fruit is born from the branch and hangs down from from the branch.[333]

Rumi goes so far as to speak of Love as being the pre-eternal Mary,[334] and sees it as a mother who tenderly looks after her children[335] (contrasted to the harlot, World, who devours her children!). Who would not suck the teats of Love?[336] And man's heart, fleeing from the depravity of mundane life, "cuddles in Love's bosom."[337] As mother, Love becomes the substitute for the whole family—it is wetnurse and father, maternal and paternal uncle.[338] Was it not Love which, though itself without form and hands, gave man his hands and his form by uniting his father and mother in the love-game?[339]

Verses about the tender, warm aspects of Love, however,

are comparatively rare. Maulana never tired of repeating that Love is meant only for the strong, not for those who want to sleep and to enjoy a comfortable life. Sleep, personified as a timid little person, has to suffer terribly from the fist of Love so that it finally runs away from the lover to join someone else's bed.[340] And, of course:

> My patience died the night when Love was born![341]

Love may be a merciless,[342] fierce lion or a bloodthirsty king, but Rumi knows and repeats the *ḥadīth qudsī* in which God promises that He, or His eternal beauty, will be the bloodmoney for those who have been slain by love for Him. And Love is a hundredfold bloodmoney for everyone who is killed by its hand.[343] This *ḥadīth qudsī* is associated with the legend surrounding the martyr of Love, Hallaj, after whose death it was revealed to his friend Shibli. It is therefore logical that Maulana states frequently:

> The lovers walk gladly to the gallows like Mansur![344]

The cruelty of Love has been described by Persian poets in numberless verses, which become increasingly perverse and disagreeable. Rumi contributed a few new images of this kind: Love is a goldsmith's shop because all those who enter it will get golden, i.e., pale, cheeks.[345] More original is the idea that Love is a mortar in which people are pounded until they lose their original, stony nature, and become *surmā*, "antimony," which is believed to enhance the eyesight.[346]

> Since we have rolled ourselves up we have become all Love:
> When antimony is beaten it is nothing but material for the vision.[347]

Not a single blind person would remain in the world if such an antimony, gained from burning one's lower soul, were available![348]

The metaphor of stones which are crushed in the mortar to be transformed into valuable medicine leads to the numerous images in which the mysterious relation between destruction and reconstruction, or, in Sufi terminology, between *fanā'* and *baqā',* is expressed in alchemical imagery. Love is often seen as a treasure,[349] but since according to Persian poetical conventions treasures are always found in ruins, the heart has first to be completely destroyed before the hidden treasure can be found (the rhyme of *ganj* (treasure) with *ranj* (pain) facilitated the composition of verses with this imagery).[350] The numerous allusions to this mystery may have reminded the listeners of the extra-Koranic Divine phrase *kuntu kanzan makhfiyan,* "I was a hidden treasure and wanted to be known, therefore I created the world." And since God had promised in another *ḥadīth qudsī:* "I am with those whose hearts are broken for My sake," similar images occur very frequently in Rumi's work.[351] He sees life as a constant series of rejuvenating deaths: to live means to be transformed. Even when he speaks at various points, particularly in the third and fourth books of the *Mathnawī,* of the development of the soul in an upward movement that leads from mineral and plant to man and angel and ends in *ᶜadam,* "positive Not-being," one should interpret these verses not as pertaining to certain philosophical theories or to metempsychosis but rather as another expression of his conviction that no part of creation can reach a higher level of existence without sacrificing itself in Love.

> Purify yourself from yourself, and become all dust
> So that grass grows out of your dust.
> And when you become dry like grass burn nicely
> So that from your burning light may shine forth,
> And when you become from burning like ashes,
> Then your ashes are the elixir.[352]

Love is the great alchemy. Its power can transform the base copper of man's lower potencies into gold, provided he endures all afflictions in its crucible—then, Love can make this transient life eternal. Even in the last decade of his life Maulana sings in the *Mathnawī:*

> From Love bitter things become sweet,
> From Love copper becomes golden,
> From Love the dregs become pure,
> From Love, pains become medicine,
> From Love, the dead are made alive,
> From Love, kings are made slaves . . .[353]

Love can even transform an Armenian into a Turk,[354] and once the lower soul, *nafs,* is in love it cannot again become *ammāra,* "inciting to evil" (Sura 12/59),[355] as the hideous demon who falls in love finally occupies a higher place than Gabriel.[356]

Love, circumscribed in ever so many new images, still escapes logical description; that is why Rumi, like numerous other mystical poets in the various religious traditions, returns to the imagery of wine and intoxication to allude to its secrets.[357] Thrown out of the well-established professorial way of life by the heady wine of Love, he uses this imagery more frequently than any other metaphor, except for fire. The red wine and the red flames sometimes become interchangeable, as in the famous poem that begins:

> I saw my friend walking around the house;
> He played a melody on his lute . . .[358]
> He was invoking the cup-bearer in the mode of Iraq:
> His object was wine, the cup-bearer was only an excuse . . .
> My beloved took [the goblet] from him, and quaffed the wine:
> Flashes of flames run over his head and face . . .

Maulana had probably read Ibn al-Farid's great ode to wine, allusions to which can be detected in some of his verses. Rumi claimed not to discern the glass from the wine due to Love, and saw Love as a winehouse or a wine-seller.[359] Like his contemporary ᶜIraqi, some of whose verse he may have known, Maulana too speaks of the cupbearer's intoxicated eye,[360] and the *sāqī,* the primordial cupbearer of Love, appears often in his *ghazals.* Of course, Rumi knows that this intoxication comes from a cup filled with affliction;[361] from a drink which is poison and antidote at the same time,[362] and yet he exclaims:

> Whoever is not drunk from its wine should have a hangover in eternity![363]

and wishes:

> Until Resurrection the eternal cupbearer, Love,
> May be coming toward me with a goblet in his hand![364]

The enrapturing and transforming character of Love can be well symbolized by fiery wine, as a result of which "everyone feels so hot that his coat seems too tight and he takes off his cap and opens his belt"—a very concrete description of what theoreticians of mysticism call *Gottesfülle!*[365] Man may feel at times like a flask or bottle of Love,[366] like a cup which is now full, now empty,[367] and he knows for certain that his intoxication is from the cup of *lā-ubālī,* "carelessness."[368] Rumi, convinced that "God has created me from the wine of Love,"[369] admonishes his reader:

> Don't be sober, because the sober one
> Is very disgraced in the assembly of Love![370]

And in one of his great rhapsodic poems in which Shams appears as the *qalandar,* he sings:

> The banquet and ruby wine and ruins [or "taverns"] and infidelity
> Are the kingdom of the *qalandar,* and the *qalandar* is beyond that![371]

Such words are reminiscent of the daring *shaṭḥiyāt* of Hallaj, who time and again pointed to the tension between *kufr* (infidelity) and *īmān* (faith) in words which were to become worn-out clichés for the mystics of a later period.

Opposed to the intoxicating wine of Love, under whose influence the whole world is transformed, stands intellect, the representative of man's form-bound, law-abiding position in this world. Intellect, *ᶜaql,* is absolutely necessary to check man's unbridled passions, but it is only a guide or a watchman whose services are superfluous once the powerful King Love enters the gate. It is therefore not surprising that Rumi's most eloquent and often grotesque descriptions are devoted to the encounter of Love and Intellect.

> Love became plump and fat and handsome—
> Reason turned toward leanness,[372]

This verse reminds us of John Donne's lines about Love's "cumbersome unwieldiness." How could the big proud camel Love squeeze into a stable built for the chicken Intellect?[373]

"Could the great jurists, Shafiᶜi and Abu Hanifa, know what Love is?" asks Rumi in a line taken over from Sana'i.[374] For Reason may know all about the religious schools, but it becomes confused by and does not know anything about the *madhhab* of Love.

> Lovers do not mix with those with intellect because
> Someone who has not been thrashed does not mix with someone thrashed.
> Those with intellect run away from a dead ant out of caution—
> Lovers trample carelessly on dragons![375]

Reason contemplates the last consequences of every act while Love calls out: "Let be whatever be!" and flies to heaven, leaving science and etiquette to Intellect.[376] There is nothing bad in Intellect, but it just does not understand what the intoxicated poet is singing about in his strange tales:

> Intellect is clever, and his dainties (*nuql*) are tradition (*naql*) or
> analogy;
> Love came as a mine of vision from the sun of "Be, and it was"
> (Sura 19/36 et al.)[377]

In other words, while Intellect is happy to nibble from the inherited sciences and traditional scholarship, Love is vision, caused by the power of the Creator in His manifestation as Sun (which leads back to Shamsuddin). The old contrast between *khabar* (information) and *naẓar* (vision) is here formulated in a pithy image.

While Love owns a rosegarden behind the veils of blood, Intellect sees only the material world and toils in it, afraid of being annihilated by an unforeseen event:

> Intellect says: "The six directions are a limit, and there is no
> way out.
> Love says: "There is a way, and I have gone it several times!"
> Intellect saw a marketplace and started business;
> Love saw marketplaces beyond that one!
> O how many hidden Mansurs, trusting the soul of Love,
> Have given up the pulpits and gone to the gallows![378]

Rumi uses in the last line a topos which was to become commonplace for almost all later Persianate poets: the only place where Love can speak up is not the preacher's pulpit but the gallows—for how could the legalistic preacher express the secret of Love? Only by becoming a martyr (*shahīd*) man can be a witness (*shāhid*) and give public testimony to Love's power.

Intellect has an important function as a guard in human society, but the guard may fall asleep, and then Love comes like a thief at night to steal everything, capturing even the drowsy intellect.[379] In Maulana's favorite, and most convenient, comparison Intellect is the *qāḍī,* the judge representing legalistic Islam. The poor *qāḍī* Intellect loses his turban[380] or even pawns it for the goblet of Love![381] A longish *ghazal* tells the strange things that happen when Love arrives in town:

> Prison became Paradise through the clamor of Love:
> Mr. Justice Intellect drunken on the judge's bench!
> They came to Professor Reason to ask:
> "Why has this terrible riot happened in Islam?"
> Mufti First Intellect answered with a *fatwā:*
> "This is the moment of resurrection—where is [the difference between] licit and illicit?"
> The preacher Love came to the ᶜ*īdgāh* of Union
> With the sword Dhu'l-fiqar and said: Praise that king
> Who strews forth from the ocean of nowhere
> Jewel-like souls . . ."[382]

Intellect may be a Plato in his own right,[383] but:

> Love took up a mace and beat Intellect's head.[384]

And worse: when Sultan Love comes, he hangs Intellect on the gallows like a thief, even though he had been a king before.[385] That is why he flees from house to house when he sees Love appear in his realm in the guise of Prince Bloodshedding, *khūnrīz-beg.*[386]

There is some hope that Intellect may one day participate in the actions of Love, although usually, like a good ascetic, he recedes into a corner when Love brings wine and roast.[387] But he may eat just one grain from Love's bait and lose immediately all his plumage,[388] or meekly crawl in the dust of Love's vestibule.[389] He may even taste some opium from Love's hand and become demented,[390] and when the lover asks him then:

"Where are you, my Intellect?" Intellect said:
"Since I have become wine—how should I behave like a sour grape?"[391]

And even stranger things may happen:

Every morning out of love for you this intellect becomes crazy,
Climbs upon the roof of the brains and plays the lute . . .[392]

This contempt for intellect leads Rumi, and other mystical poets, to extol Majnun, the demented lover, who sees his beloved Laila everywhere and may be fettered only by the chains of Love.[393] For to love means to give up "normal" life:

Everyone to whom Love has given only half a greeting
Speaks four *takbīr* [funeral prayers] over food and sleep.[394]

The complete break with the traditional values in the experience of love makes Rumi also acknowledge that Love has nothing to do with shame,[395] with *adab*[396] (the prescribed etiquette), and with honor, for the etiquette of Love is quite different from what man learns in school. Rather, it is all *bī adabī* "without proper etiquette, ill-mannered,"[397] and therefore man—provided he is a true lover in search of Love—can be called to cut the throat of shame (*ḥayā*)[398]. Such ideas were expressed more prosaically as early as c. 900 by some Baghdadian Sufi leaders.

Maulana in his personal life continued to follow the injunctions of religious law, very carefully observing fasting and prayer. Yet all these lively images point to the fact that Love is outside the religious rites and the seventy-two sects of Islam:[399]

Love entered the mosque and said: "O master and guide,
Tear the shackles of existence—why are you still in the fetters of the prayer rug?

Let your heart not tremble because of the blow of my sword;
put down your head
If you want to travel from knowing to seeing!"[400]

And he sums up his views in the line:

Love is free from the narrowness of prayer niche and cross.[401]

Love is Divine, and it therefore enables man to return to his eternal home, to the Divine beloved. In one of his grandest poems Maulana describes how the voice of Love comes from right and left to remind the soul of its eternal home and lead it to the overwhelming vision of the Divine Light. Importantly, Muhammad Mustafa is praised in this poem as the caravan leader of the souls.[402]

Given this quality of Love, it can be described as *miʿrāj,* a heavenly journey comparable to that of the Prophet.[403] Hence it is often symbolized as Buraq,[404] the heavenly mount that carried the Prophet through the heavens. As such it is easily contrasted to the stupid donkey, the material part of man which does not participate in the spiritual ascension.[405] Only Rumi could see himself, the ardent lover, weaving from his bloodied tears a satin saddlecloth for the Buraq Love.[406] Love may be a fine steed,[407] or it can appear as a camel[408] (which is usually the designation of the lover or his lower soul), but Buraq is the most convenient symbol for Love. It flies without a ladder to heaven even though it appears in other poems as a ladder or a carpenter. It has strong wings which carry the lover toward the roof of the beloved:

That is Love, to fly heavenward,
To tear a hundred veils in every moment . . .[409]

And the soul-bird, imprisoned in the cage of the body, needs the wings[410] of Love to fly away:

If my soul-bird does not fly towards Love—
The plumage of that bird may be plucked out![411]

In this flight, Love tears all veils and opens ever new horizons for the soul. "It opens sixty windows,"[412] says Rumi, who sees Love also as a key seller who has keys for the lock of the heart, either in his shop[413] or under his arm.[414]

Maulana Jalaluddin knew well that images, similes, and metaphors can never describe Love, because it is one with the Divine Essence, and also every experience of love is new and unique. The Sufis of old claimed that no one can attract Love or reject it, because it comes from God.[415] Rumi experienced this irresistable power in his own life and tried to translate it into thousands of verses. He knew that no lover can seek union unless the beloved seeks it. Just as he often spoke of prayer being a divine gift[416] and not man's action,[417] he speaks also of Love's seeking for man: not only do the thirsty seek the water but the water longs for the thirsty as well.[418] From this point of view all his images of Love are deeply meaningful—the falcon that carries away his prey, the lion or the torrent, the king who besieges the city, the musician who plays the heart's lute or flute, the devouring fire, and the loving mother. They all point to the truth that man can do nothing but answer the primordial call of Love and trust himself completely to its hands. He then experiences that God/Love, which cannot be contained in heaven and earth, is enclosed in the fragile vessel of his heart:

O Love that does not fit in the sky from bulkiness—
How is it that you fit in my veiled heart?
You leapt into the house of the heart and closed the door from inside—
My niche and my glass and my Light upon Light! (Sura 24/35)[419]

Illuminated by this light the lover will recognize that everything points to the Divine Beauty and Majesty that can never be reached by human eyes or thoughts, because the jealousy of Love hides its essence behind roses and nightingales.[420]

Rumi knew that in Love the two Divine names, *al-mumīt,* "He who kills," and *al-muḥyī,* "He who bestows life," manifest themselves. Inspired by the traditional Sufi *ḥadīth mūtū qabla an tamūtū* "Die before ye die," he sings time and again:

> He who has become the prey of Love,
> How could he become the prey of death?[421]

As Hallaj had sung, "In my being killed is my life."[422] The lover is resurrected through the trumpet of Love, not through that of Israfil,[423] and enjoys already on earth the silk and satin of Paradise.[424]

> Lovers are strange—the more they are killed the more they are alive![425]

This mystery of a rejuvenating death also underlies the symbolism of the mystical dance: Rumi, whose poetry was born out of the whirling movement of ecstatic dance, often saw Love as the great musician. Its breath fills the reedflute to make it sing of its eternal home, and its hand touches the lute of man's body to make him speak of the beloved. The beginning of the *Mathnawī* is the most famous expression of this musical imagery, and it permeates his whole work.[426] Rumi felt that Love makes man dance, and not only man, but all creatures are called forth by Love's music to stamp their feet, clap their hands, and whirl around. The love of the Sun (i.e., Shamsuddin) makes the atoms run in enthusiastic dance from nonexistence into the wide fields of existence.[427] The cosmic dance, thus inaugurated by Love, permeates everything: Gabriel and the uncouth demon ᶜIfrit dance in love, even though the object of this ugly demon's love is only a she-demon,[428] and the dust particles whirl around the gentle yet fierce central sun.

Dance expresses best the mystery of dynamic Love, and mystics in all religious traditions have seen in their visions the dance of the soul (Suso) or the cosmic dance.[429] They saw the lilies dancing at Love's music,[430] "for dancing is Love's proper exercise" (Davies)[431] and they felt like participating in the agitated yet harmonious movement which permeates the cosmos.[432] In this whirling movement the lover experiences the secret of *fanā'* and *baqā':* he is taken out of the gravitational field of the material world and annihilated in the spiritual sun's magnetic field, gaining eternal life and participating in eternal movement. The symbolism of the white robes—garments of resurrection—which appear after the Mevlevi dervishes have cast off their black coats at the beginning of the whirling dance, points to this deep secret of transforming Love. It was translated into poetry by Rumi, and was beautifully rendered into German by Friedrich Rückert in his *ghazals* (1819):

> Wer die Kraft des Reigens kennet, lebt in Gott,
> Denn er weiss, wie Liebe töte—*Allāh hū!*[433]

Four / The Voice of Love:

MYSTICAL POETRY IN THE VERNACULARS

ONE DAY IN mid-fourteenth-century Bihar, a group of people were sitting in the *dargāh* of the Firdausiyya saint, Sharafuddin Maneri, after the noonday prayer, and the minstrels began to sing, first in Persian, the language of higher education, and then in Hindwi. After the recitation the venerable saint said:

> Hindwi compositions are very forthright and frank in expression. In purely Persian verses, there is a judicious blend of allusions and what can be fittingly expressed whereas Hindwi employs very very frank expressions. There is no limit to what it explicitly reveals. It is very disturbing. It is extremely difficult for young men to bear such things. Without any delay, they would be upset. . . .[1]

This is one of the first known remarks by a mystical master about religious poetry in the folk idiom, although the use of local languages in Sufi circles goes back to the thirteenth century. If we consider the Persian quatrains of Baba Tahir ᶜUryan in the dialect of Hamadan as part of this tradition,[2] mystical poetry outside the "high" literary traditions began as early as the eleventh century in Iran, and a century later in Central Asia, where Ahmad Yasawi's *Ḥikam* are the prime examples of Turkish Sufi literature.[3] About the same time that Maneri made his remark, the Chishti master Gesudaraz (who still lived in Delhi before returning to the Deccan) spoke of Hindwi as particularly sweet and fitting for religious songs,[4] and the first romantic tale with religious flavor in Hindwi was composed in this very city of Delhi. It was Maulana Da'ud's *Lōr Chanda,* written for Feroz Shah Tughluq's vizier around 1370.[5] About two centuries later the historian Bada'uni wrote of this epic:

> When certain learned men of that time asked the shaikh saying, "What is the reason for the Hindi *mathnawī* being selected?" he answered, "The whole of it is divine truth and pleasing in subject, worthy of the ecstatic contemplation of devout lovers, and conformable to the interpretation of some of the *āyats* of the Koran, and the sweet singers of Hindustan. Moreover, by its public recitation human hearts are taken captive."[6]

His remarks are true for the numerous epics written in the regional languages of Muslim India which took up, like *Lōr Chanda,* popular love tales and transformed them into vehicles for mystical teaching. Bada'uni may even have been aware of the Chishti writer Malik Muhammad Ja'isi's Awadhi poem *Padmāvati,* which belongs to the early Moghul period.[7] But only in the centuries after his death did mystical poets in Sind and the Punjab develop the art of utilizing simple folk tales as media for mystical instruction.

Sharafuddin Maneri's statement above about the frankness of poetry in the folk idiom is applicable, to a certain degree, to popular mystical poetry in the non-Indian environment as well, for it only slowly achieved the blending of expressions pertaining to worldly and otherworldly love in which Persian poetry already excelled. But it was just this popular literature that was instrumental in carrying the message of mystical Islam to the masses. For the two main languages of Islam, the Arabic of the Koran and of the theologians and, in the Eastern part of the Islamic world, the highly sophisticated Persian of the literati and officials, were unknown to the non-elite, who thus were excluded from higher religious instruction.

About the same time—the late thirteenth and the early fourteenth centuries—we find the first songs about mystical love in Anatolia in simple Turkish verse[8] and in India in Hindwi. In the Arab world too popular mystical poetry developed during that period. Somewhat later Panjabi, Sindhi, and Pashto followed. However, Pashto religious poetry is on the whole like Balochi, more ascetic in outlook,[9] and it rarely uses the sweet generalizations of all-embracing unity which are common to Sindhi, Panjabi, and Bengali Sufi songs. Kurdish is likewise rich in religious poetry which ranges from little devotional songs to encomia for the Prophet. Muslim religious literature exists in Tamil and Telugu, and in Malayan, and from a somewhat later stage onward it even appears in Swahili[10] and other African languages. The Islamization of the Balkans also resulted in the development of religious poetry in the indigenous languages, such as Serbo-Croatian.[11]

Everywhere outside the center of the Islamic world it was the goal of mystical preachers and leaders of fraternities to reach the masses and infuse into them the love of God and His Prophet in words which they could easily comprehend, using images from their daily life. The role of these preachers and poets in the development of various Islamic languages is comparable to that of medieval German-writing mystics like Meister Eckhart and Mechtild of Magdeburg in the formation of literary German;[12] of nuns and recluses in the Netherlands, who expressed their love of Jesus in their native tongue; of the author of the *Cloud of Unknowing* and Juliana of Norwich in England; and of the Franciscan poet Jacopone da Todi who helped develop Italian. All of them flourished, like the first Muslim mystical "folk poets," in the late thirteenth and the fourteenth centuries.

Out of these religious beginnings, a nonreligious literature would develop later; in Turkey, the two currents of folk poetry and high persianized urban poetry existed side by side until our century. That religious poetry in the folk idiom could also serve political purposes is evident from the verse of the Safawid ruler Shah Isma^c^il Khata'i, the founder of the *Persian* state, whose ecstatic *Turkish* poems aimed at winning over the Turkish tribes in Western Iran and Eastern Anatolia and became an integral part of the literary tradition of the Bektashi order in Turkey.[13]

The process of the growth of popular religious poetry can be observed best in medieval India, where in both the Hindu and the Islamic traditions the sacred, liturgical languages, Sanskrit and Arabic, were inaccessible to the masses and where mystical leaders in popular Sufism as in the *bhaktī* movement reverted to the indigenous idioms for their preaching. As Pir-i Roshan, the Afghan religious leader at Akbar's time, stated:

> God speaks in every language, be it Arabic, Persian, Hindi, or Afghani: He speaks in the language which the human heart can understand.[14]

Not long before him Muhammad Saghir, in his Bengali version of a Persian epic, *Yūsuf Jalīkhā*, had written:

> People are afraid of writing *ketāb* [i.e., real books] in Bengali. Everyone will blame me but it is not right that they should. . . . If what is written is true, it does not matter what language it is written in.[15]

Similar remarks are known from Shams ul-^c^ushshaq Miranji, who is credited with some of the earliest works in Dakhni Urdu.[16]

The use of the folk language enabled the mystics to teach the core of religion without the mediation of a priestly cast (as in the Hindu case where in fact the most ardent poets in the folk idioms were shudras), and without relying upon the writings of erudite scholars who, as Imam Ghazzali had said long before, were well informed about the most complicated forms of divorce but could not tell what "trust in God" or "piety" really meant.[17]

Hence, mystical folk poetry throughout the Muslim world has a strongly anti-intellectual bias and is often directed against the ulema and their claim to be the true depositaries of the Divine Law. Of course, a certain number of Arabic expressions from the Koran and tradition were taken over into the various languages to teach the central points of the Koranic revelations. These commonly used words and sentences are found practically all over the Islamic world, and it is this Koranic heritage that gives the Muslim branches of Indian languages their distinct flavor.

One of the central concerns of mystical Islam in general, namely, attaining immediate "knowledge from God," *ᶜilm ladunnī* (Sura 18/65) plays an important role in mystical folk poetry. The poets had before them the example of the Prophet, who was called in the Koran *ummī* (Sura 7/157–158), generally translated as "illiterate." That means that his understanding of the Divine message was not marred by any intellectual, bookish knowledge.[18] Praising this state in which man is a pure vessel for Divine revelation, quite a few folk mystics too claimed (as did some masters of high Persian style) that their poetry consisted of *wāridāt,* inspired words, which descended upon them without any intellectual activity. Indeed, I myself witnessed the "birth" (*doghush*) of such folk poetry in Anatolia in the 1950's.[19] The story that this or that saint was acquainted only with the letter *alif,* the first letter of the Arabic alphabet and cipher for Allah, is commonplace in the legends of Muslim saints from Turkey to India (Yunus Emre, Shah ᶜAbdul Latif, Bullhe Shah, Bedil Rohriwaro, etc.). To know this one letter is enough for the seeker,[20] for the wisdom of all four revealed books is contained in it, as Yunus Emre sang around 1300 in

Anatolia.[21] Shah ᶜAbdul Latif in eighteenth-century Sind teaches his disciples:

> Those who remember the line which begins with *alif:*
> "There is no goal but Him in both worlds," [that is what] they think.[22]

And his Panjabi contemporary Bullhe Shah repeats in ecstatic rhythms:

> The mollas have made me read lessons,
> They have not gone beyond the *alif!*[23]

Folk poetry likes to ridicule the molla with his numerous learned books: *Kanz Qudūrī Kāfiya,* the handbooks of *ḥadīth,* jurispruḍence, and Arabic grammar,[24] which were taught in Indian madrasas for centuries. It follows that trend in Sufism in which the perusal of books, and even more the writing of books, is equated with "blackening the books of one's actions," i.e., sinning.[25] As Qadi Qadan (d. 1551) in Sind sings:

> *Lōkān naḥw ū ṣarf—*
> Leave grammar and syntax to the people;
> I study the Beloved!

He continues this thought somewhat later:

> [The letters] which I read for my own sake—
> Those letters suddenly appeared before me like crocodiles![26]

And 250 years later his compatriot Sachal Sarmast writes that:

> Those who have tasted a sip from the syrup of the ocean of love
> Cast *Kanz Qudūrī Kāfiya* in the waves,
> They say goodbye to syntax, and don't look any more at grammar![27]

It should not be overlooked, however, that there is one source from which one can derive this immediate divine knowledge, the wisdom of Love: that is the Pir, the perfect mystical guide who has lost himself in the Prophet and in God and thus becomes the embodiment of love and superhuman wisdom:

> Even if you read for a thousand years the black from the white,
> It does not work unless you reach a perfect mystical guide.[28]

The role of at least one branch of mystical folk poetry in cementing the tremendous influence of the Pir over his followers should never be forgotten. Like other mystical writers, Yunus Emre has highlighted time and again the importance of the mystical guide,[29] the true "man of God," whose "arena is higher than the Divine Throne"[30] and "whose very glance transforms dust into jewels."[31]

This emphasis on the *alif* and on immediate knowledge as derived from the living "man of God" was, of course, consoling for the illiterate villagers who were thus assured that they too could reach perfection even though they had not studied theological works and were barely aware of more than the basic duties of a Muslim. Perhaps, they thought, there might even be some saints hidden among them, since God is jealous of his saints and conceals them under his domes, as the tradition says.[32] The figure of the illiterate village saint, who may even be slightly mentally deranged and can speak to God without any restriction, plays an important role in this area of folk mysticism and its literary expression.

In order to facilitate the spread of mystical teachings among the masses, the poets resorted to an imagery taken from daily life and from the landscape that surrounded them. To be sure, a mystic like Rumi often used everyday imagery to express lofty thoughts and deep mystical experiences, but most Persian-writing mystics composed their verse in the precious style, which, though often developed out of generally used images, soon crystallized into more and more abstract patterns. The folk poets followed the Koranic injunction to find God's signs "in the earth and in yourselves—do you not see?" (Sura 51/21). In their poetry age-old symbols came to life again. Yet, in the history of mystical folk poetry too the process of repetition and fossilization of forms, topics, and images is as visible as in high poetry.

In arid areas the tree, known since ancient days as the "tree of life," is a central image. Rumi repeatedly sings of the twigs which are moved to dance by the spring breeze of love,[33] and popular Sufi poets—Shah Latif in Sind[34] as much as the Anatolian minstrel Yunus Emre[35]—see the unbeliever or the ungrateful person as a dried-up tree which cannot be moved by the breeze of Divine kindness and should be cut off and burned (a subtle allusion to Sura 111). The green tree, however, becomes the symbol of the pious one who thrives on the water of life hidden beneath the surface in the desert. This pious one constantly recollects God—as the Prophetic tradition says: "The faithful engaged in God's recollection, *dhikr,* is like a green tree in the midst of dried-up trees."[36] And as the North Indian Chishti mystic Mas^c ud Bakk in the late fourteenth century speaks of the growth of the Divine plant in man's heart,[37] the Panjabi poet Sultan Bahu some 300 years later begins his Golden Alphabet with the lines:

> *Alif:* Allah is a jasmine bud which the preceptor has planted in my heart—O Hu!
> By the water of negation and positive statement it remained near the jugular vein [cf. Sura 50/16] and everywhere—O Hu!
> It spread fragrance inside when it approached the time of blossoming—O Hu!
> May the efficient preceptor live long, says Bahu, who planted this plant—O Hu![38]

Here, the *dhikr* of the profession of faith (*lā ilāha illā Allāh*, the negative and the positive assertion as used in the Qadiriyya order, to which Sultan Bahu belonged) is the water that makes the "plant" God grow in man's heart. A century and a half earlier, we find the Divine beloved compared with a tree in the first known Sindhi poems: Qadi Qadan speaks of the Banyan tree he likes so much, because although it is only one it is at the same time a whole forest which offers shade to the wayfarer, just as the divine beloved is the protector of everyone who seeks him.[39]

The folk poet sees himself as part of nature. The stone-breasted mountains separate him from the beloved, and he asks the cloud:

> O cloud, hanging in bunches from the snow-covered mountains' head—
> Opening your hair, do you secretly secretly weep for my sake?[40]

In the hands of Love, the mystic becomes rushing like a torrent, flighty like the dust on an Anatolian road, restless like the wind. Or, if he belongs to the austere hills of Eastern Anatolia he may feel, while separated from his Divine friend, like he is dying from cold in the merciless mountains, like a lamb lost on the bare ground, or a ewe whose lamb was taken away.[41] He talks to the water wheel, *dōlāb;* the shrieking sound of the wheel is understood as the tree's complaint about its separation from the forest where its arms and legs were cut off, just as Rumi's reed flute complained of separation from its pre-eternal reedbed.

> Oh waterwheel, why do you wail?
> My grief I wail, my pain I wail.
> I fell in love with God my Lord,
> And that is why I weep and wail.
> They found me on a mountain top;

They broke my arms, they broke my limbs,
They used my wood to build this wheel:
My grief I wail, my pain I wail . . .[42]

The wandering Sufi recognizes the modest yellow flower in the stony hills as a perfect dervish who expects nothing from this world. Similarly urban poets would regard the violet as a Sufi who, in his dark blue cloak, meditates, putting his head on his knees. In a watery country like Bengal the mystic might compare his restless state to that of the little water hyacinths that tremble as the tiny waves of the river move them. The impatient worldling could be warned "not to put buds on the frying pan" in order to have them open prematurely:

Look at the Great Lord
Who waits for ages to see one bud bloom;
He is never in a hurry . . .[43]

The lover's heart is mixed with the thought of the friend, as water rushing down from a watermill is mixed with clay, and he constantly turns the thought, "How can I reach my friend?" in his mind like a boatman wriggling his boat in the river.[44] He knows that this world is like the color saffron which fades away after a few hours,[45] while true love is as steadfast as the red dye (*lāk*) that stays even when the cloth is worn to rags.[46] Love, or the Beloved, also appears not only as a washerman who mistreats the laundry by hitting it on stones,[47] but as an oilpress to squeeze out man's heart.

The *bulbul,* the nightingale of the rosegardens, appears also in folk poetry, particularly in Turkey. But more authentic is the elegant *telli turna,* the crane that dances in the Anatolian air. In Sindhi and Panjabi the *kāng,* crow, serves as messenger instead of the more urbane pigeon. As the dove in the well-trimmed Persian garden of the soul constantly asks *kū kū,* "Where, where?" the Papiha bird in the Indian plains asks during the rainy season in Hindi, *piu kahāñ*, "Where is the beloved?" And Sindhi poetry recognizes the swan that feeds on pearls as the symbol of the true Sufi.

One enjoys these poems best when one knows the country and realizes how true to life their imagery is. There occur other images in folk poetry as well, many of them taken from the world of women, who were even less educated than men but were, and still are in rural areas, the best transmitters of religious poetry, songs, and proverbs, and the depositaries of mystical lore.[48] The poets saw the women spinning, and some of the earliest Urdu poems for mystical instruction are *charkhī nāma*, spinning songs, which were popular, as Richard M. Eaton has shown, among the Bijapuri Sufis of the late sixteenth and seventeenth centuries.[49] The act of spinning could be easily compared to the *dhikr*, for regular breathing is similar to spinning, and the humming sound of the wheel reminded the poets of the sound of the *dhikr*, repeated thousands of times with low voice. By such an act the heart will, like yarn, become the more precious the more finely and regularly it is "spun," and finally God will buy it for a high price (allusion to Sura 9/112). Is not every girl called to prepare her trousseau by constant spinning? And the woman-soul who neglects this duty will find herself naked at the day of the Feast when everyone else is wearing fine new garments.[50]

> As you take the cotton, you should do *dhikr-i jālī*,
> As you separate the cotton, you should do *dhikr-i qalbī*,
> And as you spool the thread you should do *dhikr-i ᶜainī:*
> The threads of breath should be counted one by one, O sister,

sings a Bijapuri Sufi in a style typical of women's songs[51] while the Panjabi folk poet calls the woman soul:

> Quit playing, and spin the spinning wheel, young girl!
> Hurry and make the bridal gear ready, young girl!

The droning spindle moans God, O God!
The trembling and shaking in fear of the Lord.
The spindle wind breathes like the sighs—
Seems, there is a heavy load ahead, young girl![52]

Similar are the *chakkī nāma,* which take inspiration from the most important occupation of the Indian housewife, the grinding of grain. Does not the straight handle of the grain mill look like an *alif,* the symbol of God?

The *chakkī*'s handle resembles *alif,* which means Allah,
and the axle is Muhammad and is fixed there,
in this way the true seeker sees the relationship.
Ah bismillāh hū hū Allāh!
We put the grains in the *chakkī,*
to which our hands are witnesses;
the *chakkī* of the body is in order
when you follow the Divine Law . . .

That is how the Bijapuri Sufis used the image.[53]

Agriculture offered fine analogies to human life. The Koranic verses about resurrection as prefigured in the awakening of the seemingly dead earth in spring when the soil all of a sudden becomes alive again (and, as Rumi would add, looks like Paradise in its green robes)[54] were certainly in the poets' minds when they mentioned sowing and reaping. They may have thought thus of the Prophetic tradition: "This world is the seedbed for the Otherworld."[55] But there are also realistic descriptions of fields and animals that thirst for rain, of clouds gathering and finally distributing *raḥma,* mercy, to the world. Such descriptions are then ingeniously connected with praise of the Prophet who too was sent *raḥmatan lilᶜālamīn,* "as mercy for the worlds" (Sura 21/107), to quicken the dead hearts.

Poetry that was meant for the masses had to be memorable and had to have simple rhyme patterns. For this reason certain forms were favorites with the mystical folk poets. The Golden Alphabet, known from the Ancient Near East and the Old Testament, was used among the Muslims in Pashto, Panjabi, and Sindhi poetry as well as in Turkish dervish circles and Swahili religious verse.[56] It helped to memorize the sequence of the alphabet, and each letter was charged with a certain meaning. The *alif* for every Muslim is the letter pointing to God, the One and Unique. The *m* was usually connected with Muhammad. The *ᶜain* was associated with *ᶜishq,* love, or with ᶜAli ibn Abi Talib, the fourth caliph and first imam of the Shia, whose veneration plays an important role particularly in Turkish Bektashi poetry.[57] The interpretation of the other letters is more flexible, so that many Panjabi *sīḥarfī* ("thirty letter poems") use indigenous words for each letter. The form can change from short, four-lined stanzas to complicated long verses with alliteration, alliteration being typical of many "popular" poetical traditions.

While the Golden Alphabet is known all over the Muslim world, the *Bārahmāsa* ("Twelve-Months-poem") is restricted to the Indian tradition.[58] This type of poem describes the seasons of the year as seen through the eyes of a loving and longing woman. The Muslim poets sometimes replaced the Indian months by the Muslim lunar months (in recent times even Christian months are sometimes found in Sindhi *bārahmāsa*); thus the Muslim feasts and memorial days could be fitted into the framework of a love poem. Starting with the tragic events of Muharram, the soul—represented as a young woman—lives through the festive days of the year until it finally finds, in Dhu'l-hijja, the way to Mecca, the center of its longing, where the Divine Friend dwells, or to Medina, the beloved Prophet's resting place. It hopes to achieve union either with the Divine Beloved or with the *ḥaqīqa muḥammadiyya,* the archetypal Muhammad. Poems enumerating a sequence of days are also found in Sindhi folk poetry, beginning at least from Shah ᶜAbdul Latif's *Risālō*.

It should be remembered, however, that both *sīḥarfī* and *bārahmāsa*, as well as imitations of the Arabo-Persian *qaṣīda* with a very simple form of monorhyme, were used not so much for enthusiastic love songs but rather for didactic purposes (*naṣīḥatnāma*): descriptions of Muhammad's life and miracles, especially his ascension, the suffering of the martyrs of Kerbela, and the teaching of Islamic values, customs, and rituals. It is the mnemonic aspect of poetry which makes it a much more useful means of instruction than prose.

More enthusiastic folk poets revert to even simpler forms. One is the four-lined stanza in the Turkish tradition, in which the first three lines rhyme while the rhyme of the fourth line continues through the whole poem. This is related to *tarṣīᶜ* in high Persian poetry, in which the two hemistichs of a verse are split into four units, three of them with internal rhyme (a form often used by Rumi). The Turkish popular meters employ syllable counting; they are not quantitative as in the Arabo-Persian literary tradition. In Indo-Pakistan, the poets used indigenous forms such as the two-lined *dōha* with its 24 (11 plus 13, or 13 plus 11) *mātras*. Soon the *kāfī* developed, in which the first one or two lines are repeated over and over again by a chorus while the main lines of the poem are recited or sung by a single person.

Here, we touch upon an important aspect of mystical folk poetry: it was meant to be recited or sung and not to be read or studied by scholars interested in grammar. After all, it was intended for the illiterate masses and was written down, if at all, only at a very late stage. Its use in music is the reason for grammatical irregularities, strange forms, and unusual rhymes and wordings which at times defy logical analysis. Its logic is peculiar because it aims to create a certain mystical mood rather than to explain, in plain words, rational facts. John R. Walsh was the first to draw attention to the fact that many of Yunus Emre's poems were probably meant for mystical concerts (*samā*ᶜ);[59] for the *samā*ᶜ, as the Turkish verses at the end of the Mevlevi dance state, is "nourishment for the soul." Indeed, the contents of Yunus' poems in general as well as the various *radīfs* (repeated rhymes) suggest such a use, and some of the old melodies are still known. Yunus calls God:

> *Dağlar ile, taşlar ile*
> With the mountains, with the stones
>   Will I call Thee, Lord O Lord,
> With the birds in early dawn
>   Will I call Thee, Lord O Lord!
> With the fishes in the sea,
> With gazelles in deserts free,
> With the mystics' call ᶜO HE!'
>   Will I call Thee, Lord O Lord[60]

Here, he translates into poetry what the mystics experience during their visions, namely, the uninterrupted praise songs uttered by everything created in its own *lisān ul-ḥāl* ("silent eloquence"). The best introduction to Yunus' poetry seems to me Adnan Saygun's *Yunus Emre Oratoryosu,* in which some of the central repetitive verses are used as a kind of *basso ostinato: aşkīn ver şevkin ver,* "Give love to Thee, give longing for Thee," or *bana seni gerek seni,* "It's you I need, It's you I need":

> Your love has taken me from me:
>   It's You I need, it's You I need.
> I burn and burn both night and day:
>   It's You I need, it's You I need . . .
> If they should kill me, let them fling
> My ashes up into the sky,
> And there my dust would sing and sing:
>   It's You I need, it's You I need . . .[61]

For Yunus, *dhikr* is true Paradise. In one of his most beautiful poems he describes Paradise as the place where everything is engaged in repeating the word *Allāh:*

> *Şol cennetin ĭrmaklarĭ*
> *akar Allah deyu deyu*
> The rivers all in Paradise
> Flow with the word Allah Allah,
> And ev'ry loving nightingale
> He sings and sings Allah Allah[62]

so that God's name will be all in all, growing, flowing, fragrance, and smile.

The fact that such poetry was meant to be recited in the gatherings of dervishes accounts for the difficulty of finding which poems are really by Yunus. His simple but moving style has been imitated by generations of mystics who grew up in the atmosphere of a dervish *tekke,* and much of the later Bektashi poetry was inspired by his songs. A similar phenomenon can be observed in Sindhi and Panjabi religious literature.

That mystical poetry in folk idioms was first composed for *samāᶜ* assemblies is known also from the Subcontinent. The Sindhi mystics who migrated to Burhanpur at the beginning of the sixteenth century used their mother tongue for the little songs which they recited during the *samāᶜ*,[63] and the Sindhi musicians who, around 1580, tore the historian Bada'uni's heart "with grating tunes"[64] may well have belonged to this group. The use of such verse during the *samāᶜ* explains many of their formal peculiarities: "throbbing, repetitive sounds with the swaying motion of the body and the strong rhythmical element, which can be underscored by the use of drums"[65] is typical of this poetry. It would be worthwhile to study the relationship between poetry used in the *samāᶜ* and the remarkably rich tradition of imagery connected with music. For instance, the flute plays a central role in Bengali popular mystical songs. Lord Krishna's flute seems to have become interchangeable with the reed of which Rumi sang in the beginning of the *Mathnawī*.[66] The musical imagery in Shah ᶜAbdul Latif's *Risālō* culminates in King Dhyaj's offering his head to the minstrel whose ravishing melodies had kindled his love and made him forsake honor and life.[67] Rumi saw himself as an instrument in Love's hand, and the Indian popular tradition sees *viraha,* unfulfilled longing, playing the body like a lute.

In such cases, the borders between "high" and popular poetry became blurred. It should also be kept in mind that the popular poets not only used motifs taken from daily life but continued on a simpler level the traditional imagery of Persian poetry, with its numerous allusions to the Koran and tradition (in fact, some of them indulged in stating very specific facts from a legendary tradition, sometimes even mentioning the exact sources they had used!). More importantly, since folk poetry developed only after 1300, the influence of Ibn ᶜArabi's theories of *waḥdat al-wujūd,* Unity of Being, as well as the typical vocabulary of the Sufi fraternities, form an integral part of this literary genre. The contents of mystical poetry between Istanbul and Delhi are therefore so similar that one can almost translate a Sindhi poem by Sachal Sarmast into Turkish and take it for an original verse by Yunus Emre, or transplant some Bektashi verses into Panjabi and declare them to be compositions of Bullhe Shah. The feeling of the essential Unity of Being permeates all of them equally strongly.

In Arabic mystical poetry the relation between man and God was, at least in the Ibn ᶜArabi tradition, expressed in metaphors of man's longing for a beautiful maiden. In Persian, however, this relation was usually symbolized in the love between a man and a beautiful young *shāhid.* But the Indo-Muslim folk tradition has developed another peculiar facet under the influence of Hindu neighbors—the symbol of the woman soul. To be sure, classical Sufism has always represented the *nafs,* the lower soul or base instincts, as a woman, since the word *nafs* is, luckily for the ascetics, feminine in Arabic. This leads generally to a most deprecatory description of everything feminine, women being on the lowest rung of the human race. But in the tradition of the plains along the Indus and its tributaries, as in early Hindi-Urdu poetry,[68] old Indian folk tales were taken up by the mystics—tales in which the female is the seeking, longing hero who undergoes terrible hardships in the hope of being united with her Divine Beloved, who experiences the Divine Friend's various moods as did Radha and the gopis in their relation with Lord Krishna. For in the Indian popular tradition only the woman can really experience love, *prēma,* that pure devotion "which burns her without hope of satisfaction."[69] Such tales of suffering women can of course also be interpreted as allegories for the education of the *nafs* which, from lowly a beginning as *nafs ammāra,* "inciting to evil" (Sura 12/59), reaches finally the stage of *nafs muṭma'inna* "the soul at peace" (Sura 89/27), and then is reunited with her Lord. *Hīr Rānjhā* in Panjabi is the best known example of the complete spiritualization of a medieval folk tale in which the woman Hir is identified with the soul, and her beloved Ranjha with the longed-for Divine Beloved.[70]

> *Rānjhā Rānjhā kar dī niñh meñ*
> *apē Rānjhā huī—*
> Repeating Ranjha, Ranjha in my mind,
> I myself have become Ranjha.[71]

Allusions to this theme are found as early as the sixteenth century in the Panjabi verse of Madho Lal Husain, the ecstatic mystic of the Qadiri order who is buried together with his

Hindu beloved in a modest tomb near the Shalimar gardens in Lahore. The romance of *Hīr Rānjhā,* elaborated in more than a hundred versions in Panjabi, Urdu, Sindhi, and Persian, was given its final form in the late eighteenth century by Warith Shah. It is his verse which is sung, time and again, wherever Panjabis meet.[72]

In Sind, the range of folk tales utilized for mystical purposes is even wider. Early allusions to these tales appear, however veiled, in Qadi Qadan's verse in the first half of the sixteenth century. They become more obvious in Shah ᶜAbdul Karim of Bulrri's short verses,[73] and reach full bloom in the *Risālō* of his great-grandson, Shah ᶜAbdul Latif of Bhit in the eighteenth century.[74] In his poetry the woman soul appears in various guises. Since the original tales were known to everyone, he usually begins his poetical renderings with the most dramatic moment in order to describe, with remarkable psychological insight, the moods of the soul on its way to the beloved. Among these "woman-souls" is Sohni, who swims every night through the Indus to meet her beloved on an island, until the jar which she uses as a kind of life-vest is shattered and she is drowned. She thus reaches eternal union with the beloved to whom she had promised faithful love at the day of the primordial covenant. She does not fear the bloodthirsty crocodiles and sharks nor the whirlpools because the lover does not care about the obstacles on his way toward the beloved.

Her counterpart Sassui, who follows her beloved Punhun through burning deserts and over terrifying hills is not scared by blue serpents and lions. Sassui has lost Punhun because she fell asleep. During the "sleep of heedlessness"—a major sin for the Sufi—her friend was carried away. In despair she runs after him until, though she can't catch up with the swift-footed camels of his caravan, she discovers that he lives in her (as Shams lived in Maulana Rumi). Finally, she is completely transformed into Love, her voice no longer that of a woman but of Love itself.[75] Sassui is the perfect embodiment of all those qualities which were expected from someone who enters the difficult mystical path.

Marui, another poetical character, is the ideal soul. Captured from her native village by the powerful ᶜOmar of Omarkot, she resists all temptation and neglects her outward appearance to discourage his attempts at seducing her. Her heart is always with her friends—for the soul should remain unstained by the blandishments of this colorful world and seek only its eternal home and primordial beloved.

Nuri, another character, was a historical figure, the consort of the Sindhi ruler Jam Tamachi in the fifteenth century. She has reached the lofty stage of the *nafs muṭma'inna* because, though a simple fishermaid, she is devoted to the beloved king in absolute and unquestioning obedience.

Although these stories have their roots or parallels in Indian folk tales they perfectly illustrate the mystical ideal of complete devotion, of the primordial love between God and the soul and of suffering for the sake of Love. The soul assumes here the *virahini* quality of the Hindu tradition; therefore the poetical genre of *bārahmāsa* often contains allusions to the heroines of these tales or is recited by the poet, who then assumes the character of Sassui, Sohni, or Marui. Bengali Sufi poetry has utilized the imagery of the Krishna-Radha cycle in a similar way. Sindhi poets compare the silent suffering of the loving soul to the state of a potter's kiln, which is not supposed to show any flames but is supposed to keep the fire inside.[76] Bengali folk singers have the longing woman speak in similar images:

> One who has loved without weighing consequences
> Has subjected himself to a constant anguish
> Consuming him slowly, like a fire fed with rice husk

And cow-dung. I did not know before—
I have made a pen of my fingers
And ink of my tears
And parchment of my heart which I send to my beloved.
Alas, I had not known it before![77]

The imagery of the woman soul found its way into some works of high Urdu-Persian literature. It is also generally used in the *gināns* of the Ismaili community where the beloved for whom the bridal soul is waiting is the Imam. In a number of poems in the Indo-Pakistani Sufi tradition the Friend is not God but rather the Prophet Muhammad, for *fanā fi'r-rasūl,* annihilation in the Prophet, and unification with the *ḥaqīqa muḥammadiyya* was the goal of most later Sufis. The allegories of the woman soul also offered the poets the opportunity to describe God in his quality as *sattār,* the one "who covers sins": He is the husband who will return to his wife who shivers, alone, in the cold and rainy nights in her humble thatched hut, regretting her mistakes and hoping for his forgiveness.[78]

The authors of these mystical songs are of course aware that the role of woman *qua* woman is anything but positive in traditional ascetic lore, and they therefore repeatedly state that these women were in reality "men," true "men of God." Shah ᶜAbdul Latif applies to one of his heroines the famous saying of the thirteenth century Chishti saint, Jamaluddin Hanswi: *ṭālib al-maulā mudhakkar . . . ,*" He who seeks the Lord is male. . . ."[79]

Real "men" are also frequently found in popular Sufi poetry. As Sufis and laymen (and laywomen) were able to identify themselves with the heroines of these Indian tales, thus from early times onward the names of the heroes of faith were mentioned in Sufi poetry and related prose.[80] They were meant to constitute a model for the faithful, just as the pre-Muhammadan prophets and their sufferings and final triumphs in the

Koran were a model for the Prophet in his difficult task. The tradition says, "Those who are afflicted most are the prophets, then the saints, then the others," and therefore, in Sufi poetry, the suffering prophets were turned into models for the lover, who in his sad state might think of Joseph in the well and his miraculous rescue, or of Jacob, who was cured by the fragrance of Joseph's shirt. Likewise the Sufi should be willing like Abraham to sacrifice everything, including his children. He should be obedient like Ishmael, who gladly went to be slaughtered, and he should be as grateful as Job in trials and tribulations.

In popular Arabic Sufism, litanies consisting of the names of mystics who suffered at the hands of the establishment are known. A mystical poet like Shushtari (d. 1269), who no longer wrote in classical Arabic, enumerated long chains of mystical leaders and spiritual guides in a popular poetical form to remind his listeners of their spiritual ancestry.[81] One might also think of the litany of the ᶜIsawiyya in North Africa with its long list of exemplary mystical leaders.[82] Classical Sufi works, such as ᶜAttar's epics or Rumi's lyrics, but particularly the meditations of Ruzbihan-i Baqli, are replete with outcries about the suffering of the great lovers.[83] In later popular tradition the poets' complaint that God always showers visitations upon those who love Him most could without difficulty be expanded to encompass the tales of the martyrs of Kerbela: the *jārīnāma* (from Persian *zār*, "lamentation") in Bengali are typical examples of this form. In fact, the story of Kerbela formed a central topic of popular literature all over the Eastern Muslim world.[84] But there were also long lists of prophets and saints who had been executed by the unfeeling mollas who did not know that it was Divine love that made their victims speak up in daring words. A telling example is Sachal Sarmast's Sindhi poem with the beginning:

Welcome, welcome You are—
to which place will You bring me?
You will again cut off a head!
Giving a kick to Sarmad You have killed him,
You have brought Mansur on the gallows, cut off Shaikh ᶜAttar's
    head,
Now You are asking the way here![85]

And the poet goes on to speak of Zakariya, who was sawed asunder when the tree in which he was hiding was sawed by the infidel king's order;[86] and of Shams-i Tabriz, Maulana Rumi's spiritual beloved who, according to the Indian tradition, was flayed alive by the mollas in Multan where his shrine is still venerated;[87] and of Shaikh Sanᶜan, the hero of one of ᶜAttar's stories in the *Manṭiq uṭ-ṭair,* who exchanged the rosary with the infidels' girdle and began to tend the swine of his Christian beloved. Such figures also frequently appear in Turkish popular poetry.[88] Sachal adds to these generally known Sufis the names of martyred Indian religious heroes, such as Sarmad, Dara Shikoh's friend, whose daring mystical quatrains, combined with the fact that he, a convert from Judaism to Islam, walked around stark naked, aroused the wrath of Aurangzeb's judges.[89] Sachal also speaks of Shah ᶜInayat of Jhok, called the first social reformer in Sindhi Islam, who was executed by the Moghul governor in early 1718.[90]

One of the figures that always occurs in these litanies of suffering mystics, but that also plays a paramount role as an independent figure, is Hallaj, usually called by his father's name *Manṣūr,* "The Victorious."[91] It is moving to listen to illiterate folk musicians in remote corners of Sind, the country which he traversed shortly after 900 to call people to God, or to listen to *qawwāls* in the *dargāh* of Gulbarga, when they repeat his name in ecstatic songs, and claim that he was the true lover who paid with his life for his love. He was the man for whom "the gallows were the bridal bed" and who, intoxicated by the primordial wine of love, beat the big kettledrum of *anā'l-Ḥaqq,* "I am the absolute Truth," which came generally to be translated as "I am God." Because he came to symbolize the eternal struggle between Law and Love he seems to be ubiquituous: he appears in Turkish Bektashi songs and in Malik Muhammad Ja'isi's *Padmāvati* in sixteenth-century India,[92] as his name looms large in high Persian and Urdu poetry from ᶜAttar to Ghalib and Iqbal. And there is barely a poet in the popular tradition of Indo-Pakistan and Anatolia who does not sing again and again of this "martyr of love."[93] However, almost all of them saw him as the typical exponent of *waḥdat al-wujūd,* the all-embracing Unity of Being, an interpretation which is historically wrong but formed his image in the tradition of Turkish, Persian, and Indo-Muslim singers. But this very theory of *waḥdat al-wujūd* made the folk poets also eventually think that everything that happens is nothing but a manifestation of the One Reality, and finally Hallaj and his judge, Shams-i Tabriz and the molla, and Abu Hanifa and Hanuman are one and the same, and there is no longer Turk, Hindu, or Peshawari.[94]

This tenor of popular poetry in both the Turkish and the Indo-Muslim tradition led Western readers to believe, in a way similar to comparable utterances of Persian elite mystics, that Sufism is nothing but measureless pantheism—an impression which is certainly not correct but can easily be deduced from this poetry if its images are taken at face value. For the poets in this tradition liked to identify themselves with everything created and claimed that in one moment they were Jesus, in the next Moses; that they were now the flood and now Noah. Such expressions are common among Turkish Bektashi poets in the succession of Yunus Emre,[95] as in the Indo-Muslim tradition, where the Panjabi Bullhe Shah and the Sindhi Sachal

Sarmast, with their highly ecstatic songs, are the most typical exponents of this tendency.

One can of course see in these attempts to identify oneself with the various prophets an expression of the mystical theories according to which the soul has to traverse the stations of all prophets on its way towards the *ḥaqīqa muḥammadiyya* and, united with the archetypal Muhammad, it comprises all previous stations in itself. These ideas have been committed to paper by more than one Sufi. However, probably not every illiterate or semiliterate poet was fully acquainted with these speculations, at least not enough to use them consciously in his verse.

One can explain such popular poetry also as a typical expression of the state of *basṭ,* expansion, which may amount to a kind of cosmic consciousness. And one should remember that it logically grew out of the feeling to "follow the religion of Love" in which the borders of faith and infidelity were—or at least seemed to be—somewhat blurred, even though the Prophet of Islam always represents the highest manifestation of all-comprehensive love. Like numerous other poets, Yunus Emre sings:

> Love is our imam, the heart the community, the friend's face our prayer direction, and our ritual prayer is never interrupted . . .[96]
>
> We do not speak against anyone's religion. . . .[97]

The lovers have no need for "what is called religion and religious community"; they form a class in themselves, as already in the ninth century they were regarded as constituting a special group at doomsday.[98]

The tendency to spiritualize the external acts of devotion, so common with urban Sufi poets, is perhaps even more pronounced or at least expressed in more daring words in popular

Sufism: the Great Feast (*ᶜīd*) is to meet the Beloved; Mecca and Medina (and for the Sindhi and Panjabi, also Multan)[99] are inside the heart,[100] and although the necessity of the outward ritual is acknowledged, it is seen as a mere purification:

> As lungs in the body, so are fasting, feast, and ritual prayer;
> But there is still something else, namely God's presence.[101]

And often, ritual was regarded as nothing but an impediment on the Path toward the Divine Beloved, as the Bengali poet Madan cries out:

> The path that leads to you is clustered up with mosques and
> temples.
> O Lord! I have heard your call but I can't proceed.
> The *gūrūs* and the *murshids* obstruct my way . . .
> You are separated from us by so many barriers—
> The Koran, the Puranas, the Muslim and the Hindu prayer beads
> (*tasbīḥ mālā*):
> O Lord, how tragic is this! cries Madan in despair.[102]

In later Sufi tradition, the multicolored imagery of all-embracing unity and indifference toward ritual became a mere topos and could be used even by otherwise perfectly legalistic Muslims who skillfully applied the whole vocabulary of uninhibited *waḥdat al-wujūd,* with all its corollaries, to their verse. Therefore, the sharp reaction of a modern critic like Iqbal to this kind of Sufi poetry, with its sweeping generalizations which seemed to leave no room for the truly Islamic values, can be understood and appreciated.

Folk poetry, as we mentioned, developed at a time when the mystical orders and fraternities were firmly consolidated, and therefore the role of the Pir in this poetry is highly important. In fact, mystical verse in the popular languages was largely composed by members of the fraternities for missionary purposes, and thus a special genre developed which centers around the veneration of the founder of the order or the patron saint.[103] Among the founder figures, ᶜAbdul Qadir Gilani is certainly the most popular saint, and he was extolled everywhere from West Africa and Turkey to India and Indonesia.

There is no end to his miracles. It was he who, according to a Balochi folk tradition, approached the Prophet during his heavenly journey when he drew close to the Divine Presence, and while Gabriel had to recede ᶜAbdul Qadir offered the Prophet his neck to step on when descending from his heavenly mount Buraq. Gratefully, the Prophet made ᶜAbdul Qadir's foot stand on the neck of every other saint.[104] Turkish poets regarded themselves as "the honey of his bees, the rose of his garden, and the nightingale of his meadow."[105] They told how the saint, standing on one leg, used to recite the whole Koran in one night,[106] while the Panjabi folk singer praised him as "the gardener of the garden of Truth."[107] Sindhi poets saw his *baraka* extending over the whole inhabited world. The first geographical poem in Sindhi, which enumerates dozens of cities and countries as ᶜAbdul Qadir's domain, was written in the early eighteenth century in his praise.[108] It is possible that the Indian Sufi practice of assigning to each saint, and he in turn to his *khalīfa,* a spiritual territory, *wilāyat,* has prompted the poet to claim that ᶜAbdul Qadir's territory is all-comprehensive.

There are many songs in honor of other saints too,[109] because each community has hymns in praise of the mystical guide at whose shrine the *qawwāli* gather. Here was and still is the center of popular religious life. Sometimes such poems are merely rhymed accounts of the spiritual or family lineage (*silsila, shajara*) of the Pir, or they contain blessings over the saint and his family, repeating dozens of times in sweet tunes and enrapturing rhythms a formula like *as-salāmu ᶜalaika ya Bandanawāz, assalāmu ᶜalaik mērē Gēsūdarāz.*[110]

Sometimes, the statements of mystical folk poets defy rational explanation.[111] Whether we should take them as expressions of pantheistic flights into a sphere where time and space are no longer valid, or as the results of "trips" (which is possible in the case of some lower orders of Sufi poets) is not always clear. Indeed, Sufi lore, and particularly popular poetry, contains a rich store of what looks like nonsense poetry, some of which may have simply grown out of the joy of playing with words, to which Arabic roots tend to invite the poet. To be sure, paradoxes have always been used by the mystics—on the one hand because it was impossible to convey mystical experience in plain logical words and to put the endless ocean of Divine love into the fragile vessel of human expression, and on the other hand because it was dangerous to reveal the mysteries of love and union to the uninitiated.

Secrecy is an integral part of mysticism, and as the number of followers of a Sufi order grew greater, the greater was the danger of vulgarizing the lofty truths whose divulgation to the unitiated could prove detrimental for the faith of the normal believer (hence Shah Waliullah's warning that the books of Sufism may be an elixir for the elite, but dangerous poison for the uninitiated masses).[112] The Sufis therefore resorted to cryptic languages, like the mystical Suryani as it is found in prayers and incantations, or to *ishārāt,* mystical hints, or else to strange inventions. The case of the *balabailān* language, or *lisān al-muḥyī* from the sixteenth century, which was first discovered in an Ottoman manuscript by Sylvestre de Sacy, is a good example of the attempt to invent a language which could be understood only by the initiated.[113] Another case is the fragment of a "mystical kitchen vocabulary," discussed by Hellmut Ritter.[114] Again, intellectual shock therapy is often practised by the mystics, and a sentence or a poem that looks like pure nonsense may induce the listener to a supralogical understanding, as is the case with the *koan* in Zen Buddhism. The tendency of the Arabic roots to branch out into almost infinite forms was helpful to create a complicated web of associations.

On the highest level, one may think of the *shaṭḥiyāt,* the theopathic locutions or, as Henry Corbin calls them, "paradoxes" of the Sufis which grew out of "the agitation of the innermost hearts of the ecstatics when ecstasy becomes strong."[115] Such locutions transgress the normal utterances of a human being, such as Bayezid Bistami's *subḥānī,* "Glory be to me!" in which the subject seems to be God Himself who speaks through the mystic as he once spoke through the burning bush to Moses. The Lebanese poet Adonis, who stresses the surrealistic character of early Sufi literature, considers these expressions to be not only metarealistic but truly metaphysical.[116]

Strange paradoxes, sometimes in accounts of visionary experiences, are found rather frequently in the poetry of Rumi, who is a master of surprising and even shocking remarks and images.[117] The genre of what we may call true "nonsense poetry" is wellknown in the popular tradition of both Anatolia and Muslim India. We may mention in this connection also poems in which Sufis talk aggressively with God, scolding him for some apparently meaningless arrangements in this world and even more in the next, such as hellfire:

> Are You the owner of a bath house, or a *külhancĭ* [i.e., a destitute wretch that sleeps in the warm ashes of the bath house]?[118]

asks a sixteenth-century Turkish poet of the Lord. He follows Yunus Emre's example of openly questioning God's wisdom in creating the eschatological instrumentarium, such as a bridge thinner than a hair and scales to weigh the dirty sins of man.[119]

This poetry belongs to what Hellmut Ritter has called "Muslim mystics' strife with God," a genre particularly frequent in ᶜAttar's epics.[120] But in the private prayers of contemporary village "saints" one can still hear extremely daring, if not coarse addresses to God or the Prophet.

Besides such prayers and poems, which express a real concern, one finds typical nonsense verse, among which Yunus Emre's long *tekerleme* is most famous:

> *Çĭktĭm erik dalĭna üzüm toplamağa*
> I climbed upon the plum tree
> to gather there some grapes.
> The garden-owner asked me:
> "Why do you eat my nuts?"[121]

This poem has often been interpreted by Turkish writers, and its best known commentary is by the seventeenth-century mystic, Niyazi Misri, a fine poet in his own right, who in long-winded sentences interprets the prune to be outward sciences and external *sharīᶜa,* and the grapes to be inward sciences and the mystical path, *ṭarīqa,* while the walnut, the kernel of which is all sweetness and oil, symbolizes the Divine truth, *ḥaqīqa.* This explanation conforms to the general notion that the breaking of the nut refers to the sudden *Erlebnis* of the Divine, the unexpected sweetness of the mystical experience after hard labor.[122]

This very poem by Yunus contains a line which has become proverbial, *balĭk kavağa çĭktĭ:*

> The fish climbed on the poplar tree
> To eat there pickled tar.[123]

To say "when the fish climbs on the poplar tree" means in colloquial Turkish "when the pig flies," i.e., never. The same expression is found in Kabir's poetry in fifteenth-century India, and Charlotte Vaudeville has devoted a long paragraph to this type of *ultabhaṇsī* ("inverted") images, which occur frequently in Kabir's verse,[124] such as:

> The ocean is burning and consumes its prey,
> The fish is angling for the prey,

or:

> The mouse is the boatman, the cat the boat,
> And the frog is sleeping under the protection of the snake.

We cannot trace back the Turkish tradition of such topsy-turvy-world verses, while in India they go back to Vedic times and were largely used in the tantric tradition.[125] Since in Bengal the so-called "Riddles of Goraknath" are still popular among the Hindu villagers, it would be worthwhile to study Sindhi or Pashto riddles and conundrums with a view to the paradoxical (and probably often mystical) meanings which they may convey to the initiated.

The imagery of the mystical paradox does not change much in different cultures, for the tendency is to show that our sense perceptions are unreliable and more or less interchangeable, and that the seemingly weak creature is stronger than the stubborn, powerful one. When an *ultabhaṇsī* verse in India tells that:

> The cow has cut the lion in pieces and devoured him,[126]

the image immediately brings to mind a North African Sufi story which cannot possibly be related historically to the Indian verse:[127] a conceited Sufi, riding on his lion, went to visit another master. When he arrived at the convent in the mountains he was told to tether his lion in the cow's stable. Grudgingly he obeyed, and when he entered the master's room he found him surrounded by lovely damsels, so that he doubted his colleague's spiritual rank even more. But the next morning he found that his lion had been eaten by the cow. It might be interesting to study Sufi legends as projections of ideas expressed in such paradoxical verses and riddles.

The experience that in ecstasy the senses are interchangeable is well known from high poetry (Ibn al-Farid's *Tā'iyya* contains a famous example),[128] and the fact that neither the experience itself nor its contents can be properly described led the poets often to invent new oxymora. As D. T. Suzuki says: "When language is forced to be used for things of this [transcendental] world, it becomes warped and assumes all kinds of crookedness: oxymora, paradoxes, contortions, absurdities, oddities, ambiguities, and irrationalities."[129] Therefore the "bliss unspeakable," which the mystic experiences in ecstasy, can only be expressed in contradictions, be it the Sun at Midnight, the *überhelle Nacht* of Quirinus Kuhlmann and other German baroque mystics, or *ᶜadam,* the "positive not-being" of Rumi, or the *neti neti* of the Upanishads. He may see

> Eternity in an hour,

for typical of mystical experience is timelessness, which in order to express mystical writers had to use paradoxes of sorts.[130] There is not only the feeling of being contemporary with all prophets and saints, but a full inversion of the logical sequence of timebound events. When Hallaj sings in his *qaṣīda Uqtulūnī:* "Kill me, O my friends,"

> My mother has born her father,
> And my young daughters have become my sisters,[131]

he uses the same device as the *ultā bāul* poet in Bengal who sings:

> The father was born on the day of the mother's marriage,
> And the son was born two days later.[132]

Such ideas are found as early as in the Nag Hammadi texts,[133] and they have been repeated by other mystics in the Islamic world and were reflected in popular riddles.[134] ᶜAbdul Wahhab al-Bayati's third poem, "Mosaic," in his cycle on Hallaj, is a fine contemporary expression of the experience that temporal relations are no longer valid once union is achieved.

"To catch an elephant by a hair,"[135]—that is what the urban and even more the folk poets try to do in such verses. Therefore their imagery sometimes becomes weird and even obscene. For instance the poems of the Turkish Bektashi mystic Kaygusuz Abdal in the fifteenth century are anything but mystical in the traditional sense. Sometimes it sounds as if he were inventing nursery rhymes:

> *Kaplu kaplu bağalar kanatlanmiş uçmağa*
> The tur-tur-tur-tur-turtles have put on wings to fly. . . .

Then again he sings of his insatiable appetite (a topic also used by the Panjabi mystic Madho Lal Husain),[136] ridiculing or reversing the classical topic of the mystic's insatiable thirst for more and more love; or else he creates parodies of mystical love poetry by telling of his own unsuccessful affairs with a charming gentleman with peachlike cheeks who tells him to be gone; and he sees the taming of the *nafs,* the lower soul, as the cooking of a tough old goose which, even though steamed in the oven for forty days (i.e., in the forty days' seclusion) is too hard to be eaten and triumphantly sneers at the poor cook.[137]

The commentators worked hard to find the deeper meaning of such poems. As Niyazi Misri interpreted intelligently Yunus Emre's *tekerleme,* thus the *Chīstān-i rāz* or *Shikārnāma,* which was attributed to Gesudaraz in medieval India and tells of the adventures of various deformed and handicapped people who went out for hunting, has been frequently commented upon. In the early classical tradition, Dhu'n-Nun's alleged poem beginning

ᶜajab ᶜajab ᶜajab ᶜajabū
qiṭṭa saudā wa lahā dhanabū

has also found numerous commentators; this little poem about the black cat with a tail is supposed to contain alchemistic information and one has certainly to think of possible cross relations between the secret language of alchemy and apparently nonsensical expressions in mystical poetry.[138]

Popular mystical "nonsense poetry" is a very genuine expression of poets—partly literate, partly illiterate—who were confronted with the confusing world of senses and knew, either by tradition or by experience, of the world of unity behind it; of poets who often lived in restless times, and during the turmoil of wars and insurrections retired into the tranquillity of the inner life to discover the one calm and unchangeable source in which all seeming contradictions were resolved. Like their colleagues in the urban societies, they too sang of the black hair of the beloved and his/her radiant face, qualities which belong together like faith and infidelity. Their love of the Prophet was deep and sincere (see chapter 5), and inspired many of their poems. The Islam which they taught the masses was that of *tawakkul*, of complete trust in God's eternal wisdom, as reflected in many of the folk tales in the Islamic lands:

Aglatĭrsa Mevlâ yine güldürür
If the Lord makes you cry, He will make you laugh again.[139]

It was not the exclusive religion of the immutable Law but rather a religion of warm love—a love in which non-Muslims might also share, as in India Hindus participated in writing mystical poetry in honor of the Prophet and the saints. The popular Sufi poets saw the afflictions that came over their villages as signs of God's inscrutable wisdom. They knew that the lover experiences affliction, death, and resurrection already in this world by submitting completely and without question to the will of the Divine Lord and Beloved. And they firmly believed in the Koranic words: "Whithersoever ye turn there is the Face of God" (Sura 2/109).

Iy dün u gün Hak isteyen, bilmez misin Hak kandadĭr?
Her kandayĭm anda hazĭr, kanda bakarsam andadĭr [140]
O you who seek God ev'ry day,
Do you not know it, where God is?
He's present wherever I am,
Where'er I look, He's there,

sings Yunus Emre in Anatolia around 1300, and Shah ᶜAbdul Latif in eighteenth-century Sind knows that:

hika qaṣaru dara lak'ha
One castle, a hundred thousand doors,
Windows without number—
Wherever I look, there the Beloved confronts me.[141]

Five / God's Beloved and Intercessor for Man:

POETRY IN HONOR OF THE PROPHET

ONE OF THE most moving experiences in the Subcontinent is to listen to a good *qawwālī*. The musicians recite Persian or Urdu *ghazals,* beginning with a solo voice to which the group responds, and almost always a *ghazal* is sung that is usually attributed to Amir Khusrau. In

Namīdānam che manzil būd shabgāhī ki man būdam,

a mysterious nightly festivity with wine and candles is described, which all of a sudden turns into a praise of the Prophet:

Muḥammad sham^c-i maḥfil būd shabgāhī ki man būdam! [1]

This *ghazal,* as well as many others which are sung in ecstatic rhythms, is typical of one kind of poetry composed in honor of the Prophet: it leads the listener slowly into the delightful world of mystical imagery and then reveals that the beloved of whom the poem speaks and who appears as the central light illuminating our nightly world is no other than the Prophet of Islam, the *ḥabīb Allāh,* God's beloved.[2]

The love of the Prophet has been called the strongest binding force in Islam,[3] and Muslims have always regretted that most Westerners fail to understand the importance of this love for Muhammad. Tinged by centuries-old prejudices, they rarely realize that for his followers Muhammad is as much the model for the faithful, as much the infallible leader of his community as he is the beloved intercessor at Doomsday. He is the first thing created by God as well as the "seal" of all prophets, and brought with him the final and all-comprehensive revelation.[4] Wilfred Cantwell Smith has lucidly shown how important the *person* of the Prophet became particularly during the last hundred years. During that time the interest in the Life of Muhammad and his socio-political role grew among reformist and modernist Muslims, just as in Christianity during the same time the interest in *Leben-Jesu-Forschung* seemed to replace the deep mystical faith in the eternal Christ. This development however does not concern us here.[5]

Love for the Prophet has been reflected through the centuries in learned and pious treatises and voluminous books, as in the careful study of the *sunna,* his way of life, which was to form the ideal pattern for Muslim life everywhere. The Koran states: "Who obeys the messenger obeys God" (Sura 4/82), and Muhammad was called an *uswa ḥasana,* "a beautiful model" (Sura 33/21). Therefore his *sunna* became normative wherever Muslims lived, a reason for the amazing uniformity of life style and behavior in all Muslim countries. Poets in the mystical and nonmystical tradition enjoyed extolling him and singing of their love for and trust in him. The first laudatory poems for him were composed during his lifetime. Kaᶜb ibn Zuhair's famous *qaṣīda Bānat Suᶜād,* with its truly ingenious turn from the traditional description of the desert-traveler's adventures to his hope in Muhammad's forgiveness, won the Prophet's heart so that he granted the author his own *burda,* the striped coat, thus forgiving him his previous enmity.[6]

But while Kaᶜb's *Burda,* often imitated, enlarged, commented upon, and in the course of time surrounded by a special sanctity,[7] was just one more masterpiece of classical Arabic poetry.[8] Muhammad's cause was defended in various ways by Hassan ibn Thabit, who embraced Islam after the Prophet settled in Medina. He was then of mature age, and died most probably in 659.[9] His poetry is an important constituent of the *sīra,* Muhammad's biography, because he wrote extemporaneous verse in praise of the Muslim cause or denigrating the Prophet's enemies. He described events like the battle of Badr (624), in which the small group of Muslims gained their first victory over the Meccans; the Battle of the Trench (627); the fight with the Jewish tribe Quraiza, and the conquest of Mecca (630). A poem on this last occasion begins with the line:

> God spoke: "I have a servant who speaks the truth,"

thus carrying over Koranic statements into poetry.[10] Sometimes Hassan's descriptions contain remarks that sound like variations on the profession of faith:

> We know that there is no Lord but God,
> And that the Book of God has become a guide.[11]

Hassan's poetry, traditional as it is in form and imagery, already shows some elements which were to develop in later *naᶜtiyya* poetry. Thus, speaking of the battle of Badr, he plays with the word *badr,* which also means "full moon," and states that the Prophet's face shone like the full moon.[12] Incidentally, the metaphor of light occurs more frequently than any other comparison in his eulogies and descriptions.[13] Kaᶜb, too, had stated that:

> Verily the Prophet is a light by which one becomes enlightened,
> And a sharp one among God's unsheathed swords.

Hassan also used a kind of word play which became popular with later poets: he says that the name of *Muḥammad* was derived from the epithet *maḥmūd* "praiseworthy," which is a designation of God, to whom belongs *al-ḥamd,* "praise," as the *Fātiḥa* states.[14] As later theologians and mystics were very fond of pointing to this special connection, the very name of the Prophet was often praised for its *baraka.*

> Your name is beautiful, you yourself are beautiful,
> Muhammad!

sings a medieval Turkish folk poet,[15] while a modern thinker like Iqbal claims in his *Asrār-i khūdī* (written in 1915):

> All our glory is from the name of Muhammad,[16]

and he had sung a few years earlier in *Jawāb-i shikwā:*

> Light the world, too long in darkness,
> With Muhammad's radiant name.[17]

A tradition promises that on Doomsday it will be announced: "He who is called Muhammad should get up and enter Paradise thanks to the blessing of the Prophet's name!."[18] Therefore this name, or one of its equivalents (Ahmad, Mustafa, Taha, etc.) was commonly given to boys, but in order to preserve both its sanctity and its power, the word *Muḥammad* is vocalized, in some languages, differently when applied to normal human beings (thus Mehmet in Turkey, Mihammad or Mahammad in Morocco), while the full and correct vocalization is preserved for the Prophet.[19] In later times he was surrounded by numerous names derived from the Koran so that he, like God, had 99 names, similar to God's Most Beautiful Names. Sometimes, even more honorific names—up to 200!—were invented for him.

A considerable number of poems were composed on the

occasion of Muhammad's death. Among them, Hassan's threnody, considered to be one of his best poems, is particularly important because it offers allusions to his birth, which again is combined with the motif of the light which filled the whole world when he was born,[20] an idea repeated over and again in popular *maulid* poetry in later times. For the Prophet is called *sirāj munīr,* "a shining lamp" in the Koran (Sura 33/45). And even the conviction that Muhammad is the *shafīᶜ*, the intercessor at Doomsday, is found in Hassan's verse, although there is no exact Koranic sanction for it.[21] Muhammad's *shafāᶜa,* however, became the center of hope for all Muslims. A sober historian like Ibn Khaldun (d. 1406) prays:

> Grant me your intercession for which I hope
> With a beautiful pardon for my ugly sins.[22]

and an extreme mystic like ᶜAfifuddin at-Tilimsani (d. 1289) exclaims in despair:

> I have abundant sins, but perhaps
> Your intercession may save me from the flames. . .[23]

and closes his call for mercy with the words:

> I have called you, hoping for an act of grace from you—
> God forbid, God forbid that you would be called and would not answer!

Swahili folk poets trust in the Prophet's intercession,[24] and the Urdu poet Mir in the eighteenth century begins his second *Dīwān* with the consoling words:

> Why do you worry, Mir, thinking of your black book?
> The person of the Seal of the Prophets is a guarantee for your salvation,[25]

The Mamluk Sultan Qaitbay of Egypt (d. 1496) says in one of his Turkish poems:

This is God's beloved,
The physician for all pains—
Look, this noble, single one
In the midst of the field of intercession.[26]

And a popular Pashto ballad speaks of the Prophet's intercession with the refrain:

On the day of Resurrection, O Prophet,
My hand [is on] your skirt![27]

The hope in Muhammad's *shafāʿa* helped them to maintain their optimism, for would they not march behind the flag, *liwā'*, of the Prophet on the day of Judgment?[28]

Hassan's poems also contain allusions to the outward and inward perfection and beauty of the Prophet:

And a more beautiful one than you a woman has never borne,
And a more handsome one has never seen my eye.[29]

These are formulas out of which the long descriptions of the noble qualities of the Prophet, so-called *ḥilyas*, developed, which were later written in fine calligraphy to adorn the houses of the pious, and were in turn again elaborated in poetical form in Arabic, Turkish, and Urdu.[30]

Thus, Hassan ibn Thabit's verse indeed contains the germs of most later poetry in honor of the Prophet, and therefore his name became a coterminus for those who composed verse extolling the Prophet. Khaqani, the powerful Persian poet of the twelfth century proudly called himself *Ḥassān al-ʿajam*, and Azad Bilgrami in eighteenth-century India was acclaimed as *Ḥassān al-Hind* due to his glowing Arabic encomia.

The development of *naʿtiya* poetry was facilitated by the fact that it became part and parcel of Muslim piety to call God's blessings upon the Prophet, for God himself blesses him, as mentioned in Sura 33/56; and the *ḥadīth qudsī* promised that

God would bless ten times a person who blessed the Prophet once.[31] Thus, the *ṣalawāt-i sharīf* or *durūd* came to constitute an important element of the *dhikr* in some mystical groups, and is repeated hundreds of times as a protective prayer by innumerable faithful.

While the common Muslims deeply trusted in the Prophet and his message and were certain that he was able to guide them and even cure their ailments through his apparition in dreams,[32] the veneration of Muhammad as an almost superhuman figure grew predominantly in Sufi circles. The idea of the Light of Muhammad, of which Hassan ibn Thabit had spoken briefly, was elaborated, possibly in connection with trends in Shia imamology, by the mystics of the eighth and ninth centuries to form a central part of Sahl at-Tustari's theology in the late ninth century.[33] He was followed by his disciple al-Hallaj. Hallaj's hymn to the Prophet in rhyming prose in his *Kitāb aṭ-ṭawāsīn* is one of the most glowing descriptions of Muhammad ever written and states openly that the Prophet preceded everything and that his light is light from the Divine Light.[34] Such formulas were to be repeated through the centuries down to modern Sindhi folk poetry.[35] Shibli's verse:

> *Kullu baitin anta sākinuhu*
> Any house in which you dwell
> Does not need lamps,[36]

is still sung today in religious meetings to praise the Prophet, and a medieval Bengali mystic, Shaikh Chand, went so far as to tell in his *Tālibnāme:*

> The Lord of *nūr,* "light," with a stick in his hand, gazed to the East.
> The creation began with the Light of Muhammad;
> The Lord brought the light from His own heart.

He even stated that the creative word *kun,* "Be!" consists of the *k* of *kalima,* i.e., the profession of faith, and the *n* of *nūr,* Muhammad's light.[37] The idea that Muhammad radiated light and did not cast any shade is, in a certain way, an exteriorization of his *ᶜiṣma,* his freedom from faults and sins.

In the late ninth century, Tirmidhi composed his *Shamā'il al-Muṣṭafā,* talking about Muhammad's outstanding qualities, and a century later Abu Nuᶜaim wrote the *Dalā'il an-nubuwwa,* a literary genre that became very popular. The pious writers dwelt upon the Koranic remarks about the Prophet; they particularly loved the statement that he saw the Divine *qāba qausain au adnā,* "two bows' length or closer" (Sura 53/8), and the Koranic address "Did we not extend your breast?" (Sura 94/1) was developed into descriptions of his heart being taken out and cleansed, as the beginning of Sura 54, *Wa'nshaqqa'l-qamar,* was understood to point to his miracle of "splitting the moon" (a miracle by which, according to legend, some contemporary Indian kings were converted to Islam).[38] And although an eighteenth-century theologian like Shah Waliullah of Delhi tried to explain the "Splitting of the Moon" in more rational terms he could not help singing of this very miracle in glowing Arabic verse.[39] The speaking gazelle and the sighing palm trunk equally belong to the repertoire of popular preachers and sophisticated poets all over the Muslim world. Dicta of the Prophet, like: "I was a prophet while Adam was still between water and clay," i.e., uncreated, and even more importantly the *ḥadīth qudsī laulāka,* "If you had not been I would not have created the spheres," were alluded to in thousands of pious songs.

Between 900 and 1200 one witnesses a certain dearth of outstanding religious poetry in the Arabic world although important theological works were composed, as *Ash-shifā fī taᶜrīf ḥuqūq al-Muṣṭafā* by Qadi ᶜIyād of Ceuta, which assumed almost the character of a sacred book, charged with protective power.[40] But then a peculiar, and quite fanciful genre of literature developed around Muhammad's birth. Celebrations of his *maulid,* birthday, on 12 Rabi^c al-awwal, the third lunar month, are mentioned first about 1200 and soon spread into the various Islamic lands. Hafiz ibn Dihya,[41] Ibn al-Jauzi,[42] and Ibn Kathir[43] were among the first authors in the thirteenth and fourteenth centuries to devote books or treatises in prose to the Prophet's birth, and poetry soon followed.[44] In Morocco the Merinid ruler Abu Ya^cqub Yusuf introduced *maulid* celebrations in 1291, while the Mamluks in Egypt celebrated the Prophet's birthday with great splendor during the fourteenth and fifteenth centuries.[45] Lane's description of a *maulid* in Cairo in 1834 captures some of the festive atmosphere.[46] In Turkey, such celebrations must have been known in the early fourteenth century, for Yunus Emre sings:

> Those who recite *mevlûd* shall come.[47]

The first great popular poem in connection with this feast was composed in Turkey by Süleyman Chelebi, who died in Bursa in 1422. His poem, written in plain Turkish in the same simple meter as Rumi's *Mathnawī,* is still sung on the Prophet's birthday, but also at the anniversary of a bereavement or in fulfillment of a vow.[48] The night of the Prophet's birth became in the opinion of some people as important as, if not more important than, the *lailat al-qadr,* the night during which the Koran was revealed for the first time and which is "better than a thousand years" (Sura 97).[49] And like the *lailat al-qadr* in which the pious may be blessed with the vision of divine light, the night of Muhammad's birth also was luminous: for his father had been seen with a white light shining from his forehead before Muhammad was begotten, and this light—later interpreted as the creative, pre-eternal light—was carried in Amina's womb until it illuminated the world to the palaces of Bostra in Syria.[50] It was "like television, for it brought nearby and showed clearly cities far far away," as a Swahili preacher explained this miracle in 1963.[51] A white swan came to touch Amina's back (when this line is recited in the Turkish *mevlûd* all those present gently touch their neighbor's back), and ᶜAsiya (Pharaoh's believing wife), Mary, and a houri appeared to act as midwives. The Prophet was born purified and circumcised and was wrapped in white wool and green silk, and everything created began to greet him with the great *Merhaba* (Welcome):

> Welcome, O high prince, we greet you!
> Welcome, O mine of wisdom, we greet you!
> Welcome, O secret of the Book, we greet you!
> Welcome, O medicine for pain, we greet you!
> Welcome, O sunlight and moonlight of God!
> Welcome, O you who is not separated from God!
> Welcome, O nightingale of the garden of Beauty!
> Welcome, O friend of the Lord of Power!
> Welcome, O refuge of your nation!
> Welcome, O helper of the poor and destitute!
> Welcome, O eternal soul, we greet you!
> Welcome, O cupbearer of the lovers, we greet you!
> Welcome, O darling of the Beloved!
> Welcome, O much beloved of the Lord!
> Welcome, O Mercy for the Worlds!
> Welcome, O intercessor for the sinner!
> Only for you Time and Space were created . . . [etc.]

Thus all nature hailed the man who was destined to lead his followers to salvation and to intercede for them. The genre of *maulidiyyat* soon became popular in the Western Islamic world,[52] and celebrations of a *maulid* usually take place in a festive atmosphere for, as a Swahili poet says:

From the moment you set out toward the *maulid*
You have gone out to experience the raptures of Paradise.[53]

One lights candles, puts on good clothes; sometimes incense is burned and from the Maghreb to Turkey and East Africa it is customary to distribute sweets.[54] As Süleyman Chelebi's *mevlûd,* though often imitated, is still popular in Turkey, thus *maulid* are recited in Swahili (usually from the Arabic, mainly poetical versions of Barzanji's prose *maulid*).[55] In Egypt, the *maulid* of the Shadhili Sufi al-Munawi is particularly well loved, and is often played on records.[56] In other countries, different Arabic texts are recited, thus in Nigeria an acrostic *qaṣīda* of 28 × 10 × 5 = 1400 lines by one al-Fayyazi.[57] In Indo-Pakistan *maulid* literature proper is rather recent, for the 12 Rabiᶜ al-awwal was formerly mainly remembered as the day of Muhammad's death. Major *maulid* in the Subcontinent were generally composed in Persian; the genre was introduced into Bengali not long ago, although epics concerning the Prophet's life were written in Bengali as early as the Middle Ages. In Panjabi and Sindhi, the miracles of the Prophet's birth are told in balladesk or lyrical forms.[58]

But whatever the language and the poetical form may be, the recitation of a *maulid* is regarded as a highly meritorious act, and "when a person recites it there will be peace and blessing for a whole year, disasters and thieves will not come near, and you will not see the burning of his house."[59] This remark in a Swahili *maulid* could apply to *maulid* recitations all over the Islamic world, although some modernists have attacked the custom of reciting this kind of poetry because it is "filled with nonsensical tales and wrong things," as the Minister of Cultural Affairs in Egypt wrote angrily in 1934. It was no less than the noted scholar and critic Taha Husain who refuted these notions and defended the emotional importance of *maulid.*[60] Lately however *maulid* celebrations everywhere are put in the service of reformist movements and serve to remind the Muslims not so much of the traditional miracles but of the wonderful, heroic and nation-building acts of their beloved Prophet. Likewise in early times allusions to the local Arabic environment and typically Arabic traditions, as they are found in the oldest part of the *sīra,* were left out in order to give the *maulid* literature a more universal appeal.[61] Some *maulid* contain the genealogy of the Prophet, for the nobility of his descent is important; this feature is also found in the Sufi tradition where the *silsila* of the Pir is led back to Muhammad and from him to Adam.

It is not astonishing that poetry about the birth of the Prophet is so rich and colorful, for it is common to surround the birth of the founder of a religion with garlands of wonderful events. The motif of light is central in them because often the birth of a saviour (*Heilsbringer*) and his epiphany fall together.[62] Parallels to Muhammad's miraculous birth are found not only in the story of Bethlehem and the almost numberless poems on Nativity[63] but also in the wonderful birth of the Buddha as told in the *Lalita Viṣtara,* or that of Zoroaster, whose light illuminated the village from his mother's womb three days prior to his birth; the fanciful stories of Krishna's birth belong to the same literary category.

Besides the *maulid,* which remained a popular genre to our day, another event in the Prophet's life became a center of meditation for Muslim poets in the Middle Ages. That was his ascension to heaven, his *mi*ᶜ*rāj.* This kind of poetry must have been well known in the medieval mediterranean world and may account even for some ideas in Dante's *Divine Comedy,* as Enrico Cerulli has shown with great insight.[64] The *mi*ᶜ*rājiyya* seem to have reached their finest development in the Persian and Persianate tradition: classical Persian poets usually began their epics with a laud of God, which was followed by a praise of the Prophet, to which was often added a description of his heavenly journey. The story of the *mi^crāj,* developed out of the short remark at the beginning of Sura 17 and later often combined with the first half of Sura 53, offered the poets a wonderful opportunity to depict the Prophet in all his glory, flying through the heavens on his mount Buraq with a female head and a peacock tail.[65] Their descriptions inspired marvelous miniatures by the artists of Iran and Central Asia, who depicted in gold and radiant colors the Prophet's ascension between arrays of fanciful clouds, with delightful angels serving him. Sometimes, however, they showed infernal torments as mentioned in the Bengali *Mi^crājnāma* of Sayyid Sultan in the sixteenth century. Pictures of Buraq are found today on trucks and tank waggons in Pakistan, and the popular tradition tells the miracle of the ascension in similar "folkish" images:

> God sent out Gabriel:
> "My Muhammad shall come!" He said.
> "Take Buraq, draw it before him,
> My Muhammad shall mount!" He said.
>
> "He shall go to the city of Medina,
> In front of him angels shall fly,
> The door of Paradise shall open,
> My Muhammad shall enter," He said.
>
> "My Muhammad shall come, shall come,
> He shall see and look at My Throne;
> He shall pluck the roses of Paradise,
> My Muhammad shall smell them," He said. . . .[66]

Nowhere else does Islamic religious poetry come so close to myth as in these poems. It seems typical that the great masters of Persian mystical poetry, such as ^cAttar, do not dwell in their *mi^crājiyya* upon the central point of the early tradition, namely the reduction of fifty daily prayers to five, but rather upon the fact that Muhammad entered the Divine Presence alone, while Gabriel had to remain outside, "like a nightingale separated from his rose."[67] "If I would go one step further my wings would get burnt," the archangel is reported to have said.[68] That is why he becomes, for later Sufi poets like Rumi, the symbol of Intellect which must stop at the threshold of Love.[69]

Muhammad's unique position could be emphasized in the *miʿrāj* poems even more than in other forms, and an Indian poet of the early sixteenth century, Jamali Kanboh, has summed up the mystery of Muhammad's presence before God in his oft-quoted line:

> Moses went out of his mind by a single revelation of the Attributes—
> You see the essence of the Essence, and still smile.[70]

Muhammad's superiority over Moses, who swooned at the revelation on Mt. Sinai, was a topic often elaborated not only by the mystics but also by the theologians; it served them to prove that it was not intoxication and annihilation, *fanā'*, as experienced by Moses, that was the highest stage man could reach in the Divine Presence, but rather the "prophetic sobriety."[71]

It was said that Muhammad's bed was still warm when he returned, and the water in the pitcher which had tumbled over at his departure had not yet leaked out completely. That made poets and mystics understand the secret of the *nunc aeternum,* the eternal Now in God: did not the Prophet say in connection with the *miʿrāj:* "I have a time with God where even Gabriel has no access?"[72] This was understood to point to his participation in the Divine Life, where serial time no longer exists. Thus he prefigured the ideal of the mystic who hoped to perform such an ascension at least in the spirit, while the Prophet had performed it in the body.[73] The Indian tale of the seeker, who, submerged in the river, lived through a whole life in a few moments, was sometimes applied to explain the Prophet's experience.

In the Arabic world, new genres of religious poetry developed in the thirteenth century.[74] Poets began to describe the Prophet's qualities, his customs, or historical facts in the hope of gaining his help and protection. At the same time, Ibn ᶜArabi put forth his ideas of Muhammad as the *insān-i kāmil,* the Perfect Man, the point of convergence between the created world and God, the place of manifestation of the pleroma of the Divine Names, and his ideas were to permeate mystical poetry not only in the Arabic but likewise, and perhaps even more, in the Persianate world.

The poem that gained greatest fame in the thirteenth century was Busiri's long encomium, called *al-Burda,* because the ailing poet composed it in honor of Muhammad and was miraculously cured by a dream in which the Prophet put his cloak, *burda,* over his shoulders as he had done during his lifetime with Kaᶜb ibn Zuhair.[75] Busiri was a disciple of the Shadhili master Abu'l-ᶜAbbas al-Mursi, and author of both lighter poems and beautiful eulogies on the Prophet. Of these, his very poetical *Hamziyya* deserves special mention. He begins his *Burda,* officially called *Al-kawākib ad-durriyya fi madḥ khair al-bariyya,* "Luminous stars in the praise of the best of mankind," in the traditional classical style with the expression of longing for the faraway friend and a description of his own miserable state, and then (verse 34) turns to the Prophet who alone can save this frail, wretched human being. He is described in some 180 verses—verses that use the whole store of traditions, from the spider which covered him and Abu Bakr in the cave on the way to Medina to the prostration of the trees before him. The *Burda* thus constitutes a veritable compendium of medieval prophetology. For this reason it soon became the favorite poem of Muslims everywhere and could serve to elate their spirits even though they might not understand its high-flown Arabic rhetoric. At times it reaches great poetical beauty, as in the oft-imitated verse 56 which describes Muhammad:

> *ka'z-zahri fī ṭarafin wa'l-badri fī sharafin*
> *wa'l-baḥri fī karamin wa'd-dahri fī himami*
> Like a flower in tenderness, and like the full moon in glory,
> And like the ocean in generosity, and like Time in grand intentions.

Busiri rightly places Muhammad above the other prophets,

> For he is a sun of virtue and they are his stars
> Which show their lights to the people in the darkness.

And he asks for the vision of the venerated Prophet:

> O that he might grant me the grace to see his face—
> For everyone who sees him, his needs disappear.

The *Burda* soon assumed a mystical power of its own; many of its verses were believed to cure certain ailments or to protect from plague or poverty, and were therefore used in amulets or written on walls. Some reciters would repeat after each of its lines a blessing over the Prophet.[76] Understandably, the poem was soon translated into almost every Islamic language: there exist several Persian versions, among them a very fine one by ᶜAbdur Rahman Jami. The poem is available in Turkish, Urdu, Pashto, and Panjabi.[77] In the sixteenth century a Malay translation was produced, while several Swahili recensions of more recent date are in use in East Africa. The *Burda* has often been printed, and fine illuminated manuscripts exist in Cairo and elsewhere. As in the case of other "powerful" Arabic poems, later authors split its verses and filled them with their own productions (*tashṭīr*), and in Egypt alone not less than eighty quintuplet versions (*takhmīs*) were made out of it, not to mention the variations in the non-Arabic countries like India.[78] Besides, numerous imitations were written, and commentaries with high-sounding names were composed, among which that of the Egyptian theologian al-Bajuri is generally used by the students in al-Azhar. Recitations of the *Burda* in a festive setting are still practised in the Deccan.[79]

Busiri was by no means the only poet to praise the Prophet in sonorous Arabic hymns. His contemporary in Egypt, Ibn Daqiq al-ᶜId (d. 1302) is likewise known for his *naᶜt* poetry. In it he, like many other poets after him, liked to sing of the holy places in the Hijaz and of his longing for Mecca and Medina.[80] This aspect of *naᶜtiyya* poetry is worthy of mention since this "holy geography," which centers around Mecca and Medina, is also found in poetry composed in honor of the Prophet in Indo-Pakistan, in *sīḥarfīs* and *bārahmāsa.*[81] *Naᶜtiyya* poetry continued, and even increased, in the centuries after Busiri; in fact, already ath-Thaᶜlabi had discussed the expressions which were used, and soon became commonplace, in encomia for the Prophet.[82] The poets, particularly in Andalusia and North Africa, addressed the beloved Messenger in long anaphors or implored his mercy. Others, headed by Ibn Nubata (d. 1368), are noted for daring puns and poetical inventions.[83]

They indulged in complicated rhetorical play. For instance, each line of a poem might begin with the rhyming letter, or contain all the letters of the alphabet, or dazzle the reader with ever changing figures of speech.[84] Classical *qaṣīdas,* such as Imru'l-Qais' *Qifā nabki,* were filled with new verses to transform them into a *naᶜt,*[85] or popular forms like *muwashshaḥ* were used to eulogize Muhammad. The ever-growing interest in the technical aspects of *na*ᶜ*t* poetry culminates, I think, in Yusuf an-Nabhani's attempt to write sixteen praise poems on Muhammad in the sixteen classical Arabic meters, each of them containing also the name of the meter.[86] The poets—not only in the Maghreb and Egypt and Syria but also in India[87]—sometimes specialized in praising certain items connected with the Prophet, such as his sandal or his footprint.[88]

A look at the four volumes of Nabhani's *Al-majmū*ᶜ*a an-nabhāniyya fi'l-madā'iḥ an-nabawiyya,* an anthology that contains the various kinds of praise poems for the Prophet, including the author's numerous own verses, suffices to prove the enormous fertility of Arabic-writing poets when it came to singing of their beloved Prophet. But typically, the pious collector begins his anthology with a chapter which states that "the poets are incapable of praising Muhammad as it behooves and as it is necessary" because it is impossible to attain to the greatness of his rank by panegyrics. "Muhammad is beyond all description," says Busiri,[89] for God Himself has praised him in the Koran.

> The verses of the Holy Book have praised you, and how
> Could the poem of my eulogy possibly praise your greatness?

So asks the Spanish poet Lisanuddin ibn al-Khatib,[90] while Nabhani himself, who wrote a whole poetical biography of the Prophet in his long *Hamziyya,* sums up the problem in his verse:

> They say to me: "Did you not praise Muhammad,
> The Prophet of the God of everything created, the most well-shaped among them?"
> I said to them: "What shall I say in his praise
> Since his creator has praised him and has not left anything?"[91]

And yet, "the hearts long to mention his noble name and his qualities" and thus to establish a spiritual relation with him.

Therefore the poets turn again to him to express their trust in him and love for him, although this love never enters the realm of ᶜ*ishq,* erotic love, but remains in the sphere of respect. It resembles the loving veneration one feels toward a senior member of the family (Max Horten speaks of the mystical Muhammad as "the father of his community")[92] who sets the model for all those who come to know him. He is the ideal of ethical perfection which all human striving hopes to reach; and he is the loving and kind physician who can cure the ailments of body and soul.

There are an even greater number of *na*ᶜ*tiyya* poems in the Persian than in the Arabic tradition. The descriptions are certainly more colorful, culminating in glowing hyperbolas, because "to exaggerate the good qualities of the beloved is the favorite occupation of the lovers."[93] An eighteenth-century Persian poet of Sind, Mir ᶜAli Shir Qaniᶜ, expresses the importance of a proper *na*ᶜ*t* in exotic images in the beginning of his *Dīwān:*

> From the *bismillāh* ["In the name of God"], I put a comb in the curls of the *Dīwān;*
> With the scent of praise [*ḥamd,* i.e., praise of God] I made the hair of the *Dīwān* musk-exuding.
> In order to purify the confused thought of people in these days,
> Water from the fountain of *na*ᶜ*t* [eulogies for the Prophet] flows in the canal of the *Dīwān.*[94]

A modern Indian scholar claims that *na*ᶜ*tiyya* poetry "stimulates longing for the Perfect Man" and is therefore a character-building force.[95] Whether one agrees with him or not, one has to recognize that poetry in honor of the Prophet belongs to the most fascinating genres of Persian literature, and largely influenced the Ottoman Turkish and the Urdu tradition. Its founder proper seems to be Sana'i, the former court poet and, later, mystical teacher of Ghazna (d.c. 1131). He himself speaks of being a Hassani, i.e., following Hassan ibn Thabit's example. As he formerly extolled worldly rulers he then applied his whole elaborate vocabulary and immense rhetorical skill to the praise of the ruler of the Muslim community, the Prophet. Perhaps his most famous, and certainly his finest, *na*ᶜ*t* is his interpretation of Sura 93, *Wa' -ḍuḥā,* "By the Morning-light," which he improvised in a religious meeting. He begins with a verse in the rhetorical form of *laff ū nashr:*

> Infidelity and faith in darkness and purity respectively
> Have no other kingdom but Mustafa's cheek and tresses.
> If his hair and his face would not bring into the desert Divine
>   Wrath [*qahr*] and Divine Kindness [*luṭf*],
> Infidelity would remain without provision, and faith helpless.[96]

With these verses he set the stage for hundreds of similar poems in which the Prophet's radiant face is compared to the morning light, but equally to the light of faith, while his dark hair symbolizes the night as well as the darkness of infidelity.

> The radiance of your face is what one calls Morning,
> The shade of your two tresses is where you say Evening.

And commenting on the Koranic verse "And as for the favor of thy Lord, tell it," the Persian poet continues:

> Praise with your own tongue for us in Arabic
> So that our tongue may tell your praise in Persian.

For:

> As long as the breeze of your name does not rise over the garden of religion,
> The branch of religion does not grow, and the root of the *sunna* does not sprout.

In another *na*ᶜ*t* filled with Koranic names and mythical and historical figures, Sana'i sees the Prophet surrounded by his heavenly friends, the angels Michael and Gabriel, and by his servants on earth, the caliphs Abu Bakr and ᶜUmar.[97] He even introduces a conversation with the first four caliphs into one of his encomia,[98] and claims with a skillfull *tajnīs-i khaṭṭī* that the dust of Abu Dharr's foot is better than the whole glorious empire of the Persian king Nodhar,[99] and that the sandals of Bilal, Muhammad's Abyssinian muezzin, are superior to a hundred Rustams (Rustam being the unsurpassable hero of ancient Iranian history). Sana'i knows that outwardly Ahmad (that is, Muhammad) came from Adam, but in the world of the attributes:

> Adam became visible from Ahmad.[100]

That is why everything is obedient to the Prophet:

> I asked the wind: "Why do you serve Solomon?"
> It said: "Because Ahmad's name is engraved on his seal."[101]

That means his name is superior to that of all other prophets, and is the real cause for djinns and fairies, beasts and birds being obedient to Solomon.

> Those who say *lā,* No, to him, become turned over like the [crooked letter] *lā,*
> But blessed by bounty [*niᶜam*] becomes he who has said yes [*naᶜam*].[102]

Of course, Sana'i often speaks of Muhammad's quality as *raḥmatan lil-ᶜālamin,* "mercy for the worlds" (Sura 21/107), for:

> If God had not called you Mercy for the Worlds,
> Who in the whole world would see the difference between the Eternal [*ṣamad*] and an idol [*ṣanam*]?[103]

For only Muhammad defines the borderline between faith and infidelity, between the adoration of the eternal Lord and the veneration of transient, false deities. Sana'i goes on to state, in another poem, that Muhammad as "mercy for the worlds" contains help, *najāt,* and healing, *shifā',* for those who follow his *sunna,* while the noted philosopher-physician Avicenna does not possess these qualities in his learned works titled *an-Najāt* and *ash-Shifā.*[104]

An even stronger aversion to the philosophers is echoed in ᶜAttar's *naᶜt* in the beginning of the *Muṣībatnāma:*

> Indeed, two hundred worlds of the First Intellect [*ᶜaql-i kull*].
> Disappear before the majesty of one order: "Say!" [*qul*],[105]

that is, the Divine address to the Prophet as repeated often in the Koran. And he continues:

> Not a single person is farther away from the Hashimite *sharīᶜa* than a philosopher.
> *Sharᶜ* [Divine law] is to follow the order of the Prophet,
> To throw dust on the head of philosophy.

And Maulana Rumi continued in this antiphilosophical style, which is very typical for poets and mystics in the Eastern Islamic world.

Sana'i sees the whole world in the Prophet's service: the skies are kneeling down before him; the hall of Khusrau (*kisrā*) breaks (*kisr*) before him.[106] And in the chapter of his *Ḥadīqa* which he devotes to the fact "that he was preferred over the other prophets" he claims that:

> From the realm of time came to eulogize you
> Friday, the White Nights, the Night of Might, the Feast of Fast-breaking, and the *shab-i barāt,*
> And from the realm of space came, with bent statures,
> Mecca, Yathrib [Medina], [the cave of] Hira, and the *ḥarām* [around the Kaᶜba].[107]

Sana'i's glowing and inventional *naᶜtiyya* poetry has all the ingredients that were to grow in later Persian poetry. Fariduddin ᶜAttar followed his line but added some important new aspects. He too was sure that:

> His miracles cannot be described,
> The description of his essence cannot be explained.[108]

For:

> Whatever is the radiance of both worlds
> Is the reflection of his heart.[109]

The mysticism of light becomes even more dominant in ᶜAttar's poetry when he, in the introduction of the *Manṭiq ut-ṭair,*[110] describes how Muhammad's light prostrated itself before the Creator and performed in endless periods a full cycle of ritual prayer before the whole cosmos was created out of it:

> From his light are Throne and Footstool,
> Cherubim as well as spiritual powers, and the holy ones.
> This world and the next are dependent upon him,
> And the world is cheerful through the light of his essence.[111]

ᶜAttar sees the Prophet at the end of the long chains of previous prophets[112] and sees that the Prophet, who cannot read the ABCs, is yet reading from the Tablet of the Lord. For as *ummī,* illiterate, he is "silent in himself but speaking through the Lord."[113] Even the First Intellect is only part of the reflection of his soul, and:

> Paradise is one sip from his glass;
> Both worlds are from the two *m*'s of his name.
> The world, *ᶜālam,* has only one *m* as provision,
> But Muhammad has got two *m*'s in his name.
> Definitely one world is from one of his *m*'s
> And the other world from the other half.[114]

ᶜAttar begins here with speculations that became more common in the following centuries, leading up to Ahmad Sir-hindi's mystical theories about the two *m*'s of Muhammad's name. These theories form the basis of his revivalist theology.[115] It seems that also the combination of *Aḥmad* and *Aḥad* goes back to ᶜAttar: "Ahmad was the envoy of *Aḥad,* i.e., the One, God."[116] And the famous *ḥadīth qudsī* in which God attests *anā Aḥmad bilā mīm,* "I am Ahmad without the *m,* i.e., *aḥad,* One" may have its origin in ᶜAttar's mystical visions.[117] It was to become one of the favorite puns in later mystical poetry in the Persianate tradition, and Maulana Rumi alludes to it more than once, as he says in *Fīhi mā fīhi:*

> Any addition to perfection is a diminution. . . . *Aḥad* is perfect, and *Aḥmad* is not yet in the state of perfection; when the *m* is removed it becomes complete perfection.[118]

Otherwise, Maulana's prophetology is unique. As he did not open his *Mathnawī* with the traditional praise of God and the Prophet, complete *naᶜt* poems are rare in his *Dīwān,* and there is not a single *qaṣīda* among them. Many of his verses which sound like *naᶜt* or mention the Prophet in a prominent place turn then to his mystical beloved Shams, who appears as almost identical with the luminous Prophet[119] (see chapter 3). His most famous *naᶜt* is the one that is sung in ᶜItri's beautiful tune, at the beginning of the ritual dance of the Mevlevis.[120] Single verses inserted in *ghazals* contain highly poetical descriptions[121] of some of the Prophet's wonderful qualities:

> The light of Muhammad has become a thousand, yea, a thousand branches,
> And has embraced both worlds from one end to the other.
> If Muhammad tears the veil from only one branch,
> A thousand monks and priests will tear apart their infidels' girdle![122]

Or, even more poetical:

> The dervishes find their happiness from Mercy for the worlds:
> Their frocks are radiant like the moon, their shawls fragrant like roses.[123]

Muhammad's hegira from Mecca to Medina becomes for Rumi the model of the mystic's journey, for it is by leaving one's home and constant traveling that one's soul becomes purified. In a *khamriyya* dealing with the wine of mystical love, Rumi claims that everyone was intoxicated by Muhammad, but:

> Mistake; Muhammad was not the cupbearer, he was a goblet,
> Full of wine, and God was the cupbearer of the pious.[124]

This is a beautiful interpretation of the fact that Muhammad as *ummī,* illiterate, was an immaculate vessel for the Divine grace which he distributed to his followers. His name, Aḥmad, contains the names of all prophets, as Maulana says in the *Mathnawī.* One should also not overlook the fact that Rumi likes to quote Prophetic traditions both in his lyrics and in the *Mathnawī.* This shows his close connection with the Prophet, whose first and foremost interpreter was for him Shams-i Tabriz.[125]

In the purely mystical tradition Jami's *naᶜtiyya* poetry would deserve a special discussion. The poet, who could sing in very simple words:

> Lift your head from the yemenite *burda,*
> For your face is the morning of life![126]

was particularly interested in poetical elaborations of the secrets of the *ḥaqīqa muḥammadiyya,* the archetypal Muhammad, with whom the mystics hoped to reach union in their highest experience.

A special place in the development of *naᶜtiyya* belongs to Saᶜdi, whose few eulogies on the Prophet have inspired many readers.[127] In the long enumeration of the Prophet's qualities in the exordium of the *Būstān—shafīᶜun* (intercessor), *rasūlun karīm* (noble Prophet), *qasīmun jasīmun nasīmun wasīm* ("handsome, great in dignity, gentle, and elegant")—one finds the epithet *muṭāᶜ*, "who is obeyed," a word used in Ghazzali's speculations in his *Mishkāt al-anwār*. Thanks to Saᶜdi's use the *muṭāᶜ*, whose identity had caused some embarrassment to scholars, is indeed identified as the Prophet Muhammad.[128] Saᶜdi's *naᶜt* has also contributed to Islamic nomenclature, particularly in India, for all four qualities—*qasīm, jasīm, nasīm* and *wasīm*—are found as proper names, sometimes in compounds, such as Jasimuddin.

The epics of every major poet in Persian, Turkish, and Urdu contain hymns in honor of the Prophet, and sometimes four or five *naᶜts* with ever new images and metaphors follow each other.[129] Nizami's *naᶜts* in his oft-imitated epics have become models for later poets, and his descriptions of Muhammad, the ideal servant of God, show all the poetical elegance in which his epical poetry in general excels. His Indian imitator, the prolific Amir Khusrau (d. 1325), followed his example but, initiated into the Chishtiyya by his friend Nizamuddin Auliya,[130] adds more of the inherited mystical implements to his poems. Like Sana'i he too plays with the mysterious letters at the beginning of certain Koranic *sūras*, such as *yāsīn* (Sura 36) or *ṭāhā* (Sura 20), both of which were considered synonyms of Muhammad and therefore became proper names in the Muslim world.[131] The moon in the sky appears to Amir Khusrau shaped like the semicircular *n* (when the moon is a crescent) and then becomes a (circular) *m*, which shows that it is not more than a drop of dew, *nam*, from the ocean of Muhammad's beauty; and the angels' wings are used to sweep the way to his dwelling place.[132] Allusions to the *m* of Ahmad occur rather often in Amir Khusrau's poetry: the *m* is, as its shape reveals, the true seal of prophethood,[133] and everyone who has received a collar from this *m* will walk around like a ringdove in the profession of faith without ever leaving it.[134]

These last allusions came from *na*ᶜ*t qaṣīdas;* in the twelfth century this form became a favorite genre in nonmystical poetry as well. Every aspect of nature could serve the poets to praise the Prophet: spring poems in which all flowers are united in praise[135] for him are as typical as *qaṣīdas* with a highflown philosophical vocabulary.

The *na*ᶜ*tiyya* poetry of Khaqani (d. 1199),[136] who seems to be the first major panegyrist of the Prophet among the nonmystics and is therefore called *Ḥassān-i* ᶜ*ajam,* deserves a special, extensive study. In extremely artistic and powerful verse he too makes all nature serve the Prophet. The planets receive him, and his dwelling places inspired the poet to ever grander statements in which every possible rhetorical technique is displayed with breathtaking skill. The praise of the *ḥaramain,* the sacred cities of Mecca and Medina, is a specialty of Khaqani. The Kaᶜba can be compared to Muhammad Mustafa, its black stone to the Seal of prophetship, and the prophet himself becomes *dīn mushakhkhaṣ,* religion personified (as in the great poem *Tuḥfat al-ḥaramain*). Comparisons between the Kaᶜba and Muhammad, or the black stone and his mole later became commonplace in Persian poetry.[137] Like Khaqani, Fakhruddin ᶜIraqi was inspired by his stay in Medina to sing of the greatness of "the lord of al-Baṭḥā," inserting numerous Koranic statements into his encomium.[138]

Khaqani's *na*ᶜ*ts* are matched, and perhaps surpassed in difficulty, by the *qaṣīdas* which ᶜUrfi, the Shirazi artist at Akbar's court, composed and which are masterpieces of the early "Indian style." He uses simple words to tell the Prophet that he washes the book of his sins with the water of his kindness,[139] and he follows the tradition by declaring that he is not worthy to mention the Prophet's sacred name:

A thousand times do I wash my mouth with musk and rose-
 water,
And still, to speak your name is absolute impudence.[140]

But usually he describes Muhammad, the Perfect Man, in expressions that are barely translatable because he indulges in the technical vocabulary developed by the writers of the Ibn ᶜArabi school:

Until they wrote your existence to be the confluence of contin-
 gency and necessity,
The object for a common epithet could not be determined.
Destiny placed two litters on one camel:
One for the Salma of your being created in time, the other one
 for the Laila of your pre-existence. . . .

After reading some 48 of these highly sophisticated and grammatically involved verses one marvels at the poet's final statement:

I praise you through sincerity, not with the help of learning:
How could I bring forth the gazelle of the Kaᶜba from an idol-
 temple?[141]

ᶜUrfi's hyperboles are more farfetched than those of earlier writers. It was a favorite topic of *naᶜt* poets to show that Muhammad excelled over all other prophets, and in particular over the founders of Judaism and Christianity. Therefore ᶜUrfi addresses him:

Jesus is a fly and your speech
Is the sweetmeat of the shop of creation,[142]

while Khaqani had sung, somewhat more modestly:

Jesus comes down from the sky and Idris from Paradise,
For these two see victuals to be carried home from the table of
 Ṭāhā [i.e., Muhammad].[143]

The combination of Jesus and the table is of course an inversion of Jesus' heavenly table mentioned in Sura 5. The model of this kind of verse may be Sana'i's *qaṣīda,* which has a much more positive and generous ring to it:

> When you, like Moses, come onto the pulpit,
> Jesus from the fourth heaven addresses you: "Welcome, Muhammad!"[144]

It is somewhat surprising to see that ᶜUrfi's antagonist, Akbar's favorite court poet Faizi, who is usually credited with some heretic tendencies and whose verse is on the whole much more cerebral than ᶜUrfi's powerful and often tragic *qaṣīdas,* has written a rather simple *naᶜt* in which the Prophet—center of the seven spheres, who sits in the whirlpool of the first wave and is the pearl of the ocean *Laulāka,* "If you had not been . . ."—is described as coming:

> With *sharīᶜa* and Divine book: a splendid light,
> With sword and tongue: a cutting proof;
> An earthly being and yet descending on the apex of the Divine Throne,
> Illiterate [*ummī*], and a library in his heart,

and although a thousand years have passed, the palmtree of his service is still fresh and green.[145]

Among the numerous Persian *naᶜts* written in Moghul India the short poem by Qudsi Mashhadi—apparently modeled upon a bilingual *naᶜt* by Jami[146]—must be mentioned because it is still often sung in *qawwālī* sessions:

> Welcome, O Meccan, Medinan, Arabian Lord!
> Heart and soul be sacrificed for you—what wonderful surnames you have!
> Open the eye of mercy, cast a glance at me,
> O you with the surnames Quraishi, Hashimi, and Muttalibi. . . .

This is a typical expression not only of the veneration of sacred names but also of the Indian tendency to stress the Arabic aspect of Muhammad's biography. Qudsi continues with one of the exaggerations so common in poetry after Jami, who spoke time and again of the "dog of the beloved":

> I related myself to the dog, but am very distressed,
> Because to relate oneself to the dog of your street is unmannerly.[147]

And he closes his singable poem with alternating Arabic-Persian lines:

> My Lord, you are my friend and the physician of my heart—
> Qudsi has come to you in order to ask for a remedy.

This verse harks back to the traditional topos of the beloved as the true physician, which is often applied to the Prophet.

*Na*ᶜ*tiyya* poetry continued to be written everywhere,[148] and when an eighteenth-century poet in Sind wrote a *tarjī*ᶜ*band* with the refrain:

> Here is my hand, and the pure skirt of Muhammad;
> Here is my eye, and the collyrium of the dust of Muhammad,

this expression of his grasping the Prophet's hem for help and brightening his eyes with the dust of his feet "was immensely well received by the tongues of old and young, and was a means of help for those who wished to obtain their wants."[149]

This firm belief in the *baraka,* the spiritual power of a poem praising the Prophet, was widely spread. In fact the author of a Sindhi *mu*ᶜ*jizō* about Muhammad's miracles promised innumerable future rewards to those who read or recited it on a Thursday night.[150] A similar promise is connected with *na*ᶜ*tiyya* poetry in South India, and probably in other areas as well.[151] A similarly strong belief in the *baraka* of eulogies lead quite a number of poets to express the hope that their *na*ᶜ*t* would intercede, as it were, for them on the Day of Judgment. Muhsin Kakorawi, the famous Urdu poet of the late nineteenth century, closes his poem

> *Simt-i Kāshī sē chalā jānib-i Matthrā bādal*
> From the direction of Benares went a cloud toward Mathura,

with the lines:

> In the rows of resurrection your [the Prophet's] panegyrist will be with you,
> In his hand he has this enthusiastic *ghazal,* this *qaṣīda,*
> And Gabriel will say with a hint: "Now, In the name of God [recite!:]
> From the direction of Benares went a cloud toward Mathura."

The reader will certainly sympathize with him, for his poem is a very charming combination. The first part is a *tashbīb,* an erotic introduction, in the style of Indian love songs pertaining to the rainy season, in which Kakorawi uses both the imagery and vocabulary of Hindi songs; while the second part, the actual praise of the Prophet, follows the classical models and is written in highflown Urdu.

*Na*ᶜ*t*s were written even by poets who were rather worldly, and a glance at a collection of Urdu *na*ᶜ*t*s shows that almost every writer in this language has produced one or several hymns in praise of the Prophet. The greatest ruler of Golconda, Muhammad-Quli Qutbshah, composed verse in honor of Muhammad as did the last Nizam of Hyderabad and the last Moghul emperor of Delhi, Bahadur Shah Zafar.[152] Typical of *na*ᶜ*tiyya* poems by a poet who generally is regarded as anything but a paragon of piety, are the Persian encomia by Mirza Asadullah Ghalib in Delhi (d. 1869). His *na*ᶜ*t*s at times surpass even ᶜUrfi's poems in difficulty. In his most famous eulogy, which comprises 101 verses and is a masterpiece of elegant form and technical perfection,[153] he dwells once more on the old pun of *Aḥmad-Aḥad.* But he continues by stating that when the *m* is taken from *Aḥmad,* and the *alif* (the letter of Divine Unity) from the remaining *Aḥad,* the two last letters have the numerical value of *ḥ* = 8 and *d* = 4, which makes 12. Hence the very name of *Aḥmad* points at once to God's unity and unicity (*alif*); to Muhammad's stage as messenger in the temporal world, which is connected with the letter *m* with its numerical value 40 (which also implies the forty degrees between man and God); and finally to the twelve imams of the Ithna ᶜAshara Shia. Other poets had found in the chronogram of Muhammad's death, *hū* = 11 (11h/632 A.D.), the word *Hū,* "He," i.e., the Divine Ipseity into which the small "he" of the Prophet returned.[154]

As for Ghalib, he has also composed a longish but unfinished *mathnawī* about the Prophet, called *Abr-i gauharbār,* "The Jewel-Carrying Cloud," for the Prophet was often compared to the rain cloud which brings blessings all over the world.[155] One may think here of the comparison of the Buddha with the rain cloud which waters trees and grass alike, as elaborated in the Saddharmapundarika (chapter 5, 1–27), and even of Christian *Rorate* hymns. The comparison of the Prophet with the rain seems to occur more frequently, however, in folk poetry than in high poetry, while his role as *raḥmatan lilᶜālamīn* led some mystics to regard him as the manifestation of the Divine name *ar-Raḥmān,* The Merciful.[156]

Ghalib's last contribution to prophetology is a short *mathnawī* which he wrote in connection with a problem that puzzled the minds of some Indian theologians in the early nineteenth century: could God create another Muhammad or not? While one faction held that this was impossible others thought that it was basically possible but unlikely. Ghalib sided with the latter group and voiced the opinion:

> Wherever a turmoil of the worlds arises,
> There is also a Mercy for the Worlds.

That means, in case God should create other worlds with creatures endowed with intelligence He would certainly not leave them without a messenger to guide them on the right path.[157]

Many of the classical *na*ᶜ*ts*, both in *mathnawī* and *qaṣīda* as well in graceful *ghazals*, are masterpieces of rhetoric; in others the true feeling of the poet is expressed very tenderly, almost like the poet's confiding in a trusted friend. But the Prophet's "mythical" aspects often seem to gain the upper hand, as in lines composed by Nasir Muhammad ᶜAndalib, the founder of the *ṭarīqa muḥammadiyya* in Delhi in the early eighteenth century:

> O you whose light is the *basmala* of the Koran of manifestation—
> Your body is all light, and your cheek the Sura "The Light."
> Here you are the leader of the people, there the intercessor—
> O you locus of manifestation for the names "Guiding" and "Forgiving."[158]

This ᶜAndalib was one of those who had—or claimed to have—reached *fanā' fī'r-rasūl*, annihilation in the Prophet,[159] and such poets may try to voice an experience that is too high for words. Therefore Urdu writers do not in vain distinguish between the traditional *na*ᶜ*t* and a more existential kind of poetry the depth of whose contents can barely be grasped by the uninitiated.

Poetry in honor of the Prophet was not restricted to the urban poets who wrote high-soaring verse in learned languages such as Arabic, Persian, Ottoman Turkish, and Urdu, but was extremely common in the folk tradition as well. It permeates Yunus Emre's and his successors' poetry, and the various Indian languages developed a considerable *naᶜtiyya* literature—even Tamil can boast of some important praise poems in honor of the Prophet.[160] While the urban poets in India expressed their veneration of the Prophet in grandiose hymns to display their erudition, their contemporaries in the plains of Sind and the Punjab wrote tender little poems or instructive Golden Alphabets to instil love for him into the souls of the villagers. Bengali Muslim literature contains early heroic epics telling of Muhammad's journeys and battles (thus the *Rasūl viyāj*) which grew partly under the influence and in imitation of Hindu religious epics. In Bengal, Sayyid Sultan in the sixteenth century went so far as to tell a creation myth in which Brahma, Vishnu, Shiva, and Krishna are presented as prophets, and Muhammad as the fulfillment of this line of God-sent messengers.[161]

Sindhi folk poetry developed the genres of *madāḥ*, *munāqibō*, and *muᶜjizō*, all of which deal with the Prophet, the last one now and then also with saints.[162] The *madāḥ* (from Arabic *madḥ*, praise) is usually recited by professional bards who call themselves *bhān*, a word which they derive with a fanciful etymology from *Bānat Suᶜād*, Kaᶜb ibn Zuhair's famous *qaṣīda*. One of the finest Sindhi *madāḥ* was composed by one of the last members of the Kalhora dynasty, Sarfaraz Khan, who while imprisoned put in simple words his grief and fear before the "good Lord," *bhalā jām*.[163] As for the *maulid* in Sindhi, it deals not only with the Prophet's birth but is a lyrical encomium[164] with a refrain which, in singing, is repeated before every new line. It is used on festive occasions such as the *shab-i barāt* or after the *tarāwīḥ* prayers in Ramadan. The miraculous birth stories are part of the *munāqibā*, which also tell of Muhammad's battles and journeys and like to dwell upon his tender love for his ill-starred grandchildren, Hasan and Husain, "the earrings of the Divine Throne,"[165] who used to climb on his back during prayer and whose sad fate was foretold to him by Gabriel. The traditional miracle stories are elaborated in these poems in great detail so that the Splitting of the Moon or the Speaking Gazelle appear again and again, as does the story of Muhammad's healing a camel which, like his other miracles, found its way into folk tales.

> I am sighing at the Prophet's feet like the camel![166]

Most of these stories are derived from the Sindhi classic *Qūt al-ᶜāshiqīn,* which Makhdum Muhammad Hashim composed in the early eighteenth century, without caring too much whether the *ḥadīth* which he used were well founded or weak. The loving portrayal of the Prophet was more important for him and his followers than historical truth, information about which, in any case, was difficult to obtain from the literature at their disposal. It was thanks to these popularizations that allusions to the Prophet's life and miracles percolated into all levels of society and are found in lullabies and bridal songs, so that love for him is infused into a child's soul and grows as it breathes.[167]

The great mystical poets of Sind have devoted wonderful songs to the Prophet, who appears as the dawn between the night of created human life and the Divine day:

> Wondrous is the Reality of the Friend—
> One cannot call him Lord, nor creature—
> Similar to the dawn, he unites night and day.[168]

The lyrical parts at the end of many chapters in Shah ᶜAbdul Latif's *Risālō* speak of the poet's hope for Muhammad's intercession.[169] The most beautiful example among them is *Sur Sārang,* in which the poet dramatically describes the longing of all creatures for rain—rain brings fertility to the parched soil, milk to the cows, bread to the poor. Out of this description Shah Latif turns to a short, touching song in which the Prophet, once more the cloud of mercy, is praised because he will protect his community at Doomsday. And poets who followed Shah ᶜAbdul Latif's example saw this blissful rain cloud extending not only from Istanbul to Jaisalmer, from Delhi to Omarkot but from Kairouan to Rohri and from England to China.[170]

There is also some highly complicated *naᶜtiyya* poetry in the Sindhi language. The Naqshbandi mystic ᶜAbdur Rahim Girhori, who was killed when destroying a Shiva temple (1778), offers his splendid version of a Divine address to the Prophet in his poetical commentary on *Sūrat al-kauthar.* This *sūra* was, besides *Aḍ-ḍuḥā* and *An-Najm,* always a favorite of those poets who eulogized the Prophet.[171] They might even claim that *kauthar,* imagined as a paradisiacal fountain, was thirsting for the water of life which is hidden in the Prophet's blessed lips.[172]

Girhori's commentary takes up many earlier elements; thus he has God say, among other things:

> So much gift did I not give to anyone but you.
> You are the cup-bearer of the fountain: carry on now its distribution, O brave one!
> The keys of power have I given into your hand, O friend;
> The sciences of heaven and earth are a gift for Ahmad.
> The philosophers' stone have I given you, the elixir of Adam, O friend.
> To Jesus, a certain portion of grace was [given] from this elixir,
> With which the dead were quickened, the deaf became hearing,
> For the blind: seeing eyes; from the lepers fell their leprosy.
> Whatever is in the Torah is like a sip out of that ocean,
> The whole beauty of Joseph: a sign of that gift.

A small quantity only of your love, O Ahmad, has reached Zulaikha.[173]
Paradise is part of that ocean, as though it were ice of the ocean.
Hell is at your door supplicating like a beggar,
Without your permission having no strength to burn the unbelievers.
Paradise is your splendid manifestation, just a look of love.
Your look of wrath, O pure one, is Hellfire.
Heaven, earth, empyrean, God's throne, humans, djinns, and angels
Live, my beloved, always in dependence on you.
Dearest, humanity became worthy due to your light,
Thanks to your reflection, my darling, buds and flowers are blossoming. . . .

In mystical folk poetry all nature participates in the praise of Muhammad. Yunus Emre, the medieval Turkish minstrel, hears the bees humming the *ṣalawāt ᶜalā Muḥammad,*[174] and the author of a nineteenth-century Sindhi poem thinks that honey is sweet because the bees love the Prophet and utter blessings over him.[175] The rose reminds them of the Prophet because it grew from a drop of sweat that fell to earth during his *miᶜrāj:* that is why it is so fragrant.[176] And why should man be less than the weeping palm trunk which sighed when the Prophet no longer put his hand on it during his sermons? The Arab folk poet longs for the Guiding Prophet "for whom the gazelle spoke in the valley,"[177] and the Sindhi yearns for him as did Marui for her friends in her native village. Verses in his honor are found even in popular, certainly not predominantly religious, Egyptian shadow plays.[178]

Frequently Muhammad is depicted as the caravan leader, an image well known to the great mystical thinkers and poets too. We find it in Ibn ᶜArabi's *Tarjumān al-ashwāq*[179] as in Ibn al-Farid's verse,[180] and with Rumi's powerful praise of the *kārwānsālār Muṣṭafā* in one of his most ecstatic poems.[181] In areas with much water, the Prophet becomes the ferryman who brings the traveler safely to the other shore and helps him to avoid the whirlpools and sandbanks on his way to eternity:

> O Mahiya, take us over to the other shore.

This line is from a Panjabi folk song, and Bengali poets see the Prophet as the pilot or captain of the fragile boat of man's existence, as "helmsman to the far shore of truth."[182]

The image of the caravan leader offered itself easily in a culture where the pilgrimage to Mecca on long, dangerous roads was one of the duties of the faithful and where poetry describing the lonely wayfarer's adventures is part of the classical tradition. Therefore the image occurs also with implicit application to the Prophet in the work of a modern Muslim poet who has most eloquently praised Muhammad although he has never written a formal *na*ᶜ*t* in traditional style. That is Muhammad Iqbal (d. 1938).[183] Iqbal, who describes his own role as that of the caravan bell that helps guide the travelers to the central sanctuary in Mecca (as the title of his Urdu *Dīwān, Bāng-i darā,* indicates),[184] was particularly fond of the image of the caravan leader since his poetry highlights the dynamic character of religion and the constant movement of the soul to higher and higher stations. "The Arabian friend," as he calls Muhammad (like many Indian Muslim poets before him), is praised in a poem which Iqbal wrote in 1936[185] in the hope of being cured from an ailment, as he tells in a letter. He had been advised to write the poem by a dream apparition of Sir Sayyid Ahmad Khan:[186] the healing quality of the *Burda* is remembered. But even his early Urdu poems, such as *Jawāb-i shikwāh,* contain verses in praise of the Prophet, and in his first revolutionary

Persian *mathnawī Asrār-i khūdī* (1915) he has devoted some of his finest lines to Muhammad:

> We are like a rose with many petals, but with one perfume;
> He is the soul of the society, and he is one.[187]

This spiritual quality of the Prophet who is connected with the fragrance of his roselike community is emphasized from another viewpoint in the *Rumūz-i bēkhūdī,* the poetical collection which translates Iqbal's sociopolitical ideals into Persian verse. There, he appears once more, in the tradition of light-mysticism, as the lamp in the darkness of existence,[188] and his role is compared to that of the community which he has created:

> He is the seal of prophets, we that of nations.[189]

Therefore, as he was sent as mercy for the worlds, his community too should act as mercy for the worlds:

> On prophethood is our foundation in the world,
> From prophethood has our religion its ritual,
> From prophethood are hundreds of thousands of us one;
> Part cannot be separated from part.
> From prophethood all of us have received the same melody,
> The same breath, the same aim.[190]

And when he says in his last verses, which are devoted to the Hijaz, the country which he never visited:

> For us Mustafa is enough,[191]

he had gone even further in the *Jāvīdnāma,* where the daring line appears:

> You can deny God, but you cannot deny the Prophet![192]

Iqbal's prophetology has many facets: he reflects Muhammad's social and political activities in the mirror of the complaint of

Abu Jahl, one of his grimmest enemies, who defends earthrootedness, narrow patriotism and distinction of races and castes.[193] Iqbal sees Muhammad as the political leader who is able to guide people toward their destiny even in this world:

> With the key of religion he opened the door of this world,[194]

and:

> On his forehead is written the destiny of nations.[195]

But Iqbal defines also his more-than-human state with an important passage in the *Jāvīdnāma,* in a poem which he puts in the mouth of Hallaj, whose hymn in honor of the Prophet forms the actual beginning of mystical prophetology. Here he discusses the importance of the epithet *ᶜabduhu,* "His slave," which Muhammad was called in the brief allusion to his ascension in the beginning of Sura 17: *subḥāna man asrā biᶜabdihi,* "Praised be He that traveled at night with His servant!" As the mystics discovered very early, this "servanthood" must then be the highest state a human being could reach, since it was connected with the Prophet's experience of the immediate presence before God.[196] The rank of the Prophet who, as "God's servant," is distinct from God, is beyond human understanding:

> His essence is neither Arabic nor Persian;
> He is a man, and yet prior to Adam.
> "His Servant" is the painter of destinations,
> In him is the repair of ruins . . .
> "Servant" is one thing, and "His Servant" is something else:
> We all are waiting, and he is the awaited one.
> "His Servant" is Time, and Time is from "His Servant";
> We all are colors, and he is without color and scent.
> "His Servant" is without beginning, without end;
> "His Servant"—where are for him morning and evening?

> Nobody is acquainted with the secrets of "His Servant":
> "His Servant" is nothing but the secret of *illā Allāh* ([there is no deity] save God).[197]

Iqbal's prophetology combines elements of both a modern and a traditional world view: Muhammad is both the political leader of his community and the scent of the *rosa mystica;* the intercessor at Doomsday and the luminous being beyond time and space; the seal of the prophets with whom prophethood has discovered the need of its own abolition; and the mystical beloved for whose last resting place in Medina the Muslim longs,

> just like a bird who, in the desert night
> spreads out his wings when thinking of his nest.[198]

Jan Knappert, in his study of Swahili religious poetry, states that pious literature in that language "breathes a spirit of great love and devotion to the Prophet, of dedicated obedience to God's own most loved creature."[199] This sentence can be applied to poetry in honor of Muhammad in every corner of the Muslim world, for, as Iqbal says in the *Rumūz-i bēkhūdī:*

> Love of the Prophet runs like blood in the veins of the community.[200]

Abbreviations Used in Notes and Bibliography

ARW	*Archiv für Religionswissenschaft*
BEA	*Bulletin des Études Arabes*
BSO[A]S	*Bulletin of the School of Oriental [and African] Studies*
D	Rumi, *Dīwān-i kabīr,* ed. Furuzanfar. Quoted by number of poem and line.
EI	*Enzyklopädie des Islam,* 4 vols. plus Supplement. Leiden: Brill—Leipzig: Harrassowitz, 1913–1938.
*EI*²	*The Encyclopedia of Islam,* 2d ed. Leiden: Brill, since 1960.
ERE	James Hastings, *Encyclopedia of Religion and Ethics.*
GAL	Carl Brockelmann, *Geschichte der arabischen Literatur,* 2d ed. 3 vols; plus *S,* three supplements to the first edition. Leiden: Brill, 1937 ff.
GAS	Fuad Sezgin, *Geschichte des arabischen Schrifttums.* Leiden: Brill, since 1967.
GMS	*Gibb Memorial Series*
IC	*Islamic Culture*
JA	*Journal Asiatique*
JAOS	*Journal of the American Oriental Society*
JASB	*Journal of the Asiatic Society of Bengal*
JRAS	*Journal of the Royal Asiatic Society*
M	Rumi, *Mathnawī,* ed. R. A. Nicholson. Quoted by volume and line.
MW	*The Moslem (Muslim) World*
NS	(New Series)
OLZ	*Orientalistische Literaturzeitung*
REI	*Revue des Études Islamiques*

RGG	*Die Religion in Geschichte und Gegenwart*, ed. Kurt Galling et al. Tübingen: J.C.B. Mohr (Paul Siebeck), 1957–65.
S	(See *GAL* above)
WI	*Die Welt des Islam (The World of Islam)*
WZKM	*Wiener Zeitschrift für die Kunde des Morgenlandes*
ZDMG	*Zeitschrift der Deutschen Morgenländischen Gesellschaft*

Notes

INTRODUCTION

1. See Arthur John Arberry, *An Introduction to the History of Sufism;* the only brief survey of the development of Sufi poetry in the classical languages known to me is Francesco Gabrieli's "Problemi e forme della poesia mistica musulmana."

2. Karsten Harries, "Metaphor as Transcendence," in Sheldon Sachs, ed., *On Metaphor.*

3. Hermann Pongs, *Das Bild in der Dichtung* (Marburg, 1927). Quoted in Philip Wheelwright, *The Burning Fountain,* p. 376, note 20.

4. Wayne C. Booth, "Metaphors as Rhetoric," in Sachs, p. 54.

5. "The created beings of the whole world are, as it were, a book and a picture and a mirror for us, a faithful little sign of our life and death, of our state and fate." Karsten Harries, "Afterthoughts," in Sachs, p. 169.

6. Hans Heinrich Schaeder, "Die islamische Lehre vom Vollkommenen Menschen, ihre Herkunft und ihre dichterische Gestaltung," pp. 196–197.

7. Quoted in W. Jackson Bate, *Samuel Johnson* (New York and London: Harcourt Brace Jovanovich, 1979), p. 400.

8. Joseph N. Bell, *Love Theories in Later Hanbalite Islam,* p. 202.

9. Ibid.

1. FLOWERS OF THE DESERT: THE DEVELOPMENT OF ARABIC MYSTICAL POETRY

1. J. Christoph Bürgel, "Die beste Dichtung ist die lügenreichste," offers much material on this problem.

2. The best known example of this modern criticism is Altaf Husain Hali's (d. 1914) *Muqaddima-i shi*ᶜ*r o shā*ᶜ*irī* (1893), in which he mercilessly attacks traditional Urdu poetry; see Alessandro Bausani, "Alṭāf Ḥusain Ḥālī's Ideas on *ghazal.*" Hali's verdict was taken over and emphasized by Iqbal, who claimed that mystical poetry after Hafiz might prove utterly dangerous for the morals of a people; however, he admitted in his epic *Javīdnāma* (Lahore, 1932), lines 727–728:

> If the purpose of poetry is to form men,
> Poetry is the heir of prophecy.

3. Thus in *Fīhi mā fīhi,* Teheran n.d., p. 100, trans. Arthur John Arberry, *Discourses of Rumi,* pp. 85–86.

4. The Persian mystical poet Fariduddin ᶜAttar clearly defined the high rank of his own poetry by combining the word *shiᶜr,* "poetry," with the words *sharᶜ* and *ᶜarsh,* "Divine Law" and "Divine Throne," respectively, all of them consisting of the same root letters, *sh,* ᶜ, and *r.* See Hellmut Ritter, *Das Meer der Seele,* pp. 151, 156–57. Rumi's son, Sultan Walad, said about the poetry of the "men of God":

> Know their poetry as the spell of Jesus
> By which the dead gain a new life!

Waladnāma, p. 55. A good interpreter of the problem is also Khwaja Mir Dard in Delhi (d. 1785), see Annemarie Schimmel, "Mir Dards Gedanken über das Verhältnis von Mystik und Wort."

5. Hellmut Ritter, "L'orthodoxie a-t-elle une part dans la décadence?," p. 173, stresses the fact that "poetry, even much later . . . has remained a-religious," with the exception of some Kharijites and Shia Ghulat (see below, note 13). He also highlights the lack of "mythical apperception" in Arabic poetry, a characteristic which is certainly not helpful for the growth of truly "religious" verse. For the development in general see Gustave E. von Grunebaum, *Kritik und Dichtkunst.* The same author has put his finger on the theological problem connected with the proper evaluation of the "creative" work of a poet: "The theological inadmissibility of human creativeness was supported by the uncertainty of the distinction in the general consciousness between creation, artistic and intellectual, and the true *creatio ex nihilo,*" see "The Spirit of Islam as Shown in Its Literature," p. 99.

6. Philip Hitti, *History of the Arabs,* p. 90.

7. *West-Östlicher Divan,* p. 169, s.v. "Mahomet." The image of the flag suggests the concept of Muhammad's "flag of praise," *liwā' al-ḥamd,* so central in Islamic piety; Goethe, however, did not know it but intuitively chose the right simile.

8. Cf. ᶜAttar's statement in his *Muṣībatnāma* that the Prophet was too elevated for poetry, and that is why he did not write verse; see Ritter, *Meer der Seele,* p. 157.

9. Ibn ᶜArabi, *The Tarjumān al-ashwāq,* Preface, p. iii.

10. Meir J. Kister, "On a New Edition of the Dīwān of Ḥassān ibn Thābit," p. 285. A study of the Koranic influence on Arabic poetry in early Islamic times is Rahatullah Muhammad Khan, *Vom Einfluss des Korans auf die arabische Dichtung.*

11. Cf. Josef Horovitz, "Die poetischen Einlagen der Sīra"; Ibn Ishaq's poetical insertions were often incompatible with Islamic ideals, and therefore later biographers, beginning with Ibn Saᶜd, restricted the use of poetry almost exclusively to dirges on the Prophet. Omar Farrukh, *Das Bild des Frühislam in*

der arabischen Dichtung von der Hiğra bis zum Tode des Kalifen ᶜUmar, underscored the influence of the Koranic message on early poetry, a viewpoint criticized by G. E. von Grunebaum in his review, *WZKM* 45 (1938), pp. 292–95. Against Grunebaum's critique, James A. Bellamy holds that in early Islamic poetry "the influence of Islam is manifested in a variety of ways." ("The Impact of Islam on Early Arabic Poetry," p. 163.) The poetry of the Kharijites was studied in particular by Ihsan ᶜAbbas, *Shiᶜr al-khawārij* (1963).

12. Zaki Mubarak, *Al-madā'iḥ an-nabawiyya fī'l-adab al-ᶜarabī,* pp. 77–100, 106–120, deals with the early poets, among them Diᶜbil and his *tā'iyya* about Muhammad's family. The outspoken veneration of the descendants of ᶜAli and Fatima was, of course, a highly political issue during the Omayyad period. For the whole problem see the succinct article by Gustave E. von Grunebaum "The Early Development of Islamic Religious Poetry"; he rightly draws attention to the surprising fact that "Arabic literary theory never has included religious elements among the recognized motives" (p. 24).

13. Francesco Gabrieli, "Religious Poetry in Early Islam," p. 7. There is a good English translation of Qatari's most famous verse by Reynold A. Nicholson, in *A Literary History of the Arabs,* p. 213. Ibid., p. 216, remarks about Kuthayyir ᶜUzza (d. 723) and his poems on ᶜAli and his family.

14. Josef Horovitz, *Die Hāšimijjat des Kumait* (Leiden, 1904).

15. The first *zuhdiyyāt* are ascribed to one Sabiq al-Barbari in late Omayyad days; *GAS* I 635.

16. Carl Heinrich Becker, "Ubi sunt qui ante nos in mundo fuere," derives the topos from hellenistic models, while Mark Lidzbarski (*Der Islam* 8 [1918], p. 300) suggests himyarite precedents, and P. Keseling (*Der Islam* 17 [1928], pp. 97–100) stresses the Old Testament roots.

17. Ismaᶜil ibn al-Qasim Abu'l-ᶜAtahiya, *Dīwān* see *GAL* I 76, *S* I 119; R. A. Nicholson, *Literary History of the Arabs,* pp. 296–303 has a number of examples.

18. See ᶜAli Safi Husain, *Al-adab aṣ-ṣūfi fī miṣr fī'l-qarn as-sābiᶜ al-hijrī,* p. 194, about ash-Shafiᶜi's rhyming exercises. Joseph N. Bell, *Love Theories in Later Hanbalite Islam,* pp. 130–31 quotes verse *fatwās* attributed to ash-Shafiᶜi and other leaders of religious schools about the problem of the permissibility of kissing and embracing.

19. Paul Nwyia, *Ibn ᶜAṭā' Allāh et la naissance de la confrèrie šādilite,* p. 46.

20. Thus a Sindhi poet admonishes his listeners to turn "to the end of The Afternoon, *al-ᶜaṣr,*" and means with that expression the last word of the *Sūrat al-ᶜaṣr* (Sura 103), which is *ṣabr,* "patience." (Shah ᶜAbdul Latif, *Shāh jō Risālō,* Sur Kalyan III 8).

21. Paul Nwyia, *Exégèse coranique et langage mystique,* p. 187.

22. *Shaṭḥ* is explained by as-Sarraj, *Kitāb al-lumaᶜ fi't-taṣawwuf,* pp. 375–76, as comparable to "a great deal of water flowing in a narrow stream which therefore overflows, *shaṭaḥa,* its banks." This notion seems to have inspired—

perhaps subconsciously—later Indo-Muslim poets who, like Ghalib, spoke of Hallaj as an example of *tunuk-ẓarfī,* "shallowness of the vessel," because he was not able to contain the Divine secret within himself and therefore called out *anā'l-ḥaqq,* "I am the Absolute Truth," a word which was regarded by later mystics as the *shaṭḥ* par excellence. See Annemarie Schimmel, *A Dance of Sparks,* p. 105.

23. Abu Nuᶜaim al-Isfahani, *Ḥilyat al-auliyā wa ṭabaqāt al-aṣfiyā,* IX, p. 332. This saying is attributed to other mystics too.

24. Mysticism, as defined by Plotinus, is indeed "the flight of the one to the One," and the mystic cannot find the right word for the right things, for the ineffable has nothing that could express it correctly; hence the tendency of mystics everywhere either to resort to silence or, since complete silence would be destructive, to turn to oxymora and paradoxes (see Chapter 4, notes 111–135). The problem of silence has therefore been discussed by every writer on mysticism; see Friedrich Heiler, *Erscheinungsformen und Wesen der Religion,* pp. 334–39; and Gustav Mensching, *Das heilige Schweigen.*

25. Sumnun al-Muhibb, quoted by ᶜAli ibn ᶜUthman al-Hujwiri, *Kashf al-maḥjūb,* p. 137.

26. ad-Dailami, *Sīrat Ibn al-Khafīf,* ed. Annemarie Schimmel (Ankara, 1955), chapter 5, p. 90, saying by Ruwaim.

27. Abu Hamid al-Ghazzali, *Iḥyā' ᶜulūm ad-dīn,* IV, p. 266; the translation by R. A. Nicholson, *Literary History of the Arabs,* p. 234. For Rabiᶜa see Margaret Smith, *Rābiᶜa the Mystic and Her Fellow Saints in Islam.*

28. M. Smith, *Rābiᶜa,* p. 55. This exclusive love is reminiscent of sayings of Catherine of Genova: "I do not want what comes from thee but I want thee alone, O sweet love!" and Juliana of Norwich's similar statements, quoted in William Ralph Inge, *Christian Mysticism,* p. 209.

29. ᶜAbdur Rahman Jami, *Nafaḥāt al-uns,* p. 617.

30. Abu Nuᶜaim, *Ḥilya* IX, p. 387.

31. A. S. Husain, *Al-adab aṣ-ṣūfī,* p. 197. According to Edward G. Browne, *A Literary History of Persia,* Vol. 2, p. 505, R. A. Nicholson considered Dhu'n-Nun (d. 859) as the first to give to the earlier asceticism the "definitely pantheistic bent and quasierotic expression which we recognize as the chief characteristic of Sufism." This statement seems to go too far, even though Dhu'n-Nun certainly inaugurates a new period in Sufi literature.

32. Abu Nuᶜaim, *Ḥilya* IX, p. 391.

33. Victor Danner, introduction to *Ibn ᶜAṭā Allāh, The Book of Wisdom,* p. 11.

34. Ghazzali, *Iḥyā'* IV, p. 290, a statement by Yahya ibn Muᶜadh, see ibid. also a similar poem by Abu Turab an-Nakhshabi. A more artistic description of the ascetics is Ibn ar-Rumi's (d. c. 899) well-known poem quoted by Hellmut Ritter, *Über die Bildersprache Niẓāmīs,* p. 16.

35. A good example in ᶜAbdul Karim al-Qushairi, *Ar-risāla fi ᶜilm at-taṣawwuf,* p. 129:

> The stranger when he goes to a foreign land, is adorned
> By three things: they are firstly fine etiquette,
> Secondly, good morals,
> The third one is the avoidance of the doubtful.

36. Sarraj, *Kitāb al-lumaᶜ,* p. 247.

37. Ibid., p. 251.

38. Abu Nuᶜaim, *Ḥilya* X, p. 273.

39. Ibid. X, p. 166.

40. Hans Heinrich Schaeder was right when he wrote: "Islamic mysticism is the attempt to reach individual salvation through attaining the true *tauḥīd,*" in "Zur Deutung der islamischen Mystik," col. 845; the article is a diatribe against Max Horten's interpretation of Sufism as something exclusively Indian.

41. Richard Gramlich, "Mystical Dimensions of Islamic Monotheism."

42. Nwyia, *Exégèse coranique,* p. 249. Extreme Sufis went so far as to exclaim, as the last stage before complete annihilation, *lā anā illā anā,* "There is no I but I," which points to God affirming Himself through man's mouth; see Sohrawardi Maqtūl, *Ṣafīr-i sīmurgh,* p. 364–65.

43. Another member of the Baghdadian school, Ibn ᶜAta, was asked by a theologian: "How is it that you Sufis have invented expressions which sound strange to those who hear them, and have abandoned ordinary language?" For this act would imply, according to the theologian's understanding, that the Sufis have to hide some wrong views or cover some mistakes; but Ibn ᶜAta answered that they did not want to acquaint everyone with things which are precious and dear to them; for this reason they invented special expressions. Fariduddin ᶜAttar, *Tadhkirat al-auliyā,* II, p. 69.

44. W. H. Temple Gairdner, *Al-Ghazzâlî's "mishkât al- anwâr": The Niche for Lights,* p. 71.

45. Adonis, "As-suryāliyya qabla as-suryāliyya," pp. 17–19.

46. Paul Nwyia, "Massignon ou une certaine vision de la langue arabe."

47. Louis Massignon, "Le Divan d'al-Ḥallâj," muqaṭṭaᶜa, No. 80.

48. Arnold Steiger, "Función espiritual del Islam en la España medieval": "Una raiz árabe es, pues, como una lira de la que no se puede pulsar una cureda sin que vibren todas las demás, y cada palabra, además de su propria resonancia, despierta les secretos armónicos de las conceptos emparentados" (p. 42).

49. Fritz Meier, *Die schöne Mahsati,* mentions the use of the (Persian) *rubāᶜī* in *samāᶜ,* pp. 20–21; see also Benedikt Reinert, "Die prosodische Unterschiedlichkeit von persischem und arabischem *rubāᶜī,*" p. 221; he states that

all of the western representatives of the Arabic *rubāʿī* were "noted for their Sufic inclinations," p. 222.

50. Sarraj, *Kitāb al-lumaʿ*, p. 236.

51. Tor Andrae, *I Myrtenträdgården.*

52. Ghazzali, *Iḥyā'* IV, p. 298. The expression "Longer than the day of resurrection" became a topos in later poetry, poets complaining that the horrors of resurrection and judgment which the preachers described so intensely were nothing but a metaphor for their own state during the separation from the beloved; most famous is Hafiz's relevant verse, *Dīwān*, ed. Hermann Brockhaus (Leipzig, 1854–63), no. 76; the very word *qiyāmat*, resurrection, came to mean in popular idiom a state of utter confusion and unhappiness.

53. The most famous cases among Sufis are Abu'l-Hasan an-Nuri, who died in ecstasy after listening to a little song (see Sarraj, *Kitāb al-lumaʿ* p. 210), and later Bakhtiar Kaki, the Chishti leader of Delhi, who died in 1235 after listening for days to a verse by Ahmad-i Jam Zandapil. For the problem cf. Sarraj's discussion in the chapter on *samāʿ*, *Kitāb al-lumaʿ* pp. 267–99. The question to what extent, and if at all, music is permitted in Islam, continues up to this day, and has resulted in an enormous amount of treatises pro and con.

54. Walter Schubart, *Religion und Eros*, p. 139. See also Annemarie Schimmel, "Eros—Heavenly and Not So Heavenly—in Sufi Literature and Life."

55. Abu Nuʿaim, *Ḥilya* X, p. 61; trans. by Arthur J. Arberry, *Sufism: An Account of the Mystics of Islam*, p. 62 (with our change in line 3). The mention of "God's valley" leads inevitably back to Sura 26/226 with its condemnation of the poets who wander distracted "in every valley."

56. Sarraj, *Kitāb al-lumaʿ*, p. 247.

57. Abu Nuʿaim, *Ḥilya* IX, p. 377.

58. Ibid., p. 368; Sarraj, *Kitāb al- lumaʿ*, p. 368.

59. Abu Nuʿaim, *Ḥilya* X, p. 228; the poem is set in a beautiful piece of descriptive prose, a genre that was Dhu'n-Nun's forte.

60. Ibid., p. 273. Junaid heard such a verse from the ailing Sari as-Saqati.

61. Ibid., p. 310, Sumnun al-Muhibb.

62. Sarraj, *Kitāb al- lumaʿ*, p. 237. The topos of burning the paper with the fire of one's heart and/or washing off the ink with tears is widespread in Islamic poetry; for its use in Spain see Soledad G. Fenesch, "Sobre una extrano manera de escribir."

63. ʿAttar, *Tadhkirat al-auliyā*, I, p. 134.

64. Sarraj, *Kitāb al-lumaʿ*, p. 386. This topos, again, became a favorite with later poets, especially in Iran, where they would kiss not only the wall of Laila's house but even the paws of her dog (according to the *ḥadīth*, "When a faithful person loves another faithful person, he loves even his dog"). Jami, especially, indulged in this image so intensely that his translator, Friedrich Rückert, wrote ironically: "In Dschamis Gaselen wimmelt's von solchen Hun-

den, die wir meist laufen liessen, ein paarmal auch ein wenig verkleideten . . ." (Leopold Hirschberg, ed., *Rückert-Nachlese,* II, p. 402). The deeper meaning of such verses is of course that even the most despicable item that was once in touch with the beloved carries some of his/her *baraka,* and is therefore dear to the lover who impatiently waits for some sign of grace.

65. Sarraj, *Kitāb al-luma*ᶜ, p. 250, Ibn al-Khawass.

66. Abu Nuᶜaim, *Ḥilya* X, p. 372. See Abu Bakr ash-Shibli, *Dīwān,* ed. Kamil M. ash-Shaibi (Baghdad, 1967); and Emile Dermenghem, "Abou Bakr Chibli, poète mystique bagdadien." Shibli excelled in graceful little poems; famous is his verse about the approaching ᶜ*īd al-fiṭr,* when everyone is supposed to wear fine new clothes while he, separated from his beloved, has nothing but:

> Poverty and Patience, they are my two robes under which
> There is a heart which regards His company as Feasts and Friday. . . ,

again a topos which was to be used frequently by urban and rural poets.

67. Hallaj, *Dīwān,* ed. Massignon, muqaṭṭaᶜa no. 82. The poem, which is still frequently recited in the Islamic countries, is also ascribed to Shibli.

68. Sarraj, *Kitāb al-luma*ᶜ, p. 250; Abu Nuᶜaim, *Ḥilya* X, p. 310.

69. Abu Nuᶜaim, *Ḥilya* X, p. 354.

70. Sarraj, *Kitāb al-luma*ᶜ, p. 50.

71. Ibid., p. 252; Abu Nuᶜaim, *Ḥilya* X, p. 373.

72. For the problem of the Name see Gerardus van der Leeuw, *Phänomenologie der Religion,* pp. 155–170. One has to keep in mind that the Divine Name in many religious traditions (as in Israel) had to be kept secret; see also Heiler, *Erscheinungsformen,* p. 276. Furthermore, to know someone's name gives man power to use it in magic practices. A profane reason for not divulging the name of someone was, in pre-Islamic and other tribal societies the fear of becoming involved in a blood feud, see Ignaz Goldziher, "Verheimlichung des Namens."

73. Thus, Hallaj received letters from abroad in which he was called strange-sounding names; (ᶜAttar, *Tadhkirat al-auliyā* II, p. 141). Najmuddin Kubra experienced in his visions the acquaintance with his heavenly name, see Fritz Meier, ed., *Die fawā'iḥ al-ǧamāl wa fawātiḥ al-ǧalāl des Naǧmuddīn al-Kubrā,* pp. 135–37: "Himmlische Namen"; while Mir Dard claimed to be invested with ninety-nine names, ᶜ*Ilm ul-kitāb,* p. 62; cf. Annemarie Schimmel, *Pain and Grace,* pp. 83–84. For the whole question see Ignaz Goldziher, "Himmlische und irdische Namen."

74. Abu Nuᶜaim, *Ḥilya* X, p. 318, Tahir al-Maqdisi.

75. Ibid., p. 370, Abu Bakr ash-Shibli.

76. Sarraj, *Kitāb al- luma*ᶜ, p. 91.

77. For an excellent description of this development in *dhikr* see Fritz Meier, "Qušayrīs *Tartīb as-sulūk.*"

78. Jami, *Nafaḥāt al-uns,* p. 181; see Jalaluddin Rumi, D 2831.

79. Ghazzali, *Iḥyā'* IV, p. 284; the verse is also ascribed to Rabiᶜa and others. For a fine analysis of the relation between love and obedience see J. N. Bell, *Love Theories in Later Hanbalite Islam,* pp. 180.

80. Ghazzali, *Iḥyā'* IV, p. 282.

81. Hujwiri/Nicholson, *Kashf al-mahjūb,* p. 297; see also Gramlich, "Mystical Dimensions of *tauḥīd.*"

82. Abu Nuᶜaim, *Ḥilya* X, p. 310; Jami, *Nafaḥāt al-uns,* p. 96.

83. Ghazzali, *Iḥyā'* IV, p. 300: "Who dies from love shall die thus—there is nothing good in love without death."

84. Suso says in the *Büchlein der Ewigen Weisheit:* "Zur Minne gehört nach altem Recht Leiden;" as his compatriot Mechtild of Magdeburg states: "The higher a person's love, the more is he a holy martyr," quoted in Martin Buber, *Ekstatische Konfessionen,* p. 74.

85. The elaboration of the diction ascribed to the Prophet, "Who loves and remains chaste and dies, dies as a martyr" has helped to build up this tradition.

86. Louis Massignon, *La Passion d'al-Ḥosayn ibn Mansour al-Ḥallāj, martyr mystique de l'Islam.* An English translation by Herbert Mason will soon appear from Princeton University Press, Bollingen Series.

87. Friedrich A. D. Tholuck in his rather misleading and invective remarks about Hallaj goes further than this standard oriental description by calling him "the Sufi most famous by fate and fame . . . who removed the veil of pantheism with incredible audacity," *Ssufismus sive theosophia persarum pantheistica,* p. 68.

88. Louis Massignon, "Interférences philosophiques et percées métaphysiques dans la mystique hallajienne: notion de l'essentiel désir."

89. Louis Massignon, in Hallaj, *Kitāb aṭ-ṭawāsīn,* p. 132.

90. *Dīwān,* ed. Massignon, muqaṭṭaᶜa no. 27.

91. Ibid., muqaṭṭaᶜa no. 26.1.

92. Ibid., muqaṭṭaᶜa no. 1.

93. Ibid., muqaṭṭaᶜa no. 3; see al-Ghazzali, *Iḥyā',* IV, p. 267.

94. *Dīwān,* ed. Massignon, muqaṭṭaᶜa no. 9.

95. Ibid., muqaṭṭaᶜa no. 61.

96. Ibid., muqaṭṭaᶜa no. 55; the verse is also found in Louis Massignon and Paul Kraus, *Akhbār al-Ḥallāj,* no. 50.

97. *Dīwān,* ed. Massignon, qaṣīda no. 10.

98. Ibid., qaṣīda no. 6.

99. Ibid., muqaṭṭaᶜa no. 10.

100. Ibid., muqaṭṭaᶜa no. 57.

101. Ibid., muqaṭṭaᶜa no. 41.

102. Ibid., muqaṭṭaᶜa no. 48.

103. Massignon and Kraus, *Akhbār al-Ḥallāj,* no. 43; *Dīwān,* ed. Massig-

non, muqaṭṭaᶜa no. 20. Shibli's verse, quoted above (note 78) tones down this statement somewhat, as his verses usually interpret Hallaj's powerful, often shocking and offending words in a less aggressive style. The problem dealt with in this verse is that of *isqāṭ al-wasāᶜiṭ,* the abrogation of intermediaries: ritual practices are optional for those who have reached union with the Divine—a theory which could lead to dangerous consequences, particularly in social ethics, and was therefore objected to by the orthodox.

104. Massignon and Kraus, *Akhbār,* no. 12; *Kitāb aṭ-ṭawāsīn, "Ṭāsīn al-azal wa'l-iltibās."*

105. *Dīwān,* ed. Massignon, muqaṭṭaᶜa no. 7. Shibli's idea that he "became all hearts" is prefigured by Hallaj, who gives this motif the note of utter despondency:

> All of me became hearts which call You
> To wound them, and to hurry up with pains.

Ibid., muqaṭṭaᶜa no. 36.

106. Commentary on Sura 37/106; quoted in Louis Massignon, *Essai sur les origines du lexique technique de la mystique musulmane,* p. 393, no. 138.

107. Ritter, *Meer der Seele,* p. 538, states that in Hallaj's and his followers' view Satan "becomes more monotheist than God Himself." For Ahmad Ghazzali's remark, "Who does not learn *tauḥīd* from Satan, is an infidel," see Merlin S. Swartz, *Ibn al-Jawzī's Kitāb al-quṣṣās wa'l-mudhakkirīn,* p. 222; similar remarks were made by the Persian poet Sarmad at the Moghul Court, see Shaikh Mohammed Ikram, *Armaghān-i Pāk,* p. 238; the Sindhi mystic Shah ᶜAbdul Latif calls Satan "Lover": *ᶜāshiq ᶜAzāzīl, Risālō,* Sur Yaman Kalyān V 24. For the whole problem see Peter J. Awn, *Satan's Tragedy and Redemption: Iblīs in Sufi Psychology.*

108. Hans Heinrich Schaeder, "Die persische Vorlage von Goethes Seliger Sehnsucht." See Goethe, *West-Östlicher Divan: Buch des Sängers "Selige Sehnsucht."*

109. For the use of *ḥaqq* see Gerhard Böwering, *The Mystical Vision of Existence in Classical Islam,* pp. 166–172.

110. *Dīwān,* ed. Massignon, qaṣīda 1.2.

111. Muhammad ibn ᶜAbdul Jabbar an-Niffari, *The Mawāqif and Mukhāṭabāt . . . with other fragments.*

112. Annemarie Schimmel, *The Triumphal Sun,* pp. 352–66.

113. *Dīwān,* ed. Massignon, muqaṭṭaᶜa no. 17.

114. Nwyia, *Exégèse coranique,* p. 370.

115. ᶜAttar, *Tadhkirat al-auliyā,* II, p. 143: it is said that Hallaj, who had endured the stones flung at him without complaint sighed when a rose thrown by Shibli hit him; and still today the Turkish proverb says *dostun attīğī gül onar,* "The rose cast by a friend, hurts."

116. Shibli, *Dīwān,* p. 121.

117. Sarraj, *Kitāb al-luma*^{c}, p. 27.

118. Gustave E. von Grunebaum, "The Nature of the Arabic Literary Effort," p. 117.

119. A. S. Husain, *Al-adab aṣ-ṣūfī,* p. 241.

120. Ibid., pp. 221, 284.

121. Nwyia, *Ibn* ^{c}*Aṭā' Allāh,* p. 34.

122. *GAL* II 12, *S* II 4: Abu'l-Wafa ash-Shadhili and his sons.

123. A. S. Husain, *Al-adab aṣ-ṣūfī,* p. 136 and 230 ff. For instance:

> I am the nightingale of joys,
> I am the lord of the *nāmūs* . . .

or:

> My formation in love was before Adam . . .
> I was in the highest sphere with Ahmad's light . . .

The rather boring, punning poem by the Rifa^{c}i leader ad-Darimi (d. 696/1297), quoted in Husain, p. 48, belongs also to this little attractive genre of mystical verse. See also Andrae, *Die person Mohammeds in glaube und lehre seiner gemeinde,* pp. 382–83 for a similar poem by ad-Dasuqi.

124. The two basic studies which see him in this light are Hendrik Samuel Nyberg, *Kleinere Schriften des Ibn* ^{c}*Arabī* (cf. Hans Heinrich Schaeder's review in *OLZ* 28 (1925), col. 794), and Abu'l-^{c}Ala Affifi, *The Mystical Philosophy of Muḥyīd'Dīn Ibnul* ^{c}*Arabī.*

125. Marijan Molé, *Les mystiques musulmans,* p. 103.

126. Henry Corbin, *Creative Imagination in the Sufism of Ibn* ^{c}*Arabi;* Seyyed Hossein Nasr, *Three Muslim Sages.*

127. Hans Heinrich Schaeder, "Die islamische Lehre vom Vollkommenen Menschen, ihre Herkunft und ihre dichterische Gestaltung."

128. Ibn al-^{c}Arabi, *Tarjumān al-ashwāq,* no. IX.

129. The translator was Muhammad Husain Kalim, and the book was classified by his brother-in-law, the noted Urdu poet Mir Taqi Mir, as "a very difficult and subtle book which ordinary *maulwīs* cannot understand," ^{c}Abdul Hayy, *Gul-i ra*^{c}*nā,* pp. 111–12.

130. Ibn al-^{c}Arabi, *Tarjumān,* preface by R. A. Nicholson, p. vii. Cf. the articles by Muhammad Mustafa Hilmi, "*Kunūz fi rumūz*" and Zaki Muhammad Nagib, "*Ṭarīqat ar-ramz* ^{c}*inda Ibn* ^{c}*Arabī fi dīwānihi Tarjumān al-ashwāq,*" in Ibrahim B. Madkur, ed., *Al-kitāb at-tidhkārī: Muḥyīuddīn ibn* ^{c}*Arabī.*

131. Rumi, *M* VI 4022–37. Zulaikha's song is not an expression of a theoretical Unity of Being but rather translates into verse the psychological truth which the Sufis condensed in the sentence: "Who loves something mentions it often."

132. Ibn al-^{c}Arabi, *Tarjumān,* Introduction, p. 7.

133. Ibid., no. VII, commentary p. 57.
134. Ibid., no. XIII 9, commentary p. 74.
135. Ibid., no. XX 3, commentary p. 88.
136. Ibid., no. XXIX 13, commentary p. 109.
137. Ibid., no. XL 1, commentary p. 124.
138. Ibid., no. XX 3, commentary p. 88.
139. Ibid., no. XXVI 2, commentary p. 103.
140. Ibid., no. XXII 2, commentary p. 92.

141. Reynold A. Nicholson, "The Lives of ᶜUmar Ibnu'l-Fāriḍ and Muḥyi'd-Dīn Ibnu'l-ᶜArabī." Nicholson, *Studies in Islamic Mysticism,* chapter 3, is still the best introduction to Ibn al-Farid's work (pp. 199–256). See also Muhammad Mustafa Hilmi, *Ibn al-Fāriḍ wa'l-ḥubb al-ilāhī,* and A. S. Husain, *Al-adab aṣ-ṣūfī,* pp. 109–22.

142. Ibn Khallikan, *Wafayāt al-aᶜyān,* III, no. 472, pp. 126–27.

143. That happened in Muharram 875/July 1470: the Hanafite *qāḍī al-quḍāt,* Muhibbuddin ibn ash-Shihna, was the leader of the faction which claimed that Ibn al-Farid was a heretic or infidel, while the strongest defense of the mystical poet came from Jalaluddin as-Suyuti, the noted traditionist and polyhistor, who was a member of the Shadhiliyya order. The ruler, Sultan Qaitbai, who himself had some religious inclinations, sided with the latter group, and Ibn al-Farid's spiritual power manifested itself in the trials and tribulations which came over the family of Ibn ash-Shihna, as Ibn Iyas writes; this author was apparently happy with the result (Ibn Iyās, *Badā'iᶜ az-zuhūr fī waqā'iᶜ ad-duhūr,* Vol. III, pp. 44 ff).

144. Louis Massignon, *La Cité des Morts au Caire,* p. 64.

145. Nicholson, *Studies in Islamic Mysticism,* p. 201.

146. Translated by Wheeler M. Thackston, Jr., in Ilse Lichtenstadter, ed., *Introduction to Classical Arabic Literature,* pp. 312–14.

147. Emile Dermenghem, *L'écloge du vin;* Ibn al-Farid's *khamriyya* as well as his *Tā'iyya* have been commented upon by most later mystical writers, thus by al-Burini, ᶜAbdur Razzaq Kashani, Jami, and, of course, an-Nabulusi. See *GAL* II, p. 262 f.

148. Heiler, *Erscheinungsformen,* p. 250 f.; Nathan Söderblom, "Rus og religion."

149. Quoted in Ghazzali, *Iḥyā'* IV, p. 300.

150. Joseph von Hammer-Purgstall, *Das arabische Hohelied der Liebe.* The beautifully produced book was dismissed at R. A. Nicholson with the remark that "the *tā'iyya* had the misfortune of being translated by Hammer."

151. Nyberg, *Kleinere Schriften,* p. 43.

152. ᶜAttar, *Ushturnāma;* see Ritter, *Meer der Seele,* p. 42.

153. Cf. Franz Taeschner, "Das Puppentheater, nach dem Futuvvat-nāme-i Sulṭānī des Ḥusain Vāᶜiẓ-i Kāšifī (gest. 910/1504–1505)," pp. 657–60; Khwaja Mir Dard, *Dard-i dil* no. 267 and *Ah-i sard* no. 191 in *Chahār Risāla;* see

Annemarie Schimmel, *Mystical Dimensions of Islam,* p. 278, and *Pain and Grace,* p. 143. For a modern Turkish interpretation of the same idea: Samiha Ayverdi, *Ibrahim Efendi Konağı,* p. 79.

154. Sarraj, *Kitāb al-lumaᶜ,* p. 33.

155. Ibn Khallikan, *Wafayāt al-aᶜyān,* III, p. 127. See also S. A. Husain, *Al-adab aṣ-ṣūfī,* p. 177; he mentions, p. 182 f., that even Sufis of that time now and then wrote *fakāhāt,* facetiae; parallels can easily be found in the Persian tradition. For the problem see A. Schimmel, "Eros . . . in Sufi Literature and Life," p. 121; examples in Fritz Meier, *Abu Saᶜīd-i Abū l-Ḫair,* p. 205. G. van der Leeuw, *Phänomenologie,* p. 257, highlights the necessary polarity between renunciation and "unbridled behavior."

156. About him see *EI,* s.v. Tilimsani, and J. N. Bell, *Love Theories of Later Hanbalite Islam,* pp. 89–90.

157. A. S. Husain, *Al-adab aṣ-ṣūfī,* pp. 175 ff. For the didactic verses of ad-Dirini in the meter *rajaz* see *GAL* I, 2d ed., pp. 588–89.

158. An example of a mystical *muwashshaḥ* by the Shadhili poet Abu'l-Wafa, which uses the traditional symbolism of wine, is in Georg Wilhelm Freytag, *Darstellung der arabischen Verskunst,* pp. 432–33.

159. *Billīq* are strophes of three lines with one rhyme, see Reinhart Dozy, *Supplément aux dictionnaires arabes,* s.v. *blq;* Paul Kahle, *Der Leuchtturm von Alexandrien* defines *bĕlliq* as verses for singing purposes (p. 20*).

160. S. Freytag, *Arabische Verskunst,* p. 441 f., and the comprehensive study: Kamil Mustafa ash-Shaibi, *Dīwān ad-dūbait fī'l-adab al-ᶜarabī.*

161. Gustav Flügel, "Über die Versgattung Mawāliyā": a simple poem with four rhyming hemistichs, or with five hemistichs out of which one does not rhyme, based on the classical metre *basīṭ.* Freytag, *Arabische Verskunst* p. 458. The most exhaustive discussion is by Wilhelm Hoenerbach, *Die vulgärarabische Poetik al-kitāb al-ᶜāṭil al-ḥālī wa muraḫḫaṣ al-ğālī des Ṣafiy-addīn Ḥillī.* See also Pierre Cachia, "The Egyptian Mawwāl."

162. ᶜAbdul Ghani an-Nabulusi, *Dīwān al-ḥaqā'iq wa majmūᶜa ar-raqā'iq,* p. 227.

163. Ibid., p. 126.

164. Ibid., p. 261.

165. Cf. *Self Knowledge: Commentaries on Sufic Songs:* it contains a *qaṣīda* of Abu Madyan with its *takhmīs* by Ibn ᶜArabi, commentary by Ibn ᶜAta Allah and a further commentary by ᶜAbdul Qadir as-Sufi ad-Darqawi. The poetry of Abu Madyan is discussed by Ernst Bannerth, "Der Diwan des maghribinischen Sufi Šuᶜaib Abū Madjan"; it contains some of the earliest Sufi poems in nonclassical language and form. For a continuation of this tradition in North African Sufi circles see for instance the *Dīwān* of Muhammad ibn Muhammad al-Harraq (d. 1846–47), about whom a study by B. Manuel Weischer is in preparation.

166. The wealth of Arabic literature in classical forms that existed in the

Indo-Pakistan Subcontinent is often overlooked in histories of Arabic literature. See, for numerous examples of religious poetry in Indo-Pakistan, Zubaid Ahmad, *The Contribution of Indo-Pakistan to Arabic Literature;* S. Sulaiman Nadwi, "Literary Relations between Arabia and India"; Muid Khan, *The Arabian Poets of Golconda,* particularly chapter 5; Muhd. Yousuf Kokan, *Arabic and Persian in Carnatic.*

167. *Ma'sāt al-Ḥallāj* (Beirut, 1964), trans. by Khalil J. Semaan, *Murder in Baghdad.* The English title suggests that Eliot's *Murder in the Cathedral* has influenced the poet; see Khalil J. Semaan, "T. S. Eliot's Influence on Arabic Poetry and Theatre."

168. ᶜAbdul Wahhab al-Bayati, *Dīwān,* Vol. 2, pp. 9–20.

169. Nazeer al-Azma, "The Tammūzī Movement and the Influence of T. S. Eliot on Badr Shākir as-Sayyāb."

170. For translations of the above-mentioned poems see Annemarie Schimmel, *Zeitgenössische arabische Lyrik* (Tübingen 1975); and for the problem in general, Schimmel, "Mystische Motive in der modernen islamischen Dichtung."

2. TINY MIRRORS OF DIVINE BEAUTY: CLASSICAL PERSIAN MYSTICAL POETRY

1. Annemarie Schimmel, ed., *Orientalische Dichtung in Nachbildungen Friedrich Rückerts,* pp. 51–72, 182–202.

2. For the problem of translations of Hafiz' verse see Arthur J. Arberry, *Fifty Poems of Hafiz;* J. Christoph Bürgel, *Hafis, Gedichte aus dem Diwan,* has a very useful introduction; Annemarie Schimmel, "Hafiz and His Critics."

3. "It makes you great that you cannot end, and it is your fate that you never begin. Your word is turning like the starred sphere: its beginning and its end is always the same, and what is brought in the middle is apparently the same as what remains in the end and was there in the beginning." Goethe, *West-Östlicher Divan,* Buch Hafis, "Unbegrenzt."

4. This statement about Oriental music by Lois Ibsen al-Faruqi, "Ornamentation in Arabian Improvisational Music," p. 132, is true also for poetry to a large extent.

5. Rainer Maria Rilke, *Sonette an Orpheus, II,* 21.

6. For the history of Persian classical literature see Hermann Ethé, "Neupersische Literatur"; Edward G. Browne, *A Literary History of Persia;* Jan Rypka, *History of Iranian Literature;* Alessandro Bausani, "Storia della letteratura neopersiana"; Arthur J. Arberry, *Classical Persian Literature.*

7. Hermann Ethé, "Die Rubāᶜīs des Abū Saᶜīd ibn Abul Chair"; the fundamental study is now Fritz Meier, *Abū Saᶜīd-i Abū l-Ḫair.*

8. Hujwiri/Nicholson, *Kashf al-maḥjūb.*

9. Serge de Laugier de Beaurecueil, *Khwādja Abdullāh Anṣārī, mystique hanbalite;* Khwaja Abdullah Ansari, *Intimate Conversations,* Introduction, translation and notes by Wheeler M. Thackston.

10. Jami, *Lawā'iḥ,* ed. and trans. into English by Edward Henry Whinfield and Mirza Muhammad Kazwini, London 1906.

11. The best brief introduction is still E. E. Berthels, "Grundlinien der Entwicklungsgeschichte des mystischen Lehrgedichtes."

12. The Arabs had, however, the form of *muzdawij,* "the paired ones," in the meter *rajaz;* this meter was used for smaller historical reports in rhyme and particularly for didactic poetry from grammar (Ibn Malik's *Alfiyya* and *Kāfiyya*) to religion and medicine because *rajaz* was easy to memorize. See Manfred Ullmann, *Die arabische Rağazpoesie,* pp. 46–60.

13. Saᶜdi's *Būstān,* ed. first by Carl Heinrich Graf (Vienna, 1858), was translated into most Western languages; and into German by Friedrich Rückert, *Saadis Bostan* (Leipzig, 1882); latest English translation by G. M. Wickens, *Morals Pointed and Tales Adorned* (Toronto, 1974).

14. The standard work on ᶜAttar is Hellmut Ritter, *Das Meer der Seele.* See also Wolfgang Lentz, "ᶜAṭṭār als Allegoriker"; Fritz Meier, "Der Geistmensch bei dem persischen Dichter ᶜAṭṭār." For editions see the bibliography s.v. ᶜAttar.

15. *Ilāhīnāme or Book of God of Farid uddin ᶜAttar,* trans. John Andrew Boyle.

16. *Manṭiq uṭ-ṭair,* ed. Jawad Shakur, p. 287.

17. ᶜArifi, *Gūy u jaugān, The Ball and the Polostick;* Hermann Ethé, "König und Derwisch. Romantisch-mystisches Epos vom Scheich Hilali, dem persischen Original getreu nachgebildet."

18. Shabistari, *Gulshan-i rāz, The Rose Garden of Mysteries,* ed. and trans. by Edward Henry Whinfield. The work, which is best read with Lahiji's excellent commentary, evoked an interesting modern response in the 1920s: Muhammad Iqbal, *Gulshan-i rāz-i jadīd,* which he appended to his Persian *dīwān Zabūr-i ᶜajam.* See Alessandro Bausani, "Il gulšan-i rāz-i ǧadīd."

19. Baqlī, *Sharḥ-i Shaṭḥiyāt, Les Paradoxes des Soufis,* ed. Henry Corbin; *ᶜAbhar al-ᶜāshiqīn, Le Jasmine des Fidèles d'amour,* ed. Henry Corbin. See further Henry Corbin, "Quiétude et inquiétude de l'âme dans le soufisme de Rûzbihân Baqlî de Shiraz," and "Sympathie et théopathie chez les Fidèles d'amour en Islam"; Louis Massignon, "La vie et les oeuvres de Rûzbehân Baqlî."

20. Ahmad Ghazzali, *Sawāniḥ. Aphorismen über die Liebe,* ed. Hellmut Ritter, trans. Richard Gramlich, *Gedanken über die Liebe.*

21. ᶜAfif ᶜUsairan, *ᶜAinulquḍāt Hamadhānī, aḥwāl ū āthār;* Arthur J. Arberry, *A Sufi Martyr;* Hermann Landolt, "Two types of mystical thought in Muslim Iran."

22. Fakhruddin ᶜIraqi, *Kulliyāt,* ed. Saᶜid-i Nafisi.

23. E. H. W. Gibb, *History of Ottoman Poetry,* 6 vols. Among the numer-

ous Turkish anthologies: Köprülüzade Mehmet Fuat, *Eski şairlerimiz: Divan edebiyatī antolojisi.* A particularly interesting early representative of enthusiastic poetry is the Hurufi poet Nesimi, whose religious claims, expressed in daring verse in classical style, led to his execution in Aleppo in 1417; thus he indeed followed the example of the martyr mystic Hallaj, as he had always maintained in his verse. For translations see Gibb, I, pp. 336 ff.; Kathleen R. F. Burrill, *The Quatrains of Nesimi, Fourteenth-century Turkish Hurufi.* Epical poetry was modelled after Persian examples, especially the story of Yusuf and Zulaikha; Shayyad Hamza in the thirteenth century has already a *qiṣṣa-i Yūsuf,* but the most successful epics, as that of Hamdi, were written only after Jami had given the Koranic story of Yusuf and Potiphar's wife, Zulaikha, its classical form.

24. Amir Khusrau, *Dīwān-i kāmil,* ed. Mahmud Darwish; the most comprehensive biography is still Waheed Mirza, *The Life and Works of Amir Khusrau.*

25. For the development of Persian literature in various regions of the Subcontinent see Jan Marek, "Persian Literature in India"; Annemarie Schimmel, "Islamic Literatures in India"; Abdul Ghani, *A History of Persian Language and Literature at the Mughal Court;* H. J. Sadarangani, *Persian Poets of Sind;* Girdhari L. Tikku, *Persian Poets in Kashmir 1339–1846;* T. N. Devare, *A Short History of Persian Literature at the Bahmani, the Adilshahi, and the Qūtbshahi Courts-Deccan.*

26. For the history of Urdu see Garcin de Tassy, *Histoire de la littérature Hindoue et Hindoustani;* T. G. Bailey, *History of Urdu Literature;* Ram Babu Saksena, *History of Urdu Literature;* Muhammad Sadiq, *History of Urdu Literature;* for a general survey Annemarie Schimmel, "Classical Urdu Literature."

27. Abu'l-Majd Majdud Sana'i, *Dīwān,* ed. Mudarris Razawi, p. 395.

28. "Sanā'īābād", line 86, in Sana'i, *Mathnawīhā,* ed. Mudarris Razawi, p. 55.

29. Sana'i, *Dīwān,* p. 386.

30. Trans. by E. G. Browne, *Literary History of Persia,* IV, pp. 284–97. For a modern version see Sayyid Ahmad Hatif, *Tarjiᶜband. Return Ties of Existence, A Sufi Strophic Poem.*

31. Gibb, *History of Ottoman Poetry,* V, pp. 87–95. Köprülüzade, *Eski şairlerimiz,* pp. 690–94.

32. For the *rubāᶜī,* a genre most frequently discussed in connection with the *rubāᶜiyyāt* ascribed to Omar Khayyam, see particularly Fritz Meier, *Die schöne Mahsatī.*

33. Thus Hafíz's often mistreated famous line about the *turk-i shīrāzī* is not primarily important because of its contents but rather because of the delightful rhetorical plays concealed in it:

> If that Turk of Shiraz would take my heart in his hand,
> I would give for his "hindū" [i.e., black] mole Samarqand and Bukhara.

The verse contains the contrast *Turk-Hindu,* extremely widespread in Persian and related poetry, see Annemarie Schimmel, "Turk and Hindu, a Poetical Image and Its Application to Historical Fact." It further contains three geographical names: Shiraz, Bukhara, and Samarqand, and mentions three parts of the body: mole, heart, and hand, so that a multilevel *murāʿāt an-naẓīr* is achieved which is immediately destroyed when the Shirazi Turk is transformed into a "friend" or a "barmaid," or the mole is no longer called *hindū,* but simply "black." For *hindū,* besides meaning "black," denotes also the "lowly slave," so that Hafiz claims to barter in the imperial Turkish cities Samarqand and Bukhara for a low-caste blackish slave. That we have to do primarily with concepts and not with expressions of "real" experience which would allow us to compose a biography of a classical Persian poet, has been shown by Hans Heinrich Schaeder, "Lässt sich die ʿseelische Entwicklung' des Dichters Hafis ermitteln?" against an article by Karl Stolz, "Die seelische Entwicklung des Dichters Hafis." This does not exclude the possibility of detecting very personal traits in this poetry, which are, however, filtered and distilled time and again to form an immaculate work of *art* comparable to classical miniatures, where also the twist of a person's finger, or the shape of a chin, or a particular palette helps us to discover the identity of the master, who often remains anonymous. But we should not look for *Erlebnislyrik,* in the postenlightenment sense, in this poetry.

34. For the general character of Persian poetical language see Hellmut Ritter, *Über die Bildersprache Niẓāmīs,* and Jan Rypka's review in *OLZ* (1928), col. 942–45, where he states that "it is not a decorative parallel thought, but the symbolic contents are already hidden in the matter which represents the exterior situation and is interpreted metaphorically."

35. Hujwiri/Nicholson, *Kashf al-maḥjūb,* discusses the two approaches to the world: some mystics state, "I never saw anything without seeing God therein," which points to an advanced stage of contemplation because he sees the agent only, while the statement of others, "I never see anything except God," shows that he, fully enraptured, sees only the agent; pp. 9, 330.

36. ʿAttar, *Ushturnāma,* pp. 137–38.

37. Amir Khusrau, *Kulliyāt,* p. 1087.

38. E. G. Browne, *Literary History of Persia,* III, p. 511 (including a witty anecdote connected with this verse).

39. ʿIraqi, *Kulliyāt,* p. 122 (*tarjīʿband,* part 2), translation by E. G. Browne, *Literary History of Persia,* III, p. 113. Perhaps the most famous and often quoted expression of this feeling of unity is Jami's quatrain (*Lawā'iḥ* no. 21, p. 43):

> Neighbor and confident and companion—it's all He.
> In the beggar's coarse frock and in the king's satin—it's all He.
> In the crowd of separation and in the loneliness of collectedness,
> By God, it's all He! and by God! it's all He!

40. Jami, *Dīwān-i kāmil,* ed. Hashim Riza, p. 810, *rubāʿī* no. 3.

41. For the image see Toshihiko Izutsu, "The Basic Structure of Metaphysical Thinking in Islam."

42. The most famous tale, which has been reflected in fairy tales and legends from India through the Muslim world to Scottish folklore and modern German poetry (Agnes Miegel, "Die Mär vom Ritter Manuel") is retold in Heinrich Zimmer, *Maya, Der indische Mythos.* The belief in the transforming power of water and in its rejuvenating aspect underlies, lastly, even the symbolism of baptism.

43. Rumi D 469; cf. also D 1713/17391:

> Prostrating ourselves do we go toward the sea like a torrent,
> That's why we go on the surface of the ocean, foaming [or: hand clapping; *kaf zanān* has both meanings].

Cf. also Jami, *Lawāʾiḥ* no. 25, p. 61: "Existence is an ocean, eternally billowing."

44. Nyberg, *Kleinere Schriften des Ibn ʿArabī,* p. 96.

45. ʿAttar, *Dīwān-i qaṣāʾid wa ghazaliyāt,* ed. Saʿid-i Nafisi, p. 499, no. 707.

> Go out of this ocean like rain and travel,
> For without traveling you will never become a pearl.

46. ʿAttar, *Muṣībatnāma,* ed. N. Fisal, p. 355.

47. Sana'i, *Dīwān,* p. 327.

48. Sana'i, *Ḥadīqat al-ḥaqīqa,* ed. Mudarris Razawi, I, p. 60.

49. Carl W. Ernst, *"Faith and Infidelity in Sūfism,"* pp. 119–37 deals with Hallaj's sayings.

50. For examples from Maghribi see E. G. Browne, *Literary History of Persia,* III, pp. 330–44. It is due to this kind of poetry, which became known in the West prior to other Islamic works, that most Western scholars regarded Sufism as sheer pantheism, as is evident from the very title of Tholuck's pioneering thesis of 1821, *Ssufismus sive theosophia persarum pantheistica.*

51. Yusuf Husain, *L'Inde mystique au moyen age,* p. 163.

52. Evelyn Underhill, *Mysticism,* chapter 6.

53. ʿAttar, *Muṣībatnāme,* p. 62; the expression "more costly than *al-kibrīt al-aḥmar*" occurs as an Arabic proverb, see *EI* 2d ed., IV, col. 68 (*kibrīt,* Manfred Ullmann).

54. Sana'i, *Mathnawīhā,* pp. 181–316. For the topic see Reynold A. Nicholson, *A Persian Forerunner of Dante.*

55. *Sana'i, Dīwān,* p. 486. Abu'l-Wafa Kurd died in Baghdad in 1107. Uwais al-Qarani was a legendary contemporary of the Prophet, who lived in Yemen and, becoming a pious Muslim without ever having met the Prophet, is the

prototype of the *uwaisī* mystic, who enters the Path without formal initiation through a living master.

56. ^{c}Attar, *Manṭiq uṭ-ṭair,* p. 234; see also *Muṣībatnāma,* p. 63.

57. Muhammad Aslah, *Tadhkira-i shu^{c}arā-i Kashmīr,* ed. Sayyid Hussamuddin Rashdi, I, p. 370.

58. ^{c}Attar, *Muṣībatnāma,* p. 9.

59. Nizami, *Khusrau Shīrīn,* pp. 143, 144.

60. ^{c}Attar, *Dīwān,* p. 383

61. ^{c}Urfi, *Kulliyāt,* ed. ^{c}Ali Jawahiri, p. 305. For the conviction that neither the beloved nor love have an end see the anecdote about Dhu'n-Nun, who "met a woman at the sea shore and asked her: ^{c}What is the end of love?' And she answered: ^{c}O simpleton, love has no end!' And he asked: ^{c}Why?' She said: ^{c}Because the Beloved has no end!' " ^{c}Attar, *Tadhkirat al-auliyā,* I, p. 123.

62. Sana'i, *Dīwān,* pp. 806–7; cf. Browne, *Literary History of Persia,* II, pp. 321–22.

63. ^{c}Attar, *Ushturnāma,* p. 173; ibid., p. 137, the puppet player says:

> Whoever found my secret became demented,
> All at once he became estranged from intellect.

64. Sana'i, *Ḥadīqa,* IV, p. 300; cf. *Dīwān,* p. 57. Ghazzali's *Tahāfut al-falāsifa* contains a sharp criticism of Avicenna's philosophy and has probably affected the attitude of the mystics, particularly in Iran; besides, legends tell how the Prophet informed Majduddin Baghdadi (d. 1209) in a dream that Avicenna wanted to reach God without his mediation, and so he fell in the Fire. Jami, *Nafaḥāt al-uns,* p. 427.

65. Muhammad Iqbal, particularly in his *Payām-i Mashriq.* See p. 122, the poem which contrasts Avicenna and Rumi, and p. 119, the bookworm that dwells in Ibn Sina's pages and therefore lacks real experience of life and love.

66. Sana'i, *Dīwān,* p. 827.

67. Gesudaraz, *Diwān anīs al-^{c}ushshāq,* ed. Sayyid ^{c}Ata Husain, p. 9.

68. Ibid., p. 67; cf. Baqli, *^{c}Abhar al-^{c}āshiqīn,* sec. 79:

> The vision of the cosmos is the *qibla* of the ascetics,
> And the vision of Adam is the *qibla* of the lovers.

69. ^{c}Ali ibn Ahmad ad-Dailami, *Kitāb ^{c}aṭf al-alif al-ma'lūf ilā 'l-lām al-ma^{c}ṭūf,* ed. Jean-Claude Vadet, sec. 28; for the whole problem see Ritter, *Meer der Seele,* pp. 434–503.

70. Thus al-Hakim at-Tirmidhi, quoted in Nwyia, *Exégèse coranique,* p. 129.

71. Hujwiri/Nicholson, *Kashf al-maḥjūb,* p. 416 says: "Looking at youth and associating with them are forbidden practices and anyone who declares this to be allowable is an unbeliever!" The Hanbalite Ibn Qayyim al-Jauziyya

goes even farther. He writes: "The immoral among mystic lovers commit a more serious sin than either idolators or sodomites. They combine the transgression of the two groups—worshipping their minions and copulating with their idols," quoted in Joseph N. Bell, *Love Theories in Later Hanbalite Islam,* p. 143. See Ritter, *Meer der Seele,* particularly pp. 459 ff., and Ritter, "Philologika VII, Arabische und persische Schriften über die profane und die mystische Liebe."

72. Sana'i, *Dīwān,* p. 182 in a *qaṣīda.*

73. Massignon, *La Passion . . . d'al-Ḥallāj,* p. 799.

74. Rumi, D 537/5723. Although Rumi's mystical friend, Shamsuddin of Tabriz, is reported to have sharply rebuked Auhaduddin Kirmani for his *shāhidbāzī* (see Jami, *Nafaḥāt al-uns,* p. 590), *shāhidbāzī* became a legitimate topic in Persian mystical and semimystical poetry. Auhaduddin Kirmani is the most prominent exponent of this trend although in his case, as with other Sufis, it is not always certain whether the quatrains ascribed to him are really his. See Bernd Manuel Weischer-Peter L. Wilson, *Heart's Witness: The Sufi Quatrains of Auḥaduddīn Kirmānī.*

75. Ruzbihan says in the *ᶜAbhar al-ᶜāshiqīn,* sec. 4: "At the primordial covenant the souls flew in the world of Divine Love with the wings of human love," and sec. 112: "The journey [of the lovers] is nothing but Reality, the collyrium of their eyes is nothing but the dust of the street of the Divine Law."

76. Ikram, *Armaghān-i Pāk,* p. 135, but the expression *kajkulāh* is already found in ᶜAttar's *Dīwān,* ghazal on p. 27.

77. Goethe, *West-Östlicher Divan:* Buch Hafis, "Wink."

78. ᶜAttar, *Tadhkirat al-auliyā,* II, p. 193.

79. Sana'i, *Dīwān,* p. 488. The problem of the relationship between lover and beloved has been discussed by Persian, Turkish, and Indian poets over and over again; its central point is that the lover has to love without any hope of fulfillment. As Hujwiri/Nicholson, *Kashf al-maḥjūb,* p. 136, says: "It is a law that when the lover advances, the beloved retires. If the lover is satisfied with love alone, then the beloved draws near. In truth, the lover has honor only while he has no desire of union." This forms the topic of most Persian works on love, and is poetically expressed in the contrast of *nāz* and *niyāz,* coquettry and petitioning, "for the beloved ones are all created from the essence of coquettish pride," as a late Indo-Persian poet says (Mir ᶜAli Shir Qaniᶜ, *Maqālāt ash-shuᶜarā,* p. 439). In fact, I was once told that *nāz* and *maḥbūb* (beloved) are as it were interchangeable because the two words have the same numerical value, namely 58!

80. Sana'i, *Dīwān,* p. 870.

81. ᶜIraqi, *Kulliyāt,* Lamaᶜāt, no. 22.

82. Hafiz, *Dīwān,* ed. Hermann Brockhaus, no. 292. For the concept of the Sun at Midnight see Henry Corbin, *L'homme de lumière dans le Soufisme iranien.*

83. ᶜIraqi, *Kulliyāt,* Lamaᶜāt, no. 2.
84. ᶜAttar, *Muṣībatnāme,* p. 10.
85. Ibid., p. 287.
86. Sana'i, *Dīwān,* qaṣīda, p. 41.
87. ᶜAttar, *Muṣībatnāme,* p. 63; cf. ibid., p. 332:

Love is to become naughted in the beloved,
To die, means for him becoming alive.

The emphasis on annihilation, *fanā',* "Entwerden," and becoming empty in order to be able to receive the Divine is a central topic of mystical poetry: the heart has to be cleaned and emptied so that the *dulcis hospes animae* can dwell there. Seyyed H. Nasr has extended this idea also to Islamic art in his article, "The Significance of the Void in the Art and Architecture of Islamic Persia." The Koranic statement, "You are the poor and God is the Rich" (Sura 35/16) reminds man constantly of his poverty before the Lord, who owns everything and before whom the creature is so poor and insignificant that it disappears: "When *faqr* becomes perfect, it is God," as a widespread saying claims. Thus, Sufism reached an equation of *faqr,* "poverty," and *fanā',* "annihilation," which was poetically expressed by ᶜAttar in the last valley of the *Manṭiq uṭ-ṭair.* See also chapter 3, note 351.

88. Ghalib, *Urdu Dīwān,* ed. Hamid ᶜAli Khan, p. 174. The liver is the seat of emotions and appears in Persian poetry often where we would expect the heart.

89. Goethe, *Noten und Abhandlungen zum West-Östlichen Divan,* "Despotie." The head as a ball, and the tresses as a mallet are stock images, pointing to the willful submission of the lover to every whim of the cruel beloved.

90. ᶜAttar, *Muṣībatnāma,* p. 14.

91. Cf. the description of the Valley of Love in the *Manṭiq uṭ-ṭair:* "Lover is he who is like fire," p. 222.

92. Rumi, M III 1259–69. For the anamnesis of the story see Fritz Meier, "Das Problem der Natur im esoterischen Monismus des Islam, Exkurs: Zur Geschichte der Legende von den Blinden und dem Elefanten," p. 174. Sana'i's version trans. by E. G. Browne, *Literary History of Persia,* II, p. 319. Shah Waliullah uses a similar parable but speaks of the blind and a tree, *Lamaḥāt,* ed. Ghulam Mustafa Qasimi, p. 4.

93. M I 130; the expression *sirr-i dilbarān* has also become the title of more than one book dealing with mystical metaphors, see Hz. Shah Sayyid Muhammad Shauqi, *Sirr-i dilbarān.* The importance of correct symbols has been well expressed by Henry Corbin; "Le symbole garantit la correspondence de deux univers qui sont à des niveaux ontologiques différents: il est le moyen, et le seul moyen, de pénétration dans l'invisible, dans le monde du mystère, dans l'ésotérique." ("Mystique et humour chez Sohrawardi Shaykh al-ishrāq," p.

30). A contemporary Sufi exegesis of the common imagery: Dr. Javad Nurbakhsh, *What the Sufis Say.*

94. After Browne, *Literary History of Persia,* III, p. 117.

95. Bu ᶜAli Qalandar, *Dīwān,* p. 19.

96. See *ERE* VII 739 ff., "Kissing"; and RGG, 3d. ed. IV, col. 189–190 ("Kuss").

97. Gertrud Spiess, *Maḥmūd von Ghazna bei Farīd-ud'dīn ᶜAṭṭar.*

98. Herbert Duda, *Farhād und Schīrīn, Zur Geschichte eines literarischen Sagenstoffes.* Farhad, the luckless lover, who was cheated by Prince Khusrau, has become in modern progressive writings from Iqbal to Nazim Hikmet the representative of the oppressed working class.

99. Mir Taqi Mir, quoted in Dr. Syed Abdullah, *Naqd-i Mīr,* p. 117.

100. Sanā'i, *Dīwān,* pp. 30 ff. For the development of the ancient idea of the soul bird, known from primitive religions as from ancient Egypt, in the Islamic environment see Ignaz Goldziher, "Der Seelenvogel im islamischen Volksglauben"; however he does not deal with the later, mystical development. In Turkey, one still uses the expression *can kuşu uçtu,* "His soul bird has flown away," when someone has died.

101. ᶜAttar's epic is based on Ghazzali's *Risālat aṭ-ṭair* to which, however, he gave a wonderful, deeply moving end, see Ritter, *Meer der Seele,* p. 42.

102. Rumi M II 1131 ff.

103. The parrot occurs in the Indian tradition usually as a wise but often somewhat misogynic bird, as in the *Tūṭīnama,* which was reworked by the Chishti Sufi Zia'uddin Nakhshabi in North India in 1330. It became widespread in the Islamic world, and was decorated with miniatures. The most famous example is in Cleveland, see Mūhammad A. Simsar, *The Cleveland Museum of Art's Tutiname: Tales of a Parrot.* The bird's aversion to women is also reflected in some Indo-Pakistani folk tales. In other traditions, such as the Ismaᶜili classic *Dasamō Avatār* it is the parrot that introduces the wife of a demon into the mysteries of the true religion, the *satpanth* (see Gulshan Khakee, *The Dasamō Avatār*). He also teaches an Indian princess Islamic doctrines in the anonymous *Ḥujjat al-Hind* of the seventeenth century; in this work, the intelligent bird even recites long passages from Najmuddin Daya's *Mirṣād al-ᶜibād.* The green color of the parrot reminded the Sufi poets of the green robes in Paradise, and his gift for languages earned him the constant epithet "sugar chewing," so that "parrot" and "sugar" are usually found together in verse.

104. Sana'i, *Dīwān,* p. 371.

105. Annemarie Schimmel, "Rose und Nachtigall."

106. Massignon, "La vie et les oeuvres de Rûzbehân Baqlî," p. 238.

107. Irène Mélikoff, "La fleur de la souffrance, recherche sur le sense symbolique de *lâle* dans la poésie mystique turco-iranienne." In Iqbal's work, *lāla* represents the independent, vigorous plant that appears in the middle of

the desert, resembling in its shape and color the flames which Moses saw on Mt. Sinai; it is seen as a positive contrast to the traditional rose which lives in well-trimmed gardens, and thus becomes a symbol of man's striving against heavy odds to realize himself. In Turkey, the fondness of poets and painters for the tulip was explained to me by mystically minded friends with the remark that *lāla, hilāl* ("crescent"), and *Allāh* all consisted of the same four letters and had the same numerical value, namely 66, hence the tulip became a kind of religious cipher.

108. Annemarie Schimmel "Schriftsymbolik im Islam."

109. As Shelley says:

> Life, like a dome of many-colored glass
> Stains the white radiance of eternity.

Persian poets were always aware that the manifestation of the Divine needs some dense, material locus—*kathāfat,* density, is necessary for *laṭāfat* to become visible, as steel, polished to utmost clarity, can reflect the divine light.

110. William James, *The Varieties of Religious Experience.* p. 297.

111. Gesudaraz, *Dīwān Anīs al-ᶜushshāq,* p. 40. The poem is inscribed around the interior of the grand dome over his tomb in Gulbarga.

112. A good introduction to the imagery of Persian poetry, particularly the "magi," is Bausani, *Letteratura neo-persiana,* where a number of images are discussed.

113. Hujwiri/Nicholson, *Kashf al-maḥjūb,* p. 187.

114. See Kurt Goldammer, "Wege aufwärts, Wege abwärts," p. 51.

115. Rumi, M I 3192 ff.

116. Trans. by E. G. Browne, "Sufism," in *Religious Systems of the World,* p. 329.

117. D 468/4976.

3. SUN TRIUMPHAL—LOVE TRIUMPHANT: MAULANA RUMI AND THE METAPHORS OF LOVE

1. D 826/8638.

2. The literature about Jalaluddin is almost inexhaustible; see the bibliography in Annemarie Schimmel, *The Triumphal Sun;* the bibliography here s.v. Arberry, Bürgel, Gölpīnarlī, Meyerovitch, Nicholson, and Ritter. The oldest biography is by Faridun Sipahsalar, *Risāla dar aḥwāl-i Maulānā Jalāladdīn-i Rūmī;* then follows Aflaki's *Manāqib al- ᶜārifīn,* not very successfully trans. by Clément Huart, *Les Saints des Derviches tourneurs.*

3. Part translation in verse by Pir Imam Shah, Lahore 1911, fly leaf. Another Panjabi verse translation by Maulana Muhammad Shahuddin, Lahore, 1939 (see L. D. Barnett, *Panjabi,* p. 39).

4. Remarkably, one of Rumi's first interpreters in the West, the Austrian

orientalist Joseph von Hammer-Purgstall, has clearly stated the nonpantheistic character of the *Mathnawī* (*Bericht über den zu Kairo im Jahre 1835 erschienenen türkischen Kommentar des Mesnewi Dschelaleddin Rumi's*). Unfortunately, this interesting study has never been mentioned by any later student of Rumi in Europe.

5. Baha'uddin Walad, *Ma*ᶜ*ārif,* 4 vols., ed. Badiᶜuzzaman Furuzanfar; a few chapters from this work trans. in Arthur J. Arberry, *Aspects of Islamic Civilization*, pp. 227–255.

6. D 940/9918–20; *lā ḥaula,* "There is no power and strength but in God!," an exclamation uttered on a sudden emergency; *tauba,* "Repentance!"

7. D 2970/31525

8. D 2329/24655; in the next verse: "Your face is the sun in Aries."

9. D 2893; see the editor's quotations from Aflaki, *Manāqib.*

10. D 2630/27890:

> He is the king of ghazals, and all are his servants—
> Every verse of his opens [the door of] wishes, Efendi!

D 3073/32742:

> Know that I am the servant of poetry, for poetry is what *you* are saying,
> For you are the innermost soul of Israfil and the sound of the trumpet.

11. One has to remember that a new name is usually given at an initiation, be it into an order, or a conversion or baptism; Maulana, by assuming Shamsuddin's name for his poetical activity, has as it were died to himself and found a new life in the mystical beloved.

12. D 600/6330, last verse; two verses earlier: "Sun in Aries."

13. D 103/1192, last line, after a line with *khāmūsh,* "Silent!"

14. M III 3842.

15. D 757/2916–34, beginning:

> Describe that *makhdūm* even if the envious person becomes angry . . .

16. D 144/1631, in the middle.

17. D 71/846; Shamsuddin in the first line.

18. D 1196/12728, with a typical image:

> O Jalaluddin, give up dictating, talk!
> For no cheetah can enter the running course of that lion!

Shams is mentioned in vv. 12723, 12724.

19. Cf. D 24/243:

> When you mention his name, consider repetition necessary.

Then follows Shamsuddin's name in the next line. In 2229/23639 Rumi calls the friend's name "the nourishment of his intoxicated soul." Cf. for a modern example of this "magic of the name," of which the Sufis in their *dhikr* were very well aware, Gertrude Stein's remark, "If you love a name then saying that name any number of times only makes you love it more, more violently more persistently more tormentedly," quoted in Philip Wheelright, *The Burning Fountain,* p. 372.

20. D 1081/11369–70; the whole poem continues like this.

21. D 2807/29786–87, middle; in the beginning Shamsuddin is mentioned twice.

22. D 2807/29775; D 24/280; D 1374/14533 and many more, which deserve closer study.

23. D 450/4746.

24. D 2768/29430; cf. also D 2557/27149, second-to-last line:

> Shams is the purity of the Islamic soul

25. D 659/6876, second-to-last line.

26. D 882/9231:

> Infidelity became black-dressed, Muhammad's light arrived;
> The drum of *baqā* (eternal life) was beaten, the eternal kingdom arrived.

Cf. also D 341/3680, 3685:

> Muhammad came back from his ascension,
> Jesus arrived from the fourth heaven . . .

In the next line: "Once more the moon was split" (Sura 54/1).

27. D 409/4342.

28. D 25/298.

29. D 462/4910.

30. D 792/8292; cf. also D 1966/20746:

> If you want the complete fragrance and color of the Ahmadian wine,
> Rest at the gate of Tabriz for a moment, O caravan-leader!

31. D 816/8529, second-to-last line, no *takhalluṣ*.

32. D 807/8450 end.

33. D 1464/15474.

34. The scene has been painted several times, see Schimmel, *Triumphal Sun,* p. 147, a miniature from Husain Baiqara's *Majālis al-ᶜushshāq,* preserved in Berlin, Staatsbibliothek Preussischer Kulturbesitz; another interesting representation in Dr. A. Süheyl Ünver, ed., *Sevâkib-i manâkib: Mevlâna'dan hatĭralar,* p. 41, no. 17, from a manuscript in the Pierpont Morgan Library, New York, M 476, fol. 219 b.

35. D 639/6669–70, 6679.

36. D 797/8334; in 8339 Shams-i Tabriz is mentioned.

37. D 795/8306, first line:

> It was the time that a light (*żiā*) arrived from the sun,
> That a flag from Rum came to the negro "Night,"

where Salahuddin is mentioned in the end.

38. M II 3; see D 2864/30414 end: According to Aflaki, Sultan Walad mentioned that this poem was recited when Maulana chose Husamuddin as his *khalīfa*. See also D 2519/26699, where Husamuddin is called *żiā* in a longish, rather colorless poem, the preceding lines being:

> The canopus of Shams-i Tabriz does not shine in Yemen.

39. D 1210/12875, Salahuddin's name in the first line.

40. D 738 describes how everything is in ecstasy, longing for Shamsuddin, until line 7760 introduces the *anā'l-ḥaqq*. Important also is D 145/1645, where Rumi calls Husamuddin to write down his words in the second-to-last line, the last one bearing again the *takhalluṣ* Shams. A poem in which Husamuddin is fully accepted as Beloved is 533, with the *radīf*, "The intoxicated send greetings," which ends:

> O Shah Husamuddin, O pride of all saints,
> O you with whom the souls are acquainted—the intoxicated send greetings!

41. D 1839; the poem deserves a full analysis.

42. D 2364, *radīf*, "has wept."

43. M I 120–42.

44. D 3098 with the *takhalluṣ* Husamuddin may have been written during this time; the second-to-last line, 33043, says:

> Be silent, even though all the silver-breasted ones
> Write with gold whatever you have said.

45. D 2098/22165.

46. Translation by Arthur John Arberry, *Discourses of Rumi*. London 1961.

47. *Maktūbāt*, ed. Yusuf Jamshidipur and Ghulamhusain Amin; an excellent annotated Turkish translation by Abdulbaki Gölpĭnarlĭ, *Mevlâna'nin Mektublarĭ*.

48. D 1722/18026.

49. D 1326/14035–36.

50. D 683 with the *takhalluṣ* Shamsuddin; these verses are inscribed on his sarcophagus.

51. 1836/19300:

> O idol, the cooked one does not ferment [any more],
> Don't boil [me any more], for I am cooked!
> For from out the kettle my smoke goes up to the sky.

I.e., he is completely evaporated from himself. The image of the water in the kettle—which is put on the fire and at first makes noise, then finally becomes silent as steam, the form in which it comes closest to the nature of fire—has been used by Shah Waliullah to point to man's stages of approximation to God (*Saṭaᶜāt,* no. 40.)

52. See chapter 1, note 3. The poem is D 1949/20486. For the designation *Turk* for Shamsuddin cf. D 2499/26446:

> The mouth of Love laughs that I call him Turk,
> For he himself breathes into us; for we are the flute and he the flute player!

See also D 1641/17184; cf. D 1375/14549 second-to-last line, and D 1344/14222:

> Now sit and move your head and say "Yes"—
> Shams-i Tabriz will show you the secrets of the *ghazal!*

53. D 1547/16251; cf. D 2393/25282: "I spoke out of the skin," and D 538/5735:

> The heart spoke nicely this *ghazal,*
> Being out of itself from the primordial wine.

54. D 2696/28604.
55. D 35/463 end, and passim.
56. M I 1727; cf. D 2251/23859.
57. D 477/5073, second-to-last line of a long poem.
58. D 1661/17408.
59. D 981/10382–83, for it comes from the "heat of the mind."
60. D 2838/30144.
61. D 253/2857; cf. D 2025/21370.
62. D 1828/19217.
63. D 1238/13129. But he ends with the sigh:

> But what can I do? It's an old rule:
> The ocean is quiet, and the waves boiling.

Cf. D 1728/18111: "Come like the full moon and complete this!" I found a similar statement connected with Salahuddin only once, D 483/5155.

64. D 2100/22190. In the next, final verse he asks Shamsuddin to inspire him with befitting expressions.

65. D 2215/23494, a poem with the *radīf,* "Don't go!" Cf. D 2006/21211, end: "I would like to say another fifty verses," or D 2493/26355:

> The rose bush of the soul speaks in your love;
> If I were not afraid I would become like a lily, all my head tongues!

66. D 470/4998, last line.

67. D 837/8756; cf. D 1847/9487–88 (middle), D 1638/7159; grotesque is D 1188/12655:

> Quiet! This lions' milk is the light of the inner sense;
> From letters it becomes cheese for the need of cheetahs!

The cheetah, in Persian poetical tradition at least since Sana'i, is supposed to live on cheese, i.e., he is tame and meek and is kept on a meatless diet days before he is used for the hunt; he is thus contrasted to the blood-drinking, free lion. Words are as much inferior to the real sense as is a tame cheetah to a roaring lion. Another way to point to man's incapability of expressing his experience in words is, for example, D 1926/20274:

> When Love tells its own perfection,
> Man has to become a stutterer.

68. D 2667.

69. D 745/7823–29 (second-to-last line).

70. D 1946/20538.

71. D 485/5186 (second-to-last line).

72. D 2432/25640–41.

73. D 1650/17281.

74. D 49/621, according to the footnote, an allusion to a well-known anecdote.

75. D 2761/29346–47, one of Rumi's delightful personifications of the heart, which deserves special study:

> I said to my heart: "Are you thus well?"
> The heart screamed: "Yes, yes!"
> My heart took up a little rebeck
> And played it—that means, "Yes, I'm fine!"

76. D 2465/26066–67.

77. D 2309/24502, the beginning of an intoxicated poem in which also a gypsy who plays the *barbaṭ* (a kind of big lute) appears (24507).

78. D 1088/11448; another allusion to *jūᶜ al-baqar,* D 1016/10721.

79. D 45/584.

80. D 2651/28127.

81. D 551/5852. In the mystical language, God's garment means His qualities, contrary to the unqualified Numen; every trace of clothing is an impediment for full union when the soul wants to become one with the One; the Upanishads used the image of loving union for the state of highest spiritual bliss. Among the Muslim mystics Rumi, following his father's example, uses the imagery of "becoming naked" more frequently than any other poet; in the

medieval Christian tradition, Mechtild of Magdeburg is noted for her uninhibited expressions about nakedness of the soul, bridal bed, and embraces. See Heiler, *Erscheinungsformen,* p. 221.

82. D 2989/31753. In Persian poetical language, stones generally occur in two sets of images: they smash the glass, or the bottle, or they are flung by children at Majnun, the lovesick lover, as Persian miniature painters have sometimes represented; see S. Cary Welch, *Wonders of the Age,* no. 61, by Mir Sayyid ᶜAli.

83. D 2980/31632. For Rumi's technical skill, which enabled him to use complicated rhetorical devices in his spontaneous verse see J. Christoph Bürgel, "Lautsymbolik und funktionelles Wortspiel bei Rūmī."

84. D 2701/28655.

85. The allusion is of course to the well known *ḥadīth:* "This world is the seedbed of the Otherworld," which forms a pivot of Rumi's ethics. Cf. also D 2748/29228:

> Hear from the green tongue of each leaf
> That what you plant grows from the Unseen

and also D 2638/27999 where the poet asks Love to give to the earth whatever it deems right, "since the earth brings forth only what has been sown."

86. See for this feeling D 2549/27044:

> I search in both worlds a simile so that I could speak of you—
> But, O my Lord, I don't find it; you do not say whom you resemble!

87. D 1499/15800 end; cf. D 2739/29121; D 2131/22552; D 1649/17275.

88. D 1735/18197; cf. D 1157/12286.

89. M I 112–15.

90. D 213/2394.

91. D 1311; D 1308; D 1309.

92. D 232/2606, first line.

93. D 991/10484, end.

94. D 1402/14851–54, in the middle. Another charming dialogue with Love in D 2219:

> Last night I became crazy; Love saw me and said:
> "I have come, don't scream, don't tear your dress, don't speak . . ."
> etc.

95. D 2138/22624–41; *namak,* "salt," means also "elegance, charm!" Its quality to preserve organic matter by transforming it into salt has offered some Sufis a metaphor for man's annihilation in the "salt" of the Divine Beloved, and "the donkey that fell in a salt-mine" occurs from ᶜAttar to Mir Dard in mystical discourses as a symbol of "deified" man; see M II 1344; M VI 1858 f.

96. D 798/8344; D 1649/17274.

97. D 3010/31985.
98. D 3017/32070.
99. D 924/9735.
100. D 1487/15685. One is immediately reminded of the *ḥadīth* according to which "Man is between two fingers of the Merciful, who turns him as He pleases," a saying which was often poetically interpreted as man being like a pen in God's fingers (see Schimmel, *Triumphal Sun,* "Divine Calligraphy").
101. D 743/7808.
102. D 460/4886. The *tughrā* is the artistically elaborated hand sign of the ruler at the beginning of a document; it found its finest expression in Ottoman Turkey, see Ernst Kühnel, "Die osmanische Tughra." Nowadays, *tughrā* is the general term for interlaced patterns made of proper names or pious formulas.
103. D 232/2626, end after two Arabic verses; cf. D 2571/27298:

> O Love, you alone, whether you are kindness or wrath—
> Your *surnā* [a kind of oboe] complains in Arabic and Suryani.

104. D 2701/28654; D 3044/32375. The whole longish poem with its *radīf:* "What a calamity, what an affliction you are!" enumerates the contradictory aspects of Love.
105. D 698/7277; D 459/4866 says "It has neither beginning nor end," but D 183/2037: "The last station of Love is better than the beginning."
106. D 958/10110.
107. D 633/6604; cf. D 1014/10706 (Arabic):

> Travel on the roads of Love with me—
> Don't fear any error or watchdog!

108. D 983/10401.
109. D 2674/28369–72.
110. D 2392/25270 beginning; D 2163/22907.
111. D 190/2108; cf. another twist of the pun *kūh-kāh* D 58/713:

> When Love suddenly came, I was like a mountain, *kūh,*
> And became straw, *kāh,* for the ruler's horse.

112. D 1690/17713; cf. also D 13/148 a poem about roses and rose sugar, where Rumi explains:

> By "rose sugar" we mean God's grace and our existence:
> Our existence is like iron, and God's grace the magnet.

113. D 478/5089; D 790/8258 ff.; D 3099/33045, first line.
114. D 27/336–37; M III 3637; M V 3597 f.
115. D 429/4534.
116. D 2956/31390.
117. D 1657/17366.

118. D 863/9028, the Koranic quotation is slightly twisted.

119. D 2810/29838.

120. D 2/24. *Alif* denotes the straight, upright stature, while *dāl* is a bent letter which is often compared to an old, sad person.

121. D 926/9749.

122. D 1586/16627.

123. D 2785/29610.

124. M I 8.

125. D 1138/12063. For the image of fire see Heiler, *Erscheinungsformen,* p. 48 ff., with numerous examples from German mystics such as Meister Eckhart and Gertrude of Helfta; see also Richard Rolle:

> The flame of Love, who might it thole [= bear],

and his remark "luf es hard as hell," *Oxford Book of English Mystical Verse,* p. 4.

126. D 2922/31021.

127. D 2992/31799; D 2043/21540; D 368/3947.

128. D 1733/18170; cf. D 2479/26230.

129. D 1077/11333; for "fire of the face" see also D 2363/24988 and many others.

130. D 1573/16502; cf. D 1696/17772.

131. D 831/8682; cf. D 2994/31831, D 580/6142; for fire and forest, D 2912/30927, and a combination of the forest motif and Abraham, D 567/6021; the classical verse M I 10.

132. D 2031/21438; D 937/9888.

133. D 2519/26655; purification through fire belongs to ancient religious rites, cf. Origen's *purgatorius ignis,* German *Fegfeuer* for purgatory. See G. van der Leeuw, *Phänomenologie,* p. 53, esp. Baptism through fire, etc. Angelus Silesius sings:

> Wo Gott ein Feuer ist, so ist mein Herz der Herd,
> Auf welchem er den Stolz der Eitelkeit verzehrt.

Cherubinischer Wandersmann I, 66.

134. D 588/6212.

135. D 1308/13856. Angelus Silesius, too, sees God as "ein lauter Blitz," a pure lightning, II, 146.

136. D 2359/24958.

137. D 1555/16343.

138. D 2949/31322; D 2524/26766; D 2539/26958 (dry wood); D 2354/24910 (crumbs in fire).

139. D 246/2765.

140. D 2973/31556; D 491/5227; cf. D 1002/10580: "the glowing charcoal of your love."

141. D 2919/31000.

142. D 601/6336; D 1733/18170, and often in the *Mathnawī*.

143. D 2043/21544; D 338/3658. An early poem, D 2811/29843, where Shams' name occurs in the first line, has a beautiful pun on *parwāna*, "moth" and "Prime Minister":

> I requested from the candle of his love a piece of bread;
> He said: "Write a *tauqīᶜ* [diploma] for him for *parwānagī*, [i.e., the position of a moth, or of a Prime Minister].

That means, love either immolates or promotes to the highest offices those who approach it like humble beggars. A similar pun on *parwāna* in D 2803/29746. Another turn of the image is in D 1431/15141: "He burns the thought of both worlds like moths."

144. D 366/3922; cf. 33/441 (Arabic):

> Love is the lamp of the evening,
> Separation is the cook of the intestines.

For *shamᶜ* [candle] see D 743/7806.

145. D 2560/27187.

146. D 2690/28525–26; cf. D 1940/20417; D 2636/27964 with a pun on *ᶜuqāb*, "eagle."

147. M I 120; D 2274/24131 (Arabic): "Love has a light the like of which the sun has not"; *khūrshīd* D 2224/23605; D 816/8523; D 95/1060.

148. D 306/3356.

149. D 3054/32514: "transform the dark night into day by remembering Love"; cf. D 2905/30871.

150. D 2901/20828–29; cf. D 660/6891:

> When the stone heart of Love becomes soft,
> [Love] can transform the heart, if it be stone, into a jewel.

151. D 2429/25592.

152. D 1555/16344; cf. D 624/6515, beginning; D 733/7695, beginning; D 2970/31524: "the body is like dust, the soul like steam before the light of his sun." For the motif of the sun see Heiler, *Erscheinungsformen*, pp. 51–55. A beautiful contrast, which sounds almost like a line by Rumi, is used by Mechtild who speaks of "die heisse Sonne deiner lebendigen Gottheit," as contrasted to the "süsser Regen deiner Menschheit," God's *jalāl* being manifested in the scorching sun, his *jamāl* in the gentle rain (*Der stumme Jubel*, [Bonn 1926,] p. 77.

153. D 686/7132.

154. D 449/4734; cf. D 2574/27342.

155. D 52/644; D 821/8578.

156. D 1965/20732; D 1954/20636; D 310/3397; D 461/4893; D 935/9861; D 881/9222; D 1068/11249; D 2725/28947; D 1719/17997; D 798/8342:

> Love is a branch of the ocean that comes into the heart,
> The place for that ocean and the pearl is not a narrow breast!

D 2690/28534:

> I am that water which the sand of Love has swallowed—
> What sand! Rather, an ocean without shore!

157. D 1931/20298–300; D 3018/32079 "ocean of fire."

158. D 1096/11582.

159. D 270/3042.

160. D 1597/16716; cf. M I 16.

161. D 3018. Other visions of the ocean, D 2005, D 1839, D 1843 and passim; cf. also Daquqi's vision in M III 1985 ff.

162. 1931/20298.

163. D 729/7664.

164. D 2443/25792. In v. 25786 the Prophet ("O you mercy for the worlds!") is addressed as "granting pearls from the Ocean of Certitude to the dust-born creatures, and peace to the fishes," then the ocean-imagery continues briefly and tapers off. Cf. also D 2944/31280.

165. D 2980/31638; cf. M II 1366 f., also M V 199.

166. D 1433/15170. Bath houses were often decorated with wall paintings; hence the "picture in the bath house" became a topos to express something immobile and soulless. See for the Arabic tradition Heinz Grotzfeld, *Das Bad im arabisch-islamischen Mittelalter,* pp. 44–51.

167. D 1672/17520. For the motif see Annemarie Schimmel, "Der Regen als Symbol in der Religionsgeschichte."

168. D 2392/25273.

169. D 624/6525; D 1124/11868; D 3106/33130.

170. D 629/6563; D 2213/23470; D 535/5692; D 1129/11909; D 141/1609:

> The body always says to the soul: "Beware of his love!"
> The soul says to it: "How could one shun the fountain of life?"

171. D 1250/13243; but 2391/25264: "The Noah of your love."

172. D 566/16451.

173. D 1308/13857.

174. D 2400/25351.

175. D 928/9776.

176. D 455/4813.

177. D 536/5706: "The eyes of the lovers are like rain clouds behind which the moon is hidden." Cf. D 2598/27559.

178. D 2970/31523.

179. D 132/1521.

180. D 2103/22212.

181. D 888/9316; D 958/10109; D 3055/32522; D 197/2167, and many others. D 666/6953, beginning: "The meadow has no other work but your love," but mark D 2005/21201, last line:

> Shams-i Tabriz is for the garden of Love
> Moisture and growing and gardener.

182. D 2177/23085; D 78/902.

183. D 2746/29197.

184. D 886/9279, a poem in which the *lūlīs,* the cheerful but dangerous gypsies, appear. The plane tree is in Persian poetry always imagined to have hands since its leaves suggest the shape of an open hand; hence, the plane tree is supposed to hold wine cups, or jewelry, or clap its hands in enraptured dance. Likewise, the cypress is the ideal symbol of the graceful, slender beloved; both trees together form a perfect *murāᶜāt an-naẓīr.* For the whole set of images see Schimmel, "A Spring Day in Konya."

185. D 1967/20661.

186. D 395/4183.

187. D 2415/25486–87.

188. D 338/3662; D 1702/17818; D 647/6759=652/6804.

189. D 2474/26169.

190. D 470/4993.

191. D 505/5388.

192. D 2494/26367; a whole poem on Damascus as a concrete city, D 1493.

193. D 2634/27942. Egypt was a major sugar exporting country; the combination of this Egyptian sugar with the Biblical-Koranic story of Joseph, interpreted as the lovely beloved, is commonplace in Persian poetry. D 2392/25271:

> My soul has eaten so much sugar from the Egypt of Love:
> From my complaint it has blown sugar into the reed.

Combinations of the reed flute and the sugarcane (both *nay* in Persian) are frequent in Rumi's work; he sometimes adds the *qalam,* the reed pen, to this group and invents strange cross relations. See also D 2996/31848.

194. D 2634/27941 and often; several times this Baghdad is contrasted, for reasons unknown to me, with Hamadhan.

195. D 1712/17931.

196. D 1063/11221.

197. D 2276/24170, a dancing poem with the *radīf pā kūfta* "have stamped their feet"; D 436/4590, a street "where calamity is"; D 451/4760; D 2188/23217:

> Leave the *kū kū* ["Where where?"]
> Come to Love's *kū* ["street"]!

198. D 2350/24858–59.

199. D 3098/33038, a poem for Husamuddin.

200. D 2997/31867, a beautiful poem about the sky which turns, like Jalaluddin himself, out of love around the sun, or may be a pilgrim who, in his dark blue *iḥrām,* circumambulates the Kaᶜba, the House of God.

201. D 332/2589, 93.

202. D 2956/31392.

203. D 374/4013.

204. D 374/4015; D 2203/23364: fragrance comes from the cave of Love.

205. D 901/9452.

206. D 3073/32747–48.

207. D 2196/23305: the parrot Soul does not leave the sugar and the almonds of this snare. See also D 1537/16157; D 2918/30982; D 121/1377; D 66/780; D 68/804, beginning.

208. D 721/7577.

209. D 728/7641.

210. D 919/9680.

211. D 2793/29678.

212. D 1887/19850; cf. also *radīf ᶜishq.*

213. D 2796/29710. Three lines earlier, 29707: "The religion of the 72 communities be sacrificed for you"; cf. D 1394/14783; D 607/6389; D 1661/17410, "the greatest feast is Shamsuddin."

214. D 53/654; D 1019/10751; D 1814/19058; D 1720/18007; D 2807/29780. "To kill the lovers is its religion," D 1268/13424 end.

215. D 1136/12039–40; cf. D 1082/11389.

216. D 48/613; cf. D 2042/21527.

217. D 295/3223.

218. D 2330/24658.

219. D 872/9123; it is the guest for whom man's only heart is sacrificed, D 1656/17357.

220. D 2435/25669, continues:

> The soul of the kings would become a doorkeeper,
> if Love had a door!

221. D 2230/23658.

222. D 477/5056.

223. D 2102/22198–99.

224. D 723/7592.

225. D 1661/17401.

226. D 3102/33078.

227. D 1661/17404.

228. D 1006/10621. A grotesque dialogue in 2843/30200: love is "so tricky

that a thousand Juha [the arch buffoon of Persian folklore] would become its disciples."

229. D 2397/25316; D 1331/14087; D 2335/24714; D 990/10747; D 1072/11281, beginning; D 2064/21797; D 2162/22896; D 1727/18092, "sends out his hounds." In a nice pun on *shēr,* "lion" and *shīr,* "milk," Rumi compares the lovers to lion cubs who play between the paws of the lion Love and drink from his milk D 2224/23602–3.

230. D 843/8825.

231. D 674/7018.

232. D 919/9674; D 2154/22787.

233. D 3059/32569, parallel to *nihang-i faqr,* "the crocodile Poverty."

234. D 986/10440.

235. D 798/8345, end.

236. D 920/9688. See Richard Ettinghausen, *The Unicorn,* plate 3, middle. It would be interesting to find out whether Rumi's choice of images was influenced by the objects of art that surrounded him. In *Fīhi mā fīhi* he alludes to the stone lions which serve as fountains (see Arberry, *Discourses,* p. 52), and it may be that reliefs representing the Tree-of-Life or dragons on Seljukid architecture have affected his poetical imagination, since he was able to transform everything into a poetical image. For these motifs see Gönül Öney, "Das Lebensbaum-Motiv in der seldschukischen Kunst in Anatolien" and "Dragon Figures in Anatolian Seljuk Art." Rumi's most rhapsodic poetry sometimes sounds like a verbal replica of the incredibly rich foliage-like ornaments which decorate the hospital and the Great Mosque in Divriği, Anatolia, built in 1228.

237. D 471/5003.

238. D 2039/21500; D 551/5854; D 1838/19335: it scares away the dragon Sadness.

239. D 500/5321. The whole poem deals with sleep, which suffers from the fists of Love.

240. D 1331/14086.

241. D 1311/13877.

242. D 1689/17700; cf. the visionary poem about the moon-falcon, D 649. Cf. D 309/3389, the eagle.

243. D 516/5518; D 3141/33613–14.

244. D 3031/32209; the same idea in less poetical words, D 1840. Serpent and peacock are both connected with the Islamic legend of Adam's seduction in Paradise, and therefore usually appear together.

245. D 2803/29746; D 2810/29833; D 3059/32568, beginning.

246. D 378/4046. For *shāh* in general, D 760/7965 = 763/7991; D 1037/10942, end. *Pādshāh,* D 690/7177; *Khurram Shāh,* D 664/6939.

247. D 3013/32033.

248. D 983/10402.

249. D 3029/32173.

250. D 35/461; D 237/2670. See Franz Taeschner, *Zünfte und Bruderschaften im Islam,* pp. 43–52 for *ᶜayyār;* p. 280 for Rumi's relationship with the *futuwwa.* J. Christoph Bürgel has highlighted the "cosmic dimensions" of expressions like *rind, qalandar,* and *ᶜayyār* in his article "The Pious Rogue." The *qalandar,* usually a dervish of the *be-sharᶜ* type, i.e., not following all injunctions of the religious law, becomes for Rumi often the symbol for the highest mystical stage. The term is therefore applied at times to Shamsuddin (who, in fact, may have been a member of a *qalandar*-group).

251. D 843/8827; D714/7476; D 1061/11190/94; D 452/4778; D 2810/29831; D 2857/30325; D 2489/26330 end, with *takhalluṣ* Shamsuddin.

252. D 2297/24397; cf. D 848/8871; cf. D 478/5086:

> When they become Shah they suffer from the caliph's stick—
> To endure the tyranny of Love is the art of the Sultan.

253. D 366/3926.

254. D 2224/23596–600.

255. D 772/8057; D 580/6140. One may think here of Richard Crashaw's "Prayer" in which he speaks of "Love's great artillery" (*Oxford Book of Mystical Verse,* p. 50), as his powerful imagery is perhaps closest among the Metaphysical Poets to Rumi's daring verse.

256. D 2986/31715.

257. D 2140/22663.

258. D 1409/14913.

259. D 1308/13854.

260. D 48/613; D 874/9143; D 937/9883; dagger, D 751/7873; D 1571/16493.

261. D 1159/12308.

262. D 2017/21286.

263. D 2056/21715; but he knows: "He who flees from Love sheds his own blood," D 587/6203.

264. D 1926/20273; cf. D 718/7547:

> Make the soul a shield for His affliction,
> For in the hand of Love you are Dhu'l-fiqar

265. D 637/6647.

266. D 732/7688; D 1940/20414; D 2931/31099. The arrow is the most commonly used metaphor for love in both Islamic and non-Islamic literatures, whether Hindu poets compare *viraha,* "longing love," to an arrow, or St. Teresa experiences the arrow piercing her heart.

267. D 1067/11244.

268. D 59/727; D 1612/16887; cf. D 1727/18094: "The world of Love is under the flag of a certain Sultan"; D 282/3140 (Arabic). The medieval listener probably associated the "flag of Love" with the flag, *liwā',* of the Prophet (see chapter 5, note 28).

269. D 565/5988; cf. 843/8827–28.

270. D 237/2673, both hemistichs rhyming!

271. D 1710/17905; 2785/29606; D 133/1538 *tārāj;* D 416/4400, *ghārat.*

272. D 1288/13604.

273. D 2807/29798, a fine *tanāsub* with the two pre-Islamic heroes, the Persian king, Nushirwan, known for his justice, and the Arab Hatim at-Ta'i, the model of generosity.

274. D 2601/27584.

275. D 2235/23689; D 2218/23523; D 2268/24091 (Arabic).

276. D 1735/18196.

277. D 193/2125, beginning.

278. D 2288, *muṣādara,* "confiscation," is the *radīf.*

279. D 2859/30348; cf. D 779/8132; D 2718/28857, the friend's dream image is the *shiḥna-i firāq,* the police chief who does away with separation.

280. D 1643/17199.

281. D 772/8064; cf. D 224/2531: in this brand is written: "Verily, We have sent down" (Sura 9/15). The image of the mark is still very real with Rumi; one should also remember that some Sufis, particularly in India, used to inflict upon themselves branding marks as sign of complete surrender.

282. D 2859/30355; D 1012/10676, "the just ruler Love."

283. D 915/9642, a poem on the contradictory qualities of Love.

284. D 2299/24420:

> You have in every corner a Job, at every side a Jacob
> Whose doors Love has broken, and stolen all stuff from their houses!

285. D 1830/19240.

286. D 1125/11876.

287. D 2231/23651–55 f.

288. D 1100/11634.

289. D 1732/18160.

290. D 2897/30785, an imitation of Rudagi's famous poem *bū-yi jū-yi Mūliyān āyad hamī* ("The fragrance of the river Mūliyān comes all the time"), which was imitated by a great number of later poets up to Ghalib in India.

291. D 1082/11384.

292. D 1020/10763.

293. D 2801/29735. All five verses describe the fire of Love.

294. D 2751/29256.

295. D 2502/26475; in the second hemistich it offers a turban to those who have lost theirs.

296. D 924/9730. A famous quatrain attributed to Rumi, but also to others, and frequently quoted by Sufis who had to suffer for their daring utterances, begins:

> In the kitchen of Love only the good ones are slaughtered . . .

297. D 795/8310; D 824/8620: by eating bitter and sweet from Love, man will grow wings; D 1733/18168. See Heiler, *Erscheinungsformen,* pp. 248 ff., who enumerates among the symbols for "substantial union" the sacrificial meal and related phenomena. Christian mysticism abounds in this imagery. Ruysbroek says: "To eat and to be eaten, that is union" (Vom Reiche des Liebenden XXII, quoted in Underhill, *Mysticism,* p. 425). Medieval Christian mystics speak of *gustare Deum,* which logically grows out of the central role of the eucharist, and again underlies the general notion of the *coena coelestis,* see Kurt Goldammer, "Coena coelestis. Ein nicht-mystisches Überlebsel in der Sprache christlicher Mystiker." See also Angelus Silesius:

> O süsse Gasterei! Gott selber wird der Wein,
> Die Speise, Tisch, Musik und der Bediener sein!

(*Cherubinischer Wandersmann,* I, 207).

298. D 372/3999; a description of all kinds of food which the poet does not eat, but: "I eat Love, which is tasty."

299. D 2872/30493; cf. D 2755/29281, beginning; D 125/1433: love and his heart are mixed like sugar and rock sugar in *ḥalwā.* D 798/8341; cf. D 1035/10908.

300. D 902/9460.

301. D 1417; *tutmāj* is a thick broth with meat, vegetables, and a kind of noodles. The third verse is a perfect *murāʿāt an-naẓīr:* every term belongs to the kitchen-level. D 2165/22930 mentions some lowly person who "in love of *tutmāj* has become naked like garlic." See also D 133/1537:

> O you who have become the table-master of the spiritual Bughra Khan—
> On such a table, why do you pluck out morsels from the *tutmāj?*

Whether the allusion is to Bughra Khan, the first Karakhanid ruler to become a Muslim, is not certain, but possible.

302. D 482/5144.

303. D 1926/20271.

304. D 216; for the whole imagery see Schimmel, *Triumphal Sun,* pp. 157–161.

305. D 795/8307, it will be given, but D 917/9656, it should not be given, rather, they make a gown from the sun.

306. D 313/3422.

307. D 857/8943.

308. D 2250/23844.

309. D 2156/22830; D 351/3782; M I 23.

310. D 2521/26729:

> If Dr. Love had given a salve to Galen,
> Why should he then chew so much straw [= talk nonsense] because of his dry herbs?

311. D 2940/31201. Since *mufarriḥ* was prepared with a homoeopathic dose of ruby, the cross-relation between the "relaxing" medicine and the rubylike lips of the beloved is implicit for the medieval Persian reader. For theriac see D 1133/11970.

312. D 2672/28337–41.

313. D 915/9638; cf. D 2933/31112, beginning; D 405/4297, end; D 374/4017, end.

314. D 2901/30832; D 1138/12066.

315. D 2374/25101; D 2903/30850–51; D 1206/12850; D 27/323; D 541/5764; D 2919/31001; in D 408/4315, however, Love appears as Khidr, which appears more logical.

316. D 1598/16727.

317. D 1970/20807; D 405/4289.

318. D 74/863.

319. D 994/10506.

320. D 2092/22100, instead of the usual Ismaᶜil, who appears, however, in the same role in D 1237/13119.

321. D 416/4400.

322. D 202/2236.

323. D 1214/12918.

324. D 956/10085.

325. D 3092/32982.

326. D 1894/19924.

327. D 1086/11430; D 443/4670; the end of the verse is:

> Quiet! For king Love is a strange Tahamtan,

i.e., Rustam, the greatest of the heroes in the Iranian tradition as told in the *Shāhnāma*.

328. For when iron becomes soft, it can accept Love's seal, D 741/7786. But in another image, again from the sphere of Solomon:

> When Love makes the waterlike heart like iron,
> Djinns and fairies become afraid,

(D555/5896), for Solomon used to ban the djinns in iron bottles which were cast into the sea. See D 455/4809.

329. D 1158/12296.

330. D 2400/25345.

331. D 220/2488; D 881/9229.

332. D 749/7862–63; in another combination, a single glance of Love can change the four elements, D 904/9480.

333. D 566/6001; cf. 843/8824, beginning:

> You know who is alive?
> He who is born from Love!

Cf. D 1430/15120.

334. D 885/9273.

335. D 980/10374.

336. D 2405/25401; D 894/9363: the lovers suck pre-eternal light from Love's teats.

337. D 508/5425.

338. D 333/3609; D 321/3491; D 517/5527; D 2092/22101.

339. D 1126/11888–90.

340. D 500/5320.

341. M VI 4162; cf. 989/10462.

342. D 440/4616.

343. D 33/425:

> Don't give me bread, don't give me water, don't give me rest and sleep,
> O you—the thirst for whose love is the bloodmoney for hundreds like me!

D 155/1766.

344. D 2400/25349; cf. D 778/8120.

345. D 467/4967; D 2479/26230; cf. D 544/5799; D 2865/30419, end; D 2793/29685; D 140/1604, end.

346. D 990/10476; cf. D 621/6493; D 779/8130.

347. D 2942/31225.

348. D 2924/31041.

349. D 308/3384, end; D 811/8485, end; D 572/6079, end.

350. *Kharābāt,* D 2363/24992; D 2636/27970; *wīrān,* D 446/4699; D 536/5709; D 427/4493; D 1341/14196; D 937/9884.

351. Love is a strange guest that destroys the house, D 982/10391; the advice to make the house of the heart empty and diminish so that Love can grow, D 622/6504, is frequent in Rumi's verse, as it expresses the classical ideal of the Sufis that everything human has to diminish so that God's presence can increase. In the language of love mysticism, this idea was expressed by stressing the contrasting qualities of lover and beloved; they are like the green and red side of an apple (D 968/10233, an image also used by Saᶜdi); the lovers grow thinner and paler as the beloved becomes more radiant and "fat" (the most famous description is M III 4394), for the lovers are all petition, *niyāz,* the beloved all coquettish pride, *nāz* (cf. chapter 2, note 79). All these ideas work together to give the imagery of self-effacement a prominent place in Persian poetry in general, and in Rumi's verse in particular. But he can also turn the image, as in D 819/8556:

The tired, skinny ones arrive from the grazing-land of Love fat and healthy.

352. D 251/2821–23.
353. D 862/9003; D 822/8583; D 975/10339; M II 1529/32.
354. D 122/1387.
355. D 610/6412.
356. M VI 3648.
357. D 1068/11254; D 2470/26124. See D 3061/32604:

My wine is the fire of Love, especially from the hand of *Ḥaqq,* Divine Truth
Life be forbidden, if you don't make your soul dry wood!

358. D 2395. Cf. Hans Heinrich Schaeder, "Die islamische Lehre vom Vollkommenen Menschen."

359. D 67/802; D 446/4705, a wine house; D 459/4872, a wine seller.

360. Fakhruddin ᶜIraqi, *Kulliyāt,* p. 193; D 2845/30218. H. H. Schaeder once mentioned during a seminar the slim possibility that the *parda-i ᶜIrāqī* in D 2395 might perhaps point to ᶜIraqi's poetry; the poem is indeed quite close in *Stimmung* to verses of Rumi's younger contemporary.

361. D 53/649.
362. D 2634/27950.
363. D 1619/16944, beginning:

Khwaja, be my witness: I have repented from repentance—
The cup of contrition broke when I drank the wine of Love.

364. D 827/8644.

365. D 783/8174–75, beginning; G. van der Leeuw, *Religionsphänomenologie,* p. 557.

366. D 1733/18171; cf. 2131/22549; D 2394/25287–88, beginning.
367. D 3106/33133.
368. D 2728/28974.
369. D 683/7109, the verses are written on his sarcophagus.
370. D 366/3924.
371. D 3004/31927, beginning.
372. D 2190/23246.
373. D 2937/31168–69.
374. D 498/5287, see Sana'i, *Dīwān,* p. 605.
375. D 182/2030–32:

When Intellect looks still for a camel to perform the pilgrimage,
Love has already reached the hill Safa [= Purity]—

ideas which Iqbal has taken up in his lyrical poetry, particularly in the *Payām-i Mashriq*. Even more outspoken is v.2029 of the same *ghazal:*

> Far be the people of intellect from the lovers—
> Far be the stench of the dunghill from the zephyr!

See also D 2366/25018–19.

376. D 928/9783 end; D 427/4495; D 617/6462.

377. D 1940/20484, a charming pun on *naql-nuql* (*tajnīs-i khaṭṭī*).

378. D 132/1522–24.

379. D 2807/29777.

380. D 2333/24671; cf. D 748/7853. The turban is the hallmark of the intellectuals and scholars:

> Every body without love that seeks a hat,
> Has no head, and becomes all turban,

D 282/8662. Many centuries later Sa'ib (d. 1678) would complain of the ruined state of Islamdom because the scholars "are busy in building up the dome of their turbans."

381. D 1288/13605.

382. D 202/2239–43, the end of this long *ghazal* is rather uninspired.

383. D 2231/23657; D 920/9686; Abu'l-Hasan (?) is mentioned too.

384. D 1276/13496.

385. D 424/4462, also Plato; D 429/4520; cf. D 2715/28822.

386. D 2335/24711.

387. D 507/5408; cf. D 2142/22695.

388. D 2170/22988–89.

389. D 2807/29794.

390. D 1931/20296; cf. D 2398/25326; D 683/7106 and others.

391. D 2924/31040.

392. D 2601/27583. In some verses however the Beloved appears as superior to both intellect and Love, thus D 2777/29512:

> Love makes the clothes tear, Intellect stitches them with long stitches—
> The gallbladder of both of them is torn when You stitch hearts!

393. D 784/8193 "Everything becomes mad from the chains of your love," D 1037/10941.

394. D 1735/18195.

395. D 2341/24773.

396. D 232/2608.

397. D 317/3458.

398. D 213/2379, beginning.

399. D 314/3428.

400. D 2498/26406 ff. Cf. D 342/3702:

> If I gird my loins before anything but Love,
> I am a Christian, and this is the infidels' girdle!

Also D 2401/25369:

> Faith and believers are all stupefied by Love:
> The girdle of the old Christian monk got burnt!

Further, D 2601/27585:

> I passed by a monastery, the priest came forth
> And beat the wooden gong (*nāqūs*) at the door of Unity out of love for you;

perhaps an implicit allusion to Shaikh Sanᶜan's story in the *Manṭiq uṭ-ṭair*.

401. D 355/3821.

402. D 463/4911, beginning.

403. D 980/10377; D 133/1532, "toward the roof of Sultan Beauty."

404. D 228/2572; D 461/4894; D 2503/26489; D 3038/32300; D 1283/13550; this Buraq brings him to Tabriz.

405. D 2910/30917; cf. 313/3421:

> From where is the donkey, and from where the Jesus-breath of Love.

About the relation of Buraq and the donkey we find a very interesting saying in the Jewish tradition, as A. Altmann, "The Ladder of Ascension," shows at the end of his article: "It may also be taken for granted that the Jews disbelieved the legend of Muhammad's ascension to heaven and that they discounted, in particular, the story of Buraq carrying the Prophet to heaven on a stairway which amounted to Jacob's ladder. They . . . took Buraq to be an ass and nothing more. In their view, then, the story of this particular ass called Buraq climbing up on Jacob's ladder was utterly fantastic and an assertion of the impossible." Hence, this misunderstanding may be the source of the saying: "If an ass can ascend a ladder, knowledge can be found among launderers," and also of the formula found in the colophons of many a Hebrew manuscript:

> Be strong! May the copyist suffer no harm
> Either today or at any time
> Until the ass ascends the ladder
> About which our Father Jacob dreamt.

Pp. 29–31. Thus, the formula amounts to a counterpart of Yunus Emre's and Kabir's "When the fish climbs on the poplar tree" (see chapter 4, note 123), but has an important religious background.

406. D 684/7114.

407. D 288/3175; D 662/6922–23; D 2466/26088: "Love makes you ride even

though you be a pedestrian," but the other way round, D 915/9642: "We all become pedestrians when Love comes a-riding."

408. D 718/7557; cf. D 1755/18396, "I have a saddle on Love's back."

409. D 1919/20201 ff.

410. D 771/8052; D 2489/26330; D 2499/26438; D 324/3525.

411. D 827/8651.

412. D 1926/20272.

413. D 909/9531.

414. D 2336/24728.

415. See Hujwiri/Nicholson, *Kashf al-maḥjūb,* p. 398.

416. D 2733/29045:

> Who am I that I seek union?
> You draw me out of your kindness!

Cf. D 425/4471; M III 4393–94.

417. For the whole problem see Schimmel, *Triumphal Sun,* "The Problem of Prayer in Jalaloddin's Work."

418. M I 1704; the verse was translated verbatim into Sindhi poetry by Shah ᶜAbdul Latif, *Risālō,* Sur Sassui Abri I, 8. See also D 445/4691.

419. D 1460/15432–33.

420. D 1000/10565–66.

421. D 1129/11912.

422. D 1735/18202, end: "kill me."

423. D 862/9002.

424. D 1247/13220.

425. D 1075/11316; cf. D 2290/24335; and many more.

426. M I 1 ff.; see Schimmel, *Triumphal Sun,* "The Imagery of Music and Dance." In this context, Love can be personified as Zuhra (Venus), usually connected with musical activities, thus D 2486/26297:

> When the Zuhra Love cast its claw in this water-and-clay,
> Our stature became like a harp, our breast a *chaghāna* [a little stringed instrument].

427. D 686/7132.

428. D 2327/24646.

429. Quoted by Martin Buber, *Ekstatische Konfessionen,* p. 90.

430. From a medieval Belgian song, in *Der Stumme Jubel,* p. 286.

431. "Cosmic Dance" by Sir John Davies, in Wheelwright, *Burning Fountain,* p. 361.

432. For the importance of dance in the history of religions see Heiler, *Erscheinungsformen,* pp. 239–43; Gerardus van der Leeuw, *In den hemel is enen dans, RGG* 3rd. ed., VI, pp. 612–14, "Tanz." For the Mevlevi dance in the context of various forms of mystical dances in Islam see Fritz Meier, "Der

Derwischtanz"; Marijan Molé, "La Danse exstatique en Islam"; a description by Hellmut Ritter, "Die Mevlânafeiern in Konya." Abdulbaki Gölpĭnarlĭ, *Mevlâna'dan sonra Mevlevilik,* pp. 473–75, quotes Divane Mehmed Çelebi's *Risale,* in which the dervish explains:

> The *khirqa* is my tomb,
> The high hat my tombstone,

and interprets the mystical dance in terms of *fanā'* and *baqā,* an interpretation which is still current among the Mevlevi dervishes. Gölpĭnarlĭ also offers texts and melodies used in the Mevlevi ceremonies.

433. William Hastie, *The Festival of Spring,* translates this last line as follows:

> Who knows love's mazy circling, ever lives in God,
> For death, he knows, is love abounding: *Allah Hu!*

It seems fitting to quote Wheelwright's final point here: "The end of the turning wheel is the still axis which is the archê of its turning. The end of the cosmic dance is the quietude of love beyond desire. The end of dying is the ever-renewed threshold experience of potential rebirth" (*The Burning Fountain,* p. 364).

4. THE VOICE OF LOVE: MYSTICAL POETRY IN THE vernaculars

1. Sharafuddin Yahya Maneri, *Mukh al-maᶜānī,* majlis 35, information kindly supplied by Dr. Paul Jackson S.J., Patna; see also Sharafuddin Maneri, *The Hundred Letters.*

2. *The Lament of Baba Tahir, Being the ᶜRubaᶜiyat' of Baba Tahir Hamadani ᶜUryan,* Arthur J. Arberry, *The Poems of a Persian Sufi: Bābā Tahir.* See E. G. Browne, *Literary History of Persia,* I, 83–85; Jan Rypka, *History of Iranian Literature,* p. 234, and V. Minorsky, "Bābā Tāhir," *EI*² I, col. 839–43. The authorship of the quatrains is not beyond doubt, see Wilhelm Eilers, "Vierzeilerdichtung, persisch und ausserpersisch," pp. 209–49, a useful survey of all popular kinds of quatrains in Arabic and Persian dialects.

3. For the development see Mehmet Fuat Köprülü, *Türk edebiyatĭnda ilk mutesavvĭflar;* for the development of the different Turkic literatures see Pertev Nail Boratav, ed., *Philologiae Turcicae Fundamenta,* Vol. 2. The "Turkologischer Anzeiger" which appears in the *WZKM* since 1975 offers an excellent survey of recent studies in the field of Turkish classical and folk literatures.

4. Syed Athar Abbas Rizvi, *A History of Sufism in India,* p. 326–27. The first known Sufi treatises in Hindwi were composed by ᶜAinuddin Ganj ul-

ᶜilm (d. 1396 in Gulbarga), see T. G. Bailey, *A History of Urdu Literature*, no. 1; A. Schimmel, *Classical Urdu Literature*, p. 132.

5. Syed Hasan Askari, "Mulla Da,ud's ᶜChanda,in' and Sadhan's ᶜMaina Sat.' " For illustrations of this epic see Douglas Barrett and Basil Gray, *Paintings from India*, pp. 69–71; Ralph Pinder-Wilson, ed., *Paintings from Islamic Lands*, fig. 87.

6. Bada'uni, *Muntakhab at-tawārīkh*, I, trans. George S. S. Ranking, p. 333. Bada'uni also mentions at various instances Sufis who "used to sing ecstatic songs in Hindi," see ibid., III, no. 38 s.v. ᶜAbdul Wahid Bilgrami, and ibid., p. 292, Gada'i, the son of the noted Persian poet Jamali Kanboh (d. 1535), who also wrote religious songs in Hindi.

7. *Padmāvati* was probably begun in 1569. See Charlotte Vaudeville, "La conception de l'amour divin chez Muhammad Jāyasī: *virah* et *ᶜishq*"

8. Yunus Emre, *Divan*. The first Turkish verses in Anatolia were composed by Shayyad Hamza in the thirteenth century. Maulana Rumi used Turkish in some of his verses, as he interspersed others with Greek words to catch the atmosphere of the Konya bazaars. See Mecdut Mansuroglu, "Celâluddin Rumi's türkische Verse." His son, Sultan Walad, left a whole Turkish Diwan: *Dīwān-i Turkī*.

9. Good examples are found in H. G. Raverty, *Selections from the Poetry of the Afghans;* James Darmesteter, *Chants populaires des Afghans*, and Jens Enevoldsen, *Selections from Rahman Baba*.

10. Jan Knappert, *Swahili Islamic Poetry*. A survey: Ernst Dammann, "Die Überlieferung des islamischen Suahelidichtung."

11. Hamid Algar, "Some Notes on the Naqshbandi *ṭarīqat* in Bosnia."

12. Grete Lüers, *Die Sprache der deutschen Mystik des Mittelalters im Werk der Mechthild von Magdeburg*.

13. Vladimir Minorsky, "The Poetry of Shāh Ismail I"; Turhan Gandjei, *Il Canzoniere di Šāh Ismāᶜīl Ḫaṭā'ī*. Examples of his poems in Vasfi Mahir Kocatürk, *Tekke Şiiri Antolojisi*, pp. 173–78, and Sadettin Nuzhet Ergun, *Bektaşi şairleri ve nefesleri*, pp. 33–53. It is worth mentioning in passing that shortly after the turn of the sixteenth century the four major Muslim rulers indulged in poetry; paradoxically, only the Ottoman Sultan Selim Yavuz (r. 1514–1520) composed his verse in classical Persian, while the ruler of Iran, Ismaᶜil Khata'i, wrote enrapturing Turkish popular poems. The Mamluk Sultan Qansauh al-Ghuri of Egypt (d. 1516) likewise wrote Turkish, mostly devout, verse, and so did Babur, the founder of the Moghul Empire in India (r. 1526–1530), who also composed some Persian verses.

14. Alessandro Bausani, *Storia delle letterature del Pakistan*, p. 322 f. Pir-i Roshan himself wrote his *Khair ul-bayān* in rhymed prose in the four languages mentioned.

15. Qadi Abdul Mannan, *Literary Heritage of Bangladesh, Medieval Period*, p. 3. For the whole development see Maulwi ᶜAbdul Haqq, *Urdū kī nashw u*

namā meñ Ṣūfiyā-i kirām kā kām (The role of the noble Sufis in the development of Urdu).

16. Bailey, *Urdu Literature,* no. 5; for Khub Muhammad Chishti see also M. J. Dar, "Gujarat's Contribution to Gujari and Urdu," p. 30.

17. William Montgomery Watt, *Muslim Intellectual,* p. 113.

18. A number of Turkish popular mystical poets used *ümmi* as their surname: Ümmi Kemal, Ümmi Sinan, etc.

19. *Yeni Yunus Emre ve doğuşlarī;* Ismail Emre, *Doguşlar II.*

20. For the role of the *alif* see Hafiz's famous verse:

> There is on the tablet of the heart nothing but the *alif* of my friend's stature—
> What shall I do? My teacher gave me no other letter to memorize!

Dīwān, ed. Jalali Naini and Nazīr Ahmad, p. 362, *mīm* no. 9. See also Schimmel, *Mystical Dimensions,* Appendix I, pp. 417–20.

21. Yunus Emre, *Divan,* p. 308, LIX.

22. Shah ᶜAbdul Latif, *Risālō,* Sur Yaman Kalyan V, verse 21.

23. *Qānūn-i ᶜishq, yaᶜnī Halwā-e Panjāb,* commentary on the *kāfīs* of Hz. Bullhe Shah, Kafi no. 75, p. 182; cf. also no. 77, p. 184, and no. 78, p. 186. See also Lajwanti Ramakrishna, *Panjabi Sufi Poets,* p. xxx.

24. *Kanz al- ᶜummāl,* by ᶜAli al-Muttaqi al-Hindi (d. 1565), is the widely used collection of Prophetic traditions. Qudūri (d. 1037) is the author of the handiest survey of Hanafi law, while the *Kāfiya* is Ibn Malik's (d. 1274) Arabic poem on Arabic grammar. All these books were taught in Indian madrasas, although the mention of the *Kanz* in a poem from the first half of the sixteenth century is strange; one would have to find out when this collection was actually introduced in theological courses in India in order to date the verse properly.

25. The alleged aversion to writing is common also with Sufi poets in the classical tradition, who were prolific writers and yet felt the constant tension between the impossibility of expressing their experience and the urge to convey their wisdom to their disciples. Typical is Sana'i's remark (*Dīwān, ghazal* p. 801):

> First I wrote books with great pains,
> Finally I broke the pens in complete bewilderment!

26. *Qāḍī Qādan jō kalām* gives the seven verses which were hitherto known only in the appendix because they are not mentioned in the Hariyana manuscript on which this edition relies. See Sayyid Husamuddin Rashdi, *Sindhī Adab,* p. 12.

27. Sachal Sarmast, *Waḥdatnāma,* in *Risālō Sindhī,* p. 36.

28. Yunus Emre, *Divan,* p. 514, CLVI.

29. See his charming poem with the beginning:

The lands of my sheikh—
So long is the way!
The roses that bloom—
Who will gather them?

ibid. p. 528, CLXXXIII.

30. Ibid. p. 31, IV. Qadi Qadan (*Kalām* no. 23) goes even further:

You see those who have annihilated themselves:
Twenty-four hours a day they kick the Divine Throne!

31. Yunus Emre, *Divan,* p. 309, LXI.

32. Furuzanfar, *Aḥādīth-i Mathnawī,* no. 131.

33. For examples see Schimmel, "A Spring Day in Konya," p. 262.

34. Shah ᶜAbdul Latif, *Risālō,* Sur Dahar.

35. Yunus Emre, *Divan,* p. 77, IV. The Koranic remark about "a good word as a good tree" (Sura 14/24) may have been in the poets' minds. But the image is much older: cf. Psalm 1.3 and Psalm 92.13; for the symbolism of the Tree see Heiler, *Erscheinungsformen,* pp. 67–73.

36. Ghazzali, *Iḥyā ᶜulūm ad-dīn,* I, p. 265.

37. Ikram, *Armaghān-i Pāk,* p. 150.

38. Sultan Bahu, *Abyāt,* verse 1. Cf. the verse of Angelus Silesius:

Die Gottheit ist mein Saft, was aus mir grünt und blüht,
Das ist sein heil'ger Geist, durch den sein Trieb geschieht.

Cherubinischer Wandersmann, I, 81.

39. *Qāḍī Qādan jō kalām,* no. 56.

40. Yunus Emre, *Divan,* p. 252, XXVIII.

41. *Pir Sultan Abdal* (Varlik Klasikleri no. 13), p. 34:

I am like one who wore a borrowed dress
Which I received as I came in this world.
Its owner came and took it from my hands—
Now I'm a lamb, lost on the cold, bare ground.

For more translations from Yunus and Pir Sultan see Annemarie Schimmel, *Aus dem goldenen Becher,* pp. 39–49, 78–84.

42. Yunus Emre, *Divan,* p. 594, CCLXXX, trans. by Margaret Mazĭcĭ, (New York). Another *dōlābnāme* is ascribed to Kaygusuz, see Ergun, *Bektaşi şairleri,* p. 25, and Kocatürk, *Tekke şiiri,* p. 35.

43. Muhammad Shahidullah-Muhammad Abdul Hai, *Traditional Culture in East Pakistan,* p. 13.

44. Shah ᶜAbdul Latif, *Risālō,* Sur Ripa II, v. 8.9.

45. *Qāḍī Qādan jō kalām,* no. 91.

46. Ibid., no. 90.

47. Shah ᶜAbdul Latif, *Risālō,* Sur Barvo Sindhi II, v. 11.

48. An interesting account of the relation between the use of the indigenous idiom and women in c. A.D. 850 is found in Tirmidhi's Arabic autobiography (al-Hakim at-Tirmidhi, *Khatm al-auliyā*), p. 23, when the angel speaks to the Sufi's wife in *Persian* in her dream. Cf. also Dammann's remark that popular religious poetry in Swahili is often sung by women ("Überlieferung des islamischen Suahelidichtung," p. 49). Incidentally, I have learned more about Islamic piety from women in Anatolia and Sind than from most of my learned colleagues or from sophisticated books—they still cling to "the faith of the old women" as it was praised in early Islam, and represent the values of a moderately mystical Islam.

49. Richard M. Eaton, *Sufis of Bijapur,* ch. 6, "Sufis as Literati."

50. Shah ᶜAbdul Latif, *Risālō,* Sur Kapa'iti I, v. 4.

51. Eaton, *Sufis of Bijapur,* p. 164. I wonder if in some of the spinning songs an implicit allusion to Hallaj, the cotton-carder, may be intended; in high poetry, thus in Rumi's *Dīwān,* he is sometimes connected with cotton; that is the case especially in later times, after Shabistari had spoken of the "cotton of existence" when discussing Hallaj's saying, *anā'l-ḥaqq,* in the seventh problem of *Gulshan-i rāz.*

52. I owe the translation of the anonymous Panjabi spinning song to Dr. Akhtar Ahsan, Yonkers, N.Y.

53. Eaton, *Sufis of Bijapur,* p. 163. The millstone occurs frequently in ᶜAttar's and Rumi's verse, but in different settings: ᶜAttar sees the turning millstone which will then be broken and finally rest, while Rumi sometimes perceives the stone, too, as dancing, or uses the image of "grinding the grains" for man's purification by suffering.

54. For the imagery see Schimmel, "A Spring Day in Konya."

55. Furuzanfar, *Aḥādīth-i Mathnawī,* no. 338.

56. Dr. N. A. Baloch, ed. *Tih ak'haryūn;* the first known example in Sindhi occurs in Shah ᶜAbdul Latif, *Risālō,* Sur Ramakali. In Panjabi, Indian words are often used in *Sīḥarfīs,* not so much Arabic expressions; thus *alif* may begin the line *ēk alak'h bē-ant dātā,* "One endless, unlimited Lord," *d* may stand for *dikh,* "see," *sh* for *shīh,* "lion," etc. See for instance Pir Sayyid Ghulam Jilani Qadiri, *Prēm Piyālē.* In Pashto, the *Kitāb Bābū Jān* begins with a "Religious Alphabet," James F. Blumhardt and D. N. MacKenzie, *Catalogue of the Pashto Manuscripts in the British Isles,* nos. 22 and 39. See R. Siraj ud-Din and H. A. Walter, "An Indian Sufi Hymn," a metrical translation of a typical *Sīḥarfī* by one Talib, composed in Panjabi in 1317h/1899. The form is also common in Turkish, see A. Caferoğlu, *Türk Dili Tarihi II,* pp. 66–76, s.v. *Alliterasyon.* In the strophic poetry of the early Turkish poet Ashiq Pasha, all 29 poems begin

with one letter of the alphabet, each verse with the same letter, so that for instance *t* begins exclusively with Arabic *tafa^{cc}ul* nouns, see Ananias Zajączkowski, *Poezje stroficzne Ašïq Paša.* For Swahili see Knappert, *Swahili Religious Poetry,* and A. Werner, "An Alphabetic Acrostic in a Northern Dialect of Swahili." The form also occurs rarely in classical Persian, see Hadi Hasan, "Qāsim-i Kāhī, His Life and Works," p. 186–89, an *Alifnāme* for ^{c}Ali ibn Abi Talib. For a classical prose form, used for defining "Sūfism" in alphabetical terms, see Arthur J. Arberry, "A Ṣūfī Alphabet."

57. ^{c}Ali ibn Abi Talib, the first *imām* of Shia Islam, plays a particularly important role in Turkish Bektashi poetry because the Bektashis are largely Shia-oriented. See John K. Birge, *The Bektashi Order of Dervishes.* A special study: Abdurrahman Güzel, *^{c}Ali in der Bektaschi-Dichtung, namentlich jener des 16. Jahrhunderts.* In Persian lullabies too, ^{c}Ali "is more often invoked," as is natural (Jiří Cejpek, "Iranian Folk-literature," in Rypka, *History of Iranian Literature,* p. 695). However, as the early hero of Islam, who conquered the fortress of Khaibar on his white mule Duldul, ^{c}Ali also looms large in Sindhi, Panjabi, and related popular poetry, even in a non-Shiite environment.

58. Charlotte Vaudeville, *Bārahmāsa, les chansons des douze mois dans les littératures indo-aryennes.* In Panjabi, I found the Indian months almost exclusively, while Sindhi uses both Indian and Muslim and lately even Christian months (as does the contemporary poet Talib al-Maula). *Bārahmāsa* were known in early Dakhni poetry, and in Bengali at least since Muhammad Saghir's *Yūsuf Jalīkha.* There are also poems which enumerate the days of a week, or of a month, see Dr. N. A. Baloch, ed. *Haftā, dinhīn, ratiūn̄ ain mahīnā;* the first known example is again in Shah ^{c}Abdul Latif's *Risālō,* Sur Ramakali. In high Persian literature, the genre seems to have been used only in the Subcontinent: Mas^{c}ud ibn Sa^{c}d-i Salman, *Dīwān,* has a set of *māhhā-yi fārsī,* pp. 654–58, *nām-i rūzhā-yi furs,* pp. 659–67, and *rūzhā-yi hafta,* pp. 668–69. It is worth noticing that unassuming verses in connection with special days are produced by pious people all over the Muslim world; modern Turkish examples are "Hayri Bey'in Ramazan manileri," little verses for the nights of Ramadan, composed by a Turkish civil servant who died in 1941, see Erdem Yücel, in *Türk Folklor Araştïrmalarï.* That similar forms occur in Christian literature is not surprising: both the ecclesiastical year and the hours of the monastic prayer inspired the poets, as, for instance, Mechtild of Magdeburg (*Der stumme Jubel,* pp. 260, 282).

59. John R. Walsh, "Yunus Emre—A Medieval Hymnodist." Examples in Yunus Emre's *Divan* are especially found on pp. 530–41. Among the most frequently used refrains are *Hū,* "He," the "numinose Urlaut" of Islam; *madad Allahīm madad,* "Help O my God, help!"; *al-ḥamdu lillāh,* "Praise be to God." The same forms are found in Serbo-Croatian *ilāhīs,* which are modelled on Turkish songs, especially by Yunus Emre and Niyazi Misri, as Hamid Algar has shown ("Some Notes on the Naqshbandi *ṭarīqat,*" p. 186, and Appendix

II, no. 2, seven syllable four-lined stanzas with the refrain *lā ilāha illā Allāh*). See also Annemarie Schimmel, "Yunus Emre."

60. Yunus Emre, *Divan,* p. 552, CCXIX.

61. Ibid., p. 132, LX, trans. by Margaret Mazĭcĭ.

62. Ibid. p. 477, CII.

63. Rashid Burhanpuri, *Burhānpūr kē Sindhī auliyā.*

64. Bada'uni, *Muntakhab at-tawārīkh,* translation, Vol. III, p. 39.

65. Cf. Christian Poche, "Zikr und Musicology." In Gujarat, a special form of poetry called *jikrī,* from *dhikr,* developed around 1500; its most famous author was Qadi Mahmud (d. 1534), and "the *qawwāls* of Gujarat sang these *jikrī* which bore traces of rapture and love," M. J. Dar, "Gujarat's Contribution to Gujari and Urdu," p. 21.

66. For the use of the flute see Qadi Abdul Mannan, *Literary Heritage of Bangladesh, Medieval Period,* p. 11–14.

67. See Ernest Trumpp, "Eine Sindhi Sprachprobe. Sorathi, Ein Sindhi-Gedicht aus dem grossen Divan des Sayyid Abdul-Latif." The overcritical approach of the German missionary-philologist to Sindhi mystical poetry is due partly to his "protestant," violently antimystical attitude, partly also to the fact that the texts which he collected were hopelessly confused. The admittedly very cruel Hindu story of Sorathi and King Dhyaj, located originally in Svarashtra, becomes for Shah Latif an allegory of the absolute power of the mystical guide for whose sweet songs the initiate gladly sacrifices everything, including his life. Shah ᶜAbdul Latif praises also the instruments of the Yogis for their bewitching power (Sur Ramakali).

68. The first of the Sufi writers of Bijapur, Shams ul-ᶜushshaq Miranji (d. 1496), uses the motif of the woman in his treatises *Khūshnāma* and *Khūshnughz,* see Bailey, *Urdu Literature,* no. 5. The Gujarati Sufi poet Qadi Mahmud is also credited with a mystical love song put in a girl's mouth, see M. J. Dar, "Gujarat's Contribution to Gujari and Urdu," p. 25.

69. Edward Dimock, "Muslim Vaiṣnava Poets of Bengal," *Languages and Areas.*

70. Charles Frederick Usborne, *Hir Ranjha,* ed. Mumtaz Hasan. For the mystical interpretation see Mohan Singh Diwana, *An Introduction to Panjabi Literature.*

71. Thus Bullhe Shah in *Qānūn-i ᶜishq,* Kafi no. 109, p. 240.

72. L. Ramakrishna, *Panjabi Sufi Poets,* p. 24; Hafeez Hoshyarpuri, *Mathnawiyāt-i Hīr Rānjhā.*

73. Motilal Jotwani, *Shah Abdul Karim.*

74. Henry T. Sorley, *Shah Abdul Latif of Bhit, His Poetry, Life and Times;* Motilal Jotwani, *Shah Abdul Latif, His Life and Work;* Annemarie Schimmel, *Pain and Grace,* Part II.

75. He expresses Ruzbihan-i Baqli's ideal: the lover becomes completely transformed into Love, and thus writes (*Risālō,* Sur Maᶜdhuri VII, vv. 21, 22):

O voice in the desert, as though it were a wild goose:
A call from the water's depth—
It is the Ah of Love!
O voice in the desert, like a fiddle's melody:
It is the song of Love—only common people thought it
To be a woman's voice.

76. *Qāḍī Qādan jō kalām,* no. 47; Shah ᶜAbdul Latif, *Risālō,* Sur Ripa II, vv. 13–15; Sachal Sarmast, *"Waḥdat," Risālō Sindhī,* p. 37.

77. Shahidullah-Abdul Hai, *Heritage of East Pakistan,* p. 18, s.v. *bishled* songs. The imagery of tears as ink is very common in both high and popular Sufi poetry (see chapter 1, note 62), as the motif of letter-writing in general is remarkably often used in both traditions. It is indeed amazing to see the illiterate women in these poems complain time and again that no letter has reached them. This is, however, a topic also found in Sindhi folksongs recited by the young bride who is unhappy in the house of her in-laws and longs for news from home to console her: in mystical interpretation the girl is the soul, imprisoned (like Marui in the Sindhi tradition) in this colorful but treacherous world, who longs for a sign of Divine grace. One of the loveliest expressions of such a "spiritual correspondence" is found in Sachal's "Sur Malkōs," IV, vv. 1–10, in Sachal Sarmast, *Risālō Sindhī,* pp. 344–46; see also his "Marui," III, vv. 2–4. Shah ᶜAbdul Latif's heroines, who write with tears of blood (Marui II, v. 4) would like to decorate with golden threads the wings of the messenger crow that would bring news from the beloved (Sur Purab I, v. 8).

78. There is one group of popular poetry in Egypt that deals with saintly women, but these are Koranic figures like Maryam and Hagar; Enno Littmann has studied them in *Islamisch-arabische Heiligenlieder;* the verse form is, as in Turkish popular songs, the four-lined stanza, with the rhyme of the last line continuing through the poem.

79. Shah ᶜAbdul Latif, *Risālō,* Sur Sohni I, vv. 17, 18. For the origin of the tripartite saying *ṭālib ad-dunyā mu'annath—ṭālib al-ākhira mukhannath—ṭālib al-maulā mudhakkar,* "Who seeks the world, is a female; who seeks the Hereafter, is a catamite; who seeks the Lord, is a man," see Zubaid Ahmad, *Contribution of Indo-Pakistan to Arabic Literature,* p. 82.

80. One may here think of the epical elaboration of early Islamic topics such as the Hamza-Romance; or the story of Muhammad ibn al-Hanafiyya, a son of ᶜAli by another wife than Fatima (according to the tradition, a "blackish slave girl from Sind"), which is found in the Panjab, in Bengal, South India, and Malaysia; or of the tales of Tamim ad-Dari in Dakhni and Tamil as well as in Multani verse.

81. Shushtari was a disciple of the mystical thinker Ibn Sabᶜīn; therefore he starts with Hermes and Socrates and continues through Hallaj to Ibn Sina and the North African mystical philosopher Ibn Qasyi; quoted in Ibn al-Kha-

tib, *Kitāb al-iḥāṭa,* Ms. Paris, Bibliothèque Nationale, Ms. arabe 3347/2, fol. 209a–210a. See for this school of thought M. Asin Palacios, *The Mystical Philosophy of Ibn Masarra and His Followers.*

82. It leads down to al-Jazuli (d. 1463), the author of the most widely read book of blessings on the Prophet, *Dalā'il al-khairāt;* see Emile Dermenghem, *Le Culte des saints dans l'Islam maghrébin,* p. 309 ff.

83. Ruzbihan-i Baqli, *Sharḥ-i shaṭḥiyāt,* secs. 377–78.

84. Christopher Shackle, "The Multani *marsiya,*" offers an excellent analysis of popular religious poetry. Annemarie Schimmel, "The *marthiya* in Sindhi": Shah ᶜAbdul Latif, in *Sur Kēdārō* VI, vv. 10 and 11, takes up the motif of nuptials for the death of the martyrs:

> The houris wind rose chains; flower decorations for the martyrs!

For a Bengali *jārī* celebration, which is accompanied in the Mymensingh area by dancing, see Shahidullah-Abdul Hai, *Traditional Culture in East Pakistan,* with a typical example of a folk song:

> O the two imam brothers Hasan and Husain
> Are, I am told, *Rasūl*'s (i.e., the Prophet's) grandsons;
> They are the emblems of Paradise, the two brothers:
> The slave Yazid lured them away to Kerbela.

See also A. Kovalenka, *Le martyre de Ḥusayn dans la poesie populaire de l'Iraq.* The genre of *maqtal Ḥusain* was popular in India from at least the thirteenth century, as can be concluded from Amir Khusrau's remarks, and even in a predominantly Sunni country like Egypt the feast of the Hasanain is celebrated with great enthusiasm. Everywhere, Hasan is integrated into the story of Kerbela although he had died about twenty years before his younger brother was killed there in 680.

85. Sachal, *Risālō Sindhī,* p. 110; cf. also p. 81, Kafi 16. See Christopher Shackle, *Styles and Themes in the Siraiki Mystical Poetry of Sind,* p. 15 f.

86. For Zakariya cf. *The Tales of the Prophets of al-Kisā'ī.* This story has also rather frequently been illustrated; a fine miniature is in the Worcester Art Museum, Worcester, Mass. Accession No. 1935.16.

87. About the mysterious figure of Shams see Vladimir Ivanow, "Shams Tabriz of Multan."

88. The story of Shaikh Sanᶜan, from *Manṭiq uṭ-ṭair,* Maqāla 14, has been reworked by Mir ᶜAli Shir Nawa'i (d. 1501) in Chagatay Turkish, and is known in Kashmiri and Malay versions as well; it was often illustrated (see Schimmel, *Mystical Dimensions,* p. 269).

89. For Sarmad see Bashir Ahmad Kashmi, "Sarmad."

90. Annemarie Schimmel, "Shah ᶜInāyat of Jhok, A Sindhi Mystic of the Early Eighteenth Century."

91. Annemarie Schimmel, "The Martyr Mystic Hallaj in Sindhi Folk Poetry."

92. *Padmavat,* trans. A. G. Shireff, chapter 25: "The impalement of Ratan Sen"; "He like Mansur laughed as he saw the stake." In chapter 11, v. 6 Hallaj is also mentioned, with the confusing explanation in the footnote: "He was learned in the Vedanta and took the name of An-al-haq (the *so'ham* of the Upanishads, "I am He")"; the idea that "Hallaj was a Brahmanical thinker of purest water" was popularized in Europe particularly by Max Horten, *Indische Strömungen in der islamischen Mystik.*

93. Annemarie Schimmel, "Zur Verwendung des Hallaj-Motivs in der indo-persischen Poesie"; and Schimmel, *A Dance of Sparks,* "Ghalib and the tradition of Hallaj."

94. Bullhe Shah, quoted in L. Ramakrishna, *Panjabi mystical poetry,* pp. 58–59. *Turk* is the general designation of the Muslim in Indian popular tradition, as is evident from the numerous examples in Kabir and the medieval *bhakti* lyrics (see for examples Charlotte Vaudeville, *Kabir,* and Yusuf Husain, *L'Inde mystique*); the same is true for Panjabi and, less frequently, Sindhi. After all, the first conquerors of North West India and many of the later rulers, including the Moghuls, were of Turkish extraction; besides, the motif of the beautiful but cruel Turk was commonplace in higher Persian poetry.

95. A typical, though neither poetical nor attractive example of this genre, which begins in Turkey with Yunus Emre, is a *nefes* of one Fakhkhar in the fifteenth century, beginning with the statement: "I am the sultan of the sultans . . ." and turning then into a kind of grammatical exercise with the active and passive participles of Arabic verbs:

> I am the intended goal, *maqṣūd,* for those who intend, *qāṣid;*
> I am the thing known, *maᶜlūm,* for those who know, *ᶜālim;*
> I am the thing understood, *mafhūm,* for those who understand, *fāhim;*
> I am the thing asked for, *mas'ūl,* for those who ask, *sā'il,*

and so on; Kocatürk, *Tekke şiiri,* p. 95.

96. Yunus Emre, *Divan,* p. 333, I.

97. Ibid., p. 333, II.

98. Thus Sari as-Saqati, mentioned in Ghazzali, *Iḥyā ᶜulūm ad-dīn* IV, p. 254: "The nations will be called at Doomsday by the names of their Prophets . . . except for those who love God, for they will be addressed: ᶜO friends of God, quickly up to God Most High!' and then they will be utterly wonderstruck from joy."

99. *Qāḍī Qādan jō kalām,* no. 57. Multan is the resting place of the great Suhrawardi saint Baha'uddin Zakariya (d. 1267).

100. Ibid., no. 20. Yunus often uses this idea. For the combination of exercise and interior pilgrimage in the work of Khwaja Farid, a popular Siraiki poet of the late nineteenth century, see Christopher Shackle, "The Pilgrimage

and the Extension of Sacred Geography in the Poetry of Khwāja Ghulām Farid."

101. *Qāḍī Qādan jō kalām*, no. 58.

102. Shahidullah-Abdul Hai, *Heritage of East Pakistan*, p. 22.

103. Sometimes the founder of an order would leave a rhymed *waṣiya*, an exhortation for his followers; see René Brunel, *Le monachisme errant dans l'Islam*, pp. 157–60, the orally transmitted poem by Sidi Heddi who, in the midst of advice and rules promises his perambulatory disciples:

> When you roam about,
> I'll fly over your heads . . .

104. Longworth Dames, *Popular Poetry of the Baloches*, I, p. 158. The saying "My foot is on the neck of every saint" has been ascribed to ᶜAbdul Qadir in the Middle Ages. Pashto eulogies for him are mentioned in Blumhardt-MacKenzie, *Catalogue of the Pashto Manuscripts*, no. 39 (from the nineteenth century).

105. William Hickman, *Eshrefoghlu Rumi: Reconstitution of his Dīwān;* poem attributed to him, K 9.

106. Ibid., poem Y 21.

107. *Majmūᶜa Panj Ganj*, p. 4.

108. Jaman Charan (d. 1738), in N. A. Baloch, ed., *Madāḥūñ ain Munājatūñ*, p. 11.

109. In Panjabi, there are *bārahmāsa* about Fariduddin Ganj Shakar of Pakpattan (*Majmūᶜa Panj Ganj*, p. 9) and *sīḥarfī* in honor of Sultan Bahu, while in Sind, where the women often use endearing diminutives (*Pīral, Ghauthal*) in addressing the saints, we find poems in honor of Lal Shahbaz Qalandar of Sehwan, who is often implored when a woman wants a son (Annemarie Schimmel, "Hochzeitslieder der Frauen im Industal") and, in more recent times, verses devoted to the Pir Pagaro; examples for Lal Shahbaz and Pir Murad of Thatta are also found in Balochi because Baloch tribes migrate in winter into the Indus Valley; see Longworth Dames, *Popular Poetry*. An interesting West African example of popular, four-lined verses devoted to the Tijani saint, al-Hajj Omar Seydū (d. 1864): Christine Seydou, "Trois poèmes mystiques peuls du Foûta-Djalou." In Turkey, one finds poems addressing Hajji Bektash and the patron saint of Ankara, Hajji Bayram (examples in Kocatürk, *Tekke şiiri*) but also epical poems describing the miracles of saintly persons, see Franz Taeschner, *Gülschehris Mesnewi auf Achi Evran, den Heiligen von Kirschehir und Patron der türkischen Zünfte*. A modern Egyptian example with a colorful account of the saint's miracles is Enno Littmann, *Ahmad il-Bedawi, ein Lied auf den ägyptischen Nationalheiligen*. It goes without saying that classical poetry knows the same types: one may think of Amir Khusrau's eulogies for Nizamuddin Auliya, or of Fakhruddin ᶜIraqi's poems for his master Baha'uddin Zakariya Multani; in Turkey, it was particularly Maulana Rumi who inspired numberless poets to devote hymns to him, see Mehmet Önder, *Mevlâna şiirleri*

antolojisi, and Abdulbaki Gölpînarlî, *Mevlâna'dan sonra Mevlevilik*, Part IV, pp. 444–501.

110. A lovely example of poetry in honor of Gesudaraz are the verses by Sultan Ibrahim II Adilshah of Bijapur, which he inserts into his *Kitāb-i Nauras* (ed. by Nazir Ahmad), Nos. 1, 17, 28, 35, 52, and 59 (the last poem). Good examples of post-classical and modern hymns in honor of masters in the Shadhiliyya order are found in Fatima al-Yashrutiyya, *Riḥlat ila'l-ḥaqq*, esp. pp. 194 ff.

111. It would be worthwhile to explore to what extent Victor Turner's remark, "Mystical rhetoric . . . is very often characteristic of movements of egalitarism, popular protest during liminal periods of history and when social, economic, and intellectual structures . . . begin to show signs of breaking up and become objects of questioning" ("Metaphors of Anti-Structure," in *Dramas, Fields, and Metaphors*, p. 293) is valid for Sufism; it is certainly relevant for the recently growing interest of progressive writers in Islamic countries in the mystical tradition, in which they discover the predominance of Love over law and tend to interpret historical religious figures like Hallaj, Bishr al-Hafi, or Shah ᶜInayat of Jhok in the light of modern social ideals. A typical example of this tendency is the powerful set of poems about the mystical rebel Qadi Badruddin of Simawna and his conflict with the Ottoman government by the Turkish communist poet Nazim Hikmet.

112. Shah Waliullah, *Alṭāf al-quds*, p. 92, quoted in Ghulam H. Jalbani, *Shāh Walīullāh jō taᶜlīm*, p. 114.

113. Edgard Blochet, *Catalogue des manuscripts persanes de la Bibliothèque Nationale* (Paris 1928), II, pp. 246–48: *kitāb aṣl al-maqāṣid wa faṣl al-marāṣid*. See Ignaz Goldziher, "Linguistisches aus der Literatur der muhammedanischen Mystik," an article in which the problems of "mystical philology," especially the case of *suryānī*, is discussed in great depth; Alessandro Bausani, "About a Curious Mystical Language." I wonder what the *Pūrbī*, "eastern" language was, in which God according to legend addressed Nizamuddin Auliya (Vaudeville, *Kabir*, p. 90): given the connection of the East, *sharq*, in the tradition of Sufism, with the area of illumination, *ishrāq*, this Divine *pūrbī* may also belong to the "inspirational" idioms rather than being a veritable Indian dialect. With Shah ᶜAbdul Latif, *pūrab* always denotes the "mystical" East, the home of the soul, and even when the pilgrims travel to Mt. Hinglaj, which is situated west of Sind, they are said to "go East," i.e., to find illumination.

114. Hellmut Ritter, "Philologika IX," *Der Islam* 24 (1939); the manuscript is Aya Sofya 2052, fol. 53b.

115. Sarraj, *Kitāb al-lumaᶜ*, p. 375; see chapter 1, note 22.

116. Adonis, *"As-suryāliyya qabla as-suryāliyya."*

117. A study of Rumi's paradoxes would be most welcome. See in M III, v. 2609, ff., the story of the farsighted blind man, the sharp-hearing deaf per-

son, and the naked one with a long skirt, who embody certain vices. Cf. Sundardas:

> The blind man sees the three worlds and the deaf one hears various sounds,
> The man without nose smells the lotus, and the dumb one supplies much news . . .

Das Gupta, *Obscure Religious Cults,* p. 418. The *shikārnāma* attributed to Gesudaraz contains similar contradictions, as do German lying songs of the type:

> Ich will euch erzählen und will nicht lügen . . .

118. Thus ᶜAzmi, in Ergun, *Bektaşi şairleri,* pp. 201–3; when speaking of the eschatological scales, the poet asks God whether he is a greengrocer or a shopkeeper, etc. Kaygusuz, too, has a related poem:

> *Kïldan köprü yaratmïşsïn . . .*
> *Yigit isen geç a tanrï.*
> You have created a bridge [thinner than] a hair . . .
> If you are a brave young man, hey God, cross it!

119. Yunus' poem, of which also a shorter version exists (*Divan,* p. 446, LIX) has been translated in full by E. J. W. Gibb, *History of Ottoman Poetry,* I, p. 173 ff.

> O my God, if so be Thou should question me,
> Lo then, this would be mine answer unto Thee . . .
> Thou hast set a Balance evil deeds to weigh,
> Hast designed to cast me in the fire straightway.
> Scales are meet for him who may a grocer be,
> May a goldsmith, merchantman, or spicer be.
> Thou'rt omniscient, so Thou know'st mine every way;
> Where Thy need then all my actions thus to weigh?
> Since that sin uncleanst is of things unclean,
> In itself the very work of evil men,
> When shouldst Thou search out and weight that filthiness?
> This were seemly, that Thou veil it with Thy grace, etc.

120. Helmut Ritter, "Muslim Mystics' Strife with God," pp. 1–15; see also Ritter, *Das Meer der Seele,* chapter 10: "Das Hadern mit Gott. Der Narr." For the religious background of this attitude see Friedrich Heiler, *Das Gebet,* pp. 376–77.

121. Yunus' poem (*Divan* p. 131, LIX) is called *shaṭḥiyāt* in Kocatürk, *Tekke şiiri,* p. 59. It ends with the verse:

Yunus has said a word
Which does not resemble any word.
He covers the face of Inner Meaning
From the hands of the hypocrites.

The full text of the commentary in Hamza Tahir, *"at-taṣawwuf ash-shaᶜbī fī'l-adab at-turkī,"* pp. 111–46. See also Schimmel, *Mystical Dimensions,* p. 334.

122. Ernst Benz, "Die Signatur der Dinge." p. 522.

123. Niyazi Misri interprets this verse as follows: "Fish is the gnosis, *maᶜrifa,* of God, which reaches the heart through inspiration and which lives in the ocean of Divine Unity. This ocean is also in the gnostic's heart. It sometimes billows and casts the fish outside the sea toward the gnostics on the shore. By its taste, soul and heart find spiritual nourishment. 'Poplar' is a fragrant tree without fruit. Intended is the dry ascetic who claims to possess gnosis, and who is captured by the wish for authority. He learns by rote some words from the expressions and technical terms of the mighty divines (*ahl-i Allāh*) and sells these wise words as his own goods to those who, with their eyes covered, come near him. His goal is to eat and devour this [material] world. ᶜHe has eaten tar' means that neither he nor those who listen to him experience true pleasure. Now he does not have spiritual pleasure for he knows that it is not his own, and the listeners do not have true spiritual pleasure because gnosis, which does not come from the soul, has no taste. One of the perfect masters has described such people [with the Arabic verse]:

As for the tents, they are their tents,
But I see women which are other than those of the tribe."

Tahir, p. 144. The last verse, incidentally, has been quoted time and again by Sufis when they complained about the degeneration of Sufism, of which only the outward traces are left; it is found first in the introduction of Qushairi's *Risāla,* [Cairo 1912,] p. 2.

124. Cf. Vaudeville, *Kabir,* pp. 133–34. For the topic cf. Camillus Wendeler, "Die verkehrte Welt." This topsy-turvy world, known from English lying songs like "Nottingham's Fair" or the German "Dunkel war's, der Mond schien helle," is common to all peoples; it is found also in pictorial representations from the Middle Ages onward, as in thirteenth-century English tiles that show a hare riding out to hunt. It was a common theme for folk poetry in Western Europe as represented in popular prints. For the typology of lying song, nonsense tale, and their relations to the genre of Tall Tale see Gerald Thomas, *The Tall Tale and Philippe d'Alcripe,* esp. pp. 36–41.

125. Das Gupta, *Obscure Religious Cults,* Appendix E: "Enigmatic Language of the Old and Medieval Poets," pp. 413–24. The *carya*-songs of the Buddhist Siddacaryas are enigmas, and "when interpreted literally they yield the most absurd meaning, but when one obtains the key to them and learns to enter in, one gets at the true meaning hidden behind." The author com-

bines this inverted, *ultā* way of speaking with the Yoga ideal of the inversion of the bodily functions.

126. Ibid., p. 418.

127. Dermenghem, *Le Culte des saints,* p. 21.

128. R. A. Nicholson, *Studies in Islamic Mysticism,* pp. 251–52. One may think of the influence of the oft-quoted *ḥadīth an-nawāfil,* in which God promises the faithful to become "his hand with which he seizes, his eye with which he sees," etc.

129. Daisetz T. Suzuki, *On Indian Mahayana Buddhism,* p. 243.

130. See Toshihiko Izutsu, "The Paradox of Light and Darkness in the Garden of Mystery of Shabastari."

131. M. Kamil ash-Shaibī, *Sharḥ Dīwān al-Ḥallāj,* pp. 166–70. He quotes here examples from Sadruddin Qonawi as well as from the Algerian freedom fighter and mystic ᶜAbdul Qadir (d. 1882). See also Qadi Abdul Mannan, *Literary Heritage of Bangladesh: Medieval Period,* p. 9, quoting ᶜAli Raza's *Jnāna sāgar* about *ultā riti.* One may also think of the designation of Fatima as *umm abīhā,* "her father's mother," under the mystical aspect of timelessness.

132. Das Gupta, *Obscure Religious Cults,* p. 423.

133. Quoted by Gilles Quispel, "Jewish Gnosis and Mandean Gnosticism," pp. 103 ff.

134. Thus in the Pashto riddle mentioned in Darmesteter, *Poésie populaire des Afghans,* p. 114: "La mère n'était pas encore née que le fils montait au dessus du toit" = fire (the mother) and smoke (the son). Similarly the riddle about the *Maḥmal* in Egypt in the wording of a lying song "as they are told in Cairo," Enno Littmann, *Morgenländische Spruchweisheit,* p. 63. See also D. C. Phillott, "Some Persian Riddles Collected from Dervishes in the South of Persia." See also R. A. Nicholson, *Studies in Islamic Mysticism,* pp. 112–13, Jili's vision of the *rūḥ* who "spoke darkly concerning the mystery of his nature, saying: 'I am the child whose father is his son and the wine whose vine is its jar . . . I met the mothers who bore me, and I asked them in marriage. . . .' "

135. Saᶜdi advises his reader (*Gulistān,* ch. 3, p. 108):

> With a sweet tongue and kindness and silence
> Can you catch an elephant by a hair.

Later, a Bengali poet sings with a similar imagery, but in more powerful terms:

> Keep your secret love always secret
> And have your desire satisfied.
> You must make the frog dance before the serpent
> And then only are you true lovers.
> The skillful man, who can wreathe the peak of Mount Sumeru with thread

and can ensnare the elephant into the web of the spider, becomes eligible for such a secret love.

Das Gupta, *Obscure religious cults,* p. 420.

136. L. Ramakrishna, *Panjabi Sufi Poets,* pp. 24–25, a poem which shows, according to the author, his "love for intoxicating things."

137. For a translation of his poems see A. Schimmel, *Aus dem goldenen Becher,* pp. 60–66.

138. S. Manfred Ullmann, *Die Natur- und Geheimwissenschaften im Islam,* p. 196, further *GAS* I 643 and IV 273.

139. Yunus Emre, *Divan,* p. 421, XVI.

140. Ibid., p. 282, VII.

141. *Qāḍī Qādan jō kalām,* no. 31; Shah ᶜAbdul Latif, *Risālō,* Sur Kalyan, I v. 20.

5. GOD'S BELOVED AND INTERCESSOR FOR MAN: POETRY IN HONOR OF THE PROPHET

1. Ikram, *Armaghān-i Pāk,* p. 128.

2. The most important study of the development of the veneration of the Prophet is still Tor Andrae, *Die person Mohammeds in glaube und lehre seiner gemeinde,* which discusses the problem in the light of the comparative study of religions. A very useful summary of popular attitudes towards the Prophet, based mainly on the work of al-Bajuri's disciple, the indefatigable Yusuf an-Nabhani, *Wasā'il al-wuṣūl ilā shamā'il ar-rasūl* (Beirut 1310/1892) is found in Max Horten, *Die religiöse Gedankenwelt des Volkes im heutigen Islam* pp. 12–52, 135–60, 257–69. The basic Arabic source of *naᶜtiyya* poetry is Yusuf an-Nabhani, *Al-majmūᶜa an-nabhāniyya fi'l-madā'iḥ an-nabawiyya.* For a general brief survey see Annemarie Schimmel, "The Prophet Muhammad as a Centre of Muslim Life and Thought," in A. Schimmel and A. Falaturi, eds., *We Believe in One God.* A more detailed study which stresses the poetical aspects of the veneration of the Prophet, in A. Schimmel, *Und Muhammad ist Sein Prophet. Die Verehrung des Propheten in der islamischen Frömmigkeit.*

3. Constance E. Padwick, *Muslim Devotions,* p. 145. This book contains a fine analysis of Muslim prayer life, and of the veneration of the Prophet as reflected in devotional practice, particularly chapter 10b: "The Witness of Islam (*shahāda*) to the Prophet."

4. See the proceedings of the Seerat (*sīrat*) Conference in Karachi 1975: *Message of the Prophet,* where Muhammad is represented as "the model of tranquillity in a turbulent age," as "seal of prophecy," etc., but where also topics such as "The convergence of business management thought to the Holy Prophet's teaching" are discussed.

5. See Wilfred Cantwell Smith, *Islam in Modern India,* p. 65 ff. For the

development in the eighteenth and nineteenth centuries see also Annemarie Schimmel, "The Golden Chain of ᶜSincere Muhammadans.' "

6. Some orientalists have doubted the authenticity of this story because it is not found in Ibn Ishaq's *sīra;* see Rudi Paret, "Die Legende von der Verleihung des Prophetenmantels (*burda*) an Kaᶜb ibn Zuhair." The *Burda* was one of the first Arabic poems ever edited and translated in the West: G. J. Lette, *Carmen panegyricum in laudem Muhammedis* (Leiden 1748). The major annotated translation: René Basset, *La Bânat Soᶜâd;* more easily available is H. Hidayat Husain, "Banat Suᶜad of Kaᶜb bin Zuhair, translated and interpreted."

7. About the various elaborations of the poem by *tashṭīr* (inserting two verses into two original verses), *takhmīs* (filling the basic verses up to quintuplets), and imitations, see Zaki Mubarak, *Al-madā'iḥ an-nabawiyya fī'l-adab al-ᶜarabī,* p. 24 f.

8. Mubarak, *Al-madā'iḥ,* discusses the brief remark of the poet al-Aᶜsha about the Prophet; his verse however "lacks religious feeling," p. 18 ff. See the analysis of the same poem by Gustav E. von Grunebaum, who deals with the problem as to how Muhammad impressed his contemporaries and how his personality is reflected in their verse, "Von Muhammads Wirkung und Originalität" (see also chapter 1, notes 10, 11).

9. Walid N. Arafat, ed., *The Dīwān of Ḥassān ibn Thābit;* Meir J. Kister, "On a New Edition of the Dīwān of Ḥassān ibn Thābit."

10. Hassan ibn Thabit, *Dīwān,* ed. Arafat, no. 28.

11. Ibid., no. 19; cf. the beginning of no. 89:

> I witness with God's permission that Muhammad
> Is the messenger who is from above the heavens.

12. Ibid., no. 34, v. 5 ff.

13. Ibid., no. 9, v. 21; cf. nos. 152 and 132.

14. Ibid., no. 152. Especially the name *Aḥmad,* considered to be the Prophet's heavenly name, was elaborated by pious writers since it was connected in its assumed meaning, *perikletos,* with the *parakletos* of the Christian tradition; hence the importance of Sura 61/6, in which Jesus gives the good tidings of the "most praiseworthy" *Aḥmad,* who will come after him. See also Ignaz Goldziher, "Himmlische und irdische Namen." The veneration of the name is common to almost all religious traditions, see Heiler, *Erscheinungsformen,* p. 277, who speaks of the "permanence of incarnation in the name of Jesus," which finally led to the institution of the "Feast of the name of Jesus" on January 1; poems like Richard Crashaw's, "To the Name above every Name, the Name of Jesus," *Oxford Book of Mystical Verse,* p. 33 express this feeling. The repetition of the powerful name of the deity as known in Hinduism, or the *Namu Amida Butsu* in Japanese Buddhism belongs here as much as formulas of *dhikr* in Islam.

15. Yunus Emre, *Divan,* p. 562, CCXXXIII. Cf. a similar statement by the Sindhi mystic Girhori in his "Commentary Sūrat al-kauthar," see Annemarie Schimmel, "Commentaries and Translations of the Qurᶜān in the Sindhi language," p. 228.

16. Iqbal, *Asrār-i khūdī,* line 352.

17. Iqbal, "Jawāb-i shikwā," *Bāng-i Darā,* p. 231.

18. Qadi ᶜIyad, *Kitāb ash-shifā fī taᶜrīf ḥuqūq al-Muṣṭafā,* quoted in Andrae, *Die person Mohammeds,* p. 273.

19. August Fischer, "Vergöttlichung und Tabuisierung der Namen Muhammads bei den Muslimen," in Richard Hartmann and Helmuth Scheel, eds., *Beiträge zur Arabistik, Semitistik und Islamwissenschaft.* He quotes a *qaṣīda* by Safadi with the names of Muhammad derived from the Koran (p. 228); slowly the number of names grew to more than two hundred, and Horten, *Gedankenwelt des Volkes,* p. 15, mentions a thousand names, for according to ᶜAbdallah al-Mirghani, in whose *ṭarīqa* the veneration of the Prophet found its outlet in a large literature of devotion, the Prophet is called differently on every level of creation: for the devils he is ᶜAbdul Qahhar, "The Servant of the Overpowering," for the fishes ᶜAbdul Quddus, "The Servant of the All-Holy," in the Psalms he is called *al-fārūq,* etc. See also Padwick, *Muslim Devotions,* pp. 138–40. For the healing power of Muhammad's name see the touching poem which ᶜAbdur Rahim al Burᶜi, one of the most fertile panegyrists of the Prophet in the Middle Ages, composed when his young son was on the point of dying, with its closing line:

> And affliction has aggravated on my son who is named after you—
> Have mercy upon his tears which flow over his cheeks!

And the boy was healed. Nabhani, *Majmūᶜa* III, pp. 232–35.

20. Hassan ibn Thabit, *Dīwān,* ed. Arafat, no. 131, vv. 9–10; no. 132, v. 3.

21. Ibid., no. 130, v. 7 (battle of Badr); cf. Jamaluddin as-Sarsari (d.656/1258), who combines the motif of light and that of intercession in his *Hamziyya,* Nabhani, *Majmūᶜa,* I, p. 113. For the problem see T. Huitema, *De voorspraak (shafāᶜa) in den Islam.* Cf. also Padwick, *Muslim Devotions,* pp. 38–47, and Andrae, *Die person Mohammeds,* pp. 235–44.

22. Nabhani, *Majmūᶜa* I, p. 457.

23. Ibid., p. 488.

24. Jan Knappert, *Swahili Islamic Poetry,* I, p. 30 ff.

25. Mir Taqi Mir, *Kulliyāt,* p. 352.

26. A. Zajączkowski, *Ašiq Pašā,* p. 10. Understandably, the topic is common in popular poetry all over the Muslim world; for an example from the beggars' order of the Heddawa in North Africa see Brunel, *Le Monachisme errant,* p. 150.

27. Darmesteter, *Chants populaires des Afghans,* nos. 31, 32.

28. For *liwā' al-ḥamd* see Arend J. Wensinck, *Concordance et indices de la tradition musulmane,* I, p. 510.

29. Cf. Mubarak, *Al-madā'iḥ,* p. 33 f., about Hassan's composition and related traditions about the beauty of the Prophet.

30. Tirmidhi quotes the *ḥadīth:* "Whosoever sees my *ḥilya* after my death will be as if he had seen me, and whosoever sees it, longing for me, God will make Hellfire forbidden for him," see Andrae, *Die person Mohammeds,* p. 199 ff. Among the Turkish poets, Khaqani in the sixteenth century is noted for his beautiful *ḥilyā;* see E. W. J. Gibb, *History of Ottoman Poetry,* III, pp. 196–98, and Köprülü, *Eski şairlerimiz,* pp. 187–89, excerpts. In the Urdu tradition, a good example is Muhammad Lutf ᶜAli Lutf, *Sarāpā sarwar-i anbiyā.* Nabhani has described the Prophet's *shamā'il* in his long *Hamziyya* (*Majmūᶜa* I, pp. 204–97), discussing both his mystical and his worldly qualities:

> He is the light of lights, the origin of mankind,
> When there was no Adam nor Eve . . .
> He is singular, by God, and everything is from him,
> There is none second to him, and there is not a second one like him at the same time.
>
> . . .
>
> He liked all permitted food,
> And he particularly loved *ḥalwa;*
> He liked very much cream with dates, and other things
> Which he liked were melon and cucumber . . .

A good description of Muhammad's qualities in Horten, *Gedankenwelt des Volkes,* pp. 38–52.

31. Ghazzali, *Iḥyā' ᶜulūm ad-dīn,* I, p. 278. For a typical modern popular work see: Mohammad Elias Burney, *Mishkaat us-salawaat. A Bouquet of Blessings of Muhammad the Prophet* (*Peace be upon Him*). It is an anthology from widely used later handbooks, which contain formulas of blessing for the Prophet, such as ᶜAli al-Muttaqi's *Kanz al-ᶜummāl,* ᶜAli al-Qari's *Al-ḥizb al-aᶜẓam,* Gümüshkhanawi's *Majmūᶜat al-aurād wa'el-aḥzāb,* and Jazuli's *Dalā'il al-khairāt,* the most widely used collection of blessings for the Prophet (for an example from this work see Padwick, *Muslim Devotions,* pp. 146–47).

32. Nabhani, following as-Suyuti and others, has composed his *Durrat al-funūn fi ru'yat al-ᶜuyūn* about the Prophet's appearance in dreams, see Horten, *Gedankenwelt des Volkes,* Introduction, p. xxvii. Andrae, *Die person Mohammeds,* pp. 378–80, shows that among Sufis a dream of the Prophet was sometimes regarded as a kind of initiatory experience. It was commonly accepted that Satan can never assume the form of the Prophet, hence to see Muhammad in one's dream means to seem him in reality.

33. See Gerhard Böwering, *The Mystical Vision of Existence in Classical Is-*

lam, and "The Prophet of Islam: The First and the Last Prophet," in *Message of the Prophet,* pp. 48–60, particularly about the elaboration of the theory of the *nūr Muḥammad* by Sahl at-Tustari.

34. Al-Hallaj, *Kitāb aṭ-ṭawāsīn,* "ṭāsīn as-sirāj."

35. N. A. Baloch, ed., *Munāqibā,* see Schimmel, "Neue Veröffentlichungen zur Volkskunde von Sind." p. 244–48.

36. Sarraj, *Kitāb al-lumaᶜ,* p. 209.

37. Qazi Abdul Mannan, "Sufi Literature in Bengal," in *Literary Heritage of Bangladesh,* pp. 10–11. Cf. in the Arabic tradition Jamaluddin as-Sarsari's *Jīmiyya* (Nabhani, *Majmūᶜa* I, p. 564 f.) with its beginning:

> Is it your face, or the light of the morning which radiates?
> Or the Moon in the mansion of perfection which wipes out darkness,
> Or the sun on a cloudless day in his ascension? . . .

This imagery, which was very common in the Persian tradition (see note 96) was used in India as well, as becomes clear, for example, from a *naᶜt* of the South Indian poet Maulwi Ghulam Muhammad Muᶜjiz who wrote, among other eulogies for "the Nightingale of the Meadow of Unity and the Rose of the Gardens of Prophetship," a long Persian *qaṣīda* "In Praise of the Luminary of the Sky of *danā fa tadallā* [ᶜHe approached and came closer,' Sura 53/8] And the Constellation of the Zodiacal Sign *qāba qausain* [ᶜTwo bows' length or closer,' Sura 53/9], Before Whose Light the Sun and the Moon of every Evening and Dawn are smaller than the Tiny Star *Suhā,*" quoted in Muhd. Yousuf Kokan, *Khanwāda-i Qāżī Badruddaula,* I, pp. 203–5. The idea of Muhammad's omnipresent light is also applied to the dreams in which the Prophet appears; he "can be seen in dreams by many different people in the same hour . . . because he is like the sun whose light covers many countries, east and west," Fedwa Malti-Douglas, "Dreams, the Blind, and the Semiotics," p. 159. It should also be remembered that the most famous of Muhammad's prayers is the prayer for light (trans. in Padwick, *Muslim Devotions,* p. 212), which was repeated by generations of pious Muslims: a leading mystic of the eighteenth century, Mir Dard, quotes it as last prayer of his life in *Shamᶜ -i maḥfil,* no. 341.

38. S. Yohanan Friedmann, "Qiṣṣat Shakarwartī Farmāḍ": a South Indian king was converted by the miracle of the Splitting of the Moon. An epic on this event exists even in Swahili; Knappert, *Swahili Islamic Poetry,* I, p. 38.

39. Jon M. S. Baljon, trans. *A Mystical Interpretation of Prophetic Tales by an Indian Muslim: Shāh Walī Allāh's ta'wīl al-aḥādīth.* p. 60.

40. See Andrae, *Die person Mohammeds,* p. 60. For Qadi ᶜIyad see *GAL* I 455–56, S I 630–32; for al-Qastallani, whose work, *al-mawāhib al-laduniyya,* was largely based on Qadi ᶜIyad, and was then abridged by Nabhani, see *GAL* II 87–88, S II 78–79.

41. Hafiz ibn Dihya (d. 1235), *Kitāb at-tanwīr fi maulid as-sirāj al-munīr* (mark the symbolism of light in the title!); this author, who participated in

the *maulid* celebration in Arbela in 1207, also wrote a work about the names of the Prophet, see *GAL* I 310, S I 544.

42. Andrae, *Die person Mohammeds,* p. 64: Ibn al Jauzi's *maulid* is in verse and rhymed prose.

43. Ibn Kathir (d. 1372), *Maulid rasūl Allāh.*

44. The first recorded *maulid* celebrations took place in Arbela (northern Iraq) in 604/1207; see *Handwörterbuch des Islam,* s.v. *maulid.* An excellent survey is Pesah Shinar, "Traditional and reformist *maulid* celebrations in the Maghrib."

45. Annemarie Schimmel, "Some glimpses of religious life during the later Mamluk period in Egypt," pp. 370–71.

46. Lane, *Manners and Customs of the Modern Egyptians,* pp. 448–62, offers also the translation of a *muwashshaḥ* in honor of the Prophet, which Lane compares to the love poetry in the Song of Songs.

47. Yunus Emre, *Divan,* p. 575, CCL.

48. Poetical English verse translation in Gibb, *Ottoman Poetry,* I, pp. 241–48; translation by Lyman McCallum, *The Mevlidi Sharif;* Irmgard Engelke, *Süleyman Tschelebis Lobgedicht auf die Geburt des Propheten.* Hamid Algar mentions a Serbo-Croatian translation of this poem by Hafiz Salih Gašovič (for which refer to Werner Lehfeldt, *Das serbokroatische Aljamiado Schrifttum der bosnischen-herčegovinischen Muslime*), see Algar, "Some Notes on the Naqshbandi *ṭarīqa* in Bosnia," p. 177. For a poetical translation of a *maulid* of the Ottoman poet Hamdi see Gibb, II, pp. 217–20.

49. Cf. also al-Qadi Abu Bakr ibn ᶜAtiya al-Andalusi in the fourteenth century:

> The month of Rabiᶜ is preceding the months . . .
> And by God! it has one night which is resplendent
> With luminous meteors between the horizons . . .

(Nabhani, *Majmūᶜa* I, p. 450), and the Turkish popular poet Wali (d. 1695):

> The night in which that prophet was born is without doubt
> Similar to the *lailat al-qadr*

(Kocatürk, *Tekke şiiri,* p. 375).

50. Thus already in Ibn Saᶜd's *Ṭabaqāt,* see Andrae, *Die person Mohammeds,* p. 30.

51. Knappert, *Swahili Islamic Poetry,* I, p. 45.

52. See the short survey by Muhsin Jamaluddin, *Iḥtifālāt al-mawālīd an-nabawiyya fī'l-ashᶜār al-andalusiyya wa'l-maghribiyya wa'l-mahjariyya,* which also contains some related poems by Arabic writers in South America.

53. Knappert, *Swahili Islamic poetry,* I, p. 100 ff.

54. Ibid., III, p. 283; Shinar, "Traditional and Reformist *maulid* Celebrations," mentions the ᶜ*aṣīda,* a sweet which is usually distributed at childbirth.

In Turkey, candy and lemon sherbet is offered; sometimes the guests receive small amounts of sweets to take home *tabarrukan,* "for the sake of blessing."

55. Barzanji was Shafiite *qāḍī* of Medina, he died in 1765; his *maulūd* is also used in North Africa, see Shinar, "Traditional and Reformist *maulid* Celebrations," p. 395. See *GAL* II 384; *S* II 577.

56. Ernst Bannerth, *Islamische Wallfahrtstätten Kairos,* p. 15.

57. Knappert, *Swahili Islamic Poetry,* I, p. 43.

58. See ᶜAbdul ᶜAli Hafiz Jhanda, *Guldasta,* pp. 7–9, a Panjabi *qaṣīda* "Nicest commemoration of the birth of the best of mankind," in which flowers and birds praise the new-born Prophet. Muhammad Amin in sixteenth-century Gujarat, went in his *Tawalludnāma* so far as "introducing a Brahmin at the time of the Prophet's birth and his putting the sacred thread around the neck of the Prophet," Dar, "Gujarat's contribution to Urdu and Gujri," p. 33. (See also below, note 161.) This attitude is not different from that of German or Dutch painters who placed the Nativity in a northern European landscape, or that of popular Christmas carols where Bethlehem is transferred into a German rural environment (a charming example is Werner Bergengruen's *Kaschubisches Weihnachtslied*); it is the feeling of being very close to the blessed child who will emerge as the savior of all those who follow him.

59. Knappert, *Swahili Islamic Poetry,* III, p. 276 ff; Ibid., II, p. 223, a translation of the *Burda,* where the translator adds a prayer for his wife!

> Lord, help my wife!
> Let the disasters of this life avoid her,
> And tomorrow, in the other life, may she enter Paradise
> Without reckoning or blame.

Cf. in the Turkish tradition Wali (d. 1695):

> If you want to find rescue from Hell,
> come to the pure *mevlûd* of the messenger of God,

Kocatürk, *Tekke şiiri,* p. 375.

60. Mubarak, *Al-madā'iḥ,* pp. 202–6. Taha Husain wrote in 1934: "It seems most fitting not to deprive people of ideas which do not contradict religion and do not spoil them in anything of their faith. What is the danger for the Muslims when one tells them the sweet and lovely stories of these *ḥadīth* and informs them that the communities of birds and beasts competed after the birth of the Prophet because all of them wanted to look after him, but were refused because it had been decreed that the Prophet should be nursed by the blessed Halima? And what is wrong for the Muslims when they hear that djinns, men, animals, and stars congratulated each other at the birth of the Prophet, and that the trees sprouted leaves at his birth, and that the garden

blossomed at his arrival, and that the sky came close to the earth when his noble body touched the ground?" See also Joseph M. McPherson, *The Moulids of Egypt.*

61. Josef Horovitz, "Die poetischen Einlagen der Sīra."

62. G. van der Leeuw, *Phänomenologie der Religion,* p. 108.

63. A beautiful account of the annunciation in Rumi's *Mathnawī,* III, v. 3700 ff. See also Ignaz Goldziher, "Influences chrétiennes dans la littérature religieuse de l'Islam."

64. Enrico Cerulli, *Il ʿLibro della Scala' e al questione delle fonti arabo-spagnole della ʿDivina Commedia'.* The literature about the *miʿrāj* is very large. A typology is offered by Heiler, *Erscheinungsformen,* pp. 149–50; see also Mircea Eliade, "Le vol magique"; further Wilhelm Bousset, "Die Himmelsreise der Seele," *ARW* (1901)); Anthony A. Bevan, "Muhammad's Ascension to Heaven"; Bernhard Schrieke, "Die Himmelsreise Muhammads"; Josef Horovitz, "Muhammads Himmelfahrt"; Richard Hartmann, "Die Himmelsreise Muhammads und ihre Bedeutung in der Religion des Islam"; Geo Widengren, *The Ascension to Heaven and the Heavenly Book;* Abu'l-ʿAla Affifi, "The Story of the Prophet's Ascent (*miʿrāj*) in Sufi Thought and Literature"; Alexander Altmann, "The Ladder of Ascension"; Nazeer al-Azma, "Some Notes on the Impact of the Story of the *miʿrāj* on Sufi Literature" deals mainly with Ibn ʿArabi's *Kitāb al-isrā' ila maqām al-asrā;* J. R. Porter, "Muhammad's Journey to Heaven." An important Sufi work is al-Qushairi, *Kitāb al-miʿrāj.*

65. Reproduction of Sultan Muhammad's miniature of the Ascension, probably the most glorious pictorial interpretation of the event (British Library, Ms. 2265, fol. 195r) in Stuart Cary Welch, *Wonders of the Age,* no. 63, where more details are given. For another beautiful miniature see the frontispiece of Rypka, *History of Iranian Literature.* For the topic see Richard Ettinghausen, *Persian Ascension Miniatures of the Fourteenth Century.* The famous Supplement Turc 190 of the Bibliothèque Nationale, Paris, which had been translated into French by Pavet de Courteille, *Mirâdjnameh,* was recently published with all pictures: Marie-Rose Séguy, *Muhammads wunderbare Reise durch Himmel and Hölle* (English translation also available).

66. Yunus Emre, *Divan,* p. 575, CCLIV; a fine *miʿrājiyya* in ʿAttar, *Ilāhī-nāma,* pp. 12–18; a Turkish example by Thabit in Gibb, *Ottoman Poetry,* IV, pp. 22–24. The Dakhni poet Nusrati in Bijapur (d. 1684) also wrote a *miʿrājnāma.* In India and Pakistan, I found Miʿraj, or Miraj Din even as proper names, most likely for children born on the feast of *miʿrāj,* as among Turkish and North African Muslims boys may be called *maulūd* and girls *mauludiyya,* when they are born on the Prophet's birthday.

67. Thus Ghanizada, Turkey, seventeenth century, quoted in Köprülü, *Eski şairlerimiz,* pp. 353–57; this specific line is from the very colorful poem, p. 356. With a fine pun on "bow" and "arrow," the poet states towards the end:

Transgressing the station of *qāba qausain,* "Two bows' length" [Sura 53/9] like an arrow,
At that moment, the goal of "higher" and "or even closer" [*au adnā*] was achieved by him.

68. See Rumi, *Mathnawī,* Commentary, Book I, p. 86. Cf. the scene in ᶜAttar's *Ilāhīnāma,* trans. in Schimmel, *Und Muhammad ist Sein Prophet,* pp. 146–48.

69. *Mathnawī* I 1066; Yunus, like many others, also claims that "between lovers, even Gabriel is a veil," *Divan* p. 213.

70. Ikram, *Armaghān-i Pāk,* p. 158.

71. Joseph N. Bell, *Love Theories in Later Hanbalite Islam,* p. 176, discusses this question, quoting Ibn Qayyim al-Jauziyya: "The state of the prophet of Islam is undoubtedly superior to that of Moses, who fell senseless to the ground while God revealed Himself to the mountain." Paul Nwyia, *Exégèse coranique,* p. 187, mentions Jaᶜfar as-Sadiq's interpretation of the fact that Moses only *heard* God while Muhammad *saw* Him.

72. Furuzanfar, *Aḥādīth-i Mathnawī,* no. 100.

73. Cf. Knappert, *Swahili Islamic Poetry,* III, p. 25, for the mystic's ascension, an Arabic prose work by Najmuddin al-Ghiti (1896), translated into Swahili, with its description of the stages of perfection.

74. Andrae, *Die person Mohammeds,* pp. 337, 389, gives examples of ᶜAbdur Rahim al-Burᶜi's (d. 450/1058) poems.

75. The *editio princeps* by J. Uri (Leiden 1761), with Latin translation. Vincenz von Rosenzweig-Schwannau published a German translation in 1824: *Funkelnde Wandelsterne zum Lobe des besten der Geschöpfe* (Vienna, 1824); C. A. Ralfs, *Die Burda,* with Persian and Turkish translations and part translation in German (Vienna, 1860). Printed with an English version by Shaikh Faizullahbhai, *A Moslem Present; Part I: The Poem of the Scarf* (Bombay, 1893). The most widely used commentary is that by Bajuri, finished in 1814, printed in Cairo 1297/1880, with the commentary by Khalid al-Azhari (d. 1500) on the margin. Based on this, Nabhani composed his own comprehensive commentary (see above, note 2). A beautiful print with Jami's Persian poetical version and the Urdu verse translation by the noted modern architect Fayyazaddin Nizami, *Nafḥ al-warda fi sharḥ al-burda,* was issued in Hyderabad/AP 1969. The best-known translation, with commentary, into a Western language is René Basset, *La Bordah du Cheikh al-Bousiri* (Paris 1894). For a longish discussion of the poem see Mubarak, *Al-madā'iḥ,* pp. 140–51, 163 ff.; R. A. Nicholson, *Literary History of the Arabs,* devotes only a brief paragraph to the poem, p. 137.

76. When a theological dispute arose in India as to whether the blessings on Muhammad were meaningful, since he is already perfected, Shah Waliullah quoted the *Burda:*

For the virtue of the messenger of God has no limit
So that anyone who speaks could express it.

At-Tafhīmāt al-ilāhiyya, I, p. 15.

77. A fine Panjabi version with a commentary by Haji Muhammad addin Naqshbandi Mujaddidi from Bombay was published in the *Allāhwālē kī qaumī dukkān,* Lahore; it preserves the rhyme letter *m,* followed by the genitive particle *dī.*

78. Mubarak, *Al-madā'ih,* p. 163 ff.

79. I am grateful to S. S. Khusro Hussaini, Gulbarga, who arranged a special session of the "Burda" for me in his house in Hyderabad in October 1979.

80. A. S. Husain, *Al-adab aṣ-ṣūfī,* p. 217 ff., highly praises Ibn Daqiq al-ᶜId al-Manfaluti, probably because he belongs to the Egyptian tradition; Nabhani, *Majmūᶜa* II, pp. 25–27 quotes only one *naᶜt* from his pen; he was indeed more famous as a traditionist than a poet.

81. See for instance the Panjabi poem by Maulawi Ghulam Rasul (*Majmūᶜa Panj Ganj:*

Morning breeze, when you come to the resting place of God's prophet,
Inform him about my situation!

Also N. A. Baloch, ed., *Madāḥūñ ain munājātūñ,* p. 180. Booklets like one Mirza Shakur Beg's *Madīna kā ṣadaqa,* which contains *naᶜts* written by the author during his pilgrimage and visit to the Prophet's tomb, are frequently found.

82. See Mubarak, *Al-madā'iḥ,* p. 50: ath-Thaᶜlabi (d. 1035) furnished poets and writers with fitting—and of course rhyming—formulas for the description of him "who brought this community from darkness to light, and spread over them shade after heat . . . ; whose birth is blessed, and whose arrival is fortunate; whose morning is bright and whose lamp is full of light; whose wars are victorious, and whose sermons are glorious," etc.

83. S. Mubarak, *Al-madā'iḥ,* p. 188; *GAL* II (2d ed.), pp. 10–12; *EI*² III, pp. 900–01.

84. Mubarak, *Al-madā'iḥ,* speaks *in extenso* of Ibn Jabir's *badīᶜiyyāt* (p. 169). Other poets who excelled in artistic verse are Safiuddin al-Hilli (d. 1349), Ibn Hijja al-Hamawi (d. 837/1434), see *EI*² III, pp. 799–80; and as-Sarsari (d. 656/1258), about whom *GAL* I (2d ed.), p. 290, mentions that he composed a *qaṣīda* in praise of the Prophet in which every verse contains all letters of the alphabet. Nabhani quotes numerous poems by him as well as by the Spanish author Majduddin al-Witri (d. 662/1264), see *GAL* I (2d ed.), pp. 290–91.

85. Nabhani, *Majmūᶜa* III, pp. 321–23, by the famous literary critic al-Hazim al-Andalusi (al-Qartajanni) (d. 684/1285), and a similar poem by another Spanish North-African poet. See also his introductory remarks about the

various arts used in *na*ᶜ*t* poetry, I, p. 16 ff. The same rhetorical devices and forms were used in India; M. Y. Kokan, *Arabic and Persian in Carnatic,* pp. 62–65, quotes quintuplets of the *burdas* of Kaᶜb ibn Zuhair and al-Busiri.

86. Nabhani, *Majmū*ᶜ*a,* I, p. 34 ff.

87. Kokan, *Arabic and Persian in Carnatic,* p. 61 ff.: Shaikh Sadaqatullah (d. 1115/1703) in South India produced a quintuplet of Abu Bakr ibn Muhammad al-Witri's *Al-qaṣīdat al-witriyya fī madḥ khair al- bariyya* in alphabetical order plus eight additional *mukhammas* for each letter of the alphabet! See also Muᶜid Khan, *The Arabian Poets of Golconda,* pp. 102–8.

88. Poems on Muhammad's *na*ᶜ*l,* "sandal," in Nabhani, *Majmū*ᶜ*a* III, pp. 386–416; they were written as early as the thirteenth century in Andalusia. One poem is by a woman, ash-shaikha Saᶜduna umm Saᶜd al-Andalusiyya (d. 640/1238), p. 398:

> I shall kiss the picture if I do not find
> A way of kissing the [true] sandal of al-Mustafa . . .

The North African author al-Maqarri (d. 1631), devoted a whole volume to the veneration of the Prophet's sandals: *Fatḥ al-muta*ᶜ*āl fī madīḥ an-ni*ᶜ*āl.* For in some areas, Muhammad's shoe was regarded as a powerful talisman (Knappert, *Swahili Islamic Poetry,* I, p. 40).

89. *Burda,* v. 46; cf. his Hamziyya as quoted in Nabhani, *Majmū*ᶜ*a* I, p. 5.

90. Similarly Ibn al-Farid, Nabhani, *Majmū*ᶜ*a* I, p. 7.

91. Nabhani, *Majmū*ᶜ*a* I, p. 4.

92. Horten, *Gedankenwelt des Volkes,* p. 150.

93. Ghulam Dastagir Rasheed, "The Development of Naᶜtia Poetry in Persian Poetry," p. 53. The article is a useful compilation of material.

94. Mir ᶜAli Shir Qaniᶜ, *Maqālāt ash-shu*ᶜ*arā,* p. 592.

95. Ghulam Dastagir Rasheed, pp. 56, 68.

96. Sana'i, *Dīwān,* p. 34, *qaṣīda* no. 14. The formula became commonplace in *na*ᶜ*tiyya* poetry so that ᶜAshiq Pasha, one of the earliest Turkish poets to use strophic forms (d. 1332), writes in his *na*ᶜ*t* with the *radīf ver salawat Muhammad'a,* "Utter the blessings over Muhammad!" in verse 6:

> *Onun yüzü shams aḍ-ḍuḥā*
> *amber sacī leyli asjā*
> His face is the sun "By the Morning light"
> His black hair "By the Night when it falls."

Zającskowski, *Ašiq Paša,* p. 8.

97. Sana'i, *Dīwān,* p. 364.

98. Ibid., p. 167.

99. Ibid., p. 363, the letters of *Bū dharr* and *Nōdhar* are distinguished in writing only by the placement of one diacritical dot.

100. Ibid., p. 44.

101. Ibid., p. 167.

102. Ibid., p. 363.

103. Ibid., p. 374; cf. al-Busiri's poem in *ḥ:*

> If there were not the Prophet Muhammad and his knowledge,
> One would not know what to regard as good and what to blame!

Nabhani, *Majmūᶜa* I, p. 584. One has always to keep in mind that it is the second half of the profession of faith, "Muhammad is the Messenger of God," which determines Islam as a distinct religion and was understood to point to the legal aspect of Islam, while the first half, "There is no deity save God," could be accepted by most believers in the various religious traditions.

104. Sana'i, *Dīwān*, p. 43; cf. the story that Abu Hafs ᶜUmar as-Suhrawardi (d. 1234) boasted that he had washed off the ten volumes of Avicenna's *Kitab ash-shifā* (Ritter, "L'orthodoxie a-t-elle une part dans la décadence?" p. 178). See also chapter 2, notes 64, 65.

105. ᶜAttar, *Muṣībatnāma*, p. 54; Rumi, D 1793/18827, goes even further:

> O you princely rider of the order "Say!," O you before whom the Universal Soul
> Is like a child which out of childishness and ignorance chews his sleeve . . .

106. Sana'i, *Dīwān*, p. 363.

107. Sana'i, *Ḥadīqa*, ch. 3, p. 209. The "white nights" are the nights between the thirteenth and fifteenth of each month, which were sometimes used for additional fasting or other supererogatory works; the *shab-i barāt* was celebrated, from the early Middle Ages, on the fourteenth shaᶜbān; one believes that in that night the destinies for the next year are fixed.

108. ᶜAttar, *Ilāhīnāma*, p. 13. See the whole long encomium in Boyle's translation, which partly relies on a text different from that used by Ritter for his edition.

109. ᶜAttar, *Muṣībatnāme*, p. 20.

110. ᶜAttar, *Manṭiq uṭ-ṭair*, p. 18. For the idea see also Andrae, *Die person Mohammeds*, pp. 321–22.

111. ᶜAttar, *Ilāhīnāma*, p. 11.

112. ᶜAttar, *Muṣībatnāma*, p. 24.

113. ᶜAttar, *Ilāhīnāma*, p. 18.

114. ᶜAttar, *Muṣībatnāma*, p. 20. Cf. also *Ushturnāma*, ch. 12, sec. 7, p. 95 for the letter *m*.

115. See Yohanan Friedmann, *Shaikh Aḥmad Sirhindī: An Outline of His Thought and a Study of His Image in the Eyes of Posterity*, pp. 15; see also Boyle, *Ilāhīnāma*, p. 16.

116. ᶜAttar, *Manṭiq uṭ-ṭair*, p. 24.

117. Cf. Schimmel, *Mystical Dimensions*, pp. 419–20.

118. *Fīhi mā fīhi,* p. 251; Arberry, *Discourses of Rumi,* p. 226. For the problem see Schimmel, *Triumphal Sun,* "Mowlana's Prophetology," pp. 280–88.

119. Thus D 2010/21240, where *aḍ-ḍuḥā* implies again the name of Shams, or D 1966/20746:

> If you want the complete color and fragrance of Ahmad's wine,
> Then, o caravan leader, make your halting place for a moment at the gate of Tabriz.

120. Text and melody in Gölpĭnarlĭ, *Mevlâna'dan sonra Mevlevilik,* p. 503 f.

121. D 214 about the *miᶜrāj.* An interesting *naᶜt* in D 1700, where Ahmad's unique position among the prophets is stressed; in D 1649/17277 the *ḥannāna,* the sighing palm trunk; a fine allusion to the station of *mā zāgha,* "The eye did not rove" (Sura 53/17) in D 1758/18430 and at the beginning of D 1402/14846.

122. D 1137/12052.

123. D 2/22.

124. D 1135/12019.

125. Furuzanfar, *Aḥādīth-i mathnawī,* is the best introduction to the traditions used by Rumi.

126. Jami, *Dīwān-i kāmil, qaṣīda,* p. 58.

127. Saᶜdi, *Būstān,* p. 5. In Saᶜdi's *qaṣīdas,* p. 17, a rather simple *naᶜt* states that:

> The moon remains behind Muhammad's beauty,
> The cypress is not as well shaped as Muhammad.

128. For the concept of the *muṭāᶜ* see W. H. Temple Gairdner, *Al-Ghazzali's "Mishkāt al-anwār,"* pp. 37–45, and Reynold A. Nicholson, *The Idea of Personality in Sufism,* p. 44.

129. Jahangir Hashimi, *Maẓhar al-āthār,* a religious *mathnawī* from sixteenth century Sind, contains five *naᶜts.*

130. A collection of Urdu *naᶜts*: Sajid Siddiqi-Wali Asi, *Armaghān-i naᶜt;* on p. 58 a *naᶜt* in Persian ascribed to Nizamuddin Auliya, which begins: "O Morning breeze, when you pass by Medina . . ."

131. Thus Sana'i, *Dīwān,* p. 158.

132. Amir Khusrau, *Majnūn Lailā,* p. 15, lines 8–14.

133. Amir Khusrau, *Dīwān,* pp. 599, 601.

134. Ibid., p. 596. The "necklace of the dove" means the inseparable relation of two things.

135. Mir ᶜAli Shir Qaniᶜ, *Maqālāt ash-shuᶜarā,* p. 714.

136. Khaqani, *Dīwān,* contains more than a dozen *qaṣīdas* which praise the Prophet, this "Pearl of the Ocean of *k* and *n* (i.e., *Kun,* "Be!," God's creative word), from whose praise I have brought pearls into the pen, and an ocean into my fingers" (p. 258).

137. Hadi Hasan, "Qāsim-i Kāhī," p. 185.

138. Fakhruddin ᶜIraqi, *Kulliyāt,* Introduction, p. 54; see p. 74, the fine *tażādd* between morning and night:

> Since in pre-eternity the style of addressing [you] was dictated as being "By the morning-light" [Sura 93/1],
> The fixed time came that the ceremonial drumming (*nauba*) of "Praised be He who traveled at night" [Sura 17/1] was exercised.

Nauba is a group of musicians who play with fifes and drums during fixed hours at the gates of kings or grandees.

139. ᶜUrfi, *Kulliyāt,* ed. A. Jawahiri, p. 58.

140. Siddiqi-Asi, *Armaghān-i naᶜt,* p. 49 (motto of Part II).

141. ᶜUrfi, *Kulliyāt,* p. 10; see also Abdul Ghani, *Persian Language and Literature at the Mughal Court,* III, p. 119 ff., unfortunately with wrong translations of the key concepts. Salma and Laila, the names of the beloved maidens in classical Arabic poetry, are here applied to the abstract concepts of "timelessness" and "being created in time," which both apply to Muhammad who, as the Perfect Man, is the meeting point of the Divine and the created.

142. ᶜUrfi, *Kulliyāt,* p. 100.

143. Khaqani, *Dīwān,* p. 99 in the *qaṣīda Ḥirz al-Hijāz.*

144. Sana'i, *Dīwān,* p. 37. Cf. ᶜIraqi, *Kulliyāt,* p. 74:

> A slight fragrance of his beautiful character was placed in Jesus' breath,
> And from the radiance of the candle of his face, the fire of Moses was lit.

The frequent use of such images can be explained by the fact that Moses symbolizes the predominance of the Law, while Jesus represents the predominance of love and otherworldliness, while Muhammad is regarded as the prophet who preached the healthy equilibrium between these two extremes.

145. Ikram, *Armaghān-i Pāk,* pp. 174–75.

146. Siddiqi-Asi, *Armaghān-i naᶜt,* p. 52.

147. Ikram, *Armaghān-i Pāk,* p. 219. The topic of the dog of the Prophet's door is common also in folk poetry, see ᶜAli Haidar's *Sīharfī* under *m:*

> I am the dog of the family of the exalted Prophet
> And keep watch on their house,

Ramakrishna, *Panjabi Sufi poets,* p. 73. More important is the stress on the "Arabic" aspect of the Prophet which is evident in Qudsi's eulogy; this is typical of the attitude of many Indian Muslims who often felt like foreigners in the Subcontinent and found that the remedy for all ills is the Arabic tradition, as the great theologian of Delhi, Shah Waliullah, remarked. He went so far as to write in 1740: "Arabs should be given mastery of [people of all] religions, and their customs should be substituted by the customs of the Arabs," *Ḥujjat Allāh al-bāligha,* II, p. 122.

148. A good Turkish example is Nefᶜi's (d. 1635) *naᶜt,* quoted in Köprülü, *Eski şairlerimiz,* pp. 397–99.

149. Thus Ghani Tattawi (d. 1723), see Annemarie Schimmel, "The Veneration of the Prophet Muhammad, as Reflected in Sindhi Poetry," p. 132.

150. N. A. Baloch, *Muᶜjizā,* p. 176.

151. Kokan, *Arabic and Persian in Carnatic,* p. 55; see also Padwick, *Muslim Devotions,* pp. 149–51.

152. Siddiqi-Asi, *Armaghān-i naᶜt,* pp. 64, 96.

153. An analysis of this poem by Annemarie Schimmel, "Ghalib's *qaṣīda* in Praise of the Prophet."

154. Bedil Rohriwaro, *Dīwān,* p. 348.

155. For the imagery cf. the highly involved *naᶜt* of the Turkish poet Fuzuli (d. 1556) with the *radīf ṣū,* "water"; he alludes to Muhammad's prayer for rain, and hopes that "the water of his kindness" will "extinguish Hellfire"; he closes the poem with the prayer that "the fountain of union may give water to his eyes which are thirsty for the vision [of the Prophet]," Köprülü, *Eski şairlerimiz,* pp. 201–3.

156. Tor Andrae, *Die person Mohammeds,* p. 353.

157. Fazlul Haqq Khairabadi, who defended the first possibility, died in 1862 in the Andamans where he was exiled after his participation in the "Mutiny" of 1857. See also Daud Rahbar, "Ghālib and a Debatable Point of Theology."

158. Nasir Muhammad ᶜAndalib, *Nāla-i ᶜAndalīb,* II, p. 104.

159. The *Qānūn-i ᶜishq yaᶜnī ḥalwā-i Panjāb,* devotes a long chapter in mixed Persian, Urdu, and Panjabi to *fanā' fi'r-rasūl,* closing with a simple little Persian poem which one should recite "when one feels restless and harrassed"; it ends with the line:

> I am proud that I belong to your community—
> I am a sinner, yet I am lucky (p. 128).

Some of my Indian friends would quote the Urdu poetry of Muhsin Kakorawi as an example of the loftiest "existential" style in *naᶜt,* while the beautiful, tender *naᶜt*s of Akhtar Shirani would fall into the second category according to their judgment.

160. Omar Pulavar, *Sīra Purānam,* see Kokan, *Arabic and Persian in Carnatic,* p. 61. Poetical descriptions of Muhammad's life are known everywhere. In Egypt, a good example of modern popular poetry (noted down in 1938) describes Muhammad's marriage with Khadija and the miracles preceding it, see Enno Littmann, *Mohammad im Volksepos.* It begins with the line:

> O heart, say the *ṣalawāt* over the one with blackened eyes—
> He will be a help for you in the difficulties on the day of resurrection.

The topic was, however, known already in Ottoman poetry, see Abdülkadir Karahan, "Un nouveau mathnawi de la littérature turque Ottomane: Le Mevlid Haticetül-Kubra, ou la description du marriage de Khadija avec le Prophète."

161. Enamul Haq, *Muslim Bengali Literature,* p. 56; see also Qazi Abdul Mannan, *Literary Heritage of Bengal: The Medieval Period.*

162. Annemarie Schimmel, "Neue Veröffentlichungen zur Volkskunde von Sind," p. 243. One can also compare similar poems from modern Egypt, see Ernest Bannerth, "Lieder ägyptischer Meddâḥîn," who gives some examples of strophic poems in honor of the Prophet; the "licit wine of his saliva" and the "speaking gazelle" occur frequently.

163. Written in 1774. It begins:

bhalā jām,/hun[a] *ghulām/sandō suāl/sūnaj tū*
O good prince!/hear the wish/of this slave!

164. Hajji Faqir Muhammad, son of Fath Khan Macchi, wrote around 1900 a lullaby in which he enumerates all creatures that cannot sleep from joy because God's messenger is born. The Arabic refrain is the swinging verse:

Qum qum yā ḥabībī kam tanām?
Get up, get up, my friend—how long will you sleep?

165. Yunus Emre, *Divan,* p. 569, CCXLII.

166. N. A. Baloch, *Madāḥūn,* p. 25; cf. Annemarie Schimmel, trans., *Märchen aus Pakistan,* pp. 222–24.

167. Even Hindus joined the Muslims in composing *na*ᶜ*ts,* thus Sufi Bhai Asuram (d. 1941) in Sindhi (Baloch, *Madāḥūn,* p. 313); that is true for Urdu literature as well: Fani Muradabadi, *Hindū shu*ᶜ*arā kā na*ᶜ*tiyya kalām.* The first scholarly biography of the Prophet in Sindhi was also written by a Hindu teacher, Lalchand Jagtiani.

168. Hotchand M. Gurbaxani, *Luñwariā jā lāl,* p. 96; cf. Sayyid Hussamuddin Rashdi, *Sindhī Adab,* p. 54. Also interesting is the Hindi verse sung in the *band samā*ᶜ during the ᶜ*urs* in Gulbarga:

Put in water, some salt—
When it dissolves, what shall it be called?
Likewise Mustafa melted his self into God (*khudā*)
When the self is dissolved, whom could one call God?

S. S. Khusro Hussaini, "*Bund sama*ᶜ*,*" p. 183.

169. Thus *Shāh jō Risālō,* Sur Dahar II, 1–3:

Prince of Medina, hear my calling . . .
Lord of Medina, hear my calling . . .
Bridegroom of Medina, hear my calling . . .

For details see Schimmel, "The Veneration of the Prophet Muhammad, in Sindhi," p. 134 ff. It is unfortunate that the Hindu commentators on Shah ^{c}Abdul Latif's poetry failed to understand the importance of the Prophet (the same is true for Panjabi poetry); thus Lilaram Watanmal, the author of the first major biography of Shah ^{c}Abdul Latif (Hyderabad/Sind, 1889) remarks: "Shah Latif, too, has in his Risalo, in several places, impressed on his hearer the necessity of believing in Mahommad as a prophet and something more. It is true that some of the verses in praise of the prophet, somewhat vulgar in language, are not our poet's. . . . But it cannot be doubted that there are several genuine verses in which our poet has expressed his full belief in the prophet. . . . The orthodox Mahommadans [sic] might well believe him as the chief prophet of God. But the Sufis cannot, consistently with their pantheistic doctrines, say that the prophet Mahommad is the only medium of salvation. . . . It may be that Shah Latif wanted to lead the minds of his followers slowly and gradually into higher Sufism by allowing them to believe first in their prophet, and then by degrees to ascend higher and higher." These patronizing remarks (pp. 37–38) are certainly out of place.

170. Thus Hammal Faqir Laghari (d. 1887):

> *Tirmidh, Tibat ain Tatār—Bābil, Bukhārā ain Balkh—*
> *Khāwar, Khorāsān ain Khalkh . . .*

For a more detailed discussion see Schimmel, *Und Muhammad ist Sein Prophet,* pp. 66–67.

171. Schimmel, "Translations and Commentaries of the Qur'an in the Sindhi Language," p. 227. For a similar approach in Turkish popular literature see Sazayi's *ilāhī* (quoted in Kocatürk, *Tekke şiiri,* p. 402):

> You are that sun of reality for which the whole world is dust particles,
> Your existence is the reason for Being and Place, O Messenger of God,
> Those who have quaffed the cup of your love don't care for Khidr's water—
> Your love is eternal life, O Messenger of God!

172. Thus Mir Ma^{c}sum Nami, the historian, calligrapher, physician, and poet of Akbar's time, quoted in Sadarangani, *Persian Poets of Sind,* p. 30.

173. Cf. also Baloch, *Madāḥūñ,* p. 279: The love of Yusuf and Zulaikha, of Farhad, Majnun, and other lovers is only a reflection of the love of the Prophet.

174. Yunus, *Divan,* p. 524 CLXXV. A whole collection of lovely hymns in praise of the Prophet and his family, ibid., pp. 557–78.

175. Baloch, *Munāqibā,* p. 146. Trans. in Schimmel, *Und Muhammad ist Sein Prophet,* 77–78.

176. Thus also Rumi in his magnificent poem D 1348:

> This year is the year of the rose, today is the day of joy.

See also Baloch, *Madāḥūn,* p. 367.

177. A nice example in Freytag, *Darstellung der arabischen Verskunst,* p. 464. One of the fourteen major Sindhi ballads about the Speaking Gazelle trans. in Schimmel, *Und Muhammad,* pp. 81–82.

178. S. Paul Kahle, *Der Leuchtturm von Alexandrien,* where the *madīḥ,* "praise," usually occurs in the second-to-last verse of a longish strophic poem (pp. 21 and 24, Arabic text pp. 41 and 50).

179. Ibn ᶜArabi, *Tarjumān al-ashwāq,* ed. Nicholson, no. XV, v. 9.

180. R. A. Nicholson, *Literary History of the Arabs,* p. 398.

181. D 463; see also M IV 1102 and Commentary, VIII, p. 154.

182. Edward Dimock, "Muslim Vaiṣnava Poets of Bengal," in *Languages and Areas: Studies Presented to George V. Bobrinski.*

183. See Annemarie Schimmel, "The Place of the Prophet of Islam in Iqbal's Thought"; Ra'is Jaᶜfri, *Iqbāl aur ᶜishq-i rasūl.*

184. *Bāng-i darā,* p. 173 (end of *Tarāna-ye millī*); also *Asrār-i Khūdī,* line 144.

185. *Pas che bāyad kard,* p. 64.

186. Shaikh ᶜAta, ed., *Makātīb-i Iqbāl,* I, p. 414.

187. *Asrār-i khūdī,* line 305 f.; see Reynold A. Nicholson, *The Secrets of the Self,* line 305.

188. *Rumūz-i bēkhūdī,* p. 130.

189. Ibid., p. 116.

190. Ibid. pp. 116 f., 125.

191. *Armaghān-i Ḥijāz,* p. 81.

192. *Jāvīdnāma,* line 608.

193. Ibid., "Ṭāsīn of Muhammad," p. 58–60.

194. *Asrār-i Khūdī,* line 189.

195. *Pas che bāyad kard,* p. 23.

196. For the concept of *ᶜabduhu* see Qushairī, *Risāla, bāb al-ᶜubūdiyya.*

197. *Jāvīdnāma, Sphere of Jupiter,* lines 2340–55, trans. by Arthur J. Arberry, *Jāvīdnāme,* p. 99.

198. *Armaghān-i Ḥijāz,* p. 29.

199. Knappert, *Swahili Islamic Poetry,* I, p. 40.

200. *Rumūz-i bēkhūdī,* line 190.

Bibliography

^{c}Abbas, Ihsan. *Shi^{c}r al-khawārij.* Beirut: Dar ath-thaqafa, 1963.

^{c}Abd al-^{c}Alī Ḥāfiẓ Jhandā. *Guldasta-i Ḥāfiẓ Jhandā.* Lahore: Allāh-wālē kī qaumī dukān, n.d.

^{c}Abd aṣ-Ṣabūr, Ṣalāḥ. *Ma'sāt al-Ḥallāj.* Beirut: Dār al-ādāb, 1964.

Abdul Ghani, Muhammad. *A History of Persian Language and Literature at the Mughal Court.* 3 vols. Allahabad: The Indian Press, 1929; repr. 1972.

^{c}Abdul Ḥaqq, Maulwī. *Urdū kī nashw ū namā meñ Ṣūfiyā-i kirām kā kām.* Karachi: Anjuman-i taraqqī-yi Urdū, 1953.

^{c}Abdul Ḥayy, Ḥakīm Sayyid. *Gul-i ra^{c}nā.* 3d ed. A^{c}ẓamgarh: Anjuman-i taraqqī-yi Urdū, 1364h/1945.

^{c}Abdul Laṭīf Bhitā'ī, Shāh. *Shāh jō risālō,* ed. Kalyān B. Adwānī. Bombay: Hindūstān Kitābghar, 1958.

Abdul Mannan, Qadi. *The Emergence and Development of Dobhasi Literature in Bengal, up to 1855.* Ph.D. thesis, London University, 1964.

—— "Literary Heritage of Bangladesh, Medieval Period." *Learning Resources in Bengali Studies.* Mimeographed. New York, 1974.

—— "Sufi Literature in Bengal." *Learning Resources in Bengali Studies.* Mimeographed. New York, 1974.

—— "Tradition of Artificial Diction and Characteristics of Islam in Medieval Bengal." *Learning Resources in Bengali Studies.* Mimeographed. New York, 1974.

^{c}Abdullāh, Dr. Syed. *Naqd-i Mīr.* Lahore: Ayina-i adab, 1958.

Abou Shama. "Origine du ^{c}Mawlid' ou fête de la naissance du Prophète." *BEA* 5 (1945), pp. 147 ff.

Abū'l-^{c}Atāhiya, Ismā^{c}īl ibn al-Qāsim. *Dīwān,* ed. Karam al-Būstānī. Beirut: Dār Ṣādir, 1384h/1964.

Abū Nu^{c}aim al-Iṣfahānī, Aḥmad. *Ḥilyat al-auliyā wa ṭabaqāt al-aṣfiyā.* 10 vols. Cairo, 1932–1937; repr. Beirut: Dār al- ma^{c}rifa, 1967.

Adonis. "As-suryaliyya qabla as-suryaliyya." *Fikrun wa Fann, Zeitschrift für die arabische Welt* 20 (1972), pp. 17–19.

Affifi, Abu'l-Ala. *The Mystical Philosophy of Muḥyid'Dīn Ibnul-ᶜArabī.* Cambridge: Cambridge University Press, 1936; repr. Lahore: Ashraf, n.d.

—— "The Story of the Prophet's Ascent (*miᶜrāj*) in Sufi Thought and Literature." *Islamic Quarterly* 2 (1955), pp. 23–29.

Aflākī, Aḥmad ibn Muḥammad. *Manāqib al-ᶜārifīn,* ed. Tahsin Yazĭcĭ. 2 vols. Ankara: Ankara Üniversitesi yayĭnlarĭndan, 1959–1961. Turkish translation: *Ariflerin menkibeleri,* by Tahsin Yazĭcĭ. Ankara: Milli Egitim Yayĭnevi, 1964. French translation: *Les saints des dervishes tourneurs,* by Clément Huart. Paris, 1918–1922.

Ahmad, Zubaid. *The Contribution of Indo-Pakistan to Arabic Literature.* 2d ed. Lahore: Ashraf, 1968.

ᶜAinulquḍāt Hamadhānī. *Aḥwāl ū āthār,* ed. ᶜAfīf ᶜUṣairān. Tehran: Ibn-i Sīnā, 1338sh/1959.

ᶜAjabnāma: A Volume of Oriental Studies Presented to E. G. Browne. Cambridge: Cambridge University Press, 1922.

Algar, Hamid. "Some Notes on the Naqshbandi *ṭarīqat* in Bosnia." *WI* NS XIII 3–4 (1971), pp. 168–203.

Altmann, Alexander. "The Ladder of Ascension." *Studies in Mysticism and Religion Presented to Gerschom Scholem.* Jerusalem: Magnus Press, 1967; pp. 1–32.

Amīr Khusrau. *Dīwān-i kāmil,* ed. Maḥmūd Darwīsh; preface by S. Nafīsī. Tehran: Intishārāt-i jāvīdān, 1343sh/1965.

—— *Majnūn Lailā,* ed. T. A. Magerramova. Moscow: Nauka, 1964.

ᶜAndalīb, Nāṣir Muḥammad. *Nāla-i ᶜAndalīb.* 2 vols. Bhopal, 1309h/1890–91.

Andrae, Tor. *I Myrtenträdgården.* Stockholm: Albert Bonniers, 1947. German trans. by Hans Helmhart Kanus, *Islamische Mystiker.* Stuttgart: Kohlhammer, 1960.

—— *Die person Muhammeds in lehre und glauben seiner gemeinde.* Stockholm: P. A. Vorstedt og söner, 1918.

Angelus Silesius. *Der Cherubinische Wandersmann* (*Sämtliche Poetische Werke,* vol. 3), ed. Hans Ludwig Held. 3d ed. München: Hanser, 1949.

Arafat, Walid N., ed. *Dīwān of Ḥassān ibn Thābit. GMS NS XXI* 2 vols. London: Luzac, 1971.

Arberry, Arthur John. *Aspects of Islamic Civilization.* Ann Arbor: University of Michigan (Ann Arbor Paperbacks), 1967.

—— *Classical Persian Literature.* London: Allen and Unwin, 1958.
—— *Discourses of Rumi.* London: John Murray, 1961.
—— *An Introduction to the History of Sufism.* London: Longmans, Green, 1950.
—— *The Mystical Poems of Ibn al-Fāriḍ.* Ed. in transcription from the oldest extant manuscript in the Chester Beatty Collection. Chester Beatty Monographs No. 4. London: Emery Walker, 1952. English translation: *The Mystical Poems of Ibn al-Fāriḍ.* Dublin: Chester Beatty Monographs, 1956.
—— *Mystical Poems of Rumi* (1–200). Chicago: University of Chicago Press, 1968.
—— *The Poems of a Persian Sufi: Bābā Ṭāhir.* Cambridge: Cambridge University Press, 1937.
—— *More Tales from the Mathnawi.* London: Allen and Unwin, 1963.
—— "A Sufi Alphabet." *JRAS* Bombay Branch, NS 13 (1937), pp. 1–5.
—— *Sufism: An Account of the Mystics of Islam.* London: Allen and Unwin, 1950; many reprints.
—— *A Sufi Martyr: The Apologia of ᶜAin al-Quḍāt al-Hamadhānī.* London: Allen and Unwin, 1969.
—— *The Rubāᶜiyāt of Jalāluddīn Rūmī.* London: E. Walker, 1949.
—— *Tales from the Mathnawi.* London: John Murray, 1961.
ᶜArifī, *Gūy u Jaugān: The Ball and the Polostock, or Book of Exstasy,* ed. and trans. by Robert Scott Greenshield. London: Luzac, 1931–1932.
Arnaldez, Roger. *Hallaj ou la religion de la croix.* Paris: Plon, 1964.
Arnold, Sir Thomas. "Saints, Muhammadan, India." *ERE* XI, pp. 68–73.
Asin Palacios, Miguel. *The Mystical Philosophy of Ibn Masarra and His Followers.* Trans. Elmer H. Douglas and Howard W. Yoder, Leiden:Brill, 1978.
Askari, Syed Hasan, "Mulla Da,ud's Chanda,in and Sadhan's Maina Sat." *Patna University Journal* 15 (1960), pp. 61–83.
Aṣlaḥ, Muḥammad. *Tadhkirat-i shuᶜarā-i Kashmīr,* ed. Sayyid Ḥussámuddin Ráshdī. 5 vols. Karachi: Iqbal Academy, 1967–1968.
ᶜAṭṭār, Farīduddīn. *Dīwān-i qaṣā'id ū ghazaliyāt,* ed. Saᶜīd-i Nafīsī. Tehran: Sanā'ī, 1339sh/1960.
—— *Ilāhīnāma,* ed. Helmut Ritter. Istanbul-Leipzig: F. A. Brockhaus, 1940. See also Boyle.
—— *Manṭiq uṭ-ṭair,* ed. M. Jawād Shakūr. Tehran: Kitābfurūsh-i Tehrān, 1962.

—— *Muṣībatnāma*, ed. N. Fiṣāl. Tehran: Zawwār, 1338sh/1959.
—— *Tadhkirat al-auliyā*, ed. R. A. Nicholson. 2 vols. London: Luzac-Leiden: E. J. Brill, 1905–1907; repr. 1959.
—— *Ushturnāma*, ed. Mehdi Muhaqqiq. Tehran: University, 1339sh/1960.
Awn, Peter J., *Satan's Tragedy and Redemption: Iblīs in Sufi Psychology*. Ph.D. diss., Harvard, 1978; forthcoming as *Supplement to Numen* (Leiden: Brill).
Ayverdi, Samiha. *Ibrahim Efendi Konağī*. Istanbul: Fetih Cemiyeti, 1964.
Azma, Nazeer el-, "Some Notes on the Impact of the Story of the *miᶜrāj* on Sufi Literature." *MW* 63 (1973), pp. 93–104.
—— "The Tammūzī Movement and the Influence of T. S. Eliot on Badr Shākir al-Sayyāb." *JAOS* 88 (1968), pp. 671–78.
Bābā Ṭāhir. *The Laments of Bābā Ṭāhir, Being the 'Rubāᶜiyāt' of Bābā Ṭāhir Hamadānī*, ed. and trans. by Edward Heron Allen and Elizabeth Curtis Brendon. London, 1902.
Badāonī, ᶜAbdul Qādir. *Muntakhab at-tawārīkh*. Vols. I–III. Trans. George S. A. Ranking, W. H. Lowe, and Wolseley Haig. Repr. Patna: Academia Asiatica, 1973.
Bailey, T. Graham. *A History of Urdu Literature*. Calcutta, 1932.
—— "Gleanings from Early Urdu and Hindi Poets." *BSOS* 5 (1928–30), pp. 507–9, 801 ff; 6 (1930–32), pp. 201 ff., 941 ff; 7 (1933–35), p. 111 f.
Baljon, Jon M. S. *A mystical Interpretation of Prophetic Tales by an Indian Muslim: Shāh Walī Allāh's ta'wīl al-aḥādīth*. Leiden: Brill, 1973.
Balōch, Dr. Nabībakhsh A., ed. *Haftā, diñhā, rātiūñ ain mahīnā*. Hyderabad/Sind: Sindhi Adabi Board, 1961.
—— *Madāḥūñ ain munājatūñ*. Karachi: Sindhi Adabi Board, 1959.
—— *Maulūd*. Hyderabad/Sind: Sindhi Adabi Board, 1961.
—— *Muᶜjizā*. Hyderabad/Sind: Sindhi Adabi Board, 1960.
—— *Munāqibā*. Hyderabad/Sind: Sindhi Adabi Board, 1960.
—— *Ṭih akaryūñ*. Hyderabad/Sind: Sindhi Adabi Board, 1962.
Bannerth, Ernst. "Der Dîwân des maghribinischen Sufi Šuᶜaib Abû Madjan (gest. 1197–98 n.Chr.)." *WZKM* 53 (1957), pp. 28–56, 237–66.
—— *Islamische Wallfahrtstätten Kairos*. Cairo: Österreichisches Kulturinstitut, 1973.
—— "Lieder ägyptischer *meddâhîn*." *WZKM* 56 (1960), pp. 9–20.

Baqlī, Rūzbihān. *ᶜAbhar al-ᶜāshiqīn, Le Jasmine des fidèles d'amour,* ed. Henry Corbin. Tehran-Paris: Adrien Maisonneuve, 1958.
—— *Sharḥ-i Shaṭḥiyāt, Les Paradoxes des soufis,* ed. Henry Corbin. Tehran-Paris: Adrien Maisonneuve, 1966.
Barnett, Lionel D. *Panjabi: Printed Books in the British Museum.* London: British Museum, 1961.
Barrett, Douglas, and Basil Gray. *Painting of India.* Geneva: Skira, 1963.
Basset, René. *La Bordah du Cheikh al-Bousîrî, traduit par. . . .* Paris, 1894.
—— *La Bânat Soᶜâd.* Algiers, 1910.
Bausani, Alessandro. "About a Curious Mystical Language." *East and West* 4, no. 4 (1958), pp. 234–38.
—— "Alṭāf Husain Ḥālī's Ideas on *ghazal.*" *Charisteria Orientalia Jan Rypka,* ed. Felix Tauer, Vera Kubičková, and Jan Hrbek. Prague: Czech Academie of Sciences, 1956; pp. 38–55.
—— "Il Gulšan-i rāz-i ǧadīd di Muḥammad Iqbāl." *Annali del Istituto Universitario Orientale de Napoli.* NS 8 (1958), pp. 125–72.
—— "Letteratura neo-persiana." In Antonio Pagliaro and A. Bausani, *Storia della letteratura persiana.* Milan: Nuova Accademia Editrice, 1959; pp. 151–898.
—— *Persia religiosa: da Zaratustra a Bahā'ullāh* (La Cultura IV). Milan: Il Saggiatore, 1959.
—— *Storia delle letteratura del Pakistan.* Milan: Nuova Accademia Editrice, 1958.
Bayātī, ᶜAbdul Wahhāb al-. *Dīwān.* 2 vols. Beirūt: Dar al-ᶜAuda, 1972.
Beaurecueil, Serge de Laugier de. *Khwadja Abdullāh Anṣārī, mystique hanbalite.* Beirut: Dar al-machreq, 1965.
Becker, Carl Heinrich. "Ubi sunt qui ante nos in mundo fuere." *Aufsätze zur Kultur-und Sprachgeschichte, Ernst Kuhn zum 70. Geburtstag gewidmet.* Breslau: F. u. H. Marcus, 1916; pp. 87–105.
Bēdil, Mirzā ᶜAbdul Qādir. *Kulliyāt.* 4 vols. Kabul: Ministery of Education, 1962–1965.
Bēdil Rōhrīwārō. *Dīwān,* ed. ᶜAbd al-Ḥusain Mūsawī. Karachi: Sindhi Adabi Board, 1954.
Bell, Joseph N. *Love Theories in Later Ḥanbalite Islam.* Albany: SUNY Press, 1979.
Bellamy, James A. "The Impact of Islam on Early Arabic Poetry," in Alford T. Welch and Pierre Cachia, eds., *Islam: Past Influence and*

Present Challenge. Edinburgh: Edinburgh University Press, 1979; pp. 141–67.

Benz, Ernst. "Die Signatur der Dinge." *Eranos-Jahrbuch* 42 (1973); pp. 517–80.

Berthels, E. E. "Grundlinien der Entwicklungsgeschichte des sufischen Lehrgedichtes." *Islamica* 3, no. 1 (1929), pp. 1–31.

Bevan, Anthony A. "Muhammad's Ascension to Heaven," *Zeitschrift für Alttestamentliche Wissenschaft.* Beiheft *XXVII (1914).*

Birge, John K. *The Bektashi Order of Dervishes.* London: Luzac, 1937; repr. 1965.

Bleeker, C. Jouco. *Inleiding tot een Phaenomenologie van den godsdienst.* Arsen: van Gorcum, 1934.

Blochet, Edgard. *Catalogue des Manuscripts Persans de la Bibliothèque Nationale,* Vol II. Paris: Bibliothèque Nationale 1928.

Blumhardt, James Fuller, and D. N. MacKenzie. *Catalogue of Pashto Manuscripts in the Libraries of the British Isles.* London: British Museum, 1965.

Boratav, Pertev Naili, ed. *Philologiae Turcicae Fundamenta.* Vol. 2. Wiesbaden: Steiner, 1965.

Bousset, Wilhelm. "Die Himmelsreise der Seele," *ARW* (1901).

Böwering, Gerhard. *The Mystical Vision of Existence in Classical Islam: The Qur'ānic Hermeneutics of the Sufi Sahl at-Tustarī (d. 283/896).* Berlin: de Gruyter, 1979.

—— "The Prophet of Islam: The First and the Last Prophet." *The Message of the Prophet.* Islamabad: Government of Pakistan 1976; pp. 48–60.

Boyle, John A., trans. *The Ilāhīnāme, "Book of God" of Farīduddīn* ᶜAṭṭār. Manchester: University Press, 1976.

Browne, Edward Granville. *A Literary History of Persia.* 4 vols. Cambridge: Cambridge University Press 1902–1921; repr. 1957.

—— "Sufism." *Religious Systems of the World: A Contribution to the Study of Comparative Religion.* 2d ed. London: Swan, Sonnenschein, 1892; pp. 314–32.

Bruijn, J. T. P. de. "The Religious Use of Persian Poetry." *Studies in Islam* (1974), pp. 63–74.

Brunel, René. *Le Monachisme errant dans l'Islam: Sīdī Heddī et les Heddāwa.* Paris: Larose, 1955.

Bū ᶜAlī Qalandar. *Dīwān.* Lahore, n.d.

Buber, Martin. *Ekstatische Konfessionen.* Jena: Diederichs, 1909.

Bürgel, J. Christoph. "ᶜDie beste Dichtung ist die lügenreichste.' Wesen und Bedeutung eines literarischen Streites des arabischen Mittelalters im Lichte komparatistischer Betrachtung." *Oriens* 23 (1974), pp. 7–102.

—— "Lautsymbolik und funktionelles Wortspiel bei Rumi." *Der Islam* 51, no. 2 (1974), pp. 261–81.

—— *Licht und Reigen. Aus dem Diwan Dschelaladdin Rumis.* Bern: Lang, 1974.

—— "The Pious Rogue: A Study in the Meaning of *qalandar* and *rend* in the Poetry of Muhammad Iqbal," *Edebiyât* 4, no. 1 (1979), pp. 43–64.

Burhānpūrī, Rashīd. *Burhānpūr kē Sindhī auliyā.* Karachi: Sindhi Adabi Board, 1957.

Burney, Mohd. Elias. *Mishkaat as-salawaat. A Bouquet of Blessings on Muhammad the Prophet (Peace Be on Him).* Transliterated into Roman script and translated into English by M. A. Haleem Eliasi. Hyderabad/Deccan, 1978.

Burrill, Kathleen R. F. *The Quatrains of Nesimi, Fourteenth-Century Turkish Hurufi.* The Hague: Mouton, 1972.

Būṣīrī, Abū ᶜAbdallāh Muḥammad al-. *Die Burda,* ed. and trans. by C. A. Ralfs, with metrical Persian and Turkish translations. Vienna, 1860.

—— *Nafḥ al-warda fī sharḥ al-burda,* with the Persian verse translation by Jāmī and the Urdu verse translation by Fayyāżaddīn Niẓāmī. Hyderabad/Deccan, 1969. See also Basset.

Cachia, Pierre. "The Egyptian Mawwāl: Its Ancestry, Its Development, and Its Present Forms." *Journal of Arabic Literature* 8 (1977), pp. 77–103.

Caferoğlu, Ahmed. *Türk Dili Tarihi.* Vol. 2. Istanbul Üniversitesi Yayĭnlarĭndan 1964.

Cejpek, Jiří. "Iranian Folk-Literature," in Jan Rypka, *History of Iranian Literature.* Dordrecht: Reidel, 1968; pp. 607–709 [mentions poetry only in passing.].

Cerulli, Enrico. *Il 'Libro della Scala' e la questione delle fonte arabospagnole della ᶜDivina Commedia.'* Vatican City, 1949.

Chelkowski, Peter J., ed. *The Scholar and the Saint: al-Biruni/Rumi.* New York: New York University Press, 1975.

—— *Taᶜziyeh: Ritual and Drama in Iran.* New York: New York University Press, 1979.

Corbin, Henry. *Creative Imagination in the Sufism of Ibn ᶜArabi*, trans. Ralph Manheim. Princeton: Princeton University Press, 1969.

—— *L'homme de lumière dans le Soufisme iranien*. Paris: Editions Présence, 1971. English edition: Boulder: Shambala, 1979.

—— "Mystique et humour chez Sohrawardī, Shaykh al-ishrāq." In M. Mohaghegh-H. Landolt, eds., *Collected Papers on Islamic Philosophy and Mysticism*. Tehran: University, 1971; pp. 13–38.

Dailamī, ᶜAlī ibn Aḥmad ad-. *Kitāb ᶜaṭf al-alif al-ma'lūf ilā'l-lām al-maᶜṭuf*, ed. Jean-Claude Vadet. Cairo: Institut Français d'Archéologie Orientale, 1962.

—— *Sīrat Abī ᶜAbdillah Ibn al-Khafīf ash-Shīrāzī*, in the Persian translation of Junaid-i Shīrazī, ed. by Annemarie Schimmel. Ankara: Ilâhiyat Fakültesi, 1955.

Dammann, Ernst. "Die Überlieferung der islamischen Suahelidichtung." *ZDMG* 108 (1958), pp. 41–53.

Danner, Victor, trans. *Ibn ᶜAṭā' Allāh, The Book of Wisdom*. New York: Paulist Press, 1978.

Dar, M. J. "Gujarat's Contribution to Gujari and Urdu." *IC* 27 (1953), pp. 18–36.

Dard, Khwāja Mīr. *Chahār Risāla*. Bhopal, 1310h/1891–92.

—— *ᶜIlm ul-kitāb*. Delhi, 1310h/1891–92.

—— *Urdū Dīwān*, ed. Khalīl ur-Raḥmān Dā'ūdī. Lahore: Majlis-i taraqqī-e Urdū, 1961.

Darmesteter, James. *Chants populaires des Afghans*. Paris, 1888–1890; repr. Amsterdam: Philo Press, n.d.

Das Gupta, Sh. *Obscure Religious Cults*. 3d ed. Calcutta: Mukhopadhyay, 1969.

Daūdpōtā, ᶜUmar Muḥammad. *Kalām-i Girhōṛī*. Karachi: Maṭbaᶜ al-ᶜarab, 1956.

Dermenghem, Émile. "Abou Bakr Chibli, Poète mystique bagdadien." *Ann. de l'Institut d'Études Orientales d'Alger* 8 (1949–1950), pp. 235–65.

—— *Le culte des saints dans l'Islam maghrébin*. Paris: Gallimard, 1954.

Dermenghem, Émile, trans. *L'écloge du vin (al-khamriyya): Poème mystique de Omar ibn al-Faridh, et son commentaire par Abdel-ghani an-Nabolosi*. Paris: Véga, 1931.

Devare, T. N. *A Short History of Persian Literature at the Bahmani; the Adilshahi and the Qutbshahi courts—Deccan*. Poona: Mrs. S. Devare, 1961.

Dhauqī, Ḥaẓrat Shāh Sayyid Muḥammad. *Sirr-i dilbarān.* 2d ed. Karachi: Maḥfil-i dhauqiyya, 1388h/1968.

Dimock, Ed. C., "Muslim Vaiṣṇava Poets of Bengal." *Languages and Areas, Studies Presented to George V. Bobrinski.* Chicago: University of Chicago Press, 1967; pp. 28–36.

Douglas, Fedwa Malti-. "Dreams, the Blind, and the Semiotics." *Studia Islamica* 51 (1980), pp. 137–61.

Dozy, Reinhart. *Supplément aux dictionnaires arabes.* 2d ed. 2 vols. Leiden: Brill—Paris: Maisonneuve, 1927.

Duchemen, André. "Un grand mystique turc, Yunus Emre, 1248–1320, Petit livre de conseils (1307)." *Turcica* 7 (1975), pp. 73–104.

Duda, Herbert W. *Farhâd und Schîrîn. Die literarische Geschichte eines persischen Sagenstoffes.* Prague: Orientalní Ústav—Paris: Geuthner—Leipzig: Harrassowitz, 1933.

Eaton, Richard, M. *Sufis of Bijapur. 1300–1700. Social Roles of Sufis in Medieval India.* Princeton: Princeton University Press, 1978.

—— "Sufi Folk Literature and the Expansion of Indian Islam." *History of Religions* 14 (1974), pp. 117–27.

Eilers, Wilhelm. "Vierzeilerdichtung, persisch und ausserpersisch." *WZKM* 62 (1969), pp. 209–49.

Eliade, Mircea. "Le Symbolisme du 'vol magique'." *Numen* 3 (1956), pp. 1–13.

Emre, Ismail. *Doğuşlar* 2. Adana, 1965.

—— *Yeni Yunus Emre ve doğuşlarĭ.* Istanbul, 1951.

Enevoldsen, Jens. *Selections from Rahman Baba.* Herning: Paul Kristensen, 1977.

Engelke, Irmgard. *Süleyman Tschelebis Lobgedicht auf die Geburt des Propheten.* Halle: Niemeyer, 1926.

Ergun, Sadettin Nüzhet. *Bektaşi şairleri ve nefesleri.* Istanbul: Maarif kitabevi, 1944.

Ernst, Carl W. *Faith and Infidelity in Sufism. Ecstatic Expressions and their Repercussions in Medieval Islamic Society.* Ph.D. thesis, Harvard University, 1981.

Ethé, Hermann. " ᶜKönig und Derwisch.' Romantisch-mystisches Epos vom Scheich Hilali, dem persischen Original treu nachgebildet." *Morgenländische Studien.* Leipzig, 1870; pp. 197–282.

—— "Neupersische Literatur." In Wilhelm Geiger-Ernst Kuhn, *Grundriss der iranischen Philologie,* Vol. 2. Strassburg, 1901; pp. 212–370.

—— "Die Rubâ[c] îs des Abû Sa[c]îd ibn Abulchair." *Sitzungsberichte der Kgl. Bayr. Akademie der Wissenschaften, phil.-hist. Klasse.* Munich, 1875, 1878.

Ettinghausen, Richard. *Persian Ascension Miniatures of the 14th Century.* Rome: Academia dei Lincei, 1957.

—— *The Unicorn.* Freer Gallery of Art Occasional Papers, I, no. 3. Washington, 1950.

Fānī Murādābādī. *Hindū shu[c]arā kā na[c]tiya kalām.* Lyallpur, 1962.

Farrukh, Omar. *Das Bild des Frühislam in der arabischen Dichtung von der Hiğra bis zum Tode des Kalifen [c]Umar.* Phil. Diss. Erlangen, Leipzig: Druck August Pries, 1937.

Fenesch, Soledad G. "Sobre una extrane manera de escribir." *al-Andalus* 14 (1949), pp. 211–13.

Fischer, August. "Vergöttlichung und Tabuisierung der Namen Muhammads." *Beiträge zur Arabistik, Semitistik und Islamkunde,* ed. Richard Hartmann and Helmuth Scheel. Leipzig: Harrassowitz, 1944; pp. 307–39.

Flügel, Gustav (with appendix by Heinrich Leberecht Fleischer). "Über die Versgattung Mawâliya." *ZDMG* 7 (1853), pp. 365–73.

Fouchécour, C.-H. de. *La description de la nature dans la poésie lyrique Persane du XI ième siècle.* Paris: Klincksieck, 1969.

Freytag, Georg Wilhelm. *Darstellung der arabischen Verskunst.* Bonn, 1830. repr. Osnabrück: Biblio, 1968.

Friedmann, Yohanan. "Qiṣṣat Shakarwātī Farmāḍ." *Israel Oriental Studies* 5 (1975), pp. 233–58.

—— *Shaykh Aḥmad Sirhindī: An Outline of His Thought and a Study of His Image in the Eyes of Posterity.* London and Montreal, McGill University Press, 1977.

Fück, Johann. "Die sufische Dichtung in der Landessprache des Panjab." *OLZ* 43 (1940), col. 1–11.

Furūzānfar, Badī[c]uzzamān. *Aḥādīth-i Mathnawī.* Tehran: University, 1334sh/1955.

—— *Ma'ākhidh-i qiṣaṣ u tamthīlat-i Mathnawī.* Tehran: University, 1333sh/1954.

Gabrieli, Francesco. "Problemi e forme della poesia mistica musulmane." *Oriente e Occidente nel medioevo.* Rome: Academia nazionale dei Lincei, 1957; pp. 35–49.

—— "Religious Poetry in Early Islam." In Gustave E. von Grune-

baum, ed., *Arabic Poetry, Theory and Development.* Wiesbaden: Harrassowitz, 1973; pp. 1–17.
Gairdner, W. H. Temple. *Al-Ghazzâlî's "Mishkât al-anwâr": The Niche for Lights.* London: Royal Asiatic Society Monographs XIX, 1924; repr. Lahore: Ashraf, 1952.
Gandjei, Turhan. *Il Canzoniere de Šāh Ismāᶜīl Ḫaṭā'ī.* Naples: Annali dell'Istituto Orientale, 1959.
Garcin de Tassy, M. Joseph Héliodore. *Histoire de la littérature Hindoue et Hindoustani.* 3 vols. Paris, 1870–71; repr. New York, 1965.
—— *La poésie philosophique et religieuse d'après le Mantic Uttair de Fariduddin Attar.* 4th ed. Paris, 1864.
—— *Rhétorique et prosodie des langues de l'Orient musulman.* Paris, 1873.
Gēsūdarāz, Sayyid Muḥammad Abū'l-Fatḥ Husainī. *Dīwān Anīs al-ᶜushshāq.* Hyderabad/Deccan 1369h/1941.
Ghālib, Mirzā Asadullāh. *Kulliyāt-i fārsī.* Persian works in 17 vols. Lahore: University of the Punjab, 1969.
—— *Urdū Dīwān,* ed. Ḥāmid ᶜAli Khān. Lahore: University of the Punjab, 1969.
Ghazzālī, Abū Ḥāmid. *Iḥyā' ᶜulūm ad-dīn.* 4 vols. Bulaq, 1289h/1872–73.
Ghazzālī, Aḥmad. *Sawāniḥ. Aphorismen über die Liebe,* ed. Hellmut Ritter. Istanbul and Leipzig: F. A. Brockhaus, 1942. German translation: R. Gramlich, *Gedanken über die Liebe.* Wiesbaden: Steiner, 1977.
Ghulām Jīlānī Qādirī, Pīr Sayyid. *Prēm piyāla.* Lahore: Allāh wālē kī qaumī dukān, s.d. No. 200.
Gibb, Elias John Wilkinson. *A History of Ottoman Poetry.* 6 vols. London: Luzac, 1900–1909; repr. London, 1958–1963.
Goethe, Johann Wolfgang von. *West-Östlicher Divan.* Unter Mitwirkung von Hans Heinrich Schaeder, hersg. und erläutert von Ernst Beutler. Leipzig: Dieterich'sche Verlagsbuchhandlung, 1943.
Goldammer, Kurt. "Coena coelestis. Ein nicht-mystisches Überlebsel in der Sprache christlicher Mystiker." *In Deo Omnia Unum, Friedrich Heiler zum 50. Geburtstag dargebracht,* hersg. von Chr. Matthias Schröder. Munich: Reinhardt, 1942; pp. 177–99.
—— " ᶜWege aufwärts' und ᶜWege abwärts.' " *Eine Heilige Kirche* 22 (1940–41), pp. 25–56.

Goldziher, Ignaz. "Die Gottesliebe in der islamischen Theologie." *Der Islam* 9 (1919), pp. 144–58.

—— "Himmlische und irdische Namen." *ᶜAjabnama.* Cambridge: Cambridge University Press, 1922; pp. 157–62.

—— "Influence chrétiennes dans la littérature religieuse de l'Islam." *Revue de l'histoire des religions* 18 (1888), pp. 180–99.

—— "Linguistisches aus der Literatur der muhammedanischen Mystik." *ZDMG* 26 (1872), pp. 764–85.

—— *Muhammadanische Studien.* 2 vols. Halle, 1889–1892.

—— "Der Seelenvogel im islamischen Volksglauben." *Globus* (1903), pp. 301–4.

—— "Verheimlichung des Namens." *Der Islam* 17 (1928), pp. 1–3.

Gölpĭnarlĭ, Abdűlbaki. *Mevlâna Celâleddin: hayatĭ, felsefesi, eserlerinden seçmeler.* Istanbul: Inkilâp Kitabevi, 1951; 3d ed. 1959.

—— *Mevlâna'dan sonra Mevlevilik.* Istanbul: Inkilâp Kitabevi, 1953.

Gramlich, Richard, ed. *Islamwissenschaftliche Abhandlungen. Fritz Meier zum sechzigsten Geburtstag.* Wiesbaden: Steiner, 1974.

—— "Mystical Dimensions of Islamic Monotheism." *We Believe in One God,* ed. Annemarie Schimmel and Abdoljavad Falaturi. London: Burns and Oates, 1980; pp. 136–48. See also Aḥmad Ghazaālī.

Grotzfeld, Heinz. *Das Bad im arabisch-islamischen Mittelalter.* Wiesbaden: Harrassowitz, 1970.

Grunebaum, Gustave E. von. "The Early Development of Islamic Religious Poetry." *JAOS* 60 (1940), pp. 23–29.

—— *Kritik und Dichtkunst. Studien zur arabischen Literaturgeschichte.* Wiesbaden: Harrassowitz, 1955.

—— *Muhammadan Festivals.* Leiden: Brill—New York: Schuman, 1958.

—— "Von Muhammads Wirkung und Originalität." *WZKM* 44 (1937), pp. 29–50.

—— "The Nature of the Arabic Literary Effort." *Journal of Near Eastern Studies* 7 (Jan.–Oct. 1948), Chicago-London; pp. 116–27.

—— "The Spirit of Islam as Shown in Its Literature." *Islam: Essays on the Nature and Growth of a Cultural Tradition.* The American Anthropological Association, Vol. 57, no. 2, pt. 2. Menasha, Wisconsin, April 1955; pp. 95–110.

Gurbaxshānī, Hōtchand M. *Luñwariyā jā lāl.* Karachi: Educational Publishing Company, 1934.

Güzel, Abdurrahman. *ᶜAlī in der Bektaschi-Dichtung, namentlich jener des 16. Jahrhunderts.* Diss. phil. Vienna, 1972.

Hadi Hasan. "Qāsim-i Kāhī, His Life, Time, and Works." *IC* 27 (1953), pp. 99–131, 161–94, 199–224.

Hafis. *Gedichte aus dem Diwan,* Ausgewählt und herausgegeben von J. Christoph Bürgel. Stuttgart: Reclam, 1972.

Hafiz. *Die Lieder des Hafiz, persisch mit dem Kommentar des Sūdī,* hersg. von Hermann Brockhaus. Leipzig, 1854–63; repr. Osnabrück: Biblio, 1969.

—— *Dīwān,* ed. Naẓīr Aḥmad and S. M. Rażā Jalālī Nā'inī. Tehran; Sāzmān-i umūr-farhangī ū kitābkhānahā, 1971.

Ḥallāj, Ḥusain ibn Manṣūr al-, *A Commentary on the Dīwān of H.,* with an edited text and an introduction by Kāmil M. ash-Shaibī. Baghdad-Beirut; al-Nahḍa Bookshop, 1973.

—— *Kitāb aṭ-ṭawāsīn, texte arabe avec la version persane d'al-Baqlī,* ed. and trans. Louis Massignon. Paris: Geuthner 1913. See also Massignon.

Hammer-Purgstall, Joseph von. *Das arabische Hohe Lied der Liebe, das ist Ibnol Faridh's Taije in Text und Übersetzung zum ersten Male herausgegeben.* Vienna, 1854.

—— *Bericht über den zu Kairo im Jahre 1835 erschienen türkischen Kommentar des Mesnewi Dschelaleddin Rumi's,* SB. der K.u.K. Österreichischen Akademie der Wissenschaften. Vienna, 1851. Reissued in: Annemarie Schimmel, *Zwei Abhandlungen zur Mystik und Magie des Islam.* Vienna: Österr. Akademie der Wissenschaften, 1974; pp. 19–119.

—— *Geschichte der schönen Redekünste Persiens.* Vienna, 1818.

Handwörterbuch des Islam, ed. Arend Jan Wensinck and J. H. Kramers. Leiden: Brill, 1941.

Ḥarrāq, Sīdī Muḥammad ibn Muḥammad al-Ḥasanī al-. *Dīwān.* Meknes: Maktaba al-maᶜārif, n.d. (c. 1960).

Hartmann, Richard. "Die Himmelsreise Muhammads und ihre Bedeutung in der Religion des Islam." *Vorträge der Bibliothek Warburg.* Leipzig-Berlin: de Gruyter, 1928–1929; pp. 42–65.

Hashmī, Bashīr Aḥmad. "Sarmad, His Life and Quatrains." *IC* 7 (1933), pp. 663–73, and 8 (1934), pp. 92–104.

Hāshmī, Sayyid Jahāngīr. *Mathnawī maẓhar al-āthār,* ed. Sayyid Ḥussāmuddīn Rāshdī. Karachi: Sindhi Adabi Board, 1955.

Ḥassān, ᶜAbdul Ḥakīm, *At-taṣawwuf fī'sh-shiᶜr al-ᶜarabī,* Cairo: Al-maktaba al-anglo-miṣriyya, 1955.
Hastie, William. *The Festival of Spring from the "Díván" of Jeláleddin.* Glasgow: James MacLehose, 1903.
Hatif, Sayyid Ahmed. *Tarjiᶜband. Return Ties of Existence. A Sufi Strophic Poem.* Translated into interpretive free verse by Mehdi Nakosteen. Boulder: Shambhala, 1975.
Heiler, Friedrich. *Erscheinungsformen und Wesen der Religion.* Stuttgart: Kohlhammer, 1961.
—— *Das Gebet.* 5th ed. Munich: Reinhardt, 1923.
Heinz, Wilhelm. *Der indische Stil in der persischen Literatur.* Wiesbaden: Steiner, 1973.
Hickman, William. *Eshrefoghlu Rūmī: Reconstitution of his Dīwān.* Ph.D. diss., Harvard, 1972.
Hidayat Husain, Muhammad. "Bánat Suᶜād of Kaᶜb ibn Zuhair." *IC* 1 (1927), pp. 67–84 [translation and interpretation].
Ḥilmi, Muḥammad Muṣṭafā. *Ibn al-Fāriḍ wa'l-ḥubb al-ilāhī.* Cairo: Maṭbaᶜa lağnati't-ta'līf wa't-tarjama wa'n-nashr, 1945.
Hitti, Philip. *History of the Arabs.* 9th ed. New York: MacMillan, 1968.
Hoenerbach, Wilhelm, ed. *Der Orient in der Forschung. Festschrift für Otto Spies zum 5.4.1966.* Wiesbaden: Harrassowitz, 1967.
—— *Die vulgärarabische Poetik al-kitāb al-ᶜāṭil al-ḥālī wal-muraḫḫas al-ğālī des* Safīyaddīn Ḥillī, kritisch herausgegeben und erklärt. Wiesbaden: Steiner, 1956. Cf. the review by Ewald Wagner, *Der Islam* 36 (1960), pp. 78–98, for additional material.
Horovitz, Josef. *Die Hāšimijjāt des Kumait.* Leiden: Brill, 1904.
—— "Muhammads Himmelfahrt." *Der Islam* 9 (1919), pp. 159–83.
—— "Die poetischen Einlagen der Sīra." *Islamica* 2 (1926), pp. 308–12.
Horten, Max. *Indische Strömungen in der islamischen Mystik.* Heidelberg, in Kommission bei Otto Harrassowitz. Leipzig, 1927.
—— *Die religiöse Gedankenwelt des Volkes im heutigen Islam.* Halle: Niemeyer, 1917.
Hoshyārpūrī, Ḥafeez. *Mathnawiyāt-i Hīr Ranjhā.* Karachi: Sindhi Adabi Board, 1957.
Huitema, Taede. *De voorspraak (shafāᶜa) in den Islam.* Leiden: Brill, 1936.
Hujwīrī, ᶜAlī ibn ᶜUthmān al-Jullābī al-. *Kashf al maḥjūb,* trans. by

Reynold Alleyne Nicholson. *GMS* XVII. London: Luzac—Leiden: Brill, 1911; 3d ed. 1959, and often.

Ḥusain, ᶜAlī Ṣāfī. *Al-adab aṣ-ṣūfī fī Miṣr fi'l-qarn al-sābiᶜ al-hijrī.* Cairo: Dār al-maᶜārif, 1964.

Husain Khan, Yusuf. *L'Inde mystique au moyen-âge.* Paris: Adrien Maisonneuve, 1929.

Hussaini, Syed Shah Khusro. "Bund samāᶜ," *IC* 44 (1970), pp. 177–85.

Ibn ᶜArabī Muḥyīᶜddīn. *The Tarjumān al-ashwāq: A Collection of Mystical Odes by Muḥyiu'ddīn ibn al-ᶜArabī,* ed. and trans. R. A. Nicholson. London: Royal Asiatic Society, 1911; repr. with preface by Martin Lings, London: Theosophical Publishing House, 1978.

—— *Fuṣūṣ al-ḥikam,* ed. Abū'l-ᶜAlāᶜ Affīfī. Cairo: ᶜIsā al-Bābī al-Ḥalabī, 1946. Trans. by R. W. J. Austin as: Ibn al-ᶜArabi, *The Bezels of Wisdom.* Preface by Titus Burckhardt. New York: Paulist Press, 1980.

Ibn Iyās, Muḥammad ibn Aḥmad. *Badā'iᶜ az-zuhūr fī waqā'iᶜ adduhūr.* Vol. III, ed. Paul Kahle and Muhd. Mustafa. Istanbul-Leipzig: Brockhaus, 1931.

Ibn Kathīr. *Maulid rasūl Allāh,* ed. Dr. Ṣalāḥuddīn al-Munajjid. Beirut, Dār al-kutub al-jadīda, 1961.

Ibn Khallikān. *Wafayāt al- aᶜyān,* ed. Muḥammad Muḥyī'ddīn ibn ᶜAbdil Ḥamīd. 5 vols. Cairo: Maktabat an-nahḍa al-miṣriyya, 1948.

Ibn al-Khaṭīb, Lisānuddīn. *Kitāb al-iḥāṭa.* Bibliothèque Nationale, Paris. Ms Arabe, 3347/2.

Ibsen, Lois al-Faruqi. "Ornamentation in Arabian Improvisational Music: A Study of Interrelatedness in the Arts." *World of Music.* Wilhelmshaven, 1978; pp. 17–32.

Ikrām, Shaikh Muḥammad. *Armaghān-i Pāk.* Karachi: Idāra-i maṭbūᶜāt-i Pākistān, 1953.

Ikramullah, Shaista Suhrawardi. *From Purdah to Parliament.* London: The Cresset Press, 1963.

Inge, William Ralph. *Christian Mysticism.* London, 1899; New York: Meridian Books, 1956.

Iqbal, Sir Muhammad: *Six Lectures on the Reconstruction of Religious Thought in Islam,* Lahore: Ashraf, 1930 and often.

—— *Asrār-i khūdī.* Lahore: n.p., 1915.

—— *Armaghān-i Ḥijāz.* Lahore: n.p., 1938.

—— *Bāl-i Jibrīl*. Lahore: n.p., 1935.
—— *Bāng-i Darā*. Lahore: n.p., 1924.
—— *Jāvīdnāma*. Lahore: n.p., 1932.
—— *Musāfir*. Lahore: n.p., 1934.
—— *Pas che bāyad kard*. Lahore: n.p., 1936.
—— *Payām-i Mashriq*. Lahore: n.p., 1923.
—— *Rumūz-i bēkhūdī*. Lahore: n.p., 1917.
—— *Zabūr-i ᶜajam*. Lahore: n.p., 1927.

ᶜIrāqī, Fakhruddīn. *Kulliyāt*, ed. Saᶜīd-i Nafīsī. Tehran: Sanā'ī, 1338sh/1959.

—— *ᶜUshshāqnāma. The Song of the Lovers*, ed. and trans. A. J. Arberry. Islamic Research Association no. 8. Oxford: Oxford University Press, 1939.

Ivanow, Vladimir. "Shums Tabrez of Multan." *Muhammad Shafiᶜ Presentation Volume*, ed. Dr. Syed Abdullah. Lahore: University of the Punjab, 1955; pp. 109–18.

—— "Some Persian Darwish Songs." *JASB* NS 23 (1927), pp. 237–45.

Izutsu, Toshihiko. "The Basic Structure of Metaphysical Thinking in Islam." In M. Mohaghegh-H. Landolt, *Collected Papers on Islamic Philosophy and Mysticism*. Tehran: University, 1971; pp. 39–72.

—— "The Paradox of Light and Darkness in the Garden of Mystery of Shabastarī." *Anagogic Qualities of Literature*, ed. Joseph P. Strelka. University of Pennsylvania: University Park, 1971; pp. 288–307.

Jaᶜfrī, Raīs Aḥmad. *Iqbāl aur ᶜashq-i rasūl*. Lahore: Ashraf, 1956.

Jāisī, Malik Muḥammad. *Padmāvati*, trans. A. G. Shireff. Calcutta: Bibliotheca Indica no. 267, 1944.

Jalbānī, Ghulām Ḥusain. *Shāh Walīullāh jō taᶜlīm*. Hyderabad/Sind: Shāh Walīullāh Academy, 1961.

Jamāluddīn, Muḥsin. *Iḥtifalāt al-mawālīd an-nabawiyya fī'l-ashᶜār al-andalusiyya wa'l-maghribiyya wa'l-mahjariyya*. Baghdad: Dār al-Baṣrī, 1967.

James, William. *The Varieties of Religious Experience*. 1902; New York: Mentor Books, 1958.

Jāmī, ᶜAbdur Raḥmān. *Dīwān-i kāmil*, ed. Hāshim Riżā. Tehran: Pīrūz, 1341sh/1962.

—— *Lawā'iḥ*, ed. and trans. into English by Edward Henry Whinfield and Mirza Muhd. Kazwini. London, 1906; repr. with an intro-

duction by Seyyed Hossein Nasr, London: Theosophical Publishing House, 1978.
—— *Nafaḥāt al-uns min ḥaḍarāt al-quds*, ed. Mahdī Tauḥīdīpūr. Tehran: Sa ᶜdī 1336sh/1957.
Jansky, Herbert. "Der "Bektašî-Dichter Edip Harâbî (st. 1915). Ein Beitrag zur Ideengeschichte der Bektaši-Dichtung." *WZKM* 56 (1960), pp. 87–98.
Jotwani, Motilal. *Shah Abdul Karim.* New Delhi: Kumar Brothers, 1970.
—— *Shah Abdul Latif, His Life and Work.* University of Delhi, 1975.
Jubel, der stumme. Ein mystischer Chor. Bonn: Verlag der Buchgemeinde, 1926.
Kahle, Paul. *Der Leuchtturm von Alexandrien. Ein arabisches Schattenspiel aus dem mittelalterlichen Ägypten.* Stuttgart: Kohlhammer, 1930.
Kayğusuz Abdal, Hatayĭ, Kul Himmet, Varlĭk Klasikleri. Istanbul: Varlĭk, 1953.
Kazi, Elsa. *Risalo of Abdul Latif. Selections.* Hyderabad/Sind: Sindhi Adabi Board, 1965.
Khakee, Gulshan. *The Dasa Avatara of the Satpanthi Ismailis and the Imam Shahis of Indo-Pakistan.* Ph.D. thesis, Harvard, 1972.
Khāqānī, Afḍaluddīn Badīl. *Dīwān,* ed. Ziāuddīn Sajjādī. Tehran: Zawwār, 1338sh/1959.
Kister, Meir J. "On a New Edition of the Dīwān of Ḥassān ibn Thābit," *BSOAS* 39 (1976), pp. 265–86.
Knappert, Jan. "The Figure of the Prophet Mohammed According to the Popular Literature of the Islamic peoples." *Swahili,* no. 32 (1961), pp. 24–31.
—— *Swahili Islamic Poetry.* 3 vols. Leiden: Brill, 1971.
Kocatürk, Vasfĭ Mahir. *Tekke şiiri antolojisi.* Ankara: Buluş Kitabevi, 1955.
Kokan, Mohd. Yousuf. *Arabic and Persian in Carnatic, 1710–1960.* Madras: Hafiza House, 1974.
—— *Khānwāda-e Qāżī Badruddaula,* Vol. I. Madras: Dār at-taṣnīf, 1963.
Köprülüzade (Köprülü), Mehmet Fuat. *Eski Şairlerimiz; Divan Edebiyatĭ Antolojisi.* Istanbul: Ahmet Halit Kitabevi, 1931.
—— *Türk edebiyatĭnda ilk mutesavvĭflar.* 2d ed. Ankara: Universitiesi Yayĭnevi, 1966.
Kovalenka, A. *Le martyre de Ḥusayn dans la poésie populaire de l'Iraq.*

Université de Génève, Faculté des Lettres, Thèse no. 223, 1979.
Kühnel, Ernst. "Die osmanische Tughra." *Kunst des Orients* 2 (1955), pp. 69–82.
Lāhījī, Muḥammad. *Mafātīḥ al-iᶜjāz fī sharḥ gulshan-i rāz*, ed. Kaiwān Samīᶜī. Tehran: Maḥmūdī, 1337sh/1958.
Landolt, Hermann. "Two Types of Mystical Thought in Muslim Iran: An essay on Suhrawardī Shaykh al-Ishrāq and ᶜAynulqużāt-i Hamadānī." *MW* 68, no. 3 (1978), pp. 187–204.
Lane, Edward William. *Manners and Customs of the Modern Egyptians*. London, 1846.
Lawrence, Bruce B. *Notes from a Distant Flute*. Tehran-London: Imperial Academy of Philosophy, 1977.
Lawrence, Bruce B., ed. *The Rose and the Rock. Mystical and Rational Elements in the Intellectual History of South Asian Islam*. Durham, N.C.: Duke University Press, 1979.
Leeuw, Gerardus van der. *In den hemel is eenen dans*. Amsterdam: H. J. Paris, 1930.
—— *Phänomenologie der Religion*. 2d ed. Tübingen: J. C. B. Mohr (Paul Siebeck), 1956.
—— *Vom Heiligen in der Kunst*. German trans. by Annelise Piper. Gütersloh: Bertelsmann, 1957.
Lentz, Wolfgang. "ᶜAṭṭār als Allegoriker." *Der Islam* 35 (1960), pp. 52–96.
Lichtenstadter, Ilse. *Introduction to Classical Arabic Literature*. New York: Twayne, 1974.
Littmann, Enno. *Aḥmed il-Bedawî. Ein Lied auf den ägyptischen Nationalheiligen* (Abh. der Akademie der Wissenschaften und der Literatur, Mainz). Wiesbaden: Steiner, 1950.
—— *Islamisch-arabische Heiligenlieder* (Abh. der Akademie der Wissenschaften und der Literatur, Mainz). Wiesbaden: Steiner, 1951.
—— *Mohammed im Volksepos* (Det Kgl. Danske Videnskabernes Selskab, Historisk-filologiske Meddedelser XXXII, no. 3). Copenhaguen: Ejnar Munksgard, 1950.
—— *Morgenländische Spruchweisheit: Arabische Sprichwörter und Rätsel*. Leipzig: J. C. Hinrichs, 1937.
Longworth Dames, M. *Popular Poetry of the Baloches*. 2 vols. London: Royal Asiatic Society, 1907.
Lüers, Grete. *Die Sprache der deutschen Mystik des Mittelalters im Werk der Mechthild von Magdeburg*. Munich: Reinhardt, 1926.

Luṭf, Muḥammad Luṭf ᶜAlī. *Sarāpā sarwar al-anbiyā.* Cawnpore, 1869.
MacCallum, Lyman. *The Mevlidi Sherif by Süleyman Chelebi.* The Wisdom of the East Series. London: John Murray, 1943.
Macdonald, Duncan Black. "Emotional Religion in Islam as Affected by Music and Singing; Being a Translation of a Book of the Iḥyā ᶜulūm ad-dīn of al-Ghazzālī." *JRAS* (1901), pp. 195–252, 705–748; (1902), pp. 1–28.
McPherson, Joseph Williams. *The Moulid of Egypt.* Cairo: N. M. Press, 1941.
Madkūr, Ibrāhīm B., ed. *Al-kitāb at-tidhkārī: Muḥyīuddīn ibn ᶜArabī.* Cairo: Dār al-kutub al-ᶜarabī, 1969.
Majmūᶜa Panj ganj (Panjabi Mystical Verse). Lahore: Allāh wālē kī qaumī dukān, n.d. No. 195.
Maneri, Sharafuddin. *The Hundred Letters,* trans. and intro. Paul Jackson, S. J. New York: Paulist Press, 1980.
Mansooruddin, Muhammed. "Abstract of Muslim Folk Songs: An Untapped Source of Islamic History." *Proceedings All Pakistan Historical Conference* 1 (1951), pp. 368–88.
—— "Further Muslim Folksongs of East Bengal." *Proceedings All Pakistan Historical Conference* 2 (1952), pp. 316–25.
Mansuroglu, Mecdut, "Calâluddîn Rumi's türkische Verse." *Ural-Altaiisches Jahrbuch* 24, nos. 3–4 (1952), pp. 106–15.
Maqarrī, Aḥmad ibn Muḥammad al-Maghribi al-. *Fatḥ al-mutaᶜāl fī madḥ an-niᶜāl.* Hyderabad/Deccan, 1334h/1916.
Marek, Jan. "Persian Literature in India," in Jan Rypka, *History of Iranian Literature,* pp. 711–30.
Massignon, Louis. *La Cité des Morts au Caire: Qarâfa—Darb al-Ahmar.* Cairo: Institut Francais d'archéologie orientale, 1958.
—— "Le Dîvân d'al-Ḥallāj, Essai de réconstitution, ed. et. trad." *JA* 118 (Jan.–Mar. 1931), pp. 1–158. Also: Hoçeïn Mansur Hallaj. *Dîwân,* traduit et présenté par L. M. Paris: Cahiers du Sud, 1955.
—— *Essai sur les origines du lexique technique de la mystique musulmane.* 2d ed. Paris: J. Vrin, 1954.
—— "Interférences philosophiques et percées métaphysiques dans la mystique hallagienne: notion de l'essentiel désir." *Mélanges J. Maréchal,* vol. II. Paris: Desclée de Brouwer, 1950; pp. 263–96.
—— "La légende de Hallâce Mansûr en pays turcs," *REI* (1941–1946), pp. 67–117.
—— "L'oeuvre hallagienne d'Attar." *REI* (1941–1946), pp. 117–44.

—— *La passion d'al Ḥosayn ibn Manṣour Al-Hallāj, martyr mystique de l'Islam, exécuté à Bagdad le 26 mars 922.* 2 vols. Paris: Geuthner, 1922; 2d ed., 4 vols. Paris: Gallimard, 1975.

—— "Qiṣṣat Ḥusayn al-Ḥallāj." *Orientalia Suecana, Donum Natalicum H. S. Nyberg.* Stockholm: Almquist and Wiksell, 1954; pp. 102–17.

—— "La vie et les oeuvres de Rûzbehân Baqlî." *Studia Orientalia . . . Joanni Pedersen dicata.* Copenhagen: Ejnar Munksgard, 1953; pp. 236–49.

Massignon, Louis, and Paul Kraus. *Akhbār al-Hallāj, texte ancien relatif à la prédication et au supplice du mystique musulman al-Ḥosayn ibn Manṣour al-Ḥallāj.* Paris: Vrin, 1936; 3d ed. 1957.

Mas^{c}ūd ibn Sa^{c}d-i Salmān. *Dīwān,* ed. Rashīd Yāsmī. Tehran: Peirūz, 1339sh/1960.

Meier, Fritz. *Abū Sa^{c}īd-i Abū l-Ḫair, Wirklichkeit und Legende.* (Acta Iranica IV). Teheran-Liège: Bibliothèque Pahlavi—Leiden: Brill, 1976.

—— "Der Derwischtanz." *Asiatische Studien* 8 (1954), pp. 107–36.

—— *Die fawā'iḥ al-ǧamāl wa fawātiḥ al-ǧalāl des Naǧmuddīn al-Kubrā.* Wiesbaden: Steiner, 1957.

—— "Der Geistmensch bei dem persischen Dichter ^{c}Aṭṭār." *Eranos-Jahrbuch* 13 (1946), pp. 283–353.

—— "Das Problem der Natur im esoterischen Monismus des Islams." *Eranos-Jahrbuch* 14 (1946), pp. 149–227.

—— *Die schöne Mahsati. Ein Beitrag zur Geschichte des persischen Vierzeilers,* vol. I. Wiesbaden: Steiner, 1963.

—— "Qušairīs *Tartīb as-sulūk.*" *Oriens* 16 (1963), pp. 1–39.

—— "Die Wandlung des Menschen im mystischen Islam." *Eranos-Jahrbuch* 23 (1954), pp. 99–139.

Mélikoff, Irène. "La Fleur de la souffrance. Recherche sur le sens symbolique de *lâle* dans la poésie mystique Turco-Iranienne." *JA* 225 (1967), pp. 341–60.

Mensching, Gustav. *Das heilige Schweigen* (Religionsgeschichtliche Vorarbeiten). Giessen: A. Töpelmann, 1926.

Message of the Prophet. A selection of articles read at the First International Congress on Seerat 1976. Ministry of Religious Affairs. Islamabad: Government of Pakistan, 1976.

Meyerovitch, Eva. *Mystique et poésie en Islam, Djalalud-Din Rumi et l'ordre des dervishes tourneurs.* Paris: Desclée de Brouwer, 1972.

Minorsky, Vladimir. "The Poetry of Shah Ismā^c^īl I." *BSOAS* 10 (1940–1942), pp. 1006a–1053a.
Mīr Taqī Mīr. *Kulliyāt,* ed. Dr. Ebadet Brelwi. Lahore: Urdū Dunyā, 1958.
Mohaghegh, Mahdi, and Hermann Landolt, eds. *Collected Papers on Islamic Philosophy and Mysticism.* The Institute of Islamic Studies, McGill University, Tehran Branch. Tehran: University, 1971.
Molé, Marijan. "La Dance exstatique an Islam." *Sources Orientales* 6 (1963). Paris, Editions du Seuil. Pp. 145–280.
—— *Les mystiques musulmans.* Paris: Presses universitaires de France, 1965.
Mommaers, Paul. *Was ist Mystik?* Frankfurt: Insel-Verlag, 1979.
Muḥammad ad-dīn, Ḥājjī Maulānā. *Qaṣīda-i Burda Panjābī.* Lahore: Allahwālē kī qaumī dukān, n.d. Nr. 87.
Muid Khan, Muhammad A. *The Arabian Poets of Golconda.* Bombay: University Press, 1963.
Mujeeb, Muhammad. *The Indian Muslims.* Montreal-London: McGill University Press, 1969.
Nabhānī, Yūsuf ibn Ismā^c^īl an-, *Al-majmū^c^a an-nabhāniyya fī'l-madā'iḥ an-nabawiyya.* 4 vols. Repr. Beirut: Dār al-ma^c^rifa, 1974.
Nābulusi, ^c^Abdul Ghanī an-, *Dīwān al-ḥaqā'iq wa majmū^c^ ar-raqā'iq.* Bulaq, 1376h/1957. Repr. Beirut, n.d.
Nadwi, Suleiman. "Literary Relations between Arabia and India." *IC* 6 (1932), pp. 624–41; 7 (1933), pp. 83–94.
Nasr, Seyyed Hossein, ed. *Mélanges offerts à Henry Corbin.* Tehran: Wisdom of Persia Series IX, 1977.
—— *Ideals and Realities of Islam.* London: Allen and Unwin, 1966.
—— "The Significance of the Void in the Art and Architecture of Islamic Persia." *Islamic Quarterly* 16, nos. 3–4 (1972), pp. 115–20.
—— *Three Muslim Sages.* Cambridge, Mass.: Harvard University Press, 1963.
Nazir Ahmad. *Kitāb-i Nauras by Ibrāhīm Adil Shah II.* Introduction, Notes, and Textual Editing. New Delhi: Bharatiya Kala Kandra, 1956.
Nicholson, Reynold Alleyne. *A Literary History of the Arabs.* Cambridge: Cambridge University Press, 1921; repr. 1953.
—— "The lives of ^c^Umar Ibnu'l Fāriḍ and Muḥyiu'd Din Ibnu'l ^c^Arabī." *JRAS* (1906), pp. 797–824.
—— *The Mystics of Islam.* London: G. Bell, 1914; repr. 1962.

—— "Mysticism in Persian Poetry." *Proceedings of the Iran Society* 1 (1936–1938), pp. 60–69.

—— *A Persian Forerunner of Dante.* Towyn-on-Sea, 1944.

—— *The Idea of Personality in Sufism.* Cambridge: Cambridge University Press, 1923.

—— *Rumi: Poet and Mystic.* Wisdom of the East Series. London: Allen and Unwin, 1950.

—— *Selected Poems from the Dīvān-i Shams-i Tabrīz,* ed. and trans. Cambridge: Cambridge University Press, 1898; repr. 1961.

—— *Studies in Islamic Mysticism.* Cambridge: Cambridge University Press, 1921; repr. 1967.

—— *Tales of Mystic Meaning.* London: Chapman and Hall, 1931.

Nicholson, Reynold Alleyne, trans. *The Secrets of the Self.* London: MacMillan, 1920.

Niffarī, Muḥammad ibn ᶜAbdul Jabbār. *The Mawāqif and Mukhāṭabāt of . . . with Other Fragments,* ed. and trans. by A. J. Arberry. *GMS* NS IX. London: Luzac, 1935.

Niyazi Misri. *Divan.* Istanbul: Maarif Kitabevi, 1955.

Nizami, Khaliq Ahmad. *The Life and Times of Shaikh Farīd Ganj-i Shakar.* Aligarh University Press, 1955.

Nurbakhsh, Dr. Javad. *What the Sufis Say.* New York: Khaniqahi Nimatullahi Publications, 1980.

Nwyia, Paul. *Exégèse coranique et langage mystique.* Beirut: Dar el-machreq, 1970.

—— *Ibn ᶜAtā' Allāh (m. 709/1309) et la naissance de la confrèrie šādilite.* Beirut: Dar el-machreq, 1972.

—— "Massignon ou une certaine vision de la langue arabe." *Studia Islamica* 50 (1979), pp. 125–49.

Nyberg, Hendrik Samuel. *Kleinere Schriften des Ibn al-ᶜArabi.* Leiden: Brill, 1919.

Nygren, Andres. *Eros und Agape, Gestaltwandlungen der christlichen Liebe.* 2 vols. Gütersloh: Bertelsmann, 1930, 1937.

Önder, Mehmet. *Mevlâna.* Ankara: Türkiye Iş Bankasĭ, 1971.

—— *Mevlâna Bibliografyasi: 1. Basmalar; 2. Yazmaler.* Ankara: Türkiye Iş Bankasĭ, 1973, 1974.

—— *Mevlâna Şiirleri antolojisi.* 3rd ed. Ankara: Türkiye Iş Bankasĭ, 1973.

Öney, Gönül. "Dragon Figures in Anatolian Seljuk Art." *Belleten* 33 (1969). Ankara: Türk Tarih Kurumu. Pp. 193–216.

—— "Das Lebensbaum-Motiv in der seldschukischen Kunst in Anatolien." *Belleten* 32 (1968). Ankara: Türk Tarih Kurumu. Pp. 37–50.

Otto, Rudolf. *Das Heilige.* 28th ed. Munich: Biederstein, 1947.

—— *Das Gefühl des Überweltlichen.* Munich: C. H. Beck'sche Verlagsbuchhandlung, 1932.

Oxford Book of English Mystical Verse, The, chosen by D. H. S. Nicholson and A. H. E. Lee, Oxford: Oxford University Press, 1945.

Padwick, Constance E. *Muslim Devotions.* London: S.P.C.K., 1960.

Pagliaro, Antonio, e Alessandro Bausani. *Storia della letteratura persiana.* Milan: Nuova Accademia Editrice, 1960.

Paret, Rudi. *Die legendäre Maghâzî-Literatur. Arabische Dichtungen über die muslimischen Kriegszüge zu Mohammeds Zeit.* Tübingen: J. C. B. Mohr (Paul Siebeck), 1930.

—— "Die Legende von der Verleihung des Prophetenmantels (*burda*) an Ka^cb ibn Zuhair." *Der Islam* 17 (1928), pp. 9–14.

Parsram, Jethmal. *Sind and its Sufis.* Madras, 1924.

Pavet de Courteille, Abel. *Mirâdj-nâmeh. Récit de l'Ascension de Mahomet au ciel, composé AH 840 (1436–1437).* Paris, 1882; repr. Amsterdam: Philo, 1975.

Philott, D. C. "Some Persian Riddles Collected from Dervishes in the South of Persia." *JASB* NS 2 (1902), pp. 86–93.

Pinder-Wilson, Ralph, ed. *Paintings from Islamic Lands.* Oxford: Cassirer, 1969.

Pir Sultan Abdal, ed. Abdulbaki Gölpĭnarlĭ. Istanbul: Varlĭk, 1954.

Porter, J. R. "Muhammad's Journey to Heaven." *Numen* 21 (1974), pp. 64–80.

Posche, Christian. "Zikr und Musicology," *World of Music.* Wilhelmshaven, 1978; pp. 59–73.

Qāḍī ᶜIyāḍ. *Kitāb ash-shifā fī taᶜrīf ḥuqūq al-Muṣṭafā.* Istanbul, 1312h/1894.

Qāḍī Qādan jō kalām, ed. Hiro J. Thakur. Delhi: Puja Publications, 1978.

Qāniᶜ, Mīr ᶜAlī Shīr. *Maqālāt ash-shuᶜarā,* ed. Sayyid Hussamuddin Rashdi. Karachi: Sindhi Adabi Board, 1956.

—— *Maklīnāma,* ed. Sayyid Hussamuddin Rashdi. Hyderabad/Sind: Sindhi Adabi Board, 1967.

Qānūn-e ᶜishq, i.e., Ḥalwā-ye Panjāb, commentary on Bullhe Shah's *kāfīs.* Lahore: Allāhwālē kī qaumī dukān, n.d., no. 372.

Quispel, Gilles. "Jewish Gnosis and Mandean Gnosticism: Some Reflections on the Writing Brontè." *Les Textes de Nag Hammadi,* ed. Jacques-E. Ménard. Leiden: Brill, 1975; pp. 82–122.

Qushairī, ᶜAbdul Karīm al-, *Kitāb al-miᶜrāj,* ed. ᶜAlī Ḥusain ᶜAbdul Qādir. Cairo: Dār al-kutub al-ḥadītha, 1964.

—— *Ar-risāla fī ᶜilm at-ta·sawwuf.* Cairo: Dār al-kutub al-ᶜarabiyya al-kubrā, 1330h/1912.

Rahatullah, Muhammad Khan. *Vom Einfluss des Korans auf die arabische Dichtung. Untersuchung über die dichterischen Werke von Ḥassān ibn Tābit, Kaᶜb ibn Malik und ᶜAbdallāh ibn Rawāḥa.* Phil. Diss. Leipzig, 1938: Gräfenheinichen, 1938.

Rahbar, Daud. "Ghālib and a Debatable Point of Theology." *MW* 56 (1966) pp. 14–17.

Ralfs, see Busiri.

Ramakrishna, Lajwanti. *Panjabi Sufi Poets.* London-Calcutta: Oxford University Press, 1938; repr. Delhi, 1975.

Rashdi, Sayyid Hussamuddin. *Sindhī adab,* Karachi, n.d. (c. 1954).

—— "Shāh kāfī[a] jō mūjid na ahē." *Mehrān jūñ maujūñ.* Karachi: Sindhi Adabi Board, 1956. ("Shah ᶜAbdul Latif did *not* invent the *kāfī,*" see pp. 215–24.)

Rasheed, Ghulam Dastagir. "The Development of naᶜtia Poetry in Persian Literature." *IC* 39 (1965), pp. 53–69.

Raverty, H. George. *Selections from the Poetry of the Afghans.* London, 1862.

Reinert, Benedikt. "Die prosodische Unterschiedlichkeit von persischem und arabischem Rubāᶜī." *Islamwissenschaftliche Abhandlungen,* ed. Richard Gramlich. Wiesbaden: Steiner 1974; pp. 205–25.

Ritter, Hellmut. *Über die Bildersprache Niẓāmīs.* Berlin: de Gruyter, 1927.

—— *Das Meer der Seele. Gott, Welt und Mensch in den Geschichten Farīduddīn ᶜAṭṭārs.* Leiden: Brill, 1955.

—— "Muslim Mystics' Strife with God." *Oriens* 5 (1952), pp. 1–15.

—— "L'orthodoxie a-t-elle une part dans la décadence?" *Classicisme et Déclin Culturel dans l'Histoire de l'Islam* (Symposium de Bordeaux), ed. R. Brunschwig et G.E. von Grunebaum. Paris: Besson Choutemerle, 1957; pp. 167–83.

—— "Philologika VII: Arabische und persische Schriften über die profane und mystische Liebe." *Der Islam* 21 (1933), pp. 84–109.

—— "Philologika IX: Die vier Suhrawardī." *Der Islam* 24 (1939).

—— "Philologika XI: Maulānā Ǧalāluddīn Rūmī und sein Kreis." *Der Islam* 26 (1942), pp. 116–58, 221–49.
—— "Die Mevlânafeier in Konya vom 11–17. Dezember 1960." *Oriens* 15 (1962), pp. 249–70.
—— "Das Proömium des Matnawī-i maulawī." *ZDMG* 93 (1939), pp. 169–96.
Rizwi, Saiyid Athar Abbas. *A History of Sūfism in India,* Vol. I. New Delhi: Munshiram Manoharlal Publishers, 1978.
Rosenzweig-Schwannau, Vincenz von. *Funkelnde Wandelsterne zum Lobe des besten der Geschöpfe.* (German trans. of Busiri's *Burda*). Vienna, 1824.
Rückert, Friedrich. "Aus Dschamis Diwan." In Leopold Hirschberg, ed., *Rückert-Nachlese.* 2 vols. Weimar: Gesellschaft der Bibliophilen, 1911. Vol. 2, pp. 371–465.
—— *Grammatik, Poetik und Rhetorik der Perser,* hersg. von Wilhelm Pertsch. Berlin, 1874; repr. Osnabrück: Zeller—Wiesbaden: Harrassowitz, 1966.
—— *Orientalische Dichtung in der Übersetzung F.R.s,* herausgegeben und eingeleitet von Annemarie Schimmel. Bremen: Carl Schünemann, 1963.
—— *Saadis Bostan.* Aus dem Nachlass herausgegeben von Wilhelm Pertsch. Leipzig, 1882.
Rūmī, Maulānā Jalāluddīn. *Dīwān-i kabīr yā Kulliyāt-i Shams,* ed. Badīᶜuzzamān Furūzānfar. 10 vols. Tehran: University, 1336sh/1957 ff.
—— *Fīhi mā fīhi.* Tehran: Shirkat-i sihāmī-i nāshirīn-i kutub-i Irān, 1338sh/1958.
—— *Maktūbāt,* ed. Yūsuf Jamshīdīpūr u Ghulāmḥusain Amīn. Tehran: Pāyanda, 1956. Turkish annotated translation: *Mevlâna' nīn mektuplarī,* trans. Abdulbaki Gölpīnarlī. Istanbul: Inkilap ve Aka Kitapevleri, 1963.
—— *Mathnawī-i maᶜnawī,* ed. and trans. Reynold A. Nicholson. Vols. 1–6, commentary Vols. 7 and 8. *GMS* NS 4. London: Luzac 1925–1940; reprints.
Rypka, Jan. *History of Iranian Literature.* Dordrecht: Reidel, 1968.
Sachal Sarmast. *Risālō Sindhī,* ed. ᶜOthmān ᶜAlī Anṣārī. Karachi: Sindhi Adabi Board, 1958.
—— *Siraikī kalām,* ed. Maulwī Ḥakīm Muḥammad Ṣādiq Rānīpūrī. Karachi: Sindhi Adabi Board, 1959.

Sachs, Sheldon, ed. *On Metaphor.* Chicago: University of Chicago Press, 1979.
Sadarangani, H. J. *Persian Poets of Sind.* Karachi: Sindhi Adabi Board, 1956.
Saᶜdī, Muṣliḥuddīn. *Būstān–Gulistān–ghazaliyāt–qaṣā'id,* ed. from the manuscript of Muḥammad ᶜAlī Furūghī Dhakā'ul-mulk. 4 vols. Tehran, 1342sh/1963.
Sadiq, Muhammad. *A History of Urdu Literature.* London: Oxford University Press, 1964.
Sājid Ṣiddīqī and Walī Āsī, *Armaghān-i naᶜt.* Lucknow: Maktaba-i dīn ū adab, 1961.
Saksena, Ram Babu. *A History of Urdu Literature.* Allahabad, 1927.
Sanā'ī, Abū'l-Majd Majdūd. *Dīwān,* ed. Mudarris Rażawī. Tehran: Ibn-i Sīnā, 1341sh/1962.
—— *Ḥadīqat al-ḥaqīqa wa sharīᶜat aṭ-ṭarīqa,* ed. Mudarris Rażawī. Tehran: Ṭaḥūrī, 1329sh/1950.
—— *Mathnawīhā,* ed. Mudarris Rażawī. Tehran: University, 1348sh/1969.
—— *Sair ul- ᶜibād ilā'l-maᶜād,* ed. Riżā Māyil. Kabul: Ministry of Culture, 1356sh/1977 (one of the numerous publications released during the Sanā'ī-festival in 1977).
Sarrāj, Abu Naṣr as-. *Kitāb al-lumaᶜ fi't-taṣawwuf,* ed. R. A. Nicholson. *GMS* XXII. London: Luzac—Leiden: Brill, 1914; reprints.
Schaeder, Hans Heinrich. "Zur Deutung der islamischen Mystik," *OLZ* 30 (1927), cols. 834–49.
—— "Die islamische Lehre vom Vollkommenen Menschen, ihre Herkunft und ihre dichterische Gestaltung." *ZDMG* 79 (1925), pp. 192–268.
—— "Die kleineren Schriften des Ibn al-ᶜArabī." *OLZ* 28 (1925), cols. 794–99.
—— "Die persische Vorlage von Goethes Seliger Sehnsucht." *Festschrift für Eduard Spranger.* Leipzig: J. C. Hinrichs, 1942.
—— "Lässt sich die ᶜseelische Entwicklung' des Dichters Hafis ermitteln?" *OLZ* 45 (1942), cols. 201–10; against Karl Stolz, "Die seelische Entwicklung des Dichters Hafis," *WZKM* 48 (1941), pp. 97–120.
Schimmel, Annemarie. *Aus dem Goldenen Becher,* Türkische Gedichte vom 13. Jahrhundert bis in unsere Zeit. Istanbul: Milli Egitim Basĭmevi, 1973.

—— *Die Bildersprache Dschelāleddīn Rūmīs.* Walldorf: Verlag für Orientkunde, 1949.

—— "Classical Urdu Literature from the Beginnings to Iqbal." In Jan Gonda, ed. *History of Indian Literature.* Wiesbaden: Harrassowitz, 1975.

—— *A Dance of Sparks: Studies in Ghālib's Imagery.* New Delhi: Ghalib Academy, 1979.

—— "Eros—Heavenly and Not So Heavenly—in Sufi Literature and Life." *Society and the Sexes in Medieval Islam,* ed. Afaf L. S. Marsot. Malibu, 1979; pp. 119–41.

—— "Ghālib's qaṣīda in Praise of the Prophet." *Islam: Past Influence and Present Challenge.* Festschrift W. Montgomery Watt, ed. Pierre Cachia and Alford Welch. Edinburgh: Edinburgh University Press, 1979; pp. 188–209.

—— "The Golden Chain of Sincere Muhammadans." In Bruce B. Lawrence, ed., *The Rose and the Rock.* Durham, N.C.: Duke University Press 1979; pp. 104–34.

—— "Ḥāfiẓ and His Critics." *Studies in Islam* (1979), no. 1, pp. 1–33.

—— *Al-Halladsch, Märtyrer der Gottesliebe.* Cologne: Hegner, 1969.

—— "Hochzeitslieder der Frauen im Industal." *Zeitschrift für Volkskunde* 61, no. 2 (1965), pp. 224–42.

—— "The Influence of Sufism on Indo-Muslim Poetry." In Joseph P. Strelka, ed. *Anagogic Qualities of Literature.* University Park: University of Pennsylvania, 1971; pp. 181–210.

—— *Islam in the Indian Subcontinent* (Handbuch der Orientalistik, 2. Abteilung, 4, 3). Leiden-Cologne: Brill, 1980.

—— "Islamic Literatures of India." In Jan Gonda, ed. *History of Indian Literature.* Wiesbaden: Harrassowitz, 1973.

—— *Märchen aus Pakistan.* Cologne: Diederichs, 1980.

—— "The Marthiya in Sindhi Poetry." In Peter J. Chelkowski, ed. *Taᶜziyeh: Ritual and Drama in Iran.* New York University Press: 1979; pp. 210–21.

—— "The Martyr-mystic Ḥallāj in Sindhi Folk Poetry." *Numen* 9, no. 3 (1962), pp. 161–200.

—— "Mīr Dards Gedanken über das Verhältnis von Mystik und Wort." In *Festgabe deutscher Iranisten zur 2500-Jahrfeier Irans,* ed. Wilhelm Eilers. Stuttgart: Hochwacht-Druck, 1971; pp. 117–32.

—— *Mystical Dimensions of Islam.* Chapel Hill: University of North Carolina Press, 1975.

—— "Mystische Motive in der modernen islamischen Dichtung." *Weg in die Zukunft. Festschrift Anton Antweiler.* Leiden: Brill, 1976; pp. 216–28.

—— "Neue Veröffentlichungen zur Volkskunde von Sind." *WI NS* IX (1963), pp. 237–59.

—— "Ein Osten, der nie alle wird. Rilke aus der Sicht einer Orientalistin." In Ingeborg H. Solbrig und Joachim W. Storck, eds. *Rilke heute.* Frankfurt: Suhrkamp, 1975; pp. 183–206.

—— *Pain and Grace: A Study of Two Mystical Writers of Eighteenth-century Muslim India.* Leiden: Brill, 1976.

—— "The Place of the Prophet of Islam in Iqbal's Thought." *Islamic Studies* 1, no. 4 (Dec. 1962), pp. 111–30.

—— "Der Regen als Symbol in der Religionsgeschichte." *Religion und Religionen, Festschrift für Gustav Mensching.* Bonn: Röhrscheidt, 1966; pp. 178–89.

—— "Rose und Nachtigall." *Numen* 5, no. 2 (1958), pp. 85–109.

—— *Rumi: Aus dem Diwan.* Stuttgart: Reclam, 1964.

—— *Rumi: Ich bin Wind und du bist Feuer.* Cologne: Diederichs, 1978.

—— "Schriftsymbolik im Islam." *Aus der Welt der islamischen Kunst, Festschrift für Ernst Kühnel,* ed. Richard Ettinghausen. Berlin: Gebr. Mann, 1959; pp. 244–53.

—— "Shāh ᶜInāyat of Jhōk, a Sindhi Mystic of the Early 18th Century." *Liber Amicorum in Honour of C. J. Bleeker.* Leiden: Brill, 1969; pp. 151–70.

—— "Sindhi Literature." In Jan Gonda, ed. *History of Indian Literature.* Wiesbaden: Harrassowitz, 1974.

—— "Sindhi Translations and Commentaries of the Qur'ān." *Oriens* 16 (1963), pp. 224–43.

—— "Some Glimpses of Religious Life in Egypt during the Later Mamluk Period." *Islamic Studies* 4, no. 4 (1965), pp. 353–92.

—— "A Spring Day in Konya According to Jalāluddīn Rūmī." In Peter J. Chelkowski, ed. *The Scholar and the Saint.* New York: New York University Press, 1975; pp. 255–73.

—— "Tanz." *RGG.* 3d ed., cols. 612–14.

—— *The Triumphal Sun: A Study of the Works of Jalāloddīn Rūmī.* London and The Hague: East-West Publications, 1978.

—— "Turk and Hindu: A Poetical Image and Its Application to Historical Fact." *Islam and Cultural Change in the Middle Ages,* ed. Speros Vryonis Jr. Wiesbaden: Harrassowitz, 1975; pp. 107–26.

—— *Und Muhammad ist Sein Prophet. Die Verehrung des Propheten in der islamischen Frömmigkeit.* Cologne: Diederichs, 1981.

—— "The Veneration of the Prophet Muhammad, as Reflected in Sindhi poetry." *The Saviour God: Comparative Studies in the Concept of Salvation Presented to E. O. James,* ed. S. G. F. Brandon. Manchester: Manchester University Press, 1963; pp. 129–43.

—— "Zur Verwendung des Halladsch-Motivs in der indo-persischen Poesie." *Mélanges Henry Corbin,* ed. S. H. Nasr. Tehran: Wisdom of Iran, 1977; pp. 425–47.

—— "Yūnus Emre." *Numen* 8 (1961), pp. 12–33.

—— *Zeitgenössische arabische Lyrik.* Tübingen: Erdmann, 1975.

Schimmel, Annemarie, and Abdoljavad Falaturi, eds. *We Believe in One God: The Experience of God in Christianity and Islam.* London: Burns and Oates, 1979.

Schrieke, Bernhard. "Die Himmelsreise Muhammads." *Der Islam* 6 (1916), pp. 1–30.

Schubart, Walther. *Religion und Eros.* Munich: C. H. Beck'sche Verlagsbuchhandlung, 1941.

Séguy, Marie-Rose, ed. *Muhammads wunderbare Reise durch Himmel und Hölle* (Bibliothèque Nationale Paris Ms. Suppl. Turc 190). Munich: Prestel, 1977. English trans., London: The Scholar Press, 1977.

Self-Knowledge: Commentaries on Sufic Songs. Translated from the Arabic by A'isha Abd ar-Rahman al-Tarjumana. Tucson: Iqra Inc., 1979.

Semaan, Khalil J. *Murder in Baghdad.* Arabic Translation Series of the *Journal of Arabic Literature,* I. Leiden: Brill, 1972.

—— "T. S. Eliot's Influence on Arabic Poetry and Theatre." *Studies in Comparative Literature* 6 (1969).

Seydou, Christiane. "Trois poèmes mystiques peuls du Foûta-Djalon." *REI* 40 (1972), pp. 141–85.

Shabistarī, Maḥmūd. *Gulshan-i rāz: The Rose-Garden of Mysteries,* ed. and trans. by Edward Henry Whinfield. London, 1880.

Shackle, Christopher. "The Multānī *marṣiya.*" *Der Islam* 55 (1978), pp. 281–311.

—— "The Pilgrimage and the Extension of Sacred Geography in the Poetry of Khwāja Ghulām Farīd." In Attar Singh, ed., *Socio-cultural Impact of Islam on India.* Chandigarh: University of the Panjab, 1976; pp. 159–70.

—— *Styles and Themes in the Siraiki Mystical Poetry of Sind.* Multan: Bazme s̱aqāfat, c. 1976.

Shahid, Irfan. "A Contribution to Koranic Exegesis" [Sura 26/226]. *Arabic and Islamic Studies in Honor of Hamilton A. R. Gibb,* ed. George Makdisi. Leiden: Brill, 1965; pp. 563–80.

Shahidullah, Muhammad, and Abdul Hai. *Traditional Culture in East Pakistan.* Dacca: Dept. of Bengali, University of Dacca, 1963.

Shaibī, Kāmil Muṣṭafā ash-. *Dīwān ad-dūbait fī'sh-shiᶜr al-ᶜarabī.* Tripoli: Manshūrāt al-jāmiᶜa al-lībiyya, 1972.

—— *Al-Ḥallāj mauḍūᶜan li'l-adab wa'l-funūn al-ᶜarabiyya wa'sh-sharqiyya.* Baghdad: al-Maᶜārif, 1977. See also Hallāj, Shiblī.

Shiblī, Abū Bakr ash-. *The Dīwān of Sh.,* collected and ed. by Kamil M. al-Shaibi. Baghdad: al-Maᶜārif, 1967.

Shinar, Pesah. "Traditional and Reformist *maulid* Celebrations in the Maghrib." *Studies in Memory of Gaston Wiet,* ed. Miryam Rosen-Ayalon. Jerusalem: Hebrew University, 1977; pp. 371–413.

Simsar, Muhammad A. *The Cleveland Museum of Art's Ṭūṭī-nāma: Tales of a Parrot.* Graz: Akademische Druck- und Verlagasanstalt, 1978.

Sipahsālār, Farīdūn Aḥmad. *Risāla dar aḥwāl-i Maulānā Jalāluddīn Rūmī,* ed. Saᶜīd- i Nafīsī. Tehran: Iqbal, 1325sh/1946.

Siraj ud-Din and H. A. Walter. "An Indian Sufi Hymn." *MW* 9 (1919), pp. 122–31.

Smith, Margaret. *Rābiᶜa the Mystic and Her Fellow Saints in Islam.* Cambridge: Cambridge University Press, 1928.

—— *Readings from the Mystics of Islam.* London: Luzac, 1950.

—— *The Sufi Path of Love.* London: Luzac, 1931; repr. 1954.

Smith, Wilfred Cantwell. *Islam in Modern India.* 2d ed. Lahore: Minerva Bookshop, 1947.

Söderblom, Nathan. "Rus och religion." *Ur Religionens Historia.* Stockholm: P. A. Norstadt, 1915; pp. 31–56.

Sohrawardī, Shihabaddin Yahya. "Ṣafīr-i sīmurgh," in: *Oeuvres philosophiques et mystiques,* vol. 2 (Oeuvres en Persan), ed. Seyyed Hossein Nasr, commentary by Henry Corbin. Tehran-Paris: Bibliothèque Iranienne, 1970.

Sorley, Herbert T. *Shah Abdul Latif of Bhit.* London: Oxford University Press, 1940; repr. 1966.

Sources Orientales. Vol. VI: Les Dances Sacrées. Paris: Editions du Seuil, 1963.

Spiess, Gertrud. *Maḥmūd von Ghazna bei Farīd ud'dīn ᶜAṭṭār,* Phil. Diss. Basel, 1959.

Steiger, Arnold. "Función espiritual del Islám en la España medieval." *Revista del Instituto de Estudios Islámicos en Madrid* 6 (1958), pp. 41–57.

Süleyman Çelebi. *Mevlud-i şerif.* Istanbul, n.d.

Sultan Bahoo. *Abyāt,* ed. and trans. by Maqbool Elahi. Lahore: Ashraf, 1967.

Sulṭān Walad. *Dīwān-i Turkī,* ed. Kilisli Muallim Rifᶜat. Istanbul, 1341/1922–23.

—— *Waladnāma,* ed. Jalāl Humā'ī. Tehran: Iqbal, 1315sh/1936.

Suzuki, Daisetz T. *On Indian Mahayana Buddhism.* New York: Harper Torchbook, 1968.

Swartz, Merlin S. *Ibn al-Jauzī's "kitāb al-quṣṣāṣ wa'l-mudhakkirīn."* Beirut: Dar el-Machreq, 1971.

Taeschner, Franz. *Gülschehris Mesnewi auf Achi Evrān, den Heiligen von Kirschehir und Patron der türkischen Zünfte.* Wiesbaden: Steiner, 1955.

—— "Die Erlösungssehnsucht in der islamischen Mystik des Mittelalters." *Orientalische Stimmen zum Erlösungsgedanken,* ed. Franz Taeschner. Leipzig: J. C. Hinrichs, 1936; pp. 55–79.

—— "Das Puppentheater nach dem *Futuvvetnāme-i sulṭānī* des Ḥusain Vāᶜiẓ-i Kāšifī (gest. 910/1504-5). *Der Orient in der Forschung,* ed. Wilhelm Hoenerbach. Wiesbaden: Harrassowitz, 1969; pp. 657–59.

—— *Zünfte und Bruderschaften im Islam. Texte zur Geschichte der Futuwwa.* Zürich and Munich: Artemis, 1979.

Ṭāhir, Ḥamza. *"At-taṣawwuf ash-shaᶜbī fi'l-adab at-turkī." Magalla Kulliyat al-ādāb* 12, no. 2. Cairo: University, Faculty of Humanities, 1950; pp. 111–43.

Thackston, Wheeler M., trans. *Khwāja Abdullah Ansari, Intimate Conversations.* New York: Paulist Press, 1978.

—— *The Tales of the Prophets of al-Kisā'ī.* New York and Boston: Twayne, 1978.

Tholuck, Friedrich August Deofidus. *Blüthensammlung aus der morgenländischen Mystik.* Berlin, 1825.

—— *Ssufismus sive theosophia persarum pantheistica.* Berlin, 1821.

Thomas, Gerald. *The Tall Tale and Philippe d'Alcripe. An Analysis of the Tall Tale Genre with Particular Reference to Philippe d'Alcripe's "La Nouvelle Fabrique des Excellents Traits de Vérité," Together with an Annotated Translation of the Work.* St. John's: Dept. of Folklore, Memorial University of Newfoundland, in Association with the American Folklore Society, 1977.

Tikku, Girdhari L. *Persian Poetry in Kashmir, 1339–1846.* Berkeley: University of California, 1971.

Tirmidhī, al-Ḥakīm at-. *Khatm al-auliyā,* ed. ᶜOthmān Yaḥya. Beirut: Dar al-Machreq, 1965.

Trimingham, J. Spencer. *The Sufi Orders in Islam.* Oxford: Oxford University Press, 1971.

Trumpp, Ernest. "Eine Sindhi-Sprachprobe: Sorathi. Ein Gedicht aus dem grossen Dīvān des Sayyid Abd-ul-Laṭīf." *ZDMG* 17 (1863), pp. 245–315.

Tuḥfa Raḥīm Yār. Lahore: Allāhwālē kī qaumī dukān, n.d. (c. 1951).

Turner, Victor. *Dramas, Fields, and Metaphors: Symbolic Action in Human Society.* Ithaca and London: Cornell University Press, 1974.

Ullmann, Manfred. *Die Natur-und Geheimwissenschaften im Islam* (Handbuch der Orientalistik I. Abt., Ergänzungsband VI 2), Leiden: Brill, 1972.

—— *Untersuchungen zur Rağazpoesie.* Wiesbaden: Harrassowitz, 1966.

Underhill, Evelyn. *Mysticism: A Study in the Nature and Development of Man's Spiritual Consciousness.* 1911. New York: E. P. Dutton paperback, 1961.

Ünver, Dr. A. Süheyl. *Sevâkib-i menâkib: Mevlâna'nin hatĭralarĭ.* Istanbul: Organon, 1973.

ᶜUrfī Shīrāzī, Muḥammad. *Kulliyāt,* ed. Ghulāmḥusain Jawāhirī. Tehran: n.p., 1336sh/1957.

Usborne, Charles F. *Hir Ranjha,* ed. Mumtaz Hasan. Karachi: Lion Art Press, 1966.

Vajda, George. "Un libelle contre la danse des soufis." *Studia Islamica* 51 (1980), pp. 163–77.

Vaudeville, Charlotte. *Bārahmāsa, les chansons des douze mois dans les littératures indo-aryennes.* Pondichéry: Institut Francais d'Indologie, 1965.

—— "La conception de l'amour divin chez Muḥammad Jāyasi: *virah* et ᶜ*ishq.*" *JA* 250 (1962), pp. 351–67.

—— *Kabīr.* Vol. 1. Oxford: Oxford University Press, 1974.

Waheed Mirza. *The Life and Works of Amir Khusrau.* 3d ed. Lahore: University of the Punjab, 1962; repr. 1975.

Walīullāh, Shāh. *Lamaḥāt,* ed. Ghulām Muṣṭafā Qāsimī. Hyderabad/Sind: Shāh Walīullāh Academy, n.d.

—— *Saṭaᶜāt,* ed. Ghulām Muṣṭafa Qāsimī. Hyderabad/Sind: Shāh Walīullāh Academy, 1964.

—— *At-tafhīmāt al-ilāhiyya,* ed. Ghulām Muṣṭafā Qāsimī. 2 vols. Hyderabad/Sind: Shāh Walīullāh Academy, 1967, 1970.

Walsh, John R. "Yūnus Emre: A Medieval Hymnodist." *Numen* 7, nos. 2–3 (1960), pp. 172–88.

Walther, Gerda. *Phänomenologie der Mystik.* Olten-Freiburg i.Br.: Walter Verlag, 1955.

Watanmal, Lilaram. *The Life of Shah Abdullatif.* Hyderabad/Sind, 1889.

Watt, William Montgomery. *Muslim Intellectual: A Study of al-Ghazālī.* Edinburgh: Edinburgh University Press, 1963.

Weischer, Bernd Manuel. *Ghaselen und Vierzeiler des Auḥaduddīn Kirmānī.* Hamburg: Borg, 1979.

Weischer, Bernd Manuel, and Peter Lamborn Wilson. *Heart's Witness: The Sufi Quatrains of Awḥaduddīn Kirmānī.* Tehran and London: Imperial Academy of Philosophy, 1978.

Welch, Stuart Cary. *Wonders of the Age: Masterpieces of Early Safavid Painting, 1501–1576.* Cambridge: Fogg Art Museum, 1979.

Wendeler, Camillus. "Die verkehrte Welt." *Zeitschrift des Vereins für Volkskunde Berlin* 15 (1905), pp. 158–63.

Wensinck, Arend Jan. *Concordances et indices de la tradition musulmane.* Leiden: Brill, 1936–1971.

Werner, A. "An Alphabetic Acrostic in a Northern Dialect of Swahili." *BSOS* 5 (1928–30), pp. 561–69.

Wheelwright, Philip. *The Burning Fountain: A Study in the Language of Symbolism.* Bloomington: Indiana University Press, 1954.

Widengren, Geo. *The Ascension of the Apostle and the Heavenly Book.* Uppsala: A. B. Lundquist—Leipzig: Harrassowitz, 1950.

Yashruṭiyya, Fāṭima al-. *Riḥlat ila 'l-ḥaqq.* Beirut, n.d. (c. 1955).

Yücel, Erdem. "Hayri Bey'in Ramazan manileri." *Türk Folklor Araştǐrmalarǐ.* Istanbul, 1973; nos. 6778–80.

Yunus Emre. *Divan,* ed. Abdulbaki Gölpǐnarlǐ. Istanbul: Ahmet Halit Kitabevi, 1943.

Zajączkowski. *Poezje stroficzne ᶜAšïq Paša.* Warszow: Polskiej Akademie nauk, 1967.
Zakī Mubārak. *Al-madā'iḥ an-nabawiyya fi'l-adab al-ᶜarabī.* Cairo: Muṣṭafa al-bābī al-ḥalabī wa aulāduhu, 1943.
Zimmer, Heinrich. *Maya. Der indische Mythos.* Zurich: Rascher, 1952.

Index of Selected Quotations

THE KORAN

THE PROPHETIC TRADITIONS

THE ḤADĪTH QUDSĪ

THE ḤADĪTH AN-NAWĀFIL

Index of Proper Names

Index of Proper Names

Index of Technical Terms

Garden: Love as, 110, 111, 247*n*181; of the soul, 110, 144; of religion: 190
Garlic: 100, 118, 252*n*301
Garment: 119, 241*n*81; body as, 100
Gazelle, the speaking: 178, 205, 207, 289*n*162, 291*n*177
Ghauth, "Help," title of the highest member of the mystical hierarchy: 37
Ghazal, lyrical poem with monorhyme, usually not longer than 14 verses, vehicle of love lyrics, prayer poetry, and mystical songs; common in the Persian, Turkish, and Urdu tradition: 6, 7, 36, 49, 50, 57, 68, 85, 88, 89, 91, 96–98, 107, 111, 118, 125, 128, 133, 171, 194, 201, 203, 237*n*10, 240*n*52, *n*53, 256*n*382; ghazal singer, 85
Ghāzī, fighter for the true faith: Love as, 114
Ginān, religious poetry of the Ismaili community in Indo-Pakistan: 155
Gnosis: 21, 272*n*123; gnostic, 15, 38
Gold: 64, 78, 107, 122, 123, 124
Golden Alphabet, *sīḥarfī:* 142, 147, 204
Goose: 266*n*75; symbol of the lower soul, 167
Grain: dying and resurrected, 93, 94; grinding of, 146, 263*n*53
Green: color of Paradise, of the angels and the faithful, 78, 110, 146, 180, 235*n*103, 242*n*85, 254*n*351; of tree, 142; of ocean of God, 62
Guru: 160
Gypsy, *see Lūlī*

Ḥā, sixth letter of the Arabic alphabet, numerical value 8: 202
Ḥabīb Allāh, "beloved friend of God," the Prophet: 39, 171
Ḥadīth, prophetic tradition: 11, 12, 30, 132, 140, 205, 220*n*64, 242*n*85, 243*n*100, 277*n*30, 280*n*60; *ḥadīth qudsī,* extra-Koranic revelation, 20, 53, 71, 122, 123, 176, 178, 194
Ḥāl, pl. *aḥwāl,* "mystical state": 18
Hama ūst, "Everything is He": 61
Ḥamd, "praise" due to God, root of the names Muḥammad and Aḥmad: 174, 189
Ḥannāna, see Palm trunk
Ḥaqīqa, "Reality," last goal on the path, comparable to walnut: 164
Ḥaqīqa muḥammadiyya, the Archetypal Muhammad, principle of the world: 9, 36, 37, 147, 155, 159, 195
Ḥaqq, "Divine Truth": 223*n*109, 255*n*357
Ḥaram in Mecca: 192; *Ḥaramain,* the two holy cities Mecca and Medina, 197
Harp: 95, 258*n*426
Ḥilya, description of the good qualities and beauty of the Prophet: 176, 277*n*30
Hindu, as symbol of lowliness and contrasted to Turk: 114, 229*n*33
Holy War, *jihād,* against one's lowly qualities and base instincts: 30
Hudhud, the hoopoe, who acted as go-between for Solomon and the Queen of Sheba: 75
Ḥusn-i taᶜlīl, "phantastic etiology" in poetry: 58, 78
Hyacinth, connected with the dark curls: 77; water hyacinth, 144

Ice: 61, 207; the world as, 62, 107
ᶜĪd: the Feast of Fastbreaking at the end of Ramadan, *ᶜĪd ul-fiṭr,* 73, 160; the Feast of Offerings, *ᶜĪd al-aḍḥā,* 113, 221*n*66; Shamsuddin as, 248*n*213
ᶜIdgāh, place where the community gathers for the *ᶜĪd* prayers: 128
Ifshā' as-sirr, "divulgence of the secret," the greatest sin of a lover: 73
Iḥrām, garment for the pilgrimage: 248*n*200